THE McGRAW-HILL 36-Hour Course

SIX SIGMA

D0777944

THE
McGRAW-HILL
36-Hour Course

SIX SIGMA

Greg Brue
Rod Howes

McGraw-Hill

New York **Chicago** **San Francisco** **Lisbon** **London** **Madrid** **Mexico City**
Milan **New Delhi** **San Juan** **Seoul** **Singapore** **Sydney** **Toronto**

The **McGraw·Hill** Companies

Copyright © 2006 by Greg Brue and Rod Howes. All rights reserved. Printed in the United States of America. Except as permitted under the United States Copyright Act of 1976, no part of this publication may be reproduced or distributed in any form or by any means, or stored in a data base or retrieval system, without the prior written permission of the publisher.

6 7 8 9 0 FGR/FGR 0 9 8

ISBN 0-07-143008-3

This publication is designed to provide accurate and authoritative information in regard to the subject matter covered. It is sold with the understanding that neither the author nor the publisher is engaged in rendering legal, accounting, or other professional service. If legal advice or other expert assistance is required, the services of a competent professional person should be sought.

—From a Declaration of Principles jointly adopted by Committee of the American Bar Association and a Committee of Publishers.

McGraw-Hill books are available at special quantity discounts to use as premiums and sales promotions, or for use in corporate training programs. For more information, please write to the Director of Special Sales, McGraw-Hill Professional, Two Penn Plaza, New York, NY 10121-2298. Or contact your local bookstore.

To our devoted wives Kelly and Jo for their absolute support and understanding during the creation of this long-awaited book. A special thanks to all the Six Sigma zealots!

CONTENTS

PREFACE

This book is intended primarily for senior managers who are preparing to become Six Sigma champions, to be responsible for promoting the methodology throughout the company and especially in specific functional groups and for supporting project teams. Champions must understand the discipline, techniques, and tools of Six Sigma so that they can select projects, establish objectives, and serve as coaches and mentors to members of project teams. Champions do not need the intensive training that is required for black belts—the people responsible for leading the project teams—but champions must know enough about the discipline, techniques, and tools to facilitate the efforts of the black belts and their teams.

This book is intended, then, to provide an overview of Six Sigma, to explain the techniques and tools, and to outline the phases in the standard implementation model. Basically, this is a 36-hour workshop for Six Sigma champions.

Here are our basic objectives:

- You will understand the essentials of Six Sigma.
- You will know the roles and responsibilities of the people involved in Six Sigma.
- You will learn the basic vocabulary of Six Sigma.
- You will gain a high-level understanding of the methods and tools used in Six Sigma.
- You will be able to identify the benefits of Six Sigma as a methodology for improving business processes.
- You will be able to work as a champion with Six Sigma project teams, fulfilling all of the responsibilities with competence and confidence.

This book is intended for Six Sigma champions. When we address you, the reader, we are addressing you as a manager who is ultimately responsible for a Six Sigma project, although you share those responsibilities with a black belt, a master black belt, green belts, and your fellow managers as members of the executive team. How you share those responsibilities will depend on your organization and your situation. Please read with that understanding in mind.

Also bear in mind that this book is not intended as a substitute for the training that a manager should receive to become a champion. Your Six Sigma initiative should provide you with sufficient training to work with the black belts, who will be receiving more extensive training, and with a master black belt, who will have even more training and experience. In other words, you won't be doing any of this alone or without training. This book is intended as a 36-hour course to provide you with a sufficient knowledge of Six Sigma to be able to participate fully and actively in starting a Six Sigma initiative, to get maximum benefits from any training, and to work effectively and efficiently with Six Sigma project teams.

Finally, as we emphasize in Chapter 1, Six Sigma can be used for many types of business activities—production, assembly, transportation, retail, services, transactions, administration, and support. Throughout this book, we'll refer generally to products, services, and processes for the sake of convenience.

Some of the material used in this book comes from *Six Sigma for Managers,* by Greg Brue (New York: McGraw-Hill, 2002), and *Design for Six Sigma,* by Greg Brue and Robert G. Launsby (New York: McGraw-Hill, 2003). We have also consulted other sources in order to provide the balanced, comprehensive coverage of Six Sigma that you should expect from a 36-hour course.

This book consists of 14 chapters, quizzes, and a final exam.

Chapter 1 provides an introduction to Six Sigma—potential benefits and costs, myths and realities, and a basic explanation.

Chapter 2 details a general approach to preparing for a Six Sigma initiative. It includes descriptions of the primary roles and responsibilities, communication, deployment planning, and training.

Six Sigma is a methodology that is driven by data, which means that it's imperative for managers and especially champions to understand basic statistics. That's the focus of Chapter 3. The introduction to statistics transitions into business metrics in Chapter 4. It starts, most appropriately, with the customers and the characteristics that they consider critical to quality; it then shows how to convert those characteristics into criteria for business metrics, with guidelines for establishing good metrics and suggestions for avoiding problems with bad metrics.

Chapter 5 is devoted to projects—to finding potential projects, quantifying and evaluating project ideas, and making the case for a project. Chapter 6 continues with projects, discussing the procedure of prioritizing and selecting project ideas. It then outlines the standard Six Sigma methodology—Define, Measure, Analyze, Improve, and Control (DMAIC).

That discussion leads logically into the next five chapters, each covering a phase of the DMAIC model: Chapter 7—Define, Chapter 8—Measure, Chapter 9—Analyze, Chapter 10—Improve, and Chapter 11—Control. Each of these five chapters presents the purposes of the phase, outlines the steps of the phase, discusses typical barriers and countermeasures, and lists the deliverables of the phase.

After explaining in Chapters 7 through 11 how Six Sigma works, the book then moves into considering ways to keep it working, to sustain the gains and spread the success. Chapter 12 discusses critical aspects of continuing Six Sigma and building on the benefits, such as maximizing on lessons learned, communicating, focusing on the customers, developing support for the initiative, transforming the organizational culture, training, and recognizing and rewarding the people who are making Six Sigma work.

One of the ways to spread the success of Six Sigma is through Design for Six Sigma (DFSS), which applies the Six Sigma methodology to new processes, products, and services. That's the focus of Chapter 13, which explains DFSS and the standard model—Define, Measure, Analyze, Design, and Verify (DMADV). It closes with a discussion of expanding DFSS beyond the organization.

The final chapter of the book continues that expansion. Chapter 14 presents several approaches to that can work well with Six Sigma—lean, supply chain management, and knowledge management—and culminates with a system that synthesizes and synergizes these approaches: Growth Management System.

What would a book titled *36-Hour Course in Six Sigma* be without a final exam? That's how we end, with a series of questions to test your knowledge of Six Sigma. What you know could earn you a certificate of achievement from McGraw-Hill. For more information, visit the following Web site:

http://www.mcgraw-hill36-hourcourses.com

ACKNOWLEDGMENTS

I would like to thank Robert Magnan for providing this book with substance and style and a relentless pursuit to ensure accuracy.

Six Sigma has achieved incredible results in many organizations. However, not all organizations have succeeded with Six Sigma. It's not magic. It takes commitment and it takes planning. But we assure you that the results are well worth the investment.

And that investment, for you, begins with this book. We congratulate you on your decision to learn about Six Sigma—and we wish you luck in beginning this adventure!

1

INTRODUCTION TO SIX SIGMA

WHY READ THIS BOOK?

Why are you reading this book? Because your organization is considering implementing Six Sigma and you want to understand what it is and how it works? Because you're responsible in some way for a Six Sigma initiative? Because you're exploring options for improving your organization? Because you're heard and read about Six Sigma and you're curious about how it works and what results you could expect from putting it to work for your organization?

These are all good reasons for reading this book and learning about Six Sigma. Now, let's consider some of the results of Six Sigma.

WHAT RESULTS HAVE BEEN ACHIEVED WITH SIX SIGMA?

The most important results of Six Sigma are in four areas: financial, benefits for customers, benefits for employees, and effects of quality.

Financial Benefits

For most people, the most important reason for using Six Sigma is financial. So, let's start with the gains achieved by some of the companies that have invested in implementing Six Sigma:

- At General Electric, Six Sigma added more than $2 billion to the bottom line in 1999 and $2.4 billion in 2000.
- Motorola saved more than $15 billion in the first 10 years of its Six Sigma efforts.
- Allied Signal (Honeywell), from 1992 through 1996, reduced costs by $1.4 billion and reduced new product introduction time by 16 percent.
- DuPont started Six Sigma in 1998 and realized more than $1.6 billion in cost savings in four years—in addition to reducing environmental impact and/or increasing safety.
- The City of Fort Wayne is using Six Sigma in a number of departments, and the projects have resulted in over $3 million of savings or cost avoidance.
- Johnson Controls started its Six Sigma initiative in 2000. Among its success stories: in the automotive battery assembly process at its manufacturing plant in Toledo, Ohio, defects were reduced by 70 percent and costs were reduced by $800,000 per year; in the automotive interiors operation in Holland, Michigan, changes in the design and drawing processes saved an estimated $1.7 million per year in tooling costs and $943,000 per year through greater engineering productivity while saving customers an estimated $3.5 million per year.
- Mount Carmel Health System in Ohio started Six Sigma in 2000 and by the end of 2001 had realized a financial return of $2.4 million. By early 2004, the organization had saved $35.8 million—after investing only $600,000 in Six Sigma training and consulting—and even though 40 percent of its projects have not had a financial link.

Performance results through Six Sigma vary, depending on the deployment of this problem-solving methodology. But it's been estimated that you should expect a minimum return on investment (ROI) of three or four times the costs of implementing Six Sigma. How long does this take? The break-even analysis generally takes about eight months, and about 1 to 1½ years later, you will realize the ROI. The most important thing is to remain focused on your commitment to the program. The knowledge gained by solving problems for customers and process problems while increasing ROI will result in a significant competitive advantage.

Senator Everett M. Dirksen, Minority Leader of the U.S. Senate from 1959 to 1969, is credited with the following remark: "A billion here, a billion there, and pretty soon you're talking real money." That witty comment might make us laugh, but let's put it in terms of your own organization: "A thousand here, a thousand there, and pretty soon you're talking about millions." We're all familiar with the advice, "Don't sweat the small stuff." But that "small stuff" can add up to big figures. Processes—any repetitive actions—that are inefficient waste time and other resources.

Here are a few questions for you to consider for your organization:

- What is the cost of scrap?
- What is the cost of rework?
- What is the cost of excessive cycle times and delays?
- What is the cost of business lost because customers are dissatisfied with your products or services?
- What is the cost of opportunities lost because you didn't have the time or the resources to take advantage of them?
- What is the total cost of poor quality in your organization?

Do you know the answers to these questions in terms of dollars? If so, then you know how important it is to reduce process variation and defects in your organization. If not, then you need to get the knowledge that gives you the power to make the necessary changes.

As you identify and correct process variations, you save on expenses—which means money to invest in growing your business—and in further improving your processes. Although the financial results are generally the most important reason for using Six Sigma, there are other important reasons:

- Benefits for customers
- Benefits for employees
- Effects of quality

Benefits for Customers

How important are your customers? In other words, where would you be without them?

You must attract and satisfy and keep customers. Otherwise, you obviously won't stay in business long. The better you satisfy your customers (current and potential), the healthier your revenue. You know that. But what role do your customers play, besides being a source of income? Do they help you improve your products, services, and processes? Do you know how to satisfy customers most effectively—and do what you do even better?

Six Sigma focuses on the expectations of your customers: that's what matters most. By using Six Sigma management methods, your company can target the vital few factors in your processes that are allowing variations and defects that keep you from meeting the critical expectations of your customers. You can better align your business goals with the requirements and expectations of your customers.

The experiences of various organizations have demonstrated how Six Sigma management improves customer satisfaction. In every process, product, or service, there's potential for better satisfying your customers. And that translates into money.

Focusing on the customer is an absolute business requirement—especially as the pressure is increasing to perform, produce, and deliver faster, better, and cheaper. As technology has accelerated the speed of business and the quality movement has focused on the customer, customer expectations have changed. Your customers have access to the Internet and other channels of information and distribution, so they know more about what's available and they have greater freedom to choose among products and services and companies. And they tend to choose and continue to patronize companies that deliver the highest quality at the lowest price the fastest.

Six Sigma helps you get there by showing you how to find the "breakthrough points" in your processes. That means not only identifying the waste streams in your processes, but also understanding all the elements that create them.

As you meet the requirements and expectations of your customers more effectively and achieve higher customer satisfaction, you increase your income—which means money to invest in growing your business.

Benefits for Employees

The beneficial effects of Six Sigma on employees can be powerful. Let's briefly consider a few of those benefits.

Six Sigma inspires employees. When the company is committed to improving its processes, meeting customer expectations, and cutting costs, employees will naturally feel motivated to do better. After all, how many of your employees actually want to do their jobs badly, to waste time and money, and to fail to meet the expectations of your customers? Furthermore, employees play an integral role in the entire Six Sigma process—it empowers them. For example, employees are actively involved in the changes taking place. Here are the typical cultural shifts:

- Employees have a voice in the decision-making process that is heard at the leadership level.
- Employees are actively involved in making changes.
- Old organizational barriers are removed.
- Employees' presentation skills are elevated.
- Employees have higher access to data levels and information.
- Employees are allowed to voice their opinions without fear of retribution.
- Face-time from senior management to the rank and file is significantly increased.
- Strategy goals are aligned with the rank and file.
- Black belts are empowered as opposed to micromanaged.

Six Sigma promotes better morale and a higher sense of self-esteem. It gives employees the opportunity to make a difference. Every employee is important in Six Sigma. Some will be involved in special roles, of course, as black belts or green belts or champions and so forth. (We'll discuss the roles in the next chapter.) But all of them will be encouraged to provide input on the processes around them. Every one of them has the opportunity to contribute significantly to Six Sigma efforts.

Six Sigma instills a culture and an attitude. It emphasizes the importance of viewing processes, products, and services from the perspective of the customers. Because all employees are customers when they're away from work, they can identify with customers—and particularly with their dissatisfaction and frustration when there are problems with products and services. They naturally empathize with customers, so when your company focuses on the customers, your employees will feel more positive about what they are doing and about your company.

Six Sigma promotes professional development for employees. The more employees know about Six Sigma techniques and tools and the more you encourage them to think critically about processes, the more competent they become. That competence not only helps your company, but also makes employees more valuable on the job market—which is an increasingly important consideration.

Six Sigma concentrates on systematic improvement of processes. That approach will appeal to the logic of your employees, many of whom have probably wondered why certain processes work in ways that seem illogical. How many employees have you heard complain about inefficient processes? Through Six Sigma, you're providing them with opportunities to improve those systems that confuse and frustrate them.

Those are some basic benefits of Six Sigma for your employees. And they definitely have an impact on your bottom line. For example, to make a process change occur—"time to make a change" is a factor of 10, on the average. In other words, if it takes five years to make a change within an organization without Six Sigma, it will take six months if you do Six Sigma, resulting in an immediate increase in your cash flow.

Quality Advantages

Another reason for using Six Sigma is the value and impact of committing to quality as a goal in a very practical way. People who might not understand and appreciate other quality initiatives are more likely to recognize the value of Six Sigma because the focus is essentially simple, as we'll discuss soon.

But what are the advantages of improving quality, in addition to the financial benefits, the benefits for customers, and the benefits for employees? Quality is an ideal of extreme power. It instills a culture and an attitude. It creates an image in the market and the community. It attracts investors. There's something special about organizations that are among the best at what they do—and that quality pays off in many ways.

A company that reduces its costs of doing business, meets the expectations of its customers more effectively and efficiently, inspires its employees, fosters a culture of dedication and pride, and earns a reputation for quality will certainly enjoy advantages over its competitors. So, how many reasons do you need for adopting Six Sigma?

WHAT IS SIX SIGMA?

Six Sigma has at least three meanings, depending on the context.

First, it's a level of quality. *Sigma* is a statistical measure of variation in a process. Sigma (the Greek letter σ) is the symbol in statistics for *standard deviation*, a measure of the variation in a distribution of values, a concept we'll discuss in Chapter 3. Achieving a six-sigma level of quality means that processes are producing only 3.4 defects per million opportunities (DPMO). In other words, they are working nearly perfectly.

Second, Six Sigma is a problem-solving methodology that can be applied to any process to eliminate the root causes of defects and associated costs. There is also a methodology for designing processes, as we'll discuss in Chapter 13.

Third, Six Sigma is a management philosophy. It's a customer-based approach that recognizes that defects decrease satisfaction and customer loyalty and increase costs. Because the organization that provides goods and/or services of the highest value for the lowest cost is the most competitive, Six Sigma is a strategy for achieving critical results.

So, in short, Six Sigma is several things:

- A statistical basis of measurement: 3.4 defects per million opportunities
- A methodology for reducing variation in processes
- A philosophy and a goal: as perfect as practically possible

A basic concept of Six Sigma is *process*. That's any repetitive action—in any manufacturing, services, or transactional environment. The Six Sigma methodology collects data on variations in outputs associated with each process so that it can be improved and those variations can be reduced.

Another basic concept, which we will be discussing in Chapters 2, 3, 4, and beyond, is *defect*. At this point, we can define it as a measurable characteristic of the process or its output that is not within the acceptable and expected customer limits, i.e., not conforming to specifications.

Six Sigma is a methodology for using tools to reduce variation and defects in order to deliver products and services that meet customer specifications. As we'll discuss later, the sigma level of a process is calculated in terms of the number of *defects* in ratio to the number of *opportunities* for defects. Many companies believe that dealing with errors is just part of the cost of doing business. But you don't have to accept that faulty logic. The central idea of Six Sigma management is that if you can measure the variation and defects in a process, you can systematically figure out ways to reduce or even eliminate them, to approach a quality level of near zero defects, which allows you to reduce your costs and better satisfy your customers.

Now, if you want an elevator version of the explanation of Six Sigma, you could use one or more of the following:

- Six Sigma is a program that focuses on the control of a process to the point of ± six sigma (standard deviations) from a centerline, which means 3.4 defects per million items. It includes identifying factors critical to quality as determined by the customer, reducing process variation, and improving process capabilities, increasing stability, and designing systems to sustain the gains.
- Six Sigma is a methodology that provides businesses with tools to improve the capability of their processes by decreasing variation, which leads to a reduction in defects and an improvement in profits, employee morale, and quality of products and services.
- Six Sigma is a problem-solving technology that uses your human assets, data, measurements, and statistics to identify the vital few factors to decrease waste and defects while increasing customer satisfaction, profit, and shareholder value.
- Six Sigma is a disciplined, data-driven approach to process improvement aimed at the near-elimination of defects from every product, process, and transaction. The purpose of Six Sigma is to gain breakthrough knowledge on how to improve processes to do things *better*, *faster*, and *at lower cost*. It can be used to improve every facet of business, from production, to human resources, to order entry, to technical support. Six Sigma can be used for any activity that is concerned with cost, timeliness, and quality of results. Unlike previous quality improvement efforts, Six Sigma is designed to provide tangible business results, cost savings that are directly traceable to the bottom line.[1] After reading this book, it's likely that you'll be able to develop a 30-second explanation that best suits your specific situation.

MYTHS ABOUT SIX SIGMA

There are many misunderstandings about Six Sigma. Here are just a few of the myths—and the truth:

- Six Sigma works only in manufacturing settings.

[1]Parnella, Jim,. Six Sigma Discussion Forum, October 31, 2000.

- Six Sigma doesn't include customer requirements.
- Six Sigma is repackaged TQM.
- Six Sigma uses difficult-to-understand statistics.
- Six Sigma is an accounting game without real savings.
- Six Sigma is just training.
- Six Sigma is a "magic pill" with little effort.

Six Sigma works only in manufacturing settings. Although it's true that Six Sigma started in manufacturing, it has been applied successfully in all segments of business—banking, healthcare, the military, fast food chains, airlines, hotels, retail stores, and on and on and on. If there's a repetitive process with a problem, you can apply Six Sigma.

Six Sigma doesn't include customer requirements. That's totally false. Every Six Sigma project starts with the customers, with determining the factors that are critical to the customer. Those factors focus the project.

Six Sigma is repackaged TQM. Quality programs are valuable in that they can create a quality perspective and culture. But Six Sigma fixes identifiable, chronic problems that directly impact your bottom line. Six Sigma projects are selected to reduce or eliminate waste, which translates into real money. Six Sigma is not theory. It defines, measures, analyzes, improves, and controls the vital few processes that matter most, to tie quality improvement directly to bottom-line results.

Six Sigma uses difficult-to-understand statistics. Because it uses statistical terminology, Six Sigma is frequently perceived as a statistics and measurement program. This is not the case. The methodology uses statistics solely as tools for interpreting and clarifying data to derive information that can be used to drive decisions. Six Sigma practitioners also use computers and statistical software to take advantage of knowledge and speed the improvement process. Six Sigma is really more about cultural transformation than about statistics.

Six Sigma is an accounting game without real savings. To refute that myth, just return to the "Financial Benefits" section earlier and read again the gains achieved by some of the companies that have applied Six Sigma.

Six Sigma is just training. There's training, of course: practitioners are trained in the methodology and the tools. But the training that occurs with a Six Sigma program is about knowledge transfer and application. In Six Sigma we learn so that we can apply and gain a competitive advantage. That purpose keeps the focus on satisfying the customer, reducing variation and defects, and saving money. Six Sigma is far more than just training: it's a business strategy that fosters a cultural shift at all levels.

Six Sigma is a "magic pill" with little effort. Six Sigma requires commitment, planning, organization, discipline, and diligence. There's nothing magic about it—unless you consider using tools and brains methodically to be magic. MAGIC is the acronym for "Measure-Analyze-Guess-Improve-Control, but there's no G in the Six Sigma model: we don't guess; we use data and facts to drive a solution.

HOW DOES SIX SIGMA WORK?

That's the focus of this book. But here, in a few pages, are the essentials. The focus of Six Sigma is on reducing defects and variations in processes. The project team begins by identifying the attributes most important to the customers, the critical-to-quality (CTQ) elements of a process. The team then analyzes the capability of the process. (We'll discuss what capability means in terms of formulas and indexes in later chapters.) Next, the team attempts to stabilize the process by reducing or eliminating variations, focusing on the vital few factors that make the most difference, applying the basic *transfer function*—$Y = f(X)$.

This forces us to ask new questions: What is that a function of? For example, you pick a critical measurement to your business, net income, and start asking, "What is net income a function of?" The Six Sigma methodology is basically a funneling process, of narrowing down the many causal factors of a problem to the vital few. They then work on these vital few factors to improve the quality of the process, to reduce variation and costs. The Six Sigma methodology generally consists of five phases (Define, Measure, Analyze, Improve, and Control—DMAIC), a model that we will discuss in depth in Chapter 6 and use in subsequent chapters:

- Define the projects, the goals, and the deliverables to customers (internal and external). Describe and quantify both the defect and the expected improvement.
- Measure the current performance of the process. Validate data to make sure it is credible and set the baselines.
- Analyze and determine the root cause(s) of the defects. Narrow the causal factors to the vital few.
- Improve the process to eliminate defects. Optimize the vital few and their interrelationships.
- Control the performance of the process. Lock down the gains.

There are other models that are similar to DMAIC. There is also a model for designing processes, products, and services: Define, Measure, Analyze, Design, and Verify (DMADV). That will be the focus of Chapter 13. DMAIC and DMADV are the models used in most Six Sigma initiatives.

We should note that Six Sigma methodology is rigorous—but not rigid. An organization should apply Six Sigma techniques and tools according to its needs, goals, structure, cultures, and other factors. Six Sigma is *not* a recipe, but rather a road map, a guide to using the right tools for the situation. It a problem-solving method that drives a way of thinking and approaching the problem regardless of industry or function.

The method in this book uses the authors' "known success model," which has been the standard body of knowledge, established in 1994 at the pioneer deployment of Allied Signal and GE. The DMAIC phases listed above were first used at GE, after the Allied Signal deployment, which did not include the Define phase. The executive team determines the model that it will follow in its Six Sigma initiative. Then, it's the responsibility of each project team—the black belt, the master black belt, and the champion—to develop a specific plan for that specific project.

Also, as mentioned above, Six Sigma works at the optimal level only if the organization using it deploys the tools with rigor and effects a cultural transformation, with black belts and champions acting as the agents of change. Managers and employees at all levels and in all areas must think and act to identify and reduce causes of variation. Six Sigma requires a tolerance for endless questioning of the validity of beliefs, no matter how entrenched: there can be no sacred company cows. This sacred cow might include company policies set by the CEO.

THE COSTS OF SIX SIGMA

Many managers hesitate to promote quality initiatives, such as Six Sigma, because they believe that the higher the quality of the outputs, the more they have to cost to produce. This is simply not true. The real decision is *not* a cost decision, but a decision based on return on investment (ROI). If cost is the only key factor, then you have a different problem and your commitment to resolving long-term issues is *not* real. You should not contemplate doing Six Sigma; you should continue with the traditional cost-reduction approaches. However, your competitors will finally outpace your traditional efforts— and perhaps buy you in the end.

Of course, there are costs:

- Direct payroll costs: People will be devoting some or all of their time to Six Sigma.
- Consulting costs: You will likely be working with a consultant and a master black belt from that firm.
- Training costs: The key players in your Six Sigma initiative will need training, some extensive.
- Improvement costs: You'll be making changes, some perhaps quite expensive.

The prospect of those costs might make some decision makers hesitate. However, intelligent, well-directed efforts to improve quality actually reduce costs. And, in fact, there can be a direct correlation between high quality and lower costs, if your approach is in that order. When you focus on improving processes rather than on reducing costs, costs come down naturally as you reduce process waste and inefficiencies. However, if you simply cut costs without considering the effect on your outputs, you'll likely reduce quality.

Before we move on to the next chapter, let's be very clear on several points. Although some aspects of Six Sigma might present a technical challenge to master (some statistical concepts, for example), Six Sigma is for anyone with the desire to learn how to fix stuff in business for a financial benefit. Insanity is defined as asking the same question over and over and hoping for a different answer. The right questions expose the most relevant information. The right questions will take you to the most enduring solution.

SUMMARY

Six Sigma has achieved most important results in four areas: financial, benefits for customers, benefits for employees, and effects of quality. It's been estimated that an organization should expect a minimum return on investment of three or four times the costs of implementing Six Sigma. Because Six Sigma focuses on the expectations of customers, it enables an organization to target the vital few factors in its processes that allow variations and defects that keep it from meeting the critical expectations of its customers. That also translates into financial benefits. In addition, Six Sigma inspires employees and instills a culture of quality and an attitude of improvement.

Six Sigma has at least three meanings:

- It's a level of quality, based on a statistical measure of variation in processes.
- It's a problem-solving methodology that can be applied to any processes.
- It's a management philosophy, a customer-based approach to doing business.

In 25 words or less, Six Sigma is a methodology for using tools to reduce variation and defects in order to deliver products and services that meet customer specifications.

In Six Sigma, the focus is on reducing defects and variations in processes. The project team identifies the attributes most important to the customers, analyzes the capability of the process, works to stabilize the process by focusing on the vital few factors that cause the most significant variation, applying the basic transfer function, $Y = f(X)$.

The term "vital few" was coined by Joseph M. Juran, in his use of the Pareto principle, which suggests that 80 percent of the effects come from

20 percent of the possible causes. He called the 20 percent the "vital few" and the remaining causes the "trivial many"—a term that he changed to the "useful many," in recognition of the fact that in improving quality no problems are truly trivial.

The Six Sigma methodology generally consists of five phases—Define, Measure, Analyze, Improve, and Control (DMAIC). There are other models that are similar to DMAIC. There is also a model for designing processes, products, and services—Define, Measure, Analyze, Design, and Verify (DMADV).

Here is an example showing how the five phases in the DMAIC problem-solving method work.

Define

A large service center is responsible for the overhaul of specialized equipment. Serial numbers of components on this equipment must be recorded and tracked through the life of the equipment. Currently, for every three pieces of equipment returned for service, one piece will have a component serial number incorrectly recorded.

Measure

Process and work-flow maps were constructed to examine the flow of information from receipt of the equipment for overhaul through to dispatch. In addition, some overhaul work is done in the field, so it was also necessary to retrieve records of this work. The short-term sigma value for the current records generation and management process, allowing for all the opportunities for error, was 1.7 sigma, or 45,000 defects per million opportunities (DPMO).

Analyze

Inventory record sheets were manually completed on arrival of the equipment for overhaul. These records were copied and distributed to the Records Center, Customer Service, Disassembly, Work in Progress Storage, and Assembly. The Records Center compares the inventory record sheets against the original condition as shipped and makes corrections in conjunction with all parties involved. Errors made included transcription errors, handwriting misinterpretation, wrong parts linked to serial numbers, obsolete data on forms, lateness of copies, and paper copies lost in the service areas.

Improve

A portable data entry and retrieval system was developed in conjunction with all concerned personnel, incorporating the inventory record sheets, the original shipping records, and previous service events. A wireless link to the main computer, together with speech software for feedback of serial numbers, provided mistake proofing.

Control

The project is being integrated into a paperless overhaul records system.

Results

A fivefold reduction in the DPMO to 8,000, or 2.42 sigma, with a savings of $120,000 per year.

By the way, people are always putting their feet in their mouths by making the famous statement, "I could have told you that was the answer." My follow-up question is "Well, why didn't you? And, by the way, how could you with that foot in your mouth!"

The basic work, the data collection, and the steps of DMAIC force the problem resolution. Making something hard look simple is hard work. There are no shortcuts or magic pills.

REVIEW QUESTIONS

1. What is Six Sigma?
    a. Problem solving
    b. Culture change
    c. Knowledge generator
    d. All the above

2. Where do you start Six Sigma?
    a. It's a bottom-up approach
    b. From the quality director
    c. Middle management
    d. The CEO decides

3. What is a defect?
    a. Something that the customer is willing to pay for
    b. A feeling that the process is causing a problem
    c. Something we should ignore if possible
    d. A measurable characteristic not conforming to a customer requirement that costs money–it's waste!

4. Achieving Six Sigma quality means your business is
   a. Producing 500,000 defects per million opportunities (DPMO)
   b. Producing 100,000 DPMO
   c. Producing 25,000 DPMO
   d. Producing 3.4 DPMO maximum

5. What is a process?
   a. A system used in manufacturing
   b. A Six Sigma computer application
   c. Any repetitive action in a business environment
   d. The opposite of a concess

6. What is standard deviation?
   a. A measure of variation
   b. A normal perversion
   c. A behavioral aberration that is considered typical
   d. An acceptable modification of a process

7. What is the standard model for the Six Sigma methodology?
   a. BACI
   b. CIADF
   c. DPMO
   d. DMAIC

8. What is $Y = f(X)$?
   a. A quadrilateral equation
   b. The Six Sigma transfer function
   c. One variation of $X = f(Y)$ and $Y = x(F)$
   d. An algorithm for controlling DMAIC

9. All of the following are phases in the Six Sigma DMAIC model except
   a. Measure
   b. Continue
   c. Define
   d. Analyze

2

HOW TO GET STARTED WITH SIX SIGMA

S IX SIGMA CAN GENERATE very impressive results, as we showed and explained in Chapter 1—but only if the people in the organization are ready and willing to commit to the effort. The top leaders of your company must be committed to the Six Sigma process. This means that they must fully embrace what you're doing. They must realize that the Six Sigma approach to management and process improvement is not a quick fix and that implementing this approach will require many changes in the conventional ways of operating. They must be committed on two levels:

- They must commit company resources to help the Six Sigma initiative succeed.
- They must commit their time and energy to actively promote the initiative.

It's not enough to just be involved in Six Sigma; you must be committed to making it work.

You've got to give it your all. Company leaders and other managers must be engaged; they need to function as champions and provide the support—financial and otherwise—to make the effort succeed. When you start Six Sigma, it's no longer business as usual—for anyone on the organizational chart. Now let's consider if your company is ready to do Six Sigma.

COMMITMENT VERSUS INVOLVEMENT

It's like making bacon and eggs:

- The hen is involved.
- But the pig is absolutely commited.

We as leaders need to be more like the pig and less of a chicken.

ARE YOU AND YOUR COMPANY READY?

To determine whether your company is ready for Six Sigma, you need to ask certain key questions. By asking them at the beginning of the Six Sigma process, you can gauge how you're doing now and later how far you've gone.

- Does your company have a clear strategic course?
- Are the people in your company ready and willing to accept and react to changes?
- How effectively does your company focus on meeting customer expectations?
- Are you ready to begin measuring the defect levels and yields for each service, product, and process?
- Are you ready to begin reducing defect rates by at least 50 percent over time?
- Are you ready to begin looking at how much you spend in fixing mistakes—the cost of poor quality?
- Are you ready to reduce the cost of poor quality (the cost of doing it wrong) by 25 percent over time?
- Are you ready to reduce your process cycle times by 50 percent over time?

By asking such key questions, you can gauge if your company is ready to determine the impact of defects and reduce the cost of poor quality—which Juran estimated to be in most companies between 20 percent and 40 percent of sales—and cycle time. Getting answers takes time, research, and careful analysis. It's not easy and it's not quick—but the results are worth the effort and time.

Assess Your Readiness for Six Sigma

Are you ready to put Six Sigma to work for your organization? Use the checklist below to quickly assess your readiness. If you agree with the following statements and can answer the questions, you might already be on the Six Sigma journey.

1. "Customers have critical-to-quality expectations."

   What are your customers' top four expectations?

   (1) _____

   (2) _____

   (3) _____

   (4) _____

2. "We are in business to achieve a phenomenal customer satisfaction rate that exceeds critical-to-quality expectations."

   Can you quantify your customers' current level of satisfaction? Yes __ No __

   If yes, how would you rate it on a scale of 1-10? ____

   How has it changed over the last five years? _____

3. "We strive to produce profitable bottom-line results. We are in business to make money!"

   List your company's profits for the last five years:

   Year 1 $ _____

   Year 2 $ _____

   Year 3 $ _____

   Year 4 $ _____

   Year 5 $ _____

4. "We have repetitive processes in our business that create products and services for our customers."

   List four major repetitive processes in your business:

   Process #1 _____

   Process #2 _____

   Process #3 _____

   Process #4 _____

   How many times do you do these processes per year?

   Process #1 _____

   Process #2 _____

   Process #3 _____

   Process #4 _____

5. "Our goal is to create knowledge about our processes and take action to reduce cycle time, defects, and variations."

For Processes #1 and #2 listed above, give the reduction of cycle time, defects, and variation.

	Cycle Time	Defects or Yield
Process #1		
Baseline:	_____	_____
Currently:	_____	_____
Process #2		
Baseline:	_____	_____
Currently:	_____	_____

6. "We create knowledge about our processes by collecting data and stating the problem in statistical terms, such as the mean and standard deviation of the process."

   Does your company know the vital statistics of Processes #1-4 listed above?

   Yes __ No __

7. "We validate the data collected through the Measure phase of the Six Sigma DMAIC model."

   Is your data validated? Can it be trusted? Yes __ No __

   Can you test the data for repeatability and reproducibility by others? Yes __ No __

   Is the data accurate and precise? Yes __ No __

   If yes, then what are the results of the test? _____ percent R&R (repeatable and reproducible)

8. "We use the data to determine the vital few factors that are the root of the quality problem through the Analyze phase of the Six Sigma DMAIC model."

   For Process #1 what are the vital few factors?

   Factor #1: _____

   Factor #2: _____

   Factor #3: _____

9. "In the Improve phase of the Six Sigma DMAIC model, we create a predictable equation or relationship between the process variables (vital few) and output of the product with a low defect level."

   Can you calculate a result equation for Process #1?

   What is $Y = f(X)$? _____

10. "We sustain the reduction in defects while always quantifying our bottom-line result."

If Process #1 is in the Control phase of the Six Sigma DMAIC model, what are the controls?

What is the financial result of the project? $_____

You should show the money benefit.

11. "We share our knowledge to ensure that everyone understands and benefits from that knowledge."

    How does your company transfer knowledge?

    What velocity is involved in that knowledge transfer?

    Is there an infrastructure in place? (i.e., intranet or database sharing?)

12. "We as a company achieve our goals, which results in sustained and satisfied internal and external customers."

    What are the goals that have been met in the last two years?

    Goal #1 _____

    Goal #2 _____

Were you able to understand and answer every question? If no, then your company is an excellent candidate for doing Six Sigma.

Requirements

Six Sigma can stand alone and still get results, but there are fundamental requirements and foundational training aspects to its process management tools that are necessary. You need to accurately survey your company's knowledge, to identify the gaps or misconceptions and determine how you can best provide training in the methodology to ensure correct implementation. Surveying your knowledge base is as individual as your company culture. Every organization is different in terms of how prepared its people are to use Six Sigma tools and begin to work with the data. Most important of all is to find out what your black belt candidates know about Six Sigma.

You can find out how well your people understand Six Sigma by asking them if they are familiar with any of the following statistical tools, which are essential for implementing Six Sigma. Once you know how much they know, you can best prepare for their training experience.

- Check sheet—a list of check-off items for quick and easy collection of data in a simple, standardized format.
- Histogram—a bar chart for displaying the frequency of data in subgroups or categories.
- Brainstorming—a method for getting people to openly exchange ideas for specific problems or opportunities.

- Process mapping—a graphical view of your process steps for a given situation, showing inputs and outputs and flow.
- Pareto chart—a bar graph used to break down a problem into the relative contributions of its components, to identify the vital few elements on which you should focus.
- Run chart—a chart that displays any given measurement over a specified time sequence.
- Cause-and-effect (fishbone) diagram—a figure used to identify and classify causes of a given effect.

Once you and your staff fully understand these tools and their value, you can use them to identify the defects and waste in your processes. (We'll discuss all of these tools and more in later chapters.)

KEY PLAYERS

Six Sigma is about techniques and tools and statistics—but the results of Six Sigma depend on the people applying the techniques and tools and statistics. In Six Sigma initiatives, there are five key players:

- Executive leaders: to commit to Six Sigma and to promote it throughout the organization
- Champions: to fight for the cause of black belts and remove barriers
- Master black belt: to serve as trainer, mentor, and guide
- Black belts: to work full-time on projects
- Green belts: to assist black belts part time

Regardless of the roles played by participants in the Six Sigma initiative, they must all have full responsibility for their individual areas. Simply put, to be responsible is to be accountable, trustworthy, and dependable. It's important that all your participants recognize this as their charter: from green belts to executive leaders, they need to exercise responsibility in all that they do to achieve optimum outcomes.

It's vital to understand and define key operational roles from the start. All the key players should know what's expected of them and how all of the roles work together in the Six Sigma initiative. Each of the roles has a clearly defined set of responsibilities.

Roles of the Executive Leaders

The key role of executive leaders is to decide to do Six Sigma and to publicly endorse it and promote it throughout the organization. They must reinforce the comprehensive scope of Six Sigma to engage everyone's support and participation. It's important that the Six Sigma initiative involve the entire organization: that point cannot be emphasized enough. As you begin your initiative, visible and vital leadership is crucial. It rallies the employees, it lends legitimacy to your projects, and it sends the clearest signal that you are committing to Six Sigma to achieve major company priorities.

Leaders should show determination. They need to be resolute in believing that Six Sigma will succeed. So, after the initial fanfare of introducing Six Sigma, executives should be determined to get the training, understand the savings, perpetuate the use of metrics, showcase black belt achievements, mark key milestones, and keep the overall initiative on track.

Jack Welch, the CEO who started Six Sigma at General Electric, called Six Sigma "part of the genetic code" of future leadership at that company. Welch could be considered the ideal executive leader for Six Sigma because an executive's responsibility, ultimately, is to make sure that Six Sigma becomes part of the "genetic code" of the company. From the top down and throughout the organization, executive leaders can inspire and promote a Six Sigma culture that continually produces results. For example, General Electric has encouraged its executives to promote Six Sigma by linking it to compensation, tying part of the bonuses for top executives to Six Sigma implementation. That incentive sends the message about the importance of Six Sigma and ensures commitment from the top levels down.

Executives also need to actively display confidence—not only in Six Sigma, but also in the people charged with making it work. By actively showing their confidence with rewards and incentives, company leaders inspire sustained commitment and effort. When an executive lets employees know that she believes in them, supports their success, and applauds their talents, employees will try to live up to those expectations. Confidence is a powerful motivator.

And that confidence isn't expressed only in compliments and congratulations. It can be supported by project metrics: executives can point to specific outcomes as proof that validates their confidence in a given champion, black belt, or project team.

Executives must also show integrity. They need to do what they say they're going to do. This puts substance behind the statements. By following through on commitments and staying true to a stated purpose, executives demonstrate a high level of ethical leadership. Integrity stimulates loyalty and respect, both of which motivate and inspire employees across the organization.

Finally, executive leaders should be models of patience. This might be very hard to do in a business environment that demands immediate answers and quick results. Six Sigma projects take time; skipping steps or rushing the process will jeopardize the results.

If a company has been functioning at a four-sigma level or lower for the last decade, then surely company leaders can allow six months for projects that will bring its performance up to a six-sigma level. That seems logical—but too often executives and managers are impatient for results.

But to fix problems properly, you need to invest the time to do it right—and that takes patience.

Company executives have a golden opportunity to develop their relationship with employees when they demonstrate their determination, confidence, integrity, and patience. By "walking the walk" as well as "talking the talk," they stand out from the crowd and they show that they're actively leading and facilitating exciting changes in the organization and that they fully support the employees driving those changes.

Roles of the Champions

A champion is a senior-level manager who promotes the Six Sigma methodology throughout the company and especially in functional groups. A champion understands the discipline and tools of Six Sigma, participates in selecting projects, establishes objectives, serves as coach and mentor, removes barriers, and dedicates resources to support black belts. A champion is closest to the process and "owns" it—monitoring projects and measuring the savings realized.

Champions are critical to the success or failure of any Six Sigma project. The concept of "champion" dates back to the Middle Ages: a champion was someone who took the field to battle for a cause. In Six Sigma, a champion is an advocate who fights for the cause of black belts and overcomes obstacles—functional, financial, personal, or otherwise—so that black belts can do their work.

Depending on the size of a company, champions are drawn from the ranks of the executives and managers. Generally, a champion should be a senior manager who:

- Understands at least the basics about the tools and techniques used in Six Sigma
- Understands and supports Six Sigma
- Has direct access to other senior managers
- Is responsible for the area that is the focus of the Six Sigma project
- Is able to remove barriers for the team and committed to doing so

Champions are responsible for monitoring and managing each critical element in a Six Sigma project. They need to report up to senior managers about project progress and they need to support their teams. Champions must be sure that the projects they select align with the executive strategy and can be readily understood and embraced by project teams.

Champions select black belt candidates, identify project areas, and establish clear and measurable goals for projects. They do whatever it takes to keep the projects on schedule. They must be fully engaged in the process, allotting at least 20 percent to 30 percent of their time to ensuring that black belts are making progress on their projects and effecting lasting changes.

The champion acts as advocate and defender, as mentor and coach. The champion is ultimately responsible for the Six Sigma project. The black belt and project teams hunt defects and waste, but it is the champion who selects the project and monitors progress. Champions must thoroughly understand the strategy and discipline of Six Sigma and be able to educate others about its tools and implementation. Champions direct and mobilize the teams to make lasting change. They also ensure that the teams share what they learn; they transfer the knowledge into other areas and increase the results exponentially.

It should be mentioned that champions are sometimes called *project champions* to distinguish them from *deployment champions*. The latter is a senior-level manager, normally reporting to an executive, who is responsible for managing the deployment plan.

What makes a good champion? Here's a quick example. At a manufacturing company implementing Six Sigma, a champion regularly met with his black belts. At one Six Sigma review (when black belts report to senior-level management), a black belt informed him that she needed to purchase and install a table for sorting defects off-line. It would cost about $17,000, but it would provide an alternative to shutting down the entire line, which would cost far more. The controller told her to go through the normal requisition process and she'd have her table in about four months. That delay would have killed the project right then and there: to submit the project to "business as usual" would have shown little real commitment to supporting Six Sigma. So the champion asked for the data that backed up her request, analyzed it, agreed with it, and then got immediate executive signoff on securing a table the following week.

This is the stuff of a good champion: removing barriers and sending a clear signal that he and upper management are aligned and committed to Six Sigma. The champion does whatever it takes to support the black belts.

Roles of the Master Black Belts

This role requires the highest level of technical proficiency. It is often fulfilled initially by someone working with your implementation partner, an outside expert engaged in introducing, training, and supporting your Six Sigma initiative. The master black belt serves as your trainer, mentor, and guide. He teaches executive managers the basics, helps them select the right people for the project teams, and helps them screen and select projects.

The master black belt is an expert in Six Sigma tools and tactics and a valuable resource in terms of technical and historical expertise. Teacher, mentor, and lead agent of change, the master black belt ensures that the necessary infrastructure is in place and that black belts are trained. Master black belts focus 100 percent of their efforts on process improvement. Because the master black belt is responsible for training and coaching, teaching and communications skills should be considered as important as technical skills in selecting candidates.

A key aspect of the master black belt role is the ability to skillfully facilitate problem solving without actually taking over a project. In this way, your team members have the security of knowing that you've chosen the best project, that you're correctly using the tools, and that you will find the causes of variations—all without losing autonomy, responsibility, or the ability to direct change.

Master black belts are invaluable assets as you begin your Six Sigma initiative. They coordinate and collaborate with the executive managers, and particularly with the champions. They meet regularly and as needed with black belts and green belts, advising and coaching and mentoring them. They keep the executive managers and champions focused on what's important in selecting projects and implementing Six Sigma.

Once you have your Six Sigma initiative well under way, once you've established all the necessary elements, designated and trained people in their roles, started projects, and garnered some results, you can graduate some black belts to the ranks of master black belts. The best candidates for this promotion are black belts who have led projects successfully and who have been strong leaders and change agents. The best master black belts are black belts who are good thinkers, both creative and analytical. Of course, they should also really want to commit more fully to the Six Sigma initiative.

Growing your own master black belts ensures that your initiative will not only survive, but also succeed and be sustained. Six Sigma initiatives must be self-perpetuating; as your team members gain experience and some become master black belts, you're well on your way to sustaining Six Sigma results.

Roles of the Black Belts

A black belt leads a team on a selected project on a full-time basis, working strictly on defining, measuring, analyzing, improving, and controlling processes to reach desired outcomes. Black belts do nothing else; their only responsibility is to root out variation and identify the vital few factors. They devote 100 percent of their energies to the projects, supported by project team members.

Some organizations use their black belts only part time. This is a business decision that depends on the situation, particularly on the urgency of the motivation for implementing Six Sigma. However, you can't expect the greatest results if you don't commit the resources necessary to achieve them.

Although champions are responsible for getting the bottom-line results, because they select the projects and monitor progress, black belts are responsible for doing the work. They are selected to solve problems within the Six Sigma framework and they are trained to be technical leaders in using Six Sigma tools and methods to improve quality. As team leaders and project heads, black belts are central to Six Sigma success.

So, why the martial arts terminology? Because a black belt's sole function is to focus on disciplined problem solving, practice specific skills, use a defined set of tools, and defeat the enemy—variation.

SELECTING BLACK BELTS

How does a champion select employees to be black belts? Here's an organized approach to evaluating your employees in terms of their black belt potential. (This survey tool was validated with 100 successful black belts to correlate threshold value.)

Rate the employee in each of these 11 key areas on a scale of 1 to 5 (5 = excellent; 4 = above average; 3 = average; 2 = below average; 1 = unacceptable).

Process and product knowledge _____

Basic statistical knowledge _____

Knowledge about your organization _____

Communication skills _____

Self-starter, motivated _____

Open-minded _____

Eager to learn about new ideas _____

Desire to drive change _____

Team player _____

Respected _____

Results track record _____

Total: _____

A candidate who scores at least 38 has excellent black belt potential. Successful black belts generally share the following traits:

- They work well on their own and also in groups.
- They remain calm under extreme pressure.
- They anticipate problems and act on them immediately.
- They respect their fellow workers and are respected by them.
- They inspire others.
- They are able to delegate tasks to other team members and coordinate their efforts.
- They understand and recognize the abilities and limitations of their fellow workers.
- They show a genuine concern for others, for what they need and want.
- They accept criticism well.
- They are concerned about the current processes and results, and they want to improve the system.

(Continued)

> - They have the intelligence and are interested in learning how to apply the Six Sigma tools.
>
>   Choose your black belt candidates carefully. It takes certain qualities to be a black belt; training develops these qualities, but it can't create them. It's essential to choose the right people for these roles that are central to Six Sigma.

Empower your black belts and assure them of your total support for their projects. Their access to information or data, from within your company and from outside, and their interpretation of it must be unrestricted. By applying Six Sigma statistical tools in tandem with critical data, black belts can mine hidden dollars. As long as you and other champions and your implementation partner are available on-site to mentor them, black belts will provide the return on investment you want.

Roles of the Green Belts

Green belts assist black belts in their functional area. They work on projects part time, usually in a limited, specific area. They apply Six Sigma tools to examine and solve chronic problems on projects within their regular jobs. In this way, knowledge is being transferred and used in even narrow applications.

They also help black belts accomplish more in less time. They might help collect or analyze data, run experiments, or do other important tasks in a project. They are team members with enough understanding of Six Sigma to share the tools and transform company culture from the ground up. Working in a complementary fashion with the charter of executive leadership, champions, and black belts, green belts are essential "worker bees" driving bottom-line results. Depending on the organization and the situation, green belts can be responsible for forming and facilitating Six Sigma teams and managing projects.

Roles of the Project Team Members

Finally, we have the employees who work as members of project teams. They come from various functions and they work part time on projects. They are very familiar with the processes, the "resident experts." They have the least training in Six Sigma, maybe none at all. They are accountable as individuals and together for specific tasks and, when they are responsible for a specific aspect of a project, they will often make decisions.

Recognition and Rewards

There's one important note to interject here. In discussing requirements, roles, and responsibilities, we should also emphasize two more R's—recognition and rewards. The executive team should create rewards that employees can earn in the short term for exceptional efforts and rewards for team members who meet their individual and team goals.

It's idealistic to think that employees will support and promote Six Sigma simply because it's a way to satisfy the customers and to make bigger profits. After all, how many CEOs would buy that line? They'd expect to share in the financial gain of any initiative in which they've participated. The same is true of employees. They expect and deserve recognition and, of course, rewards.

Rewards can take the form of advancement. For example, choose master black belt and black belt candidates from among your top performers and make Six Sigma a path to promotion and for managerial advancement for managers who are in charge of motivating people.

Another reward to offer is a compensation plan. To cover the full scope of Six Sigma activities, create compensation plans and progression plans for a full two years. Here's an example. To engage everyone throughout GE in Six Sigma, Jack Welch made the following statements:

1. To get promoted, you must be trained in Six Sigma.
2. 40 percent of top management bonuses are tied to Six Sigma goals.
3. Stock options are tied to Six Sigma performance.

In his comments in the 1997 GE Annual Report, Welch made the following statement: "Six Sigma is quickly becoming part of the genetic code of our future leadership. Six Sigma training is now an ironclad prerequisite for promotion to any professional or managerial position in the Company—and a requirement for any award of stock options."

As a result of this measure and others, GE had few problems engaging managers and employees in its Six Sigma initiative.

Roles of the Consultants

It might be wise to hire an outside consultant to help you start with Six Sigma. If you decide to do so, here are some suggestions for making the most appropriate choice.

First, you need to work with someone who preaches and practices Six Sigma. When you're talking about implementing a strategy that's going to change not only your outcomes, but also your processes and the deployment of your people, you'd better do it right. You need to choose an outside partner who's demonstrated an ability to help organizations get the most out of Six Sigma. After all, you want your investment to pay off as fast and as effectively as possible. Your consultant should help you plan and structure your initiative so you can move toward self-sufficiency quickly.

The consultant should be focused on knowledge transfer, on showing you how to solve problems through the most effective methods and fix process defects with the right tools, so you can transfer that knowledge throughout your organization.

A quick way to distinguish among outside consultants is to look at how they structure their own employee reward systems. We all need to make money, of course. But here's a big difference. Some consultants are rewarded for time, on the basis of their billable hours. Others are rewarded for results, on the basis of the speed and size of the client's return on investment. Both groups of consultants are committed to your success in theory, but only the latter consultants are investing in the financial results with you.

Finally, when choosing an outside consultant for Six Sigma, check credentials. Lots of organizations purport to be Six Sigma experts, so you should ask for proof of their claims: request references and actual case studies from clients. You want to know how they contributed to the outcomes. You want proof of results—that's what Six Sigma is all about.

Role of the Controller

The controller is an often neglected but important player in Six Sigma initiatives. It's crucial to get advance buy-in from your controller and important—especially since projects involve company money—to be "in sync" with the controller. You need to be operating from the same monetary baseline: you both need to agree on how you calculate real savings and how you distinguish between hard dollars and soft dollars. In general, *hard dollars* are savings that are tangible and quantifiable, such as reduced hours, reduced inventory levels, etc., and *soft dollars* are savings that are intangible, expenses that you avoid, such as not increasing hours, inventory, or physical workspace. If you work together with the controller, she can verify your results, which further validates all your Six Sigma work.

The average black belt improvement project results in a return to the bottom line of about $175,000. A black belt, if deployed properly, will complete four to six projects per year—saving between $600,000 and $1 million. So it's important not to let the controller waffle about calculating the savings. Controllers who refuse to acknowledge soft versus hard dollar savings can really hurt a Six Sigma project.

Include controllers in your Six Sigma initiative from the outset. They need to know that your executive leadership expects them to cooperate and support your efforts. Make sure you and the controller are in agreement on how you define and assign savings to your projects.

Sometimes controllers can be barriers, as they fear their budgets will be cut if they report the money saved by your projects. For instance, in some companies, if a project saves $10 million in a $100 million budget, the savings will be eliminated, forcing controllers to operate with a $90 million budget. You need to stress that the purpose of Six Sigma projects is to save "hidden" money, not to eliminate it. Although you want to drive that hidden revenue to the bottom line, you will also use it in other areas. When the controllers understand that Six Sigma projects work to reduce costs, not to slash budgets, they will probably want projects to succeed as much as you do.

PLANNING FOR THE SIX SIGMA INITIATIVE

Once you've determined that you're ready to start Six Sigma, you need to know how to plan for it. There are certain phases in Six Sigma planning that serve as the foundation for any implementation; in each phase, there are certain steps that build sequentially to launch your projects. Here we'll discuss how to launch the initiative; in Chapters 6 and 7 we'll discuss how to plan for a project.

The most important time in a Six Sigma initiative is the beginning. If you start out poorly, it's likely to be very difficult to recover and start again. Even a temporary setback can generate skepticism and resistance.

Essential to a successful beginning are the following:

- Communication about the initiative
- An overall deployment plan (strategy)
- An initial list of projects
- Training for members of the executive team, champions, black belts, and green belts

COMMUNICATION

At this point the executive team should start involving the rest of the organization in the Six Sigma initiative by communicating about it. The best way to build awareness about Six Sigma through a companywide communication from your CEO or president. It should do the following:

- It should explain Six Sigma.
- It should explain why the organization is implementing Six Sigma.
- It should list the business goals the executive managers have set for the initiative.
- It should outline the deployment plan.
- It should make the point that Six Sigma depends on all team members, regardless of how they are involved early on or later. From the start, it should show that the executive managers consider every employee a potential black belt or green belt: the more employees understand the Six Sigma initiative, the more likely they are to show an interest and to commit. Even employees who do not become black belts or green belts can contribute by working as members of project teams and/or by suggesting ideas for projects.

The following sidebar shows a sample letter, a "serving suggestion."

An effective way to kick off Six Sigma is a letter of introduction by the CEO or president that's distributed to every employee, to communicate the importance of Six Sigma and executive commitment to its success.

From: [President, CEO, or other executive staff member]
To: All Employees
Subject: Six Sigma Success

The world in which our organization is competing is far different from even a decade or two ago. Competition is stronger than ever, customers have more choices and are demanding higher quality and faster delivery, and profit margins are shrinking across our industry. To compete effectively in this environment, we need to explore new ways to improve our performance, to develop a better strategy.

That strategy is Six Sigma. Six Sigma is the best way for us to break through to the next level, to delight our customers and reduce our costs dramatically by greatly improving our performance, processes, products, and services. Our goal is to be a high-growth company and our first target is to become a $_____ company.

The term "Six Sigma" is a measurement that is more than 99 percent perfect. Yet it is far more than just a measurement. Six Sigma is a method that we'll use to take our productivity and profitability to the next level.

You will all have the chance to learn about the Six Sigma methodology and receive essential training. In addition, some of you will receive further training and lead teams in applying Six Sigma to projects. Six Sigma will require us to ask questions about our processes and think differently. I ask you to consider the great opportunities here and I urge you to support our Six Sigma initiative. We can make our company the highest-quality, lowest-cost provider of goods and services in our industry. As we reach our goals, you will be recognized and rewarded for your dedication to the initiative's success.

The executive staff is committed to the program and will soon be training in the methodology. We will continue to train participants at all levels and will begin training "black belts" on [date]. Black belts are the designated project leaders who will assemble teams and begin Six Sigma projects in various areas. In the beginning, we will be working with people from [company name]. With their expertise and experience, they will be training us and guiding us in our Six Sigma initiative.

It is crucial that you understand our goals and support our initiative. Together, we can improve our performance and achieve the results we're seeking. Please join me in this exciting and challenging venture!

Thank you.

This initial communication is followed by many more, continuously. The executive team should use all of the tools available, such as the company intranet and newsletter. The team should post information on what, how, and when it plans to kick off the Six Sigma projects and publicize the roles and responsibilities of every person participating in the initiative. Communications should clearly state the purpose of all Six Sigma projects, in terms of the outcomes expected and the benefits for the entire organization.

DEPLOYMENT PLAN

Also at this point the executive team should have a deployment plan ready. The deployment plan should include the following elements, at least, scheduled in phases:

- Workshops for the executive team
- Workshops for the champions
- Selection of initial projects
- Selection of initial black belt and green belt candidates
- Training for finance personnel
- Training for potential black belt and green belt candidates
- Goals for the initiative
- Strategy for the initiative
- Roles of executive team members, champions, master black belts, and black belts
- Criteria for selecting projects
- System for evaluating and prioritizing project ideas
- System for tracking projects
- Reward and recognition plan
- Communications plan

In most organizations, the executives will not be ready and able to develop a solid deployment plan without a good understanding of Six Sigma and assistance from people who have experience with Six Sigma. This is why it's wise to begin with workshops for the executive team, during which the first draft of the deployment plan will be developed.

Figure 2-1 is a sample deployment plan. It details the communication and the training provided at all levels.

The first version of the deployment plan is finalized in the following weeks by the management team as a regular part of their management meetings. A key part of this work is the refinement of the list of project areas and associated champions.

	Task	Duration	Start	Finish
1	Present final proposal.	1 day	6/7	6/7
2	Approve and sign final proposal (includes legal approval and review).	34 days	6/10	7/25
3	Define and hold first leadership core team meeting (monthly 1- to 3-hour meeting).	1 day	8/5	8/5
4	Project selection and validation.	25 days	8/5	9/6
5	Select key business units to start.	7 days	8/5	8/13
6	Meet with all key business unit leaders for overview and actions to start identifying projects and resources.	15 days	8/12	8/30
7	Compile list of champions.	5 days	8/26	8/30
8	Compile list of projects.	10 days	8/26	9/6
9	Compile list of black belts.	7 days	8/26	9/3
10	Executives' 1-day event. (Select a date.)	14 days	8/26	9/12
11	Order training material.	21 days	8/12	9/9
12	Notebook computers selected for purchase and use. (Internal IT department will configure.)	28 days	8/26	10/2
13	E-mail access and badge setup.	14 days	8/19	9/5
14	Selection of first project list complete.	1 day	9/6	9/6
15	Finalize list of champions.	1 day	9/6	9/6
16	Communication and invite to first champions class.	2 days	9/9	9/10
17	Send out prereading prior to class.	3 days	9/9	9/11
18	Send first champions a selection criteria sheet for black belts, attached to invitation. Champions to fill out.	3 days	9/9	9/11
19	Collect and compile lists of black belt candidates from first champions, using the selection criteria worksheet.	18 days	8/26	9/18
20	Consultant conducts phone interviews to aid in preselecting black belts.	24 days	8/26	9/26
21	Schedule key executives to kick off first champion session the morning of July 8, 2002. (15 minutes minimum.)	14 days	8/19	9/5
22	First champions training sessions (two one-day sessions).	3 days	9/27	10/1
23	First champions class, Session 1 of 2.	1 day	9/27	9/27
24	First champions class, Session 2 of 2.	1 day	10/1	10/1
25	Project improvement tracker (database) installed and set up with IT department.	60 days	9/4	11/26
26	Logistics for training sites.	21 days	8/19	9/16
27	Finalize wave-1 black belt class.	4 days	9/19	9/24
28	Communication and invitation for black belt candidates ("You been selected" memo).	4 days	9/19	9/24
29	First round of champions to have one-on-one with black belts (setup for success) prior to class. (Hand off project assignment.)	4 days	9/19	9/24
30	Arrange date for key executives to make one-hour visit during Six Sigma reviews.	60 days	8/26	11/15

FIGURE 2-1   Sample Six Sigma deployment plan

	Task	Duration	Start	Finish
31	Wave-1 black belt class (Measure phase), Session 1. (Class size 10-20.)	4 days	10/14	10/17
32	Six Sigma team training sessions 10 days after Measure phase of each wave.	5 days	10/28	11/1
33	Communication plan created for both internal and external PR.	191 days	8/19	5/12
34	Internal ongoing communication plan (newsletters, intranet, etc.).	100 days	8/19	1/3
35	External communication to flow through corporate communications.	120 days	11/26	5/12
36	Wave-1 black belt class (Analyze phase), Session 2.	4 days	11/11	11/14
37	Wave-1 Six Sigma Review 1.	1 day	11/11	11/11
38	Training week for Analyze (Session 2).	4 days	11/11	11/14
39	First black belts class (Improve phase), Session 3.	4 days	12/9	12/12
40	Wave-1 Six Sigma Review 2.	1 day	12/9	12/9
41	Training week for Improve (Session 3).	4 days	12/9	12/12
42	First black belts class (Control phase), Session 4.	4 days	1/20	1/23
43	Wave-1 Six Sigma Review 3.	1 day	1/20	1/20
44	Training week for Control (Session 4).	4 days	1/20	1/23
45	Wave-2 prework, including champion class and black belt selection along with project assignment.	25 days	12/13	1/16
46	Quarterly executive review of Six Sigma improvement activity, status, and update. Agenda is structured for 2.5 hours with Q&A.	1 day	1/27	1/27
47	Second champions class.	2 days	1/24	1/27
48	Second champions class, Session 1 of 2.	1 day	1/24	1/24
49	Second champions class, Session 2 of 2.	1 day	1/27	1/27
50	Wave-2 of black belts (Measure, Analyze, Improve, and Control) (class size 10-20).	64 days	2/10	5/8
51	Beginning of wave 2, session 1 (Measure).	4 days	2/10	2/13
52	Wave-2 Six Sigma Review 1 (Analyze).	1 day	3/10	3/10
53	Wave-2 Six Sigma Review 2 (Improve).	1 day	4/7	4/7
54	Wave-2 Six Sigma Review 3 (Control).	1 day	5/5	5/5
55	Wave-2 last training week (Control), Session 4.	4 day	5/5	5/8
56	Six Sigma team training sessions 10 days after Measure phase of each wave.	5 days	2/24	2/28
57	Wave-3 prework, including champion class and black belt selection along with project assignment.	25 days	4/8	5/12
58	Quarterly executive review of Six Sigma improvement activity, status, and update. Agenda is structured for 2.5 hours with Q&A.	1 day	4/21	4/21
59	Third champions class.	2 days	5/16	5/19
60	Third champions class, Session 1 of 2.	1 day	5/16	5/16

FIGURE 2-1   (*Continued*)

	Task	Duration	Start	Finish
61	Third champions class, Session 2 of 2.	1 day	5/19	5/19
62	Wave-3 of black belts (Measure, Analyze, Improve, and Control). (Class size 10-20.)	59 days	6/9	8/28
63	Beginning of wave-2 Session 1 (Measure).	4 days	6/9	6/12
64	Wave-3 Six Sigma Review 1 (Analyze).	1 day	6/30	6/30
65	Wave-3 Six Sigma Review 2 (Improve).	1 day	7/28	7/28
66	Wave-3 Six Sigma Review 3 (Control).	1 day	8/25	8/25
67	Wave-2 last training week (Control), Session 4.	4 days	8/25	8/28
68	Six Sigma team training sessions 10 days after Measure phase of each wave.	5 days	9/8	9/12
69	Wave-1 of green belts, prework for training.	5 days	7/29	8/4
70	Wave-1 of green belts.	30 days	9/4	10/15
71	Wave-2 of green belts, prework for training.	1 day	8/5	8/5
72	Wave-2 of green belts, coteaching with training department. (Class size 10-20.)	30 days	8/6	9/16
73	Waves-3 and 4 of green belts, prework for training.	10 days	9/30	10/13
74	Waves-3 and 4 of green belts. (Class size 10-20.)	45 days	8/26	10/25
75	Wave-4 prework, including champion class and black belt selection along with project assignment.	25 days	6/13	7/17
76	Quarterly executive review of Six Sigma improvement activity, status, and update. Agenda is structured for 2.5 hours with Q&A.	1 day	8/21	8/21
77	Fourth champions class.	2 days	8/15	8/18
78	Fourth champions class, Session 1 of 2.	1 day	8/15	8/15
79	Fourth champions class, Session 2 of 2.	1 day	8/18	8/18
80	Wave-4 of black belts (Measure, Analyze, Improve, and Control). (Class size 10-20.)	65 days	9/8	12/5
81	Beginning of wave-2 session 1 (Measure).	4 days	9/8	9/11
82	Wave-4 Six Sigma review 1 (Analyze).	1 day	10/6	10/6
83	Wave-4 Six Sigma review 2 (Improve).	1 day	11/3	11/3
84	Wave-4 Six Sigma review 3 (Control).	1 day	12/1	12/1
85	Wave-2 last training week (Control), session 4.	4 days	12/2	12/5
86	Six Sigma team training sessions 10 days after Measure phase of each wave	5 days	9/22	9/26
87	Master black belts program. (This is only 8–12 master black belts, your internal consultants for sustainment, includes training department.)	1 day	8/26	8/26
88	Supplier base option. Client will help populate key suppliers that will work on projects to benefit both parties. Key leveraged suppliers will share 50% of cost savings with client.	1 day	8/26	8/26

FIGURE 2-1   (*Continued*)

During this time, the executive team should also start to identify, evaluate, and prioritize potential projects. The members should be familiar enough with processes throughout the organization to identify those that the Six Sigma teams should investigate and improve. The implementation partner should help evaluate and prioritize projects in terms of their impact on customers and finances. We'll discuss this process in Chapter 5.

TRAINING

Next, Six Sigma is further introduced in key sessions to executives and managers, to ensure that they understand the basics and support the initiative.

For Executives

Executive training should be offered to all senior managers. Ideally, it should include all members of the executive team, regardless of the initial focus of the initiative. In particular, the heads of the following functions must participate in the workshop and be active in the deployment:

- Finance, because it is responsible for determining the dollar impact of the projects and creating a system to track the tangible results
- Human resources, because it is responsible for reward and recognition systems and the career paths of the champions, master black belts, black belts, and green belts
- Information technology, because it is responsible for developing computer systems to collect measurement data from the projects and for providing technological support for improvements

Executive training typically takes two days. It should include an initial pretest to gauge the current knowledge base, an overview of Six Sigma, a review of case studies, a definition of the roles of executive team members, a discussion of deployment strategies, an exploration of scientific tools and methods, a presentation of statistical analysis and measurements, a discussion of management controls, development of a draft deployment plan, a posttest of the material, and identification of areas to target for improvement and the champions of these areas.

After introducing Six Sigma to executives and managers and determining who will receive executive and champion training, the next steps in this planning phase are to order training materials, select black belt candidates, and schedule training. As you compile your list of black belt candidates, you develop "job descriptions" for their new roles and coordinate with your human resources department to post them. Human resources should also benchmark compensation plans that reward black belts and their teams upon the completion of projects.

The executive workshop is followed in approximately one month by a workshop of three to five days for the people identified as champions during the executive workshop. This workshop uses as input the initial deployment plan and the project areas that were outputs of the executive workshop and refined in subsequent weeks.

This workshop is particularly important because inactive or ineffective champions are often identified as the root cause of project failures. If the executives and the champions do not take this role seriously or do not properly understand it, the champions can become the weak link in the Six Sigma initiative, with devastating consequences.

For Champions

Champion training should be offered to managers at all levels. Champion training provides the managerial and technical knowledge necessary to plan and implement Six Sigma and mentor black belts. The goal is to transfer and reinforce fundamental Six Sigma strategies, tactics, and tools necessary for achieving the breakthrough in key processes. Training covers the principles, tools, and applications of Six Sigma, including deployment tactics and strategies for establishing metrics, selecting black belts and projects, and implementing Six Sigma. A champion must understand what his black belts are working with in order to best facilitate their progress. At a minimum, a champion must be trained in the following:

- Project selection methods
- Basic statistics
- Capability analysis
- Measurement systems analysis
- Process mapping
- *XY* matrix
- Hypothesis testing
- Design of experiments

A champion who knows what her black belts are doing can better understand all their findings in their final reports and, in turn, present and explain those results to upper management.

After their training workshop, the champions meet with the black belt candidates to discuss the projects and make any refinements needed. Refinements are often needed because the black belts have detailed data and insights that were not available when the project charters were developed. (Project charters will be discussed in greater detail in Chapter 7.)

For Black Belts

Once you've selected your black belts, determined how they will be rewarded, and decided what your projects will entail, it's time to kick off the training phase. This involves coordinating all logistics for the training sites, ensuring that you and your executive team are ready to serve as champions and that your training materials and instructors are ready to go. Then you communicate with black belts about the training schedule and prepare them for their first day of class.

Black belt training usually follows the champion workshop by approximately one month. The black belts are expected to bring their project charters to the training and work on their actual projects as part of the training. They will learn and deliver results at the same time. Such an approach is consistent with the principles of adult learning.

The crucial point to keep in mind is that training of black belts and green belts should be thorough but not overwhelming. Also, as much as possible, it should be just in time. A tool should be taught just before the training participants need to use it. Then they should be guided in using it. That way, they are exposed only to what they will need in the immediate future, they are more motivated to learn, and they learn better because they're applying what they've learned and they're understanding directly the value of the tools.

The goal in training black belts is to create an independent thinker, technical leaders, advanced practitioners, and teachers of Six Sigma. Black belts should learn the philosophy of Six Sigma, tactics for applying it, and group dynamics.

Training for black belts basically follows the DMAIC sequence. They learn about measuring, analyzing, improving, and controlling processes in intensive, hands-on training sessions that take eight hours a day, five days a week, for a month—30 days of non-stop immersion in Six Sigma.

Here's a typical black belt training agenda:

- Measure (Week One)—Black belts are introduced to Six Sigma. They are assigned projects, and they are taught process mapping, FMEA matrices, statistics, capability studies, measurement systems, and project application. (We'll get into these matters in Chapter 8.) They are also assigned regular homework.
- Analyze (Week Two)—Black belts learn how to analyze distributions, graphically plot data, conduct multivari analyses, do hypothesis testing, and plan project applications (more in Chapter 9) while completing regular homework assignments.
- Improve (Week Three)—Black belts learn the design of experiments method, understand correlation studies, conduct full factorial experiments, and continue to plan and execute project plans. (We'll get into these tools in Chapter 10.)
- Control (Week Four)—Digging into all the control tools, black belts now review the methodology, learn how to implement statistical methods of control and mistake proofing, and finalize their project work.

Your aim in training black belts is to create technical leaders, advanced users, and teachers of Six Sigma. They should learn its philosophy, application tactics (including statistics, benchmarking, process-control techniques, diagnostic methods, and experiment design), and group dynamics. Then, once you've trained your black belts, you assign them to the projects you've selected.

Critical to the success of your black belts is the on-site support of an experienced master black belt, usually provided by the outside consultant. A master black belt will guide and coach the black belt candidates and work with champions to help overcome barriers and obstacles. A master black belt also builds relationships with company leaders to inform and educate them on the progress of their Six Sigma initiative.

It's important that employees understand that they will be able to transition back into their regular job responsibilities if they do not continue on working as black belts or do not move up to become master black belts. Some might be concerned that involvement in the Six Sigma initiative might slow down their career progress or even sidetrack them. It's important to recognize contributions to the Six Sigma initiative and make them advantageous to careers, perhaps even required for advancement, but it's also important for employees to be able to commit temporarily without fear of risking it all.

For Green Belts

Green belts also receive training in the methodology, so they can help and support the black belts. They must have at least a working knowledge of the methodology, but their training is not as rigorous or detailed as that of the black belts. Green belts are provided enough training to develop their technical knowledge to the point that they become local experts at solving problems.

PLANNING AND COURAGE

These planning stages can be considered as the steps necessary to laying the foundation for Six Sigma. Each Six Sigma deployment follows essentially the same success model for implementation. The specifics of your particular situation, the projects you select, and the champions and black belts will determine how you create a plan and a schedule for all activities.

In case you're wondering how all of this gets done, remember that your outside consultant is there to direct, train, and execute the critical elements of the planning process. Your implementation partner can help you orchestrate all responsibilities, roles, and schedules to make a smooth transition from planning to implementation.

It takes courage to decide to do Six Sigma. It takes courage to implement it, to use the Six Sigma techniques and tools, to persevere, to make changes. You can't find that courage in a methodology; you have to encourage and promote it in the people who use Six Sigma.

The success of Six Sigma relies on the people who are responsible for implementing it. Six Sigma provides some powerful techniques and tools, but success depends on the people who play the primary roles and assume the central responsibilities for putting those techniques and tools to work.

Six Sigma necessarily upsets the status quo, as job descriptions are redefined and activities are radically changed. This must happen to make any real, permanent improvements.

SUMMARY

Plan well. There are many steps in a Six Sigma initiative and many players to prepare and coordinate to ensure the best possible outcomes.

Survey how much you and your people actually know about basic Six Sigma tools to gauge the extent and depth of training you will all need before starting.

The top leaders of your company must be committed to the Six Sigma process and to changing the conventional ways of operating. They must commit company resources to help the Six Sigma initiative succeed and they must commit their time and energy to actively promoting the initiative.

To begin a Six Sigma initiative properly, you need to survey your company's knowledge, to identify the gaps or misconceptions, and to determine how you can best provide training. Surveying your knowledge base is as individual as your company culture.

The results of Six Sigma depend on the people in the following five roles:

- Executive leaders
- Champions
- Master black belt
- Black belts
- Green belts

Executive leaders are responsible for deciding to do Six Sigma and for publicly endorsing it and promoting it. They must reinforce the comprehensive scope of Six Sigma to engage everyone's support and participation. Involve executive managers in leading the Six Sigma initiative throughout the organization. Their leadership is crucial to success.

Champions are responsible for promoting the Six Sigma methodology throughout the company and especially in functional groups. Champions are closest to the processes. They understand the discipline and tools, help select projects, establish objectives, coach and mentor, remove barriers, and dedicate resources to support black belts. Champions must own the process in question and be dedicated to doing whatever it takes to make it easier for the black belts to achieve results.

The master black belt is responsible for teaching executive managers the basics and helping them select the right people for project teams and screen and select projects. An expert in Six Sigma tools and tactics, the master black belt teaches and mentors black belts and green belts. Use the expertise and experience of a master black belt wherever and whenever possible. These skilled practitioners can be extraordinarily valuable in helping you launch your initiative.

Black belts are responsible for leading project teams full time. They do nothing else but root out variation and identify the vital few factors. Choose your black belt candidates with care. It takes certain qualities to be a black belt; training develops these qualities, but it can't create them. Pick the right people to lead your Six Sigma project teams—and empower those key players. Make sure that your black belts and team members have the essential quality tools for a particular project.

Green belts are responsible for helping black belts in their functional area, working on projects part time, usually in a limited, specific area related to their regular jobs. They also help black belts do more in less time—collecting or analyzing data, running experiments, or doing other important project tasks. They are team members with enough understanding of Six Sigma to transform company culture from the ground up.

Recognition and rewards are essential. The executive team should create rewards that employees can earn in the short term for exceptional efforts and rewards for team members who meet their individual and team goals.

Outside consultants can help start Six Sigma initiatives. If you decide to work with an implementation partner, engage one with the demonstrated qualifications to best lead your Six Sigma initiative. Your consultant should help you plan and structure your initiative, select the right projects, train your people so you can move toward self-sufficiency quickly, and be focused on knowledge transfer and on showing you how to solve problems most effectively, so you can transfer that knowledge throughout your organization. Check credentials: request references and actual case studies from clients. You want to know how they contributed to the results.

The controller is responsible for verifying the bottom-line results of Six Sigma projects. Champions and the controller need to be operating from the same monetary baseline, in agreement on how to calculate real savings and to distinguish between hard dollars and soft dollars.

Your primary resources are your people, particularly the ones who will play the key roles in your Six Sigma projects. Define the key roles from the start. All the key players should know their responsibilities and how all of the roles work together. Six Sigma success depends on you, your team, and the unqualified support of executive leaders. They must be committed to making it work. They need to lead, understand, and support the initiative throughout the organization.

Six Sigma focuses on real, tangible financial results. You and your staff need to learn how to implement it and get started. There should not be seminar after seminar to further develop their Six Sigma skills. Of course, they need to know what they're doing, but once they're trained as black belts and using what they've learned, they'll know exactly how and what they need to do. It's all about getting bottom-line results.

The best way to build awareness about Six Sigma through a company-wide communication from your CEO or president. Make sure you and your executives regularly communicate why, when, and how you are undertaking Six Sigma projects so that everyone in the organization is committed to your efforts. Tell everyone what you're doing and what you intend to accomplish.

The executive team should prepare a deployment plan, outlining training, goals, strategy, roles and responsibilities, criteria and procedure for selecting projects, a system for tracking projects, a plan for rewards and recognition, and a communications plan.

A big part of implementing Six Sigma is necessarily training. But, although you want to train your people well, particularly your black belts, you don't want to spend excessive time "tweaking" training materials to fit your exact business model. You should certainly relate training materials to your business focus, but recognize the overall and adaptable nature of Six Sigma and get busy applying it, not discussing it. Keep the focus on getting results.

It's also very important to communicate and celebrate each milestone of success. This keeps your team's enthusiasm high and demonstrates how Six Sigma is working. Tell employees, upper management, customers, and vendors; they need to know the value of your efforts every step of the way.

It takes courage to decide to do Six Sigma. You can't find that courage in a methodology; you have to encourage and promote it in the people who use Six Sigma. The success of Six Sigma relies on the people who are responsible for the primary roles in the initiative.

CASE STUDY

This case study is a real-life example showing the outcome of a good start and the benefits of keeping the momentum going. BHP Billiton is one of the world's top three producers of copper and a leading producer of lead and zinc.

"To remain competitive in our marketplace," Bradford A. Mills, the president and CEO of Base Metals, stated in his letter in March 2003, "we must be the lowest cost and highest quality provider in the market today." That's why Six Sigma is one of "the three main pillars" of the company's "Base Metals Culture Change Program."

For its Six Sigma initiative, BHP Billiton originally set a goal of $90 million annually of net cost savings or revenue enhancements within two years. However, Mills said that the company had underestimated the power of Six Sigma. "When we benchmarked ourselves against the better-deployed Six Sigma programs, that goal might actually be too low an expectation." So, the company decided to redesign and relaunch its Six Sigma program in two phases, in a "revitalization effort to re-ignite the desire to drive to the next higher level":

- Phase one: "We will evaluate the current program in order to establish what it will take to achieve the results we are seeking."
- Phase two: "We will launch the deployment plan generated in the design phase."

As part of that revitalization effort, the company appointed a Six Sigma program director and engaged an implementation partner to maximize the gains from implementing Six Sigma. The company set what Mills called "an aggressive but achievable schedule" in order to include the program in the upcoming budget cycle.

He closed his letter with the following exhortation:

The fundamentals of teamwork and team contribution are a basic foundation for every significant undertaking, and this is no exception. It is imperative that we operate as a team as we develop synergy between our key success strategies of Six Sigma, Zero Harm, and BHP Billiton Charter over the next year, as we endeavor to set the new standards for our industry.

REVIEW QUESTIONS

1. A black belt works on Six Sigma projects part-time.

   a. True

   b. False

   c. Only if you have part-time problems

   d. Both a and c

   e. Both b and c

   f. None of the above

2. What is the average annual savings per black belt?

   a. We don't measure it

   b. $10,000–$20,000

   c. $40,000

   d. $175,000

   e. $600,000 and $1 million

3. Hard dollars are

   a. Money that's difficult to earn

   b. Savings that are tangible and quantifiable

   c. Silver coins

   d. U.S. currency in a global economy

3

SOME STATISTICS

NOW THAT YOU HAVE a general idea of the methodology of Six Sigma and understand who plays what roles in a Six Sigma initiative, we reach the point where we must get into something that many people dread about Six Sigma—statistics. So, we'll discuss a few basic concepts in this chapter that will allow us to move into business metrics in Chapter 4.

Because it uses statistical terminology, Six Sigma is frequently perceived as a statistics and measurement program. This is not the case.

The Six Sigma approach to management uses statistics solely as tools for interpreting and clarifying data. Data is not information. You have to torture it before it tells all it knows. (Most of us will have little difficulty with the analogy between statistics and torture, when we recall our student days.) The issue is not so much "What data do we have?" as "Which statistical tool should we use to explore the information hidden in the data?" You focus on tool selection and the use and interpretation of data to drive decisions.

You need to understand and use statistical data and respect its value. Statistics and statistical tools are essential to Six Sigma. But Six Sigma practitioners also use computers and statistical software to take advantage of knowledge and speed the improvement process. You do not need to spend exorbitant amounts of time reviewing stats. With the systems and software available, you'll have the critical formulas and equations at your fingertips so you can let technology and training work together to yield results. Your implementation partner usually provides such training systems. So, it's not about becoming a master of statistics, but of achieving six-sigma performance—systems and processes that are as perfect as possible, functioning at their highest performance level.

VARIATION

Variation is the basis of Six Sigma. It's defined as the fluctuation in the output of a process. Sometimes it's called *noise*—but it can be very expensive noise. It is a truism of Six Sigma that every repeatable process exhibits variation.

Any improvement of any process should reduce variation, so that the process can more consistently meet expectations—of either internal customers (such as the employees responsible for subsequent processes) or external customers. In Six Sigma, teams must approach all projects from the perspective of understanding the variation in the inputs of a process, controlling them, and reducing or eliminating the defects.

But in order to reduce variation, we must be able to measure it.

So, how do we measure variation? There are several ways, each with advantages and disadvantages. Let's take a very simple example to show how these methods work.

Your company produces widgets. There are two lines that assemble the components, A and B. You want to reduce the variation in assembly times so that the workers who package the components can work most efficiently—not waiting for finished widgets, not falling behind, and not being forced to work so quickly that they make mistakes.

The first step is to track assembly times. You gather the following data:

Process A: 3.7, 6.5, 3.2, 3.2, 5.7, 7.4, 5.7, 7.7, 4.2, 2.9
Process B: 4.7, 5.3, 4.7, 5.4, 4.7, 4.4, 4.7, 5.8, 4.2, 5.7

Now, what do those figures mean? We can compare the two processes in several ways, using common statistical concepts. (In reality, you would be collecting much more data—hundreds or even thousands of measurements.)

Mean, Median, Mode, and Range

If we use the mean (the average, also known as the arithmetic mean or the simple average), we find that line A averages 5.02 minutes and line B averages 4.96 minutes. By that measure, the times measured for the two processes would be very close. But we don't know which process varies more.

We can calculate the median value (the midpoint in our range of data). For A it's 4.95 and for B it's 4.7. By that measure, again, the two processes would be close, although not quite as close as when we use the mean.

We can also calculate the mode (the value that occurs most often). For A, it would be either 3.2 (two times) or 5.7 (two times) and for B it's 4.7 (four times). So, what does the mode tell us? Not much.

Based on these three measurements, what do we know about the variations in our two widget assembly lines? How do they compare? Which statistical concept best represents the variation in each line?

We quickly come to the conclusion that we don't know much about our variation at this point. Fortunately, there are two more concepts that we can use: range and standard deviation.

Range is easy to calculate: it's simply the spread of values, the difference between the highest and the lowest. The range for A is 4.8 (7.7 – 2.9) and the range for B is 1.6 (5.8 – 4.2). Now, that measure shows a considerable discrepancy between A and B. The variation in process A is much greater than in process B—at least if we use the range as our measure.

But range is a rough measure because it uses only maximum and minimum values. It seems to work OK in this case. But what if we had a third process, for which we measured the following values?

Process C: 3.2, 6.5, 3.4, 6.4, 6.5, 3.3, 3.7, 6.4, 6.5, 3.5

The range for this set of values is 3.3 (6.5 – 3.2), which suggests that there's less variation in process C than in process A (range = 4.8) and more variation than in process B (range = 1.6). But common sense tells us that the values for C vary more than the values for A, even if less widely, and that they vary only a little more than the values for B. But that's just common sense; we need to quantify the variation for each process.

We need another concept, something more accurate than range for calculating and representing process variation. That concept is standard deviation.

Standard Deviation

The most accurate measure for quantifying variation is standard deviation, which is an indicator of the degree of variation in a set of measurements or a process calculated by measuring the average spread of the data around the mean. Calculating the standard deviation is more complicated than calculating the mean, the median, the mode, or the range, but it provides a far more accurate quantification of variation.

As with many formulas, the formula for the standard deviation seems more difficult because it uses symbols. But you already know one of those symbols, sigma (the Greek letter σ), which is the symbol in statistics for standard deviation, as you remember from Chapter 1. Another symbol is really simple: capital sigma (the Greek letter Σ) is used to indicate the sum of some values. The third symbol is X, which stands for values. For the fourth symbol, we place a bar over the X and call it (logically) *bar X* and use it to represent the arithmetic mean, which, as we mentioned above, most of us know more commonly as the average. The final symbol in the equation for standard deviation is n, which stands for the number of times we measure something. OK, now we're ready for that formula.

Standard deviation measures the variation of values from the mean, using the following formula:

$$\sigma = \frac{\sqrt{\sum (X - \bar{X})^2}}{n}$$

where Σ = sum of, X = observed values, $\bar{X}$ = arithmetic mean, and n = number of observations. That formula might seem complicated, but it's actually simple to understand if we break it down into steps:

1. Find the average of the process values.
2. Subtract the average from each value.
3. Square the difference for each value (which eliminates any negative numbers from the equation).
4. Add all of these squared deviation values.
5. Divide the sum of squared deviations by the total number of values.
6. Take the square root of the result of that division.

So, when we do the calculations for process A, process B, and process C (fortunately, there are software applications that can crunch these numbers for us.), we get the following results:

A: standard deviation = 1.81
B: standard deviation = 0.55
C: standard deviation = 1.61

These figures quantify what we observed, that the variation in process A is considerably greater than the variation in process B and slightly greater than the variation in process C. Our simple example uses only 10 values for each process, so it might seem that calculating standard deviation doesn't help us much more than simply using common sense. But when our measurements give us many more values and when we want to use the figures to track the progress of our efforts to improve our processes, it's much more useful to calculate standard deviation—and we appreciate even more the software that does all of these calculations for us.

Another measurement of the spread of a distribution is *variance*, which is the square of the standard deviation. The variance is calculated as the sum of the squared deviations of n measurements from their mean divided by $(n-1)$.

DISTRIBUTIONS AND CURVES

If we plot the values for a process and we have a large number of values, we'll likely find that the distribution of values forms some variant of a bell-shaped curve—high in the middle around the mean and tapering off on both sides

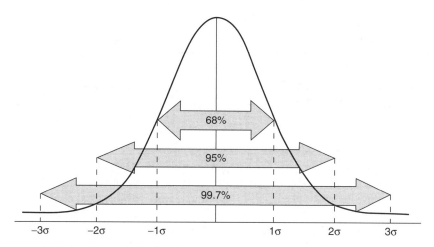

FIGURE 3-1   Normal distribution

more or less symmetrically. (See Figure 3-1.) This distribution pattern is considered normal. These are the characteristics of a normal curve:

- A normal distribution can be described in terms of two parameters— its mean and its standard deviation.
- A normal distribution is symmetrical around its mean.
- In a normal distribution, the mean, the median, and the mode are equal.
- 68 percent of the values lie within 1 standard deviation (± 1 sigma) of the mean.
- 95 percent of the values lie within 2 standard deviations (± 2 sigma) of the mean.
- 99.73 percent of the values lie within 3 standard deviations (± 3 sigma) of the mean.

Historically, 3 sigma has been the standard. It has been reflected in design specifications and control charts where tolerances and acceptable boundaries have often been arbitrarily set at plus or minus 3 standard deviations (± 3 sigma). That makes sense: after all, 99.73 percent of the values in a normal distribution lie within 3 standard deviations of the mean. So, if a process is good enough that 99.7 percent of the outputs are acceptable, that should be enough, right?

Well, yes—until Six Sigma changed the standard. But we'll get into that complication a few pages from now.

Applying Statistics

Now that we've covered the basic statistics, let's apply those concepts to our situation of assembling widgets. Your goal is to reduce the variation in your widget assembly processes. So you first need to determine how much variation is acceptable to your customers, the employees in the widget packaging group. Then, you use those values to set a lower specification limit (LSL) and an upper specification limit (USL). These are the lower and upper boundaries within which your assembly processes must operate, the values beyond which the performance of the processes is unacceptable. (The spec limits are sometimes also called the upper tolerance limit—UTL—and the lower tolerance limit—LTL.)

If an aspect of a process, a product, or a service that customers consider critical to quality exceeds either spec limit, it's considered a defect. (Remember, from Chapter 1, that a defect is defined as a measurable characteristic of the process or its output that is not within the acceptable and expected customer limits, i.e., not conforming to specifications.)

In our example, you might determine that the customers think that it would be ideal if the assembly lines took exactly 5 minutes per widget but they would be happy if the time were between 4 and 6 minutes (within 1 minute either way of the ideal time of 5 minutes). So, you set an LSL of 4.0 and an USL of 6.0 around a mean of 5.02 minutes for line A and a mean of 4.96 for line B (Figure 3-2).

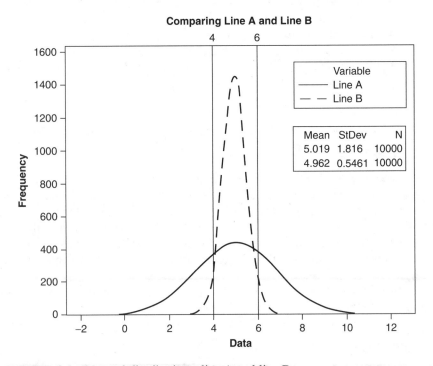

FIGURE 3-2   Normal distributions, line A and line B

Because the standard deviation for A is 1.81, we're quite far from our goal because the standard deviation is greater than the interval between the LSL and the mean (1.02) and the interval between the USL and the mean (0.98).

On the other hand, because the standard deviation for B is 0.55, we're already meeting our goal, because the standard deviation is greater than the interval between the LSL and the mean (0.96) and the interval between the USL and the mean (1.04). Of course, we already knew that line B was meeting the customer's expectations, at least according to our 10 measurements, because we measured no times above 6 minutes or below 4 minutes. However, the times of 4.2 and 5.8, very close to the LCL of 4 and the UCL of 6, should make us wonder if it might be wise to take some more measurements.

Our objective is to ultimately reduce the variation in the processes so that 99.99966 percent of the outputs will fall between the LSL and the USL. In other words, the processes will be producing at most 3.4 DPMO.

CAUSES OF VARIATION

There are two categories of causes of variation—common and special. A *common* cause is any source of unacceptable variation that is part of the random variation inherent in the process, when unknown factors result in a steady but random distribution of output around the average of the data. For this reason, it is also known as a *random* cause; common-cause variation is also called random variation, inherent variation, noise, noncontrollable variation, and within-group variation. Common cause variation is the result of many factors that are usually part of the process, acting at random, each independently— many X's, each with a small impact. Common-cause variation is the standard deviation of the distribution. It is a measure of the process potential, how well the process can perform without any special cause variation.

A *special* cause is any source of unacceptable variation that lies outside the process. A special cause is sometimes also called an *assignable* cause. Special-cause variation is the result of a nonrandom event, intermittent and unpredictable, and the changes in the process output are occasional and unexpected—a nonrandom distribution of output, a shift of a sample mean from the target. Also called *assignable variation* or *exceptional variation*, special-cause variation is a shift in output caused by a specific factor, such as environmental conditions or process input parameters—few X's with a big impact.

Here's another way of expressing the difference between common causes and special causes. Variation from common causes is natural and variation from special causes is unnatural: on control charts, natural variation is variation between the UCL and the LCL and unnatural variation is variation above the UCL or below the LCL.

Why is it important to distinguish between the two? Because each category requires a different approach, different strategies. Common causes require a long-term strategy of process management to identify, understand, and reduce them. Special causes of variation require immediate action.

It's estimated that approximately 94 percent of problems are caused by common-cause variation. The less well-defined a process is, the more vulnerable it is to random variation and the more defects result. However, if there is any special cause of variation, the Six Sigma team must first eliminate it before working to stabilize the process, bring it into statistical control, and then improve it. If there are only common causes of variation, the output of a process forms a distribution that is stable over time.

If there are special causes of variation, a process cannot be stable over time. The team must first identify any special causes and eliminate them to bring the process into statistical control.

PROCESS CAPABILITY

In addition to the lower and upper specification limits, there's another pair of limits that should be plotted for any process—the lower control limit (LCL) and the upper control limit (UCL). These values mark the minimum and maximum inherent limits of the process, based on data collected from the process. If the control limits are within the specification limits or align with them, then the process is considered to be capable of meeting the specification. If either or both of the control limits are outside the specification limits, then the process is considered incapable of meeting the specification.

Process capability is a statistical measure of inherent variation for a given characteristic in a stable process. In other words, it's the measure of the ability of a process to produce outputs that meet the specifications. It expresses the range of the natural variation as determined by common causes.

If you place the control limits on a process capability curve and the LCL is three sigma to the left of center and the UCL is three sigma to the right of center, the process capability is three sigma. The area of the curve between the two control limits represents the percentage of products or services that meet the specifications—99.73 percent. The area outside the control limits is the percentage that is out of spec—0.27 percent. That percentage equates to 2,700 DPMO.

Shift

That might seem simple enough, but then statisticians add the complication of a shift. They've found that processes tend to shift from center over time. A process that has been improved is generally at its best immediately after the improvement. Data for the project is collected over a period of months;

discrepancies are likely when it's collected over years. Also, because the project team should exclude special cause variation in order to focus on common cause variation, the short-term data will usually indicate a higher process capability than the long-term data, which is likely to be affected by special cause variation. Consequently, a process that's really six sigma immediately after the project team has improved it would likely suffer some losses over time.

Controlling a process so that it remains on target in the longer term can be difficult. That's why, in discussing process capability, it is common to distinguish between *short-term* capability and *long-term* capability. This distinction can seem complicated, but it's a simple idea.

The standard deviation and sigma level of a process are considered short-term values because the data is collected by the project team over a period of months and it shows the results of common-cause variation only. In contrast, data collected over years will show the results of common-cause variation and special-cause variation.

The Six Sigma pioneers at Motorola recognized this difficulty and adjusted for it. They calculated that, under the worst conditions, the performance of a process might suffer a degradation of as much as 1.5 sigma. So, they decided to allow in their calculations for this worst-case scenario and, to compensate, they corrected in advance for a possible shift of 1.5 sigma. If you consult a standard normal distribution table, you'll find that 6 sigma actually equates to about 2 defects per *billion* opportunities (0.002 DPMO). The figure usually used for 6 sigma, as in this book—3.4 defects per *million* opportunities—really equates to 4.5 sigma. In other words, although statistical tables show 3.4 DPMO when the distribution between the mean and the closest specification limit is 4.5 sigma, the target is raised to 6.0 sigma to compensate for process shifts over time and still achieve a maximum of only 3.4 DPMO.

Shifts in process averages will not always be as great as 1.5 sigma, but that figure allows enough leeway to ensure that the process will meet the goal of 3.4 DPMO over the long term.

There's nothing sacred about 1.5 sigma. Some practitioners advocate a lower figure. It's possible to use a different figure when setting your sigma target for a process, if you have data from experiences with similar processes. However, it's simpler and safer to use the figures that have been adjusted to accommodate shifts of as much as 1.5 sigma. So, when a process that's at 3 sigma shifts 1.5 sigma from center, the capability declines from 99.73 percent to only 93.32 percent, as 6.68 percent of the area is now outside the control limits. This equates to 66,807 DPMO.

The goal of Six Sigma is to reduce the standard deviation of your process variation to the point that 6 sigma (six standard deviations) can fit within your specification limits. At that level of process capability, a shift of 1.5 sigma from center results in a defect rate of only 3.4 DPMO.

Capability Indices

Various indices are used to represent process capability. These indices are calculated by a process capability study, which is a preliminary statistical test of process output to predict the quality level that can be expected from that process. A process capability index uses process variability and process specifications to determine how capable a process is. As mentioned above, process capability is a measure of a process that is stable; capability indices have meaning only for processes that exhibit statistical control.

There are two capability indices with which you should be familiar: *Cp* and *Cpk*. These two are the most widely used of all the capability indices. (*Cpk* is sometimes called *process performance,* to distinguish it from *Cp, process capability.*)

Cp can be used if the mean of the process is centered on the target value. *Cp* is a measure of the width of a distribution of outputs of the process. It tells us how nearly we can repeat product characteristics. *Cpk* tells us the same thing, but also how close the average value is to the target value.

To calculate *Cp* and *Cpk*, we use the *spec width* and the *process width.* The spec width is the difference between the upper specification limit (USL) and the lower specification limit (LSL), a.k.a. upper tolerance limit (UTL) and lower tolerance limit (LTL), which we defined earlier as the upper and lower boundaries within which a process must operate, the values beyond which the performance of the process is unacceptable. So we subtract the LSL from the USL to get the spec width.

The process width is the difference between the upper control limit (UCL) and the lower control limit (LCL). These two limits indicate how well the process is doing. So we subtract the LCL from the UCL to get the process width. The process width can also be calculated by multiplying the standard deviation of the process by 6.

The *Cp* of a process is usually expressed as *spec width* divided by *process width*:

$$Cp = \text{spec width/process width} \quad \text{or} \quad Cp = USL - LSL/6\sigma$$

So, what do the results mean? Simply, the higher your *Cp*, the less variation in your process. A *Cp* of 1 is acceptable. A Cp less than 1 is bad: the process is not acceptable. A *Cp* greater than 1 is good. A *Cp* of 1.33 is standard. (The two process capability indices, *Cp* and *Cpk*, have counterparts in two process performance indices, *Pp* and *Ppk*. We'll discuss these two and a related pair of capability ratios in Chapter 13.)

Let's return to our example of the widget assembly lines. The means for our sampling of 10 values were A = 5.02, B = 4.96, and C = 4.94. The standard deviations were A = 1.81, B = 0.55, and C = 1.61. Our LSL is set at 4.0 and our USL is set at 6.0. Because we allow ±1 minute from the ideal mean difference, reaching a quality level of 6 sigma would mean reducing the standard deviation of both process A and process B to about 0.166. The *Cp* of process A is 1.105, the *Cp* of process B is 3.636, and the *Cp* of process C is 0.207.

Cp is a measure of variation; however, it does not consider how well the output measured is centered on the target value. Figure 3-3 shows two distributions that have *Cp* of 2.0 but are quite different in terms of their relation to the process center, the target. Because *Cp* does not take into account the process mean (where the process is centered), if the process mean is not located at the midpoint between the USL and the LSL, *Cp* has little meaning.

That's why we need *Cpk*. It measures how well the output is centered on the target value. *Cpk* is an adjustment of *Cp* for the effect of noncentered distribution. In essence, *Cpk* splits the process capability of *Cp* into two values. *Cpk* = the lesser of these two calculations:

$$\text{USL} - \text{mean}/3\sigma \quad \text{or} \quad \text{mean} - LSL/3\sigma$$

We calculate 0.180478821 or 0.187845304 for *A*, 0.63030303 or 0.581818182 for *B*, and 0.219461698 or 0.194616977 for *C*. Taking the lesser of the two figures for each, we have these *Cpk*'s: *A* = 0.180478821, *B* = 0.581818182, and *C* = 0.194616977.

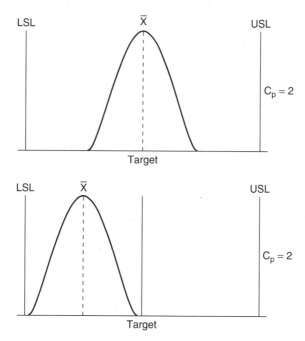

FIGURE 3-3 Two distributions with a Cp of 2.0

Cp	Quality Level
0.167	0.5 sigma
0.333	1.0 sigma
0.50	1.5 sigma
0.667	2.0 sigma
0.833	2.5 sigma
1.00	3.0 sigma
1.167	3.5 sigma
1.33	4.0 sigma
1.500	4.5 sigma
1.66	5.0 sigma
1.833	5.5 sigma
2.00	6.0 sigma

FIGURE 3-4   *Cp* values and sigma levels

Comparing *Cpk* and *Cp* for a process will show how far that process is off center. If the process is centered on the target value, that is, if the process mean is midway between the USL and the LSL, then *Cp* and *Cpk* will be identical.

Here's a simple way to think of *Cp* and *Cpk*. If you plotted the values measured for a process, the *Cp* would show how closely together they cluster (indication of precision), while *Cpk* would show how close the values come to the target specification (indication of accuracy).

The higher the *Cpk* of a process, the better the process should be. Figure 3-4 shows how *Cp* values correspond with sigma levels. A *Cpk* less than 1 indicates that the process is out of spec. A *Cpk* of 0 indicates that the process center is at one of the spec limits. A Cpk less than 0 indicates that the process center is outside one of the spec limits.

Our three lines don't fare so well: a *Cpk*-sigma conversion table shows that A (0.180478821) is between 0.500 and 0.625 sigma, B (0.581818182) is just under 1.750 sigma, and C (0.194616977) is a little under 0.625 sigma. We don't need to carry the calculations out beyond the first decimal place to recognize that all three processes are very defective.

Process Capability: Two Simple Examples

To show the purpose of process capability indices, we can use as an example the performance of the field goal specialist on a football team. He must kick the ball between the goal posts: those are his specification limits. Any result between those limits is good. Any result outside those limits is a defect. We establish a baseline by having the kicker attempt a field goal 100 times. The number of successful kicks out of those 100 attempts is his capability.

The scoreboard registers only successes, but that's not good enough for us because we want to improve his kicking process. So we want to measure his accuracy in terms of the exact center of the goalposts. The less his kicks deviate from that ideal, the more confidence we can have in our kicker.

So, we track the distribution of the kicks through the uprights. That allows us to calculate the capability index Cp—the distance between the goal posts divided by six times the standard deviation of his 100 kicks. Also, if the kicker tends to pull to one side or the other, we might measure this shift in the process with the capability index Cpk.

Now we not only know the percentage of correct outcomes, but also understand how we need to work on his kicking process to make it more reliable, less susceptible to circumstances that might cause variation, such as wind or wet turf.

We can also imagine aiming at a target, whether shooting a gun or arrows or throwing darts. If you're hitting consistently within a small area on the target, your Cp would be high. However, that area of closely bunched hits could be anywhere on the target. If you're hitting on or around the bull's-eye, your Cpk would also be high. If you're hitting closer to the edge, your Cp would be low.

ROLLED THROUGHPUT YIELD

Six sigma is a performance target that applies to a single critical-to-quality characteristic (CTQ), not to an entire process, product, or service. A process capability of 6 sigma means that, on average, there will be only 3.4 defects in a critical-to-quality characteristic per million opportunities for a defect in this characteristic. The more complex a process, the more likely a defect will occur at some point.

As complicated as the concepts and formulas might be for sigma and process capability, they are simple calculations, actually, because the issue of variation is simple—when we talk about a process as being simple. The sigma levels and DPMOs that we've been discussing apply to only one step and one specification. That is *first-time yield* (FTY)—the number of good units coming out of a process or a step divided by the number of total units going into the process or step. (*Yield* is the percentage of units coming out of a process free of defects.)

However, virtually all processes consist of more than one step and involve more than one specification. Because variation is additive, we must consider and calculate cumulative effects of variation in each part of a process. In other words, we must think in terms of what could be called the worst-case scenario of variation. In Six Sigma, this is called *rolled throughput yield* (RTY).

RTY, also known as the *rolling effect*, is the probability that a single unit can pass through all the steps in a process free of defects. It's the net result of the effect of all of the steps in a process.

In a five-step process in which each step has a first-time yield of 93.32 percent (three sigma), the process as a whole is not at 93.32 percent good. Instead, we must calculate the *RTY* as follows:

$$RTY = \text{Step1 yield} \times \text{Step 2 yield} \times \text{Step 3 yield}$$
$$\times \text{Step 4 yield} \times \text{Step 5 yield}$$

or

$$RTY = 0.9332 \times 0.9332 \times 0.9332 \times 0.9332 \times 0.9332 = 0.707739852$$

The *RTY* of 70.8 percent means that you have a 70.8 percent chance of getting through this five-step process without a defect. That's just a little over 2 sigma at 69.1 percent, definitely not the 3 sigma (93.32 percent) of each step. In other words, the process would have a 29.2 percent improvement gap, a 29.2 percent probability of creating a defect—far from the 6.68 percent for each of the five steps in the process.

Now, imagine a process that consists of 50 steps, or of 100 steps, or of even more. What sigma levels would you need for each step in order to achieve a *RTY* that's even acceptable, let alone impressive? Figure 3-5 shows some interesting calculations.

- What do the calculations in Figure 3-5 mean? Here are two examples. If you're processing loan applications and the process consists of 30 steps, if each step of the process is at a 4 sigma level, only 82.95 percent of your applications will meet specifications.
- If you're building a widget and the process consists of 100 steps, a process capability of 4 sigma for each step means that only 5 percent of your widgets will meet specifications.

If you didn't appreciate the huge differences between one sigma level and the next, you might appreciate it now, as that difference is magnified when the process in question consists of many steps. And even if these figures confuse you, it's easy to understand that the fewer steps in a process, the less the *RTY* will decline.

For example, if you reduce the loan application process from 30 steps to 25 steps, you raise the success rate of your four-sigma process from

Percent per Step	RTY, 10 Steps	RTY, 20 Steps	RTY, 30 Steps	RTY, 100 Steps
69.15% (2 sigma)	2.50%	0.06%	0.00%	0.00%
93.32% (3 sigma)	50.09%	25.09%	0.00%	0.00%
99.379% (4 sigma)	93.9607%	88.286%	82.9542%	53.6367%
99.9767% (5 sigma)	99.7672%	99.535%	99.3034%	97.69667%
99.99966% (6 sigma)	99.9966%	99.9932%	99.9898%	99.9660%

FIGURE 3-5   Rolled throughput yield calculations for five sigma levels

82.95 percent to 85.58 percent. That's a good increase, considering that you didn't even do anything to improve any of the steps. That's money for nothing.

THE COST OF POOR QUALITY: A KEY METRIC

Many believe that the cost of improving processes makes reaching six-sigma quality (3.4 defects per million opportunities for a defect) impractical. However, those companies that are striving for six sigma have realized that the net "cost" to reduce defects actually lowers as they approach six sigma, because as they dramatically reduce defects they can also dramatically redirect the resources they currently put into finding and fixing defects. In fact, the highest-quality producer of goods or services is actually the lowest-cost producer. One major reason is the metric called the cost of poor quality (COPQ).

This is one of the key business metric concepts of Six Sigma—the cost of doing things wrong. The COPQ represents the visible and less visible costs of all the defects that exist in our processes. Every time we have any result that is not what the customer of a process needs, we consume time and resources to find, fix, and try to prevent these defects—such as scrap, rework, inspection, warranty claims, and lost customer loyalty.

The COPQ represents opportunities for Six Sigma. The Six Sigma approach to managing is all about helping you identify ways to reduce the errors and rework that cost you time, money, opportunities, and customers. Six Sigma translates that knowledge into opportunities for business growth. As you improve the capability of your processes and boost your RTY, you not only decrease variation and defects, but also reduce the cost of running your process, sometimes dramatically.

Figure 3-6 shows the cost in sales for five sigma levels. Note: This chart includes a 1/5 sigma shift, i.e., 6 sigma is 4.5 sigma.

Sigma Level (Process Capability)	Defects per Million Opportunities	Cost of Poor Quality (% of Sales)
2	308,537	30%–40%
3	66,807	20%–30%
4	6,210	15%–20%
5	233	10%–15%
6	3.4	<10%

FIGURE 3-6   Cost of poor quality at five sigma levels

Consider an operation at a three-sigma level—the baggage-handling process of a good airline. For every million pieces of baggage that airline handles, there's a problem with more than 66,000 pieces. For each piece reported missing, the airline workers have to process a report, locate the piece, retrieve it, and deliver it—which means time and money wasted just to right the wrong, to correct the defect. And the airline might not be able to recover the confidence of the passenger. When you translate the 6 percent probability gap of missing baggage into monetary terms, the hard cost of this defect can be much higher than 6 percent of the overall cost of handling baggage.

And the COPQ might not be completely obvious. Consider a typical manufacturer. What is the COPQ? There are warranty claim costs reported every month and maybe maintenance costs incurred to fix failures in the field. There's also the cost of scrap and rejects—a waste of material, labor, and machine time, utilities, and wear. Add to that the cost of reworking defective parts. Then there are costs that are less obvious.

For example, when a process produces a lot of defective components, the time required to get completed components through the system increases. This increase in cycle time has a cost in terms of additional labor hours to get the work done. There is also the cost of all inspection and testing to try to catch the defects. Then, because some defects somehow escape detection, there's the cost of lost customers and reduced customer loyalty—important but hard to quantify.

To discover the COPQ, as in this example, might take a structured approach, such as the following:

- *Internal failure*—costs resulting from defects found before the customer receives the product or service (examples: scrap, rework, reinspection, retesting, downgrading, downtime, reduced productivity, failure analysis)
- *External failure*—costs resulting from defects found after the customer receives the product or service (examples: warranty charges, complaint adjustments, returned material, allowances, replacements, compensation, damage to reputation)
- *Appraisal*—costs of determining the degree of conformance to quality requirements (examples: inspection, testing, process control, quality audits)
- *Prevention*—costs of minimizing failure and appraisal costs (examples: quality planning, policies and procedures, new design reviews, in-process inspections and testing, supplier evaluations, education and training, preventive maintenance)
- *Non-value-added activities*—costs of any steps or processes that don't add value from the customers' perspective.

This approach can be deployed using a step-by-step technique, or it might use a concurrent method to expedite the process.

The cost of poor quality usually has a personal side as well. People who work in an organization that has problems with quality might be affected in various ways: poor morale, conflicts, decreased productivity, increased absenteeism, health problems related to stress, burnout, and higher turnover. These human consequences add to the cost of poor quality.

Costs That Are Hidden—and Even Accepted and Allowed

Sometimes it seems that the only people who recognize or suspect that there are "hidden" losses are CEOs—and some employees closest to the processes. Are they just worrying too much, being too suspicious? After all, surely any loss will be exposed in some kind of reconciliation exercise. Well, maybe. But consider the following.

The traditional way to measure process performance is end yield (not rolled throughput yield). Mature processes have predictable end yields and known process step yields. When you know what the individual process step yields are, you also know what their losses are. The losses become predictable.

In traditional unit cost calculations, losses are accounted for by applying a loss factor, such as material losses and reject levels. When these predicable losses (scaled for production forecasts) become factors, they become invisible. From there, they are built into budgets. For example, in a manufacturing environment, a typical loss factor might be that 10 percent of the units produced would be considered as a loss; in a fast-food restaurant, it might be an over-capacity of labor cost of 20 percent caused by an inability to predict customer demand levels.

Middle managers are responsible for maintaining their budgets. So, not only are the losses invisible, the managers actually allow for them. There is no incentive for middle managers to reduce these losses. They are both hidden—and even accepted and allowed. It doesn't matter what kind of business you are in. Any hidden waste streams in any of your processes ultimately siphon off dollars that should be going to your bottom line.

As you implement the core Six Sigma methodology, you will be armed with the tools that enable you to identify, correct, and control the critical-to-quality (CTQ) elements so important to your customers and reduce the cost of poor quality (COPQ). Once you start implementing the method full-time with your black belts and project teams, your projects will start revealing costs that are hidden and returning that money to the company.

Money is generally the most important reason for using Six Sigma. Processes that are inefficient waste time and other resources—and organizations pay a lot for poor quality: the COPQ for traditionally managed organizations has been estimated at between 20 percent and 40 percent of budget. This means that a company that has annual revenues of $1 million has waste and defects in its systems that are costing between $200,000 and $400,000 in potential benefit. That would seem to be enough of a "burning platform" to convince the people at the top to start Six Sigma immediately.

We conclude this discussion of COPQ with a warning: don't focus solely on COPQ. Consider the experience of one company that implemented Six Sigma. During the first year of implementation, the teams focused on COPQ alone. Then they realized that it was smart to broaden their focus, because they were finding that focusing on COPQ alone drove them to work on internally focused projects. That just makes sense, because COPQ is the voice of the business, about saving money, and not the voice of the customers. The company discovered that internally focused projects were not resulting in the breakthrough impact that it was expecting.

Are You Committed to Quality?

Business leaders often say, "We are committed to quality." That's a standard claim. But what does it mean exactly? How can you verify that? How do you quantify that?

You measure the extent to which goods and services are meeting customer expectations. After all, that's the basic criterion for quality. You measure every aspect of the goods, services, and processes that affect quality. By doing this, you remove opinions and emotions from the equation and replace them with facts and figures that verify or refute that claim of commitment to quality.

Traditional management often operates by the "seat of the pants"—by tradition, impression, reaction to events, gut instincts. The essence of Six Sigma management is to use objective data to make decisions.

Enough Already!

A friend who was studying statistics had a young daughter who referred to the subject as "sadistics." From the mouths of babes. . . .

At this point, you might not be able to perform all of these calculations and others used in Six Sigma. That's why there's statistical software. The industry standard that is used pervasively throughout the Six Sigma world is MINITAB™. You might not understand all the ins and outs of these concepts. That's why training is essential to any Six Sigma initiative.

What's important here is that you understand the basic concepts of Six Sigma measurements and better appreciate the importance of establishing metrics to track variation so you can improve processes. With that quick overview of the essentials, we can leave our imaginary example of widgets and return to the very real situation of your business.

SUMMARY

Because it uses statistical terminology, people tend to believe that Six Sigma is a statistics and measurement program. This is not true. Statistics are used only for interpreting and clarifying data, to turn it into information.

Variation is the basis of Six Sigma. It's defined as the fluctuation in the output of a process. Every repeatable process exhibits variation. Any improvement of any process should reduce variation so that the process can more consistently meet the expectations of the customers. To reduce variation, it's first necessary to be able to measure it. There are several ways, each with advantages and disadvantages—mean, median, mode, range, standard deviation, and variance.

If a large number of values for a process are plotted, the distribution of values will generally form some variant of a bell-shaped curve—high in the middle around the mean and tapering off on both sides more or less symmetrically. This is considered a normal distribution.

A normal distribution can be described in terms of its mean and its standard deviation. A normal distribution is symmetrical around its mean and the mean, the median, and the mode are equal. In a normal distribution, 68 percent of the values lie within one standard deviation (± 1 sigma) of the mean, 95 percent of the values lie within two standard deviations (± 2 sigma) of the mean, and 99.73 percent of the values lie within three standard deviations (± 3 sigma) of the mean.

A lower specification limit (LSL) and an upper specification limit (USL) are set as the boundaries within which a process must operate, the minimum and maximum values beyond which the performance of the process is unacceptable to the customers—a defect. The objective is to reduce the variation in the processes so that 99.99966 percent of the outputs will fall between the LSL and the USL. In other words, the processes will be producing at most 3.4 DPMO.

There are two categories of causes of variation—common and special. A *common* cause is any source of unacceptable variation that is part of the random variation inherent in the process. A *special* cause is any source of unacceptable variation that lies outside the process. Variation from common causes is natural and variation from special causes is unnatural: on control charts, natural variation is variation between the UCL and the LCL and unnatural variation is variation above the UCL or below the LCL. Each category requires a different approach: special causes of variation require immediate action and common causes require a long-term strategy of process management. If there are special causes of variation, a process cannot be stable over time. The team must first identify and eliminate any special causes to bring the process into statistical control.

The lower control limit (LCL) and the upper control limit (UCL) mark the minimum and maximum inherent limits of a process, based on data collected from the process. If the control limits are within the specification limits or align with them, then the process is considered capable of meeting the specification. If either or both of the control limits are outside the specification limits, then the process is considered incapable of meeting the specification. Process capability is the measure of the ability of a process to produce outputs that meet the specifications.

Over time, processes tend to shift from center, and special causes are likely to occur. In order to compensate for this shift, the Six Sigma pioneers at Motorola calculated for a worst-case scenario shift of 1.5 sigma. So, sigma capability charts generally allow for this 1.5 sigma difference.

Two indices are most commonly used to measure process capability—*Cp* and *Cpk*. (*Cpk* is sometimes called *process performance,* to distinguish it from *Cp, process capability.*) Cp is a measure of the width of a distribution of outputs of the process. *Cpk* tells us the same thing, but also how close the average value is to the target value.

Six sigma is a performance target that applies to a single critical-to-quality characteristic, not to an entire process, product, or service. It's actually a measure of *first-time yield*—the number of good units coming out of a process or a step divided by the number of total units going into the process or step. The more complex a process, the more likely a defect will occur at some point. That's why a better metric is *rolled throughput yield*— the probability that a single unit can pass through all the steps in a process free of defects. It's the net result of the effect of all of the steps in a process.

The cost of poor quality is one of the key business metric concepts of Six Sigma—the cost of doing things wrong, the total of all the costs of all the defects in the processes. COPQ represents opportunities for Six Sigma project teams.

CASE STUDY QUESTION

"One accurate measurement is worth a thousand expert opinions."

—GRACE MURRAY HOPPER, REAR ADMIRAL, U.S. NAVY

This case study shows how GE saved millions by using data and basic statistics—and getting away from "I think, I believe, and I feel."

At the General Electric appliance plant in Louisville, Kentucky, I helped a black belt address a chronic problem: the washing machine agitator didn't fit. It took two factory assembly people to force the agitator into place, using a big cross-patterned auger. This was a source of carpal tunnel syndrome for the employees, a safety-related issue, and a cost of poor quality as there were two people doing what should have been a one-person job.

If the agitator did fit, it was often too tight. If the washing machine leaked in the field, the repair person couldn't remove the agitator, so the whole machine had to be taken in for the repair. The customer wasn't happy with the washing machine or with GE.

Some of the agitators didn't fit at all and became scrap. Sometimes the production line was stopped to make adjustments. The production, warranty, and service costs all increased because of this chronic problem of poor fit.

This problem added up to about $1 million annually. To solve it, we (Greg and the black belt) had to measure what was happening and understand the whole process. The black belt identified a strong correlation between the weight of the agitator and the fit. If it weighed just right, it would fit perfectly, with only one person doing the installation.

To really understand the problem, it's sometimes necessary to imagine that you are the defective part. In this case, imagine that the agitator is asking the question, "Why don't I fit?" The answer is "If I am the right weight, I fit perfectly."

Then the question is "Why aren't all the agitators the right weight?"

We went to the supplier of the agitator for the answer. The agitators had never been weighed before, but because we now knew that there is a correlation between the weight of the agitator and the fit, we had to weigh them. Remember: $Y = f(X)$. Simply stated, fit is a function of weight.

In the past, thinking about this problem was through brainstorming sessions, with "I think, I feel, I believe" statements. We were now getting away from that and actually weighing the agitators. Then we did a comparison of the 10 injection-molding cavities used to make the agitators. The question we asked (the hypothesis) was "Are all 10 plastic-molding cavities producing agitators of the same weight?"

GE had never asked that question of the supplier before. We had to analyze it, to break the problem down into parts.

First, we had to demonstrate that we could actually weigh things consistently and accurately, which we did. With this data, we identified the vital few issues. (See Figure 3-7.)

When the agitators were weighed, it was clear that cavities 1 through 4 produced agitators whose weight was within specifications for a "good" weight—between 29.5 and 30.5 pounds. Fit is a function of weight. Only agitators from cavities 1 through 4 fit.

The weight of each agitator is a function of each of the 10 cavities. Now, leaving the world of "I think, I feel, I believe," we enter the world of facts and data or the "confidence interval question." We can say, "I am 95 percent confident of this," based on data that has been validated. A confidence interval is a computed interval with a given probability—usually 90 percent, 95 percent, or 99 percent—that the interval contains the value of a certain statistic, such as a mean, a proportion, or a rate.

We were 95 percent confident that the first four molding cavities (represented in Figure 3.7) were going to produce properly weighted agitators. A correct agitator weight meant no warranty costs for repair, no carpal tunnel syndrome in the employees, and only one person per shift required to install the agitator. Controlling these costs would result in $1 million in additional cash for GE. The other six cavities were problem producers.

Now GE had identified one of the "vital few" sources of the problem. But what could GE do to fix the problem that comes from the supplier? GE managers told the supplier they would purchase only agitators made from

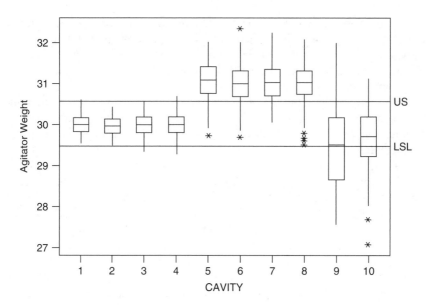

FIGURE 3-7   Which agitators fit?

the first four cavities. The supplier then had to adjust the other six and prove
that they were producing agitators that met GE's weight specifications.

In the Measure and Analyze phases we contained the problem at the
supplier level, by limiting the agitators to the first four cavities. The supplier didn't like the solution, but he was not consistent with his production,
so he had to fix the problem of the cavities of the other six machines if he
wanted to continue to work with GE. From that point forward, he only supplied cavities that conformed with GE's specifications. The benefit to GE
for fixing this defect exceeded $1.5 million.

REVIEW QUESTIONS

1. What is variation?

   a. The fluctuation in the output of a process

   b. Something that every repeatable process exhibits

   c. Something that any improvement of any process should reduce

   d. All of the above

   e. None of the above

2. Mean is

   a. A calculation consisting of adding the lowest and highest values in a series

   b. A representation of the sense of a Six Sigma principle

    c. The average of a series of numbers

    d. The disposition of the average Six Sigma practitioner

3. What is the midpoint in a range of data?

    a. Median

    b. Mode

    c. Discrete data

    d. Mean

4. Standard deviation is

    a. An indicator of the degree of variation in a set of values calculated by measuring the average spread of the values around the mean

    b. The sum of the mean, median, mode, and range of a set of values divided by four

    c. A defective variation that has become accepted as inevitable

    d. The usual workaround when data is unavailable for a process

5. Which of the following statements is/are true for a normal distribution?

    a. The mean, the median, and the mode are equal.

    b. 68 percent of the values lie within one standard deviation (± 1 sigma) of the mean.

    c. It can be described in terms of its mean and its standard deviation.

    d. a and b

    e. b and c

    f. a and c

    g. a, b, and c

    h. None of the above

6. A common cause is

    a. A source of variation that is found most frequently

    b. A source of variation found in all processes

    c. A source of variation that unites project team members

    d. A source of variation that is inherent in a process

7. First-time yield (FTY) is

    a. The gain achieved from applying Six Sigma to a project initially

    b. The number of good units coming out of a process or a step divided by the number of total units going into it

    c. The gain achieved by a project team new to Six Sigma

    d. A concession by a project team in its initial efforts

8. Rolled throughput yield (RTY) is

   a. The probability of getting through the entire process free of defects
   b. The percentage of units that finish without a defect out of the number of units started
   c. A means of calculating DPMO
   d. A means of calculating sigma level

9. What is the rolled throughout yield for a three-step process with a 90 percent yield for each step?

   a. 90 percent
   b. 81 percent
   c. 72 percent
   d. 63 percent

10. What is the cost of defects in a company with revenues of $1 million?

   a. Nothing
   b. Between $200,000 and $400,000
   c. $100,000
   d. About 10 percent

BUSINESS METRICS FOR SIX SIGMA

"When you can measure what you are speaking about, and express it in numbers, you know something about it; but when you cannot measure it, when you cannot express it in numbers, your knowledge is of a meagre and unsatisfactory kind. It might be the beginning of knowledge, but you have scarcely, in your thoughts, advanced to the stage of science."

—WILLIAM THOMSON, LORD KELVIN (1824–1907)

THIS CHAPTER RELATES closely to the discussion of process metrics in Chapter 3. Together, these two chapters should prepare you for Chapters 5 and 6.

If you don't have measurements, you can't progress intelligently and efficiently because you don't know where you are. Quite simply, we need ways to keep score. In business, the most important scorecard is profit. However, money is not a sufficient metric in itself because it leads businesses to be penny-wise and pound-foolish.

A business metric is any unit of measurement that provides a way to objectively quantify a process in ways that make sense and dollars for your organization. Any measurement that helps managers understand their operations might be a business metric.

Most businesses have some version of measurement. After all, managers and executives need to calculate profits and losses, the cost of goods or services sold, and return on investment. But beyond the basics, how exactly do managers go about making decisions and changes that reduce costs, improve profitability, and foster growth?

Many managers simply accept and communicate and operate according to certain beliefs that they hold as truths. However, when managers are pressed to objectively justify their beliefs and explain how they provide appropriate guidance, they're often at a loss. And, as quality guru Edwards Deming said, "Without data, all anyone has is an opinion."

Metrics should be a fundamental part of running any business. Measurement is a fundamental value and belief of Six Sigma.

Every Six Sigma project depends on metrics, whether you call the set of metrics your scorecard or your dashboard or whatever. Improving processes— whether for products or services or operations—requires improving how we do things. This means looking at how we track what we're doing.

Business metrics provide data that Six Sigma managers can use to better understand their processes and identify target areas for improvement. If you can measure your processes, you can understand them. If you can understand them, you can correct, control, and improve them and thus reduce costs while improving the quality of your outputs.

Six Sigma metrics might include customer satisfaction, percent of defects from a process, number of products completed per hour, hours required to deliver a certain number of outputs or provide a service, the cost of poor quality, the cost of goods or services sold, and so on. These metrics quantify the effects of those factors that matter most.

How do we measure our progress? Are those metrics appropriate? Are they effective? Before you undertake any Six Sigma project, you must ask and answer the big question: what should we measure?

IT ALL STARTS WITH THE CUSTOMERS

"The best Six Sigma projects begin not inside the business but outside it, focused on answering the question—how can we make the customer more competitive? What is critical to the customer's success? . . . One thing we have discovered with certainty is that anything we do that makes the customer more successful inevitably results in a financial return for us."

—JACK WELCH

What do your customers want and expect from you? How do your customers understand quality?

The answers to those questions provide the basis of any Six Sigma project. The first step toward improving processes, products, or services is determining what your customers consider critical to quality. The critical-to-quality (CTQ) concept in Six Sigma allows you to focus on improving quality from the perspective of the customers. This is often called "voice of the customer" (VOC). VOC confirms and validates the CTQ, or in some cases, the VOC might change the CTQ. We'll discuss it in depth in Chapter 7.

Managers and employees all have some ideas about what constitutes quality for their products and services. That's good—but it's not what matters most, because managers and employees don't put cash in the coffers. Find out which aspects of your products and services are vital to the customer and in what ways. Then managers and employees can devote themselves to finding ways to improve those products and services by improving the processes behind them.

Here's a quick and simple example. Most of us have used the drive-through window at McDonald's. So, as a customer, what would you consider the CTQs for McDonald's drive-through process? How long it takes to deliver your order? Whether the order is correct? Whether the Happy Meal contains a toy? We know that taste is not a CTQ for most normal adults going through the McDonald's drive-through. We know that it's not the hot spot to take a date. So, if you have to wait long for your order, that's a defect. If the employees get your order wrong, that's a defect. If the Happy Meal is missing the toy, that's a defect.

Now, the manager and the employees might have ideas about how they would like to improve the drive-through process, but what matters most is what you and the other customers consider important. Those CTQs should be the basis of any improvement efforts. Those CTQs are the terms by which customers understand defects. The defects defined by those CTQs should be what managers focus on analyzing, to identify and reduce or eliminate the factors that cause those defects. A general guideline to set CTQs are by customer expectations that can be measured both financially and at internal/external defect levels.

Here's another example. At a conference in a hotel, I asked participants what they expected in their coffee breaks. The answer: "lots of good, hot coffee!" When I asked the hotel banquet staff what they needed to provide, they agreed on good, hot coffee. But the two groups differed in their CTQ expectations.

Beyond coffee, the staff was concerned with providing linens, china, attractive displays, and extra snacks. However, the customers wanted a fast line for refills, high-capacity restrooms nearby, and access to telephones. Of course, customers don't want dirty cups or grubby linens, but they don't care much about ice sculptures.

So, here's the bottom line. The hotel is putting time and money into things that matter less to the customers and missing out on things that customers expect. Although the English author and diplomat James Bryce was not referring to Six Sigma, his comment seems very apt here: "Three-fourths of the mistakes a man makes are made because he does not really know what he thinks he knows."

CRITERIA FOR BUSINESS METRICS

So what are the criteria for establishing business metrics? The answer is surprisingly simple. The criteria relate to why you're in business and why you want to implement Six Sigma—to improve customer satisfaction and reduce costs. With that in mind, you need to establish metrics to help you achieve these goals.

Measurement is crucial to the success of your Six Sigma initiative. Your business metrics show you the ways to achieve dramatic improvements in your processes. They apply statistical tools to any process to evaluate and quantify its performance. They continually ask what outcome, or dependent variable, is a function of another, independent variable, to dig out the information that improves your performance.

It's a fundamental principle of the Six Sigma philosophy that you cannot improve quality unless you can measure it. This applies to any aspect of Six Sigma. If you're going to invest in measuring customer satisfaction, then you need to have a quality measurement system to track performance. In other words, your business metrics constitute your scorecard, the way you figure out where you are. To use another term, they form your dashboard.

The Dashboard Concept

The business dashboard as a metaphor for critical metrics to measure business performance originated years ago at General Electric. Just as you use the speedometer, oil gauge, battery indicator, fuel gauge, and other instruments to monitor the status of your vehicle as you drive, so you want to keep track of key indicators of the performance of your company. Like the dashboard gauges, your metrics allow you to continually assess your progress and detect any potential problems.

Your choice of business metrics and the importance you give them show what you value. If you value customer service, for example, you make it central to your business metrics. You put it on your scorecard. You include it in your dashboard.

Conversely, if you don't measure quality and don't follow up on any measurements, you give the impression that you don't care about customers or profitability. That impression affects the behavior and productivity of everyone in the department, division, or organization.

By instituting key business metrics across functions and groups and at every level, you directly link individual performance to measurable outcomes. This sends a clear message that not only do you care about customers and revenue, but so should all team members because they are accountable for the results measured by their particular metrics. In the end, what we are talking about is establishing the proper "dashboard" of measures to help us understand our quality situation and to create urgency to take the actions needed to address the root issue: defects.

QUESTIONS ARE KEY

When you create metrics, you need to ask questions—new questions—and search for new results. If you keep asking the same questions, you'll keep generating the same measurements. That brings to mind that adage: "The height of insanity is doing things the same way and hoping for a different result." How many companies exemplify that insanity in managing their processes?

How do new measures arise? Fundamentally, new measures arise when new questions are asked.

If we ask questions about outputs, not inputs, we get a lot of focus and measures on outputs. If we get questions on budgets, we measure budgets. How many of our questions are focused on process and product quality? How many of our questions are focused on causes and inputs versus results and outputs?

Questions are key. To get new metrics—and new behaviors—we must ask new questions.

There's another quote to keep in mind:

"Genius, in truth, means little more than the faculty of perceiving in an unhabitual way."

—WILLIAM JAMES (1842–1910)

Six Sigma allows and even requires you to be a genius. The key to "perceiving in an unhabitual way" is asking questions—and then questioning the answers.

When you begin setting up new business metrics and asking questions, you should begin with the fundamentals:

- Why do we measure this?
- Why do we measure it in this way?

- What does this measurement mean?
- Why is this measurement important?

Ask questions. Challenge answers. Put assumptions to the test. Confront conventions. At this stage you should tap people who are known for their critical thinking skills, whether they're familiar with the processes or not. Encourage them to question and to challenge. That approach might be unusual in your company, but to do otherwise would be the height of insanity.

Another behavior that's insane is to make decisions without using metrics. Sometimes managers trust their instincts or play their hunches or just guess at what might be wrong and how to solve the problems suspected. But why would you simply guess at ways to improve products, satisfy customers, and increase revenue? Sure, you might find a way to reduce expenses in a given process without using metrics. But how will the change affect customer satisfaction? Are there ways to improve the process as well as cut costs? Is the process even necessary?

Measure first and measure often. It's the best way to improve processes, meet customer expectations, and reduce costs. And, to offer one more quote, artist Edward Simmons said, "The difference between failure and success is doing a thing nearly right and doing it exactly right."

LEARN FROM YOUR CUSTOMERS

Here's how you can best proceed to get the most from your Six Sigma initiative. From metrics to project selection, as long as you follow the basic principles expressed in the following list, you can ensure that your efforts are working at maximum capacity for lasting results.

Start to ask questions—different questions—and really desire to seek out data that counts. Use the simple customer-based management survey tool (Figure 4-1) to promote awareness. Everything yo do or produce affects more than one customer. Who are your customers and what are their top three requirements?

If your company is like most others, this process will clearly show that you are stuck in four sigma or less, along with most of your competitors. You are just *average*—and that is nothing to celebrate. Especially when you realize that one of your new competitors is in the Six Sigma group of *world-class* companies. You might suddenly understand why this competitor is giving your sales manager such difficulties in the marketplace. They aren't dumping their product at an artificially low price. Instead, they are able to underprice you because *the highest-quality provider of goods and services is the lowest-cost provider.*

Customers	*Requirements*
Shareholders (analysts)	1. _____ 2. _____ 3. _____
Customer base	1. _____ 2. _____ 3. _____
Employees	1. _____ 2. _____ 3. _____
Union	1. _____ 2. _____ 3. _____
Suppliers	1. _____ 2. _____ 3. _____
Federal government	1. _____ 2. _____ 3. _____
State/local government	1. _____ 2. _____ 3. _____
Other	1. _____ 2. _____ 3. _____

FIGURE 4-1 Customer-based management survey

MOVING FROM CRITERIA TO METRICS

How do you actually select appropriate metrics? You need to measure what's important, what's critical to your business. You know that key criteria are customer satisfaction and revenue. So, let's start with customer satisfaction. For every product or service, you need to determine the expectations of your customers, particularly the CTQ factors. What aspects of the product or service are key to your customers? For each aspect, what are your customers' expectations?

If you're producing widgets, for example, you might consider the following aspects: size, weight, durability, price, ease of use, versatility, colors, styles, availability, maintenance, service, warranty, and so on. For each of these aspects, you would determine expectations. How many sizes of widgets do they expect? Which sizes do they expect? How long do they expect a widget to last? What price do they expect to pay? How easy to use do they expect a widget to be? How long do they expect it to take to repair a widget? Do they expect a loaner widget?

For every product or service, there could be dozens or even hundreds of aspects. Focus on the aspects that are most important to your customers. For every key aspect, there could be several or many expectations. Once you determine the essential expectations, figure out ways to measure how well your product or service is meeting those expectations. Then, work backward through the process, to establish metrics for activities that are critical to meeting those expectations.

Make sure that all measurements are linked to bottom-line results. For example, if you're working on making your super widget more durable, you should focus on metrics for raw materials and assembly, but not on metrics for painting or packaging. For every metric, ask this question: How does this metric link to the bottom line?

With Six Sigma, this is a continual question—because Six Sigma is based on tangible financial results. Measurements must result in an identifiable impact on the bottom line.

Identifying CTQ factors is generally a laborious process. In one company, the Six Sigma team analyzed 800-1,000 processes, each of which had 100-120 specifications. It identified the most critical factors that would lead to greater customer satisfaction, lower costs, and/or greater ease of assembly. The team then mapped and prioritized CTQ factors to be targeted in Six Sigma projects.

Process Mapping

Mapping processes is extremely valuable. A process map is an illustrated description of how a process works, a flowchart of the steps in a process— operations, decision points, delays, movements, handoffs, rework loops, and controls or inspections.

It takes a lot of time and effort to identify CTQ factors, but without mapping each and every CTQ process, you won't get the information necessary to target areas for improvement and fix problems.

Process maps allow a team to visualize the flow of products or the sequencing of activities. In so doing, it can locate steps that don't add value to the process. Eliminating such steps is an easy way to reduce cycle time and cut costs.

Value-Added versus Non-Value-Added

A key step in making improvements that matter to the customers is to determine which processes add value and which do not—from the customers' perspective. The concept of distinguishing between value-added activities and non-value-added activities is simple: any part of a process for which the customer is willing to pay is value-added, while any part for which the customer is not willing to pay—such as moving or storing raw materials or approvals by managers between processes—is non-value-added. Because non-value-added activities do little or nothing to satisfy customers and only add costs, they should be targets for elimination. In addition, whenever an activity can be eliminated, complexity is reduced. That means lower costs and fewer opportunities for errors.

However, it can be difficult to work with that distinction between value-added activities and non-value-added activities, particularly when the processes have been in place for a while and/or the people involved are secretive, defensive, and/or territorial. Nonetheless, Six Sigma enables you to show how much time and money the organization can save through eliminating non-value-added activities.

Are there any non-value-added activities in your organization? Bet on it! It's been said that all processes accrete additional activities and complications that add little or no value, just as the hull of a ship accumulates barnacles, which make it less efficient. So, think of this part of the Six Sigma process as scraping the hulls of your business processes to gain efficiencies relatively easily.

Waste

Waste is essentially anything that customers don't want to pay for when they buy your products or services. Here are some examples.

Activity. Sometimes, even often, activity is work only because the employees are being paid for it. The activity is adding no value to your products or services. Maybe it's because a process is inefficient. Maybe it's because a step is unnecessary. For each of your processes, think about what it's intended to do, about the inputs and the required outputs, and then imagine designing a process to turn those inputs into those outputs. That zero-based thinking can help you identify steps in your current process that are adding no value, steps that are waste.

Waiting. When people or products or documents must spend time doing nothing between value-added steps, that's waste. There's waste in many processes—but that doesn't mean that it must be tolerated, or that it cannot be eliminated.

Excess. Sometimes this type of waste is overproduction—making more of something than required by the next process or making it sooner than required by the next process. It's waste when it takes people or equipment or materials away from more immediate tasks or when it necessitates inspection, storage, and/or transportation. In some cases, the product might not even be necessary and must be sold at a discount or scrapped. Occasionally, excess products get damaged or go missing. Sometimes excess is a problem when employees order more materials or supplies than are necessary within a given period—especially when the money used for those materials or supplies is needed for other purchases or when the need for those materials or supplies ends before the inventory is exhausted.

Transportation. Whether you've got forklifts moving widgets or inter-office mail moving documents, extra steps that do not add any value to your products or services are waste. Don't work at improving the transportation; work at minimizing it.

Under-utilization of people. This can be a big waste—and it can be easy to neglect because the cost is usually in soft dollars—opportunities lost—rather than in hard dollars. Who could be doing things that would benefit the organization more and possibly allow the employees to feel more satisfied and improve morale? What abilities is the organization not tapping and developing? If conventional thinking, restrictive politics and culture, poor personnel policies and practices, little or no developmental training, or other factors are keeping your organization from taking advantage of the experiences and skills and enthusiasm of any employees, it could be missing out a lot.

These are the main types of waste in most organizations. When you map your processes and examine every activity in terms of adding value to your products and services from the perspective of your customers, you can probably identify a lot of waste. And, once you identify waste, you can work toward eliminating it.

LESS IS MORE

When setting metrics, keep the numbers of measurements small. As you get into the Six Sigma mind-set, it's natural to want to measure everything. Don't! The key here is quality over quantity. Select only a true set of indicators that will give you the information you need about process factors that affect customer satisfaction and revenue. When establishing a metric, you need to know why you're measuring it, why it's important, and what's causing the results.

Think back to the dashboard analogy. Driving would be more difficult if the dashboard contained too many indicators. The same is true with too many metrics. Select and limit measurements carefully. The essential indicators will provide the information you need.

Your metrics should provide data that enables you to identify and solve performance problems in your processes as quickly as practical. They should also, consequently, be sufficiently sensitive to reveal changes or variations that are significant.

What's "significant?" That depends on your baselines and your goals. It's important that your metrics capture change with enough sensitivity to enable you to take action.

For a simple example, let's take our widgets. If the cycle time for the process of molding components averages three hours and seven minutes, a metric that tracks minutes might be sensitive enough. If the cycle time for the process of assembling those components averages 11 minutes and 54 seconds, then we'd want a metric that tracks seconds. If the cycle time for the process of packaging widgets averages four seconds, then our metric should be sensitive to at least tenths of a second.

Metrics need to "slice and dice" in increments that capture small but significant changes and track them in terms of cost, time, and quality. They indicate the ability of a process to achieve certain results—your process capability index, as explained earlier in this chapter.

UNIVERSAL STANDARD

One of the innovations of Six Sigma is to establish metrics in terms of opportunities for defects. You'll recall from Chapter 1 that sigma levels are based on the number of defects per million opportunities (DPMO). That is a metric that managers can use to apply Six Sigma thinking to any business process, because "defects" can be anything that causes customer dissatisfaction and "opportunities" can be any possibility for a defect. By calculating quality levels according to the complexity of the product, service, or process, Six Sigma allows for metrics that make it easier and more realistic to compare performances of products, services, or processes that differ.

Here's a simple example. William and Mary both work for Acme Wax Fruit Company. William runs the apple production line, which melts wax cubes, pours the wax into molds, and then dips the resulting item into a wax bath of another color. Mary manages the shipping department for the citrus fruit division; she's responsible for the employees who handle the inventory (oranges, lemons, and limes) in the warehouse, the employees who load the trucks, and the truckers who deliver the goods. The processes that William and Mary manage vary greatly, but because some of the metrics established for them are in terms of DPMO, it's possible to know that they are currently at 81,900 DPMO and 74,700 DPMO, respectively, and set a goal for next year of three sigma—66,8000.

And that's how, with metrics using DPMO, you can compare apples and oranges!

FINANCIAL LINKAGE OF METRICS AND RESULTS

There are two main concepts governing metrics. The first is *knowledge*. Your metrics provide knowledge about your processes and help you develop better metrics. The second concept is *alignment*. Your metrics must align with your strategic goals for performance.

When implementing business metrics, it's critical to link them to your overall performance. This is the key. If your metrics don't align with your performance, then they can't possibly tell you anything you really need to know.

Here's an example. A direct-order clothing company sets forth its basic performance goals in a series of "principles of doing business." These principles establish the following points:

- The company does everything possible to make its products better and never reduces the quality of any product to make it cheaper.
- The company accepts any return for any reason at any time. It guarantees its products unconditionally: there's no fine print and no arguments.
- The company ships all quickly: items in stock ship the day after the order is received; customized orders take a day or two longer.
- The company trains its sales and service employees to know its products, to be friendly and helpful, to spend the time necessary to take care of customers.
- The company has lower prices because it operates efficiently.

These principles frame, in straightforward terms, the company's performance goals. The metrics should align with these goals. Because product quality is important, the company might assess conformance of raw materials with specifications, but not focus on cycle time. Because products are guaranteed unconditionally, the company might not calculate the value of returns, but should concentrate instead on reasons for those returns. The company promises next-day shipping; it would necessarily track turnaround time, to ensure keeping its promise but not to try to reduce that time. The company encourages employees to take care of the customers; if it measured contact time, that metric would not be in alignment with the performance goal of complete customer care. Because the company keeps its prices low through efficiency, it would have a series of metrics to measure factors throughout its operations, but probably not in areas that affect quality or attention to customers.

This quick example shows how your metrics should link to your performance goals. Otherwise, you won't be getting the knowledge about your processes that you need to improve them—or you'll be working on making improvements that won't matter to your customers or could even disappoint, frustrate, or anger them. It's a simple point, but worth repeating: if your metrics don't align with your performance, then they can't possibly tell you anything you really need to know.

LEADERSHIP AND METRICS

Establishing metrics requires dedication, focus, and logic. It also requires leadership. Managers at all levels must serve as models of critical thinking and courage to challenge the status quo and underlying assumptions. You must ask yourself and people in your division and even throughout the company why all of you are doing the things you do. When you challenge, when you ask new questions and start measuring the answers, you demonstrate leadership that gets positive financial results from digging into the hidden streams of waste. You need to know exactly what a particular process is actually providing, its cost of goods or services sold, and its capability. By always asking about the function of each metric and linking it to your key criteria, you'll know where you are and where you need to go. Here are some basic questions to ask as you establish metrics:

- What are our business metrics?
- What are the measurement criteria?
- Do the metrics link to the criteria?
- Do the metrics correlate to competitive advantage?
- If the metrics don't correlate, what must we change?

These questions might be obvious, but they help keep you and your staff on target for Six Sigma results. As long as you can answer these questions, then you're setting your business metrics right. Remember: if you don't ask the right questions, whatever answers you get won't be right.

The importance of humility and active listening in this process is vital—listening to both internal and external customers. Without humility and active listening, we have barriers to questioning how we currently do things. We need to ensure we have an environment where we can question the status quo.

BASELINES

After you've determined the metrics that will provide you with the most important information about your processes, you use them to establish baselines. A baseline is a standard for comparisons: it shows the current status of your performance and serves as a reference for measuring progress in improving a process.

In a way, baselining is similar to the thorough physical examination that you would undergo before beginning an exercise regimen. Just as your doctor would check out basic indicators of health, your baseline activity should measure key input variables, key process variables, and key output variables.

The focus of Six Sigma lies in the transfer function, a simple three-part formula: $Y = f(X)$. This formula represents the basic truth of a process: output Y is a function of input X. This is just a mathematical way to state that variables or changes in inputs and the process will determine outputs.

The inputs—the X's—are independent variables, at least in terms of the specific process, and the outputs—the Y's—are dependent variables, because they're factors that depend on other factors. In the equation $Y = f(X)$, you can't adjust the dependent variable Y (the outcome); since it depends on the independent variable X, you must adjust the X to change the Y. We establish the transfer functions and then we identify the vital few factors, the elements that we must we work to isolate and then control. In other words, understand and manage the inputs (X's) and the outputs (Y's) will follow.

The activity provides not only baselines, of course, but it also serves as a good test of your metrics. As you apply your metrics to establish baselines, you might find problems with some of them: Maybe you need to modify metrics, drop metrics, and/or add metrics. Sometimes metrics that make sense on the drawing board just don't work as well when we put them to use.

BENCHMARKING

You've determined the value content of your processes, you know which affect CTQ customer issues, and you've established your baselines. Now you can move on to understanding how your processes measure up and figuring out where you want to go with your processes. You do that through benchmarking, both internal and external. Benchmarking is basically a method for comparing a process, using standard or best practices as a basis, and then identifying ways to improve the process. Through benchmarking, you can establish priorities and targets for improving the process and identify ways to do so.

At this point, you know what processes you want to benchmark and you've got your metrics. Now what?

The next step is generally to identify benchmarks for your target processes and to gather benchmark data to show how your processes could be performing. The benchmarks might be internal or external. Because most Six Sigma initiatives use benchmarks outside the company and because that's a more complicated practice, external benchmarking will be our focus here. (If you decide to use benchmarks within your company, it's considerably less difficult.) Whether you benchmark internally, externally, or both, it's essential to ask key questions about why your performance differs and to determine how you measure defects and yield rates.

How do you identify benchmarks? First, you consider your competitors. Which among them has target processes that perform better than yours? You might know that through competitive intelligence or through media reports. Also, as you probably realize, the Web has become a great source of information on companies. Articles that would have gone unnoticed in small, local publications or data that would have been buried in a report are now out there for you to access.

After you've identified the benchmarks to use, you collect data on the target processes. How you do this depends on the processes, the benchmarks identified, and the sources of information. Use your creativity and investigative instincts and skills.

Think Creatively

Choose your benchmarks carefully. Don't benchmark only very similar processes in the same industry unless you want to quickly improve a very defective process. Also, be cautious about benchmarking your competitors: that makes sense only if you know that their processes are better.

Think in terms not of the *process*, but of the *purpose* for the process. That way, you can identify dissimilar processes from which you can learn.

Here's an example. An airline has problems with its baggage-handling process. It could benchmark other airlines, of course. But the project team could also think beyond baggage and study national package delivery services. Another good example for benchmarking is a company that was preparing to move its corporate manufacturing to another location across the country. The managers asked the question, "Who's the best in the world at moving?" They selected rock band "roadies" as the benchmark for excellence in moving a complex setup efficiently from city to city! They studied the practices of this "best of the best" and adapted them to their particular situation.

To briefly show how benchmarking works, let's consider a bank, specifically the residential loan processing department. Imagine that you're a customer waiting for the department to process your application. You're in a hurry. In other words, your CTQ requirement is promptness. But one week passes, then two, and then three …

The lending institution, by not meeting your CTQ requirement, risks alienating you (and probably many other customers) and increases its cost of services sold (COSS). Of course, if it raises its fees to cover those costs, it's likely to lose even more customers.

Each functional group in the organization—customer service, sales and marketing, finance, information technology, accounting—plays a part in delivering what the customer wants. Each group has processes that should work together to serve the customer. Are those processes the best they can be? Clearly not, because loans are delayed by nearly a month. So the residential loan department needs to benchmark its processes against processes in other divisions to discover waste, so it can work to eliminate it.

Greg, the manager of the residential loan department, decides to start benchmarking internally. He determines which loan department is processing the most loans with the lowest defects. Then it's a question of studying how the processes in that department work better and finding ways to improve his department's processes.

Greg could also examine how the loan process works in competing companies. Maybe one aspect is better with Alpha Savings and Loan, another with Big Money Loans, and yet another with Consumer Loans.

You might be able to get information for benchmarking from public domain sources, through the library or the Web. Some companies provide information in white papers, technical journals, conference presentations, panel discussions, and so forth, or in materials for vendors and customers or advertisements. There is a lot of information available about what you are trying to benchmark from public domain sources. These sources include the following:

Library databases	Inquiry service
Internal publications	Literature searches
Industry publications	Internal reviews
Functional trade publications	Professional associations
Industry data firms	Special industry reports
University sources	Seminars
Newspapers	Industry experts
Newsletters	Company "watches"
Customer feedback	Advertisements
Original research	Networks
Telephone surveys	Web site searches

An excellent organization that can help with your benchmarking exercise is the American Productivity and Quality Center (APQC). You can reach them at www.apqc.org or by phone at (713) 685-4670.

You might need to develop questions for a survey to be conducted by mail, by telephone, by fax, or by e-mail. You might decide to take the most direct approach, to contact companies and arrange site visits. You could also enter into a benchmarking partnership, in which each partner would gain information about the others in exchange for sharing information on its own processes. Another possibility is to work with a competitive intelligence firm.

Keep It Legal and Ethical

Benchmarking can be risky business. To minimize the likelihood of misunderstandings, ethical slips, and legal problems, you should follow the simple Code of Conduct scripted by the International Benchmarking Clearinghouse, a service of the American Productivity & Quality Center (www.orau.gov/pbm/pbmhandbook/apqc.pdf). It provides guidance through outlining the following eight principles:

- Legality
- Exchange
- Confidentiality
- Use
- Contact
- Preparation
- Completion
- Understanding and action

Once you've completed your benchmarking studies, you should have data for each of your key metrics for the targeted processes. Then, you're ready for the next step.

To sum up the benchmarking process, here are the basics:

- Select a topic for which to establish a benchmark.
- Estimate the costs of doing a benchmarking study.
- Select and train a team to complete the study.
- Choose the key metrics you want to study.
- Select or design a survey and develop questions.
- Develop tools to collect the data.
- Test the methods you plan to use to analyze the data.
- Analyze your own process for the key metrics.
- Identify companies and contact them.
- Collect and analyze data from public domain sources.
- Formulate a benchmark plan and analyze information.
- Conduct gap analysis.
- Develop recommendations and plan to implement.
- Identify departments that are needed for support.
- Present the plans to management.
- Implement the plan and monitor the progress.
- Collect data on benchmark subjects.

GAP ANALYSIS

You've used your key metrics to establish baselines for your target processes. You've gathered benchmark data to show how your processes could be performing. Now, you compare. In technical terms, you do a gap analysis, to quantify the gaps between where you are now and where you want to be.

Your gap analysis enables you to set goals for improving your processes and to develop strategies for improvement. You might not be able to set goals for improving every aspect of every process; you might need to prioritize. You might not be able to set ideal goals; especially early in Six Sigma implementation, you might want to set goals that allow you to achieve important gains quickly, to prove the value of Six Sigma. Then you can set your sights on breakthrough goals.

GUIDELINES FOR METRICS

Here are some steps to help you select, set up, measure, and get results from your metrics. These guidelines will help you realize the financial connection of your metrics effort. They are simple, internal things you can do to get the metrics in place and get the information you need. You must go through all of these steps to set up the proper metric system.

Get leaders involved. Because they set company strategy, they need to be involved in how the metrics are linked to achieving it. We cannot stress enough how important it is for executive leadership to actively support you. Your Six Sigma initiative will require a companywide commitment of human and other resources. When upper managers are engaged, you've got the freedom to make real changes, based on what the metrics tell you and the entire organization.

Visually represent your metrics. Prominently display them in charts, graphs, and diagrams, to show your employees what you're trying to do and how they are involved in delivering information and correcting the processes.

Metrics must respond quickly. Your measurement systems must provide feedback promptly, so you can identify problems and correct them as soon as possible. They should not be cumbersome or take a long time to yield data.

Metrics must be simple. They must clearly communicate the CTQ information you need. Avoid setting up complex measurements that are difficult to use. You want direct information to take direct action.

Metrics should drive only important activities. Make sure they relate to regular activities and processes. You need to assess the most important factors to measure—both in terms of COPQ and COGS/COSS—and then make sure that what you examine will result in information that's relevant. Your goal is to get at waste and defects and correct the processes to reduce costs. Your metrics must reflect that, no matter what.

Limit the number of metrics. Generally, you should implement no more than 10 metrics at a given time. Why? You want fast feedback. Metrics exist for this purpose only. If you get bogged down in measurements, you can lose time and focus, employees will get confused, and upper managers might lose track of what you're doing. Don't get flooded with metrics that clog the entire activity stream. Ten or fewer—that's the rule!

Take corrective action. Once you have feedback, you and your team should take corrective action as soon as possible. You want to maintain the momentum of your Six Sigma initiative and have it pay off as soon as possible. Act quickly, then move on to your next project and set new metrics.

PROBLEMS WITH METRICS

It's easy to get caught up in measuring things, so that you focus so much on quantifying defects that you forget about also quantifying the effects. Here's an example: If you're setting metrics for your administrative assistants, you might include a measurement of typos in terms of 1000 characters (opportunities). So you determine that George averages five typos, Sarah averages seven, and Pat averages eight. Well, obviously George is the most accurate, right? Yes—if you quantify defects only. But what about the effects on your customers? George generally has more problems with names, while Sarah and Pat check names carefully. Because customers are usually more bothered by mistakes with their names than mistakes with other words, George would suffer by comparison with Sarah and Pat. That's one of the problems with being too focused on counting defects alone.

Along these lines, we should caution against focusing on averages. The usual way to represent a series of figures is by finding the average. But consider the potential complication. Here's an example: your goal is on-time deliveries. For your three delivery drivers this month, you calculate averages of 15.3 minutes late, 24.7 minutes late, and 6.3 minutes late. So, you conclude, Driver 3 has the best average. That's true, but the averages don't show everything. They don't show that Driver 3 is often as late as Drivers 1 and 2, but occasionally arrives 20 to 30 minutes early. That helps compensate for being late—but it inconveniences the customer when dock workers have to cut their lunch short to unload the truck. The averages also don't show that Driver 1 has several times been late by 45 minutes, while Driver 2 has been late by 20 minutes at most. Six Sigma allows you to measure variation in a process, to calculate standard deviations from the mean, so you have a more accurate picture of the process.

A final point to make here is that metrics should use units that everybody understands. If, for example, we want to establish metrics for incomplete shipments, what constitutes "incomplete?" Does it matter how many items are missing? Do you account for the relative importance of the items to the customer? If so, how? The problem of an incomplete shipment is worse if the customer refuses delivery, but how do you measure that effect? How do you establish a metric that doesn't require any of the employees to make judgments when they track the data?

How do you establish appropriate, accurate metrics? You tap the experience of the employees who are closest to the processes. You hold meetings to discuss your attempts at establishing metrics, and you encourage everyone to find fault with them. Then, finally, as you use your metrics, encourage one and all to report any questions or problems with them.

HOW TO AVOID BAD METRICS

When developing metrics, beware of the following:

- Metrics for which you cannot collect accurate or complete data.
- Metrics that are complex and difficult to explain to others.
- Metrics that complicate operations and create excessive overhead.
- Metrics that cause employees to act not in the best interests of the business just to "make their numbers."

A fundamental element of Six Sigma philosophy is that unless we are prepared to invest in the measurement of quality, we cannot improve quality; if we don't measure quality, and don't follow up on these measures, then we are sending a signal that we really don't value quality. This, in turn, affects day-to-day behaviors and activities of all employees.

Generating new measures requires new questions. If we continue to ask the same questions, we will continue to ask for and generate the same measures. It is an issue of leadership to ask new questions about the quality of our products and processes, new questions that will lead to new research and new measures.

Here's a summation of the basic steps in setting metrics:

1. *Start with your customers.* What expectations are important, critical to quality?
2. *Establish key, consistent metrics.* What metrics belong on your dashboard?
3. *Determine baselines.* What is the current state of your processes?
4. *Benchmark processes.* Who's doing the same or similar things better than you?
5. *Set goals.* Easier goals can give you quick successes; more ambitious goals can help sustain your Six Sigma initiative.

SUMMARY

A business must have metrics in order to progress intelligently and efficiently. A business metric is any unit of measurement that provides a way to objectively quantify a process in ways that make sense.

Metrics should be a fundamental part of running any business. Measurement is a fundamental value and belief of Six Sigma. Every Six Sigma project depends on metrics. If you can measure your processes, you can understand them. If you can understand them, you can correct, control, and improve them and thus reduce costs while improving the quality of your outputs.

Measurement is crucial to the success of your Six Sigma initiative.

The first step toward improving processes, products, or services is determining what your customers consider critical to quality. The criteria for establishing business metrics must relate to improving customer satisfaction and reducing costs.

Your business metrics constitute your scorecard, your dashboard: They allow you to continually assess your progress and detect any potential problems. Also, your choice of business metrics and the importance you give them show what you value.

When you create metrics, you need to ask questions—new questions—and search for new results. To get new metrics—and new behaviors—you must ask new questions. Begin with the fundamentals. Why do we measure this? Why do we measure it in this way? What does this measurement mean? Why is this measurement important?

Start with customer satisfaction. For every product or service, what aspects are key to your customers? For each aspect, what are your customers' expectations? You must really know what customers want, not go by what you think they want. Ask what's important to them. What are their CTQ criteria? Once you determine the essential expectations, figure out ways to measure how well your product or service is meeting those expectations. Then, work backward through the process, to establish metrics for activities that are critical to meeting those expectations. Then, for every metric, ask this question: How does this metric link to the bottom line?

Mapping a process allows a team to examine how all of the steps in a process work together and to visualize the flow and sequencing. In so doing, it can locate steps that don't add value to the process and eliminate them to reduce cycle time and cut costs.

When setting metrics, keep the numbers of measurements small. The key here is quality over quantity. Select only a true set of indicators that will give you the information you need about process factors that affect customer satisfaction and revenue. When establishing a metric, you need to know why you're measuring it, why it's important, and what's causing the results.

Your metrics should provide data that enables you to identify and solve performance problems in your processes as quickly as practical. They should be sufficiently sensitive to reveal changes or variations that are significant.

One of the innovations of Six Sigma is to establish metrics in terms of opportunities for defects. Defects per million opportunities (DPMO) is a metric that managers can use to apply Six Sigma thinking to any business process, because defects can be anything that causes customer dissatisfaction, and opportunities can be any possibility for a defect.

Two main concepts govern metrics. Your metrics provide knowledge about your processes and help you develop better metrics. Your metrics must align with your strategic goals for performance.

After determining the metrics that will provide the most important information about your processes, you use them to establish baselines, standards for comparisons that show the current status of your performance and serve as a reference for measuring progress in improving a process.

The focus of Six Sigma lies in the transfer function: $Y = f(X)$. Output Y is a function of input X. This is just a mathematical way to state that variables or changes in inputs and the process will determine outputs. Establish the transfer functions and then identify the vital few factors, the inputs (X's) that you must isolate and then control in order to control the outputs (Y's). The transfer functions serve as a good test of your metrics.

Then move on to understanding how your processes measure up and figuring out where you want to go with your processes. Do that through benchmarking, a method for comparing a process using standard or best practices as a basis and identifying ways to improve the process.

After you've used your key metrics to establish baselines for your target processes and gathered benchmark data to show how your processes could be performing, you compare. In technical terms, you do a gap analysis to quantify the gaps between where you are now and where you want to be. Your gap analysis enables you to set goals for improving your processes and to develop strategies for improvement.

CASE STUDY

There are a lot of variables involved in setting business metrics. Here's an example to show how they might all come together.

In a recent study, I found that a particular company's SG&A (Selling, General, and Administrative expenses) was 500 percent higher than that of the nearest competitor in its peer group. Why? What was the difference?

We determined that the company was overstaffed—way overstaffed! By first benchmarking its performance and figuring out its baseline, we had the knowledge to select the metrics necessary to realign the company.

The first thing the company had to do was to set a new short-term direction to get to a minimally acceptable level of performance. That was the goal for creating a new company baseline, which in turn set in motion the actions that translated the goal into a real, better baseline.

At that point, the company was ready to ask more searching questions or, in other words, to set up metrics. It could ask questions about why competitors performed better with less and how they sustained their performance.

At the same time, it could examine its own processes and functions to yield the crucial answers—or data—that improve profitability.

Six Sigma allows you to achieve the constancy of purpose that is the secret to success, by focusing your efforts on understanding the variations in your processes and the defects that result. Here are the basic results: money, customer satisfaction, quality, impact on employees, growth, and competitive advantages.

Six Sigma focuses on the critical-to-quality (CTQ) expectations of your customers: That's what matters most. By using Six Sigma management methods, your company can target the vital few factors in your processes that are allowing variations and defects that keep you from meeting the CTQ expectations of your customers. You can better align your business goals with the requirements and expectations of your customers. The critical-to-quality (CTQ) concept in Six Sigma allows you to focus on improving quality *from the perspective of the customer.* Managers and employees all have some ideas about what constitutes quality for their products and services. That's good—but it doesn't put cash in the coffers. Find out which aspects of your products and services are vital to the customer and in what ways. Then you can set standards for delivering quality that matters to your customers.

REVIEW QUESTIONS

1. What is a business metric?

    a. A measurement of the difference between the current state of a process and the future state

    b. Any characteristic that is critical to quality for customers

    c. A means of distinguishing between processes or steps that add value for customers and those that do not

    d. Any unit of measurement that provides a way to objectively quantify a process in terms of objectives

2. In the transfer function $Y = f(X)$, which letter represents the dependent variable?

    a. Y

    b. f

    c. X

    d. None of the above

3. This is a technique by which an organization measures the performance of a process against similar best-in-class processes in other organizations, determines how those organizations achieve their performance levels, and uses the information to improve its process.

    a. Six Sigma

    b. Cause-and-effect diagram

    c. Benchmarking

    d. Gap analysis

4. A baseline is

    a. A Six Sigma synonym for the bottom line

    b. A standard for comparisons, the current performance of a process

    c. The lowest limit in a series of data points

    d. A synonym for gap analysis

5. If we know $Y = f(X)$, then we know

    a. Key questions to ask

    b. The function of the problem

    c. That X is the dependent on Y

    d. That Y is a function of the X's, which are independent

    e. None of the above

6. What is the concept of a "dashboard"?

    a. It shows what happened after the fact.

    b. It shows how to improve a metric.

    c. It shows the metrics of the business shown like that of a car.

    d. It shows the critical metrics to monitor.

    e. All the above

SEARCHING FOR PROJECTS AND DEVELOPING A PORTFOLIO

HERE'S A BUSINESS reality that is all too common—a problem that screams for Six Sigma.

When I went to the production site of new client for an assessment visit, I found a Six Sigma project immediately. The company made a four-foot control cable for cruise control, which is made from a half-dozen or so single-strand wires. Looking around, I saw hundreds of four- to six-inch pieces of cable lying near the cutting process. These pieces had been trimmed because their process was not capable enough to get the correct length on the first pass.

As I laid these pieces out end to end, I asked the plant manager, "What do you see?"

He had no answer until the lengths approached the full measure of the final cable, when he finally realized that the waste on the floor represented a whole lot of complete cruise control cables. At six cents per foot, each four- to six-inch wasted piece was worth about two or three cents. When you add that up over time, it amounted to a $193,000 waste of money. I told him I saw money!

This was lower than low-hanging fruit. I refer to this type of cost savings as rotted fruit. Your normal quality and cost-control system should address rotted fruit. This kind of rotted fruit proves that Six Sigma projects are right in front of us; we are so close to them that the defective activity is accepted as part of the process.

Project selection will make or break the success of a Six Sigma deployment.

Just like building a house brick by brick, Six Sigma is a project-by-project journey with a set of resources focused on the bottom line.

As your Six Sigma initiative takes off and your black belts are ready to get to work on projects, the big question that remains is deciding how to select projects that will be most successful, that will return the maximum result. There are certain criteria that must come into play when choosing a project. Although this might seem obvious, it's important to remember why you're undertaking the work. It's easy to be enthusiastic and feel ready to apply Six Sigma virtually everywhere you look, but not every business scenario warrants the label of "project."

Project selection for Six Sigma needs the following:

1. A problem
2. A process
3. A financial benefit
4. A metric and a goal
5. A customer metric

Does your industry have 1 through 5? If not, then you are a Six Sigma enigma.

Project selection can affect the organization dramatically. If the choice is good, the organization will realize the many benefits cited in Chapter 1. If the choice is bad, however, there might be less support for the project, members of the team might feel ineffective, or, worse, morale in general might suffer, and the outcomes of the project might be less than expected.

Your approach to selecting projects should be as rigorous as your approach to applying the Six Sigma methodology to working on those projects. In a way, it's like that classic distinction between a manager and a leader: A manager is concerned with doing things right. A leader is concerned with doing the right things. You want to be doing projects right—but you must first be doing the right projects.

The success or failure of any Six Sigma initiative depends on selecting projects that can be completed within a reasonable time and will result in quantifiable business benefits, in terms of financial impact or customer satisfaction or both. It is important to select those projects that will be most successful, that will return the maximum result.

The same attention to detail, the same objectivity in measuring and assessing, and the same sensitivity about the human aspects that will maximize the benefits of the Six Sigma approach are essential when selecting projects. In other words, Six Sigma begins as soon as people start thinking about where they want to implement it.

FINDING POTENTIAL PROJECTS

The first question to be considered here is basic: Who chooses? That, like so many decisions, depends on the organization. It is generally the responsibility of senior managers, including champions and the Six Sigma director or implementation leader, if any. For the sake of simplicity, we'll refer to this group as the executive team. The outside consultant should also be able to help find potential projects.

The executive team develops a list of possible projects, assesses the possibilities, and then approves some of them for the project portfolio from which projects will be chosen for implementation. How does the team choose projects for the portfolio? There are various ways, but we'll outline the basic possibilities.

It seems appropriate here to reiterate a point mentioned earlier that will be repeated at times throughout this book: The methodology of Six Sigma is rigorous but not rigid. Intelligence and judgment—and even creativity—are needed all along, from the very beginning, from launching the initiative, and selecting the first project. Those key elements cannot be found in any book or distributed in any training. Six Sigma provides a basic methodology and numerous tools, but decisions about applying that methodology and using those tools must be based on the particular situation, in respect of the goals and the strategies and the culture of the organization.

One final point to make before we discuss criteria for selecting projects: Not every improvement decision is a Six Sigma project. As good as the methodology is, it is not appropriate to apply it to every improvement project.

Here's an example. Your business is consolidating some of its operations and you need to reduce your facilities from two to one. It's not necessary to allocate Six Sigma resources and collect data and put black belts and project teams to work; you know what has to happen. You need to sell one building and move the contents into the other.

The purpose of Six Sigma is to improve processes by solving problems. If you already know the solution to a problem, then the problem is not a Six Sigma project. Apply Six Sigma only to problems for which you do not already know the solutions.

Establish Basic Criteria

The process of selecting Six Sigma projects should begin with some basic criteria. Here are a few general guidelines:

- There must be the potential to save money by reducing variation and defects; the fundamental criterion is the opportunity to turn the cost of poor quality (COPQ) into bottom-line savings.

- You should select projects that allow the Six Sigma team to attack and reduce or even eliminate costs. Whether in sales, marketing, manufacturing, or other areas, every process has a connected cost.
- It must be possible to define and delimit the project, which includes identifying inputs and outputs.
- Any process involved in a project must be stable, i.e., the amount of money that could be saved cannot vary more than 5 percent, or the project team must be able to stabilize it. You cannot improve a process unless it is stable and you know its capability.
- It must be possible that management will approve the project.
- The project must be both small enough to be manageable and big enough to be important (and maybe impressive and/or interesting to the stakeholders).
- The project must relate directly to the organization's mission.
- The project must be appropriate to the Six Sigma approach of understanding the causes of variation and reducing or eliminating them in order to minimize the defects.
- The project must be limited enough to allow for rigorous data collection and analysis within a reasonable time with a reasonable commitment of resources. The interpretations of "narrow" and "reasonable" will vary, but focus is central to a Six Sigma project.
- The project must involve recurring events, repetitive processes—generally, more is better. The more often a process is repeated, the more performance will be hurt by variation and wasted time and resources and the more defects will occur.
- The project should be doable in four to six months. This time frame is not carved in stone, but it's important to keep the organization interested and committed to the project. Projects that would require more than six months are better divided into subprojects of shorter length.

These basic criteria are minimum requirements for any Six Sigma project. Then, you add criteria—a lot or a few, stringent or flexible, specific or general—depending on your situation, the goals of the organization, the resources available, and how long or how short you want your list of possible projects to be.

The criteria will also depend on your approach. The majority of these criteria are derived from these perspectives:

- *Top down.* Criteria based on the metrics used in the goals and objectives of the organization's strategic plan and/or operating plan
- *Bottom up.* Criteria based on budget limitations and/or expectations, the costs of doing business
- *Outside in.* Criteria based on the voice of the customer and the requirements that your customers consider critical to quality

If the organization is new to Six Sigma, and especially if commitment to Six Sigma is not yet ensured, use these criteria to guide you. Again, you should consider the difficulty of the project, the time frame, the resources needed, and the risk involved in completing the project.

Here is a rule of thumb in selecting projects for Six Sigma training: Target projects with minimal effort for learning purposes. Basically, you should choose projects that fit the criteria of offering relatively high-value outcomes with high visibility to help engage the company and build momentum.

Long List or Short List?

The executive team might want to start by generating a long list of project possibilities and then narrowing down those possibilities by developing a second list of criteria. Or it might make more sense to first add more criteria to the list of basic requirements and then draw up a shorter list. For the purposes of this explanation, we will start with the basic criteria listed above, move to generating project ideas, and then list additional criteria that could be used to shorten the list of possible projects.

LIST POSSIBLE PROJECTS

Now that the executive team established the minimum requirements for projects to be listed for consideration, the team members look for possibilities. Logically, the same perspectives that guided them in establishing the basic criteria for projects can guide them in looking for projects to meet those criteria.

- *Top down.* Projects that are most closely aligned with the goals and objectives of the organization's strategic plan or operating plan
  - Did any senior managers recommend or even just mention any possible projects when they were discussing initiating Six Sigma?
  - Ask the CEO and others at the top what they consider the greatest issues facing the organization. Then, find projects directly related to those issues.
  - Start with financial goals for the organization or key divisions and look for projects that would allow you to make the most progress toward those goals.
  - If the organization has a balanced scorecard or a dashboard or other such way of tracking metrics toward goals, that's half the battle. Such a system makes picking projects much easier.
- *Bottom up.* Projects that improve processes that are incurring excessive costs
  - What processes are generating higher scrap rates, falling below capacity requirements and/or performance expectations, and/or resulting in large numbers of customer complaints?

- Start in the area that's most important financially. What's keeping it from being even more important?
- Start in the area that's least important financially. What's keeping it from being more important?
- What are employees complaining about around the water cooler and the lunch tables? Are they complaining about any processes as being unnecessary, time-consuming, confusing, or otherwise "not how I would run this company?"
- Do inspections reveal any serious problems with meeting specifications?

- *Outside in.* Projects that would matter most to the customers, projects that would address concerns raised by audits or cited by regulatory agencies, projects that result from comparisons with competitors, projects that develop from suggestions made by suppliers
  - Are there any customer complaints that stand out as more serious or more common? Check complaint logs and files. Talk with your customer service representatives.
  - Ask your customers what they consider the biggest problem with the products or services they receive from your organization.
  - Are there any trends, now or expected, that might change the needs of your customers?
  - Call former customers and ask why they stopped doing business with you.
  - Call current customers and ask what they like least about your products or services.
  - Have any audits (internal or external, financial or regulatory) revealed any issues?
  - In what ways is the organization possibly, probably, or even definitely inferior to any competitors?
  - Have any of your suppliers offered suggestions? Ask—especially if they also supply any of your competitors.

- Miscellaneous
  - Start in the heart of your organization, the area that's most important in terms of employee pride, name recognition in the community, and so on. A success in this area would have a big impact psychologically as well as financially.
  - Start in the area the champion knows best.
  - Which projects would generate results most easily?
  - Which projects would generate results fastest?
  - Which projects would require the least resources, in terms of money or assets or humans?
  - Which projects would affect the most people within the organization?
  - Which projects would offer the best opportunity for before-and-after comparisons on direct and indirect costs and/or benefits?

- Which projects would be easiest? Which could the team give to your Six Sigma teams to illustrate some successful experiences before taking on the big projects?
- Bring together employees from various divisions and/or functions as a focus group to brainstorm.

To find potential Six Sigma projects, members of the executive team can also go through the organization from function to function and look for indications of problems such as the following:

- High variation in the outputs of processes
- Expenses that are excessive and/or vary greatly out of line with any changes in productivity
- Scrap from production processes
- Process capacity lower than expectations and/or benchmarks
- Customer complaints
- Downtime
- Overtime
- Rework, such as with invoices, proposals, contracts, and other paperwork
- Cycle time in excess of expectations and/or benchmarks
- Throughput lower than expectations and/or benchmarks
- Rolled throughput yield lower than expectations and/or benchmarks
- Unnecessary transportation of products or paperwork
- Processes in which there are many handoffs between individuals or functions
- Processes producing less than expected
- Expenses for expedited shipping and other costs resulting from delays

Finally, here are some project ideas by business function:

- Sales
  - Increase sales by unit volume
  - Increase orders from current customers
  - Reduce the time required to enter orders
  - Reduce the errors and rework in processing orders
  - Improve the process for checking customer credit
- Marketing
  - Expand sales through company Web site
  - Improve cross-sell opportunities
- Customer service
  - Increase the efficiency of handling calls received
  - Improve customer service representative knowledge of products and services
  - Reduce number of call transfers

- Shipping/receiving
  - Improve on-time delivery to customers
  - Improve the accuracy of documentation
  - Reduce inventory damage and loss
  - Decrease production delays due to inventory problems
  - Improve inspection processes
- Information technology
  - Reduce system downtime
  - Improve employee access to network from remote locations
  - Coordinate applications to reduce data entry time
- Accounting and finance
  - Reduce the cycle time for closing (month, quarter, year)
  - Improve collection processes
  - Improve processing of payments to suppliers
  - Improve cash management processes
  - Reduce electronic financial transaction costs
  - Reduce the cycle time for reconciliation
  - Improve the accuracy of financial forecasts
- Human resources
  - Reduce the cycle time for hiring
  - Reduce the cycle time for entering a new hire into the system
  - Improve employee orientation processes
  - Improve efficiency of training
  - Improve the value and perception of employee performance reviews

Project Selection Using Process Entitlement

Process entitlement represents the best that a process, a product, or a service can be at any given time. Knowing what is possible defines the short-term target for both defect and dollar levels.

If a process achieves a higher level of performance at more than three points over time, it demonstrates what is possible. It is not a freak accident that it achieved that level. It indicates what you should be entitled to expect from that process. It's the process entitlement.

For example, if there are three points at which a process has produced 500 units in a day, when the average baseline performance is 350 units per day, you have a "gap to entitlement" that can generate major cost benefits. You know what the process can achieve, so why isn't it achieving it consistently? This "gap to entitlement" marks this as a must-select project.

Look at all your business metrics and start looking for entitlement levels. If a process has demonstrated a higher level of achievement than it averages, this is your internal benchmark. Then, go look at external benchmarks. Maybe your level of entitlement is even higher than the process has demonstrated. In other words, if your competition is achieving higher levels using the same process, you know you are entitled to more.

Let's get an understanding from a personal point of view regarding entitlement. We all have a weight that is considered ideal for a healthy life. Some of us have achieved that target weight. However, some keep gaining weight, for one reason or another. Why can't we achieve and maintain that healthy target weight? We know we can do it, because we've done it on occasion. In a sense, we're entitled to that ideal weight. In Six Sigma terms, we need to make it a project that consists of working with the transfer function, $Y = f(X)$, to identify the reasons that have caused us to vary upward from that target weight and reduce or eliminate them.

If we know the entitlement levels of our processes, that is, if we know the quality that we can expect from them, we cannot be satisfied with less than that. We also cannot spend more to increase capacity until we have identified the causes that are keeping us from our entitlement level and are ready to work to fix the problems.

Quantifying Projects

As a step toward prioritizing projects, the executive team might find it useful to create Pareto charts to quantify and prioritize issues within potential projects. The results can often help teams understand and shape projects.

A Pareto chart is used to display the relative importance of the multiple items (defects, causes, or other aspects of a situation) and track the cumulative weight of the items. When the executive team identifies a problem, it might seem too large and/or complicated to be treated as a project at this point. It might be necessary to drill down and identify the actionable items within that could be listed as projects. A tool that's useful at this point is the Pareto chart. Pareto charts are good for initially focusing a project.

The charts are based on the Pareto principle, named after Vilfredo Pareto, a nineteenth-century economist who noticed that around 80 percent of the wealth in Italy was held by around 20 percent of the population. This observation was extended by pioneers of the quality movement into a rule of thumb, also known as the 80-20 rule: in many situations, 80 percent of the effects result from 20 percent of the causes.

A Pareto chart is basically a bar chart in which the bars that represent the items being measured and compared are ordered by size, starting from the left with the highest bar, the most important item. The measurement data are tracked cumulatively as a percentage by means of a line. If the Pareto principle holds true, after you measure the impact of the most important 20 percent of the items, the cumulative percentage should reach 80 percent.

Here's how Pareto analysis works. First, determine the categories of problems that are to be compared. It's usually best to have no more than 10. Next, decide on a standard measurement for quantifying the problems, such as frequency or number or size. Set a period of time for collecting the data that will serve as the basis for the comparison. Then, collect and tabulate the data in a three-column table, with headings for the problem category, the measurement, and the percent of the total. In the first column, list the categories of problems. In the second column, list for each problem category the data measured. For the third column, divide each number in the second column by the total of measurements, to arrive at the percentage of the total.

The next step in the Pareto process is to construct the bar chart. Draw a horizontal axis and label along it the categories of problems, beginning with the one with the highest percentage and continuing in descending order of importance. Then, at each end of the horizontal axis, draw a vertical axis. Mark the left axis with increments for the measurements used in the analysis. Mark the right axis with increments for percentage, from 0 to 100 percent, so that each percentage increment matches the appropriate point along the left axis.

The Pareto selection method is a very handy tool for getting to the heart of the issues in advance of initiating a project. When you conduct the analysis, you can drill down to arrive at defects and then frame a project that will focus on those defects, resulting in a financial benefit.

Poor Choices for Projects

Bad projects generally rate as poor choices because they have little or no business impact, the effort expended is not justified by the results, and the probability of success that they will save enough money is not high. But how does one determine if a potential project is a poor choice? We'll look at several aspects below.

Impact
First, let's look at four aspects that make a project a poor choice with regard to its overall impact on business.

1. *Revising reports.* It might be interesting to create and revise reports for projects, but such activity doesn't make any money: There's no tangible, bottom-line outcome. Don't get lost in project materials management; stay focused on the explicit objective.
2. *Quantifying the performance of a process.* This is the "getting ready to get ready" scenario, where a champion or a black belt spend time assessing without actually fixing any problems. Again, there's no tangible, positive result. Your energies would be much better invested in actually working on the problem.
3. *Improving a supplier's performance without sharing in the benefit.* Imagine you depend on a supplier for a key component and it's defective, so you decide to help the supplier improve that component. That's logical—but not necessarily right. While it makes sense to have your supplier fix the component so your processes are improved, why just give away that corrective measure to the supplier? When you share your knowledge, there has to be something in it for you.

4. *Reducing cycle time for an operation that's not critical.* A common mistake is to work at reducing cycle time for an operation that's not a bottleneck. If it's not hurting you, don't fix it. Six Sigma is about getting financial results, not about improving processes which don't need improvement.

Effort

Second, a project can be considered to be poor in terms of the effort it requires. Here are some examples:

1. *Installing a company-wide computer network.* This is a huge undertaking with a long time horizon. It does not require a black belt to initiate the DMAIC phases to manage it. It's not a problem; it's a business decision. You just need to do it! Deploy your Six Sigma teams elsewhere.
2. *Improving the profitability of an entire product line.* This project is so massive and complex that you probably won't get the results you want in a defined time span. This scale of project will frustrate you when you're trying to get fast, quantifiable results.
3. *Fixing the annual planning process.* Strategic actions such as these are not appropriate for Six Sigma projects. Why? You don't need to assign a black belt to lengthy, administrative tasks; his or her efforts are much better spent on tactical, results-oriented activities.

Probability of Success

Finally, a poor project can be evaluated with regard to its probability of success. A project is unlikely to succeed if any of the following conditions holds:

- If it involves improving a process that won't show any substantial benefits for several months, beyond the three- to six-month period discussed earlier.
- If it depends on the completion of other risky projects.
- If it requires assistance from extremely busy people.
- If it is not aligned with management objectives.

Again, this type of effort lacks definition, schedule, or clear measurement. Without a disciplined, targeted approach and clearly defined and quantified objectives, poorly chosen projects likely won't yield the hidden dollars you want.

EVALUATING PROJECTS

Now the executive team has a list of projects—maybe a dozen, maybe several dozens. All of them have met the basic requirements. Every one of them merits consideration, each in its own way. The possibilities are bewildering, even overwhelming. Now the team must evaluate those potential projects.

Making the Case

For each potential project on the list, the executive team needs to make the business case. This means defining the project initially or scoping the project. (The team does not fully define any projects at this point. That level of effort is appropriate only for projects that the executive team selects; then the champion and the project team do it fully in the Define phase of the Six Sigma model). It also means quantifying the benefits of potential projects and prioritizing them based on financial metrics.

It's important to understand the concept of scope for Six Sigma projects. This term is more specifically defined as the boundaries of the process that the project team is working to improve, the limits within which it will be focusing its efforts. For example, although a process might impact other areas of the entire business, the project should focus on one business unit only. In other words, let's say a project in accounts receivable aims to fix an "aging" defect greater than 120 days. This project will be restricted to that department only. The object is to focus on that area only to resolve the problem, then replicate it by expanding the boundaries into other areas of the business.

The executive team can engage black belts and/or green belts in breaking down potential projects into processes, with assistance from champions and a master black belt, in order to determine the areas on which to focus the Six Sigma efforts. This breakdown ensures that a project team is concentrating on the best opportunities for improvement. The team defines the scope, sets boundaries, quantifies financial benefits, and determines basic objectives for the potential project.

These are the most important questions to guide the team during this activity:

- What is the process to be considered as a project?
- What are the boundaries? What is to be included in the process and what is to be excluded?
- Where does the process start and where does the process end?
- What is the impact? Who would be affected by improvements? Who are the owners, shareholders, customers, suppliers?
- What are the benefits?
  - Financial benefits, in terms of the criteria—resources, time, defects
  - Benefits for customers of the process
  - Benefits for other people affected by improvements
  - Other benefits (depending on the situation—e.g., the organizational culture, the status of the Six Sigma initiative), such as showing the value of the Six Sigma initiative or improving morale

Then the black belts and/or green belts gather data on the current state of the processes. While working on making the case for a project, the team might discover possibilities for other projects to consider at a later time. It might also realize that a possibility on the list might not require Six Sigma, that it might be a simpler improvement project. If the team identifies an improvement or a solution, the project should be handled instead by a project manager instead of through Six Sigma.

Next, the team makes estimates about the outcomes to be expected from improving the processes—the process entitlement. The team should determine entitlement for all key process performance measures of a process, such as rolled throughput yield, defect rate, waste, capacity, the cost of poor quality, cycle time, and downtime. The best performance might be based on experience, claims by equipment manufacturers, calculations by engineers, benchmarking, and any other means appropriate for the process in question.

The team then examines the gap between baseline performance (current state) and entitlement (desired state). Next, it scopes the project in order to determine the best way to narrow or close the performance gap within four to six months. If a team cannot close the gap between baseline performance and entitlement in a single project, it might outline further projects. Then, it makes the case for each of those projects to be evaluated and prioritized individually.

For every project under consideration, the executive team must set general objectives. A Six Sigma project should have one or more of the following objectives:

- Reduce variability
- Reduce defects
- Improve customer satisfaction
- Reduce costs
- Reduce cycle time
- Improve first-pass yield
- Improve rolled throughput yield
- Shorten lead time
- Optimize process performance
- Optimize the supply chain

Each objective should be stated precisely, with metrics. Metrics that allow for comparison are better, such as first-pass yield and rolled throughput yield. Wherever possible, every metric should be accompanied by a translation into dollars. The determination of the project impact is the responsibility of the financial personnel working in cooperation with the black belt and the champion.

All Six Sigma projects are rigorously evaluated for financial impact. The CFO is an important member of the executive management team; as mentioned in Chapter 2, a project team should generally have the controller or some other member from finance who documents the financial impact.

Take, for example, an objective such as "Reduce downtime of X production line by at least 30 percent, from a monthly average of 27 hours to a monthly average of 18.9 hours or less." That objective might be impressive, but the impact is greater and more widely and easily understood if you calculate the dollar equivalent of that metric, if you show the value of that reduction by multiplying the hours by the salaries and benefits of the employees on that production line, the share of overhead, the cost of lost productivity, and so forth. Then, the difference of 8.1 hours a month on the one production line becomes $2,607. That's a metric that everyone can understand.

Once the team has determined what success is possible for a project and stated those outcomes in terms of objectives and metrics, it must estimate what it will take to achieve those outcomes. It estimates the time, the skills, the money, and the other resources that the project would require. It also includes whatever other information would qualify the project according to the criteria for selecting projects.

You should exclude from further consideration at this point any projects that do not (at least yet!) fit the following requirements of a good Six Sigma project:

- It should be well defined.
- The scope should be realistic.
- The current status (baseline should be established).
- The objectives and goals should be clear in terms of the process performance metrics and expected outcomes, and focused.
- There should be clear quantitative measures for assessing progress toward the objectives.
- The importance to the organization should be established so that people from management on down will support the project.
- The executive team makes the business case for the projects— which brings us to the subject of the next chapter, selecting projects and planning for the five phases of the DMAIC model.

SUMMARY

Project selection can affect the organization dramatically. A good choice can save the organization time and money, build company morale, and improve customer relationships. If the choice is bad, however, there might be less support for the project, members of the team might feel ineffective or worse, morale in general might suffer, and the outcomes of the project might be less than expected.

The success or failure of any Six Sigma initiative depends on selecting projects that can be completed within a reasonable time and will result in quantifiable business benefits. Your approach to selecting projects should be as rigorous as your approach to applying the Six Sigma methodology to working on those projects.

The responsibility of selecting Six Sigma projects belongs to senior managers, including champions and the Six Sigma director or implementation leader, if any—the executive team—and the outside consultant.

Some basic criteria are minimum requirements for any Six Sigma project. Then, you add other selection criteria depending on your situation, the goals of the organization, the resources available, and the number of possible projects you want to undertake.

A sure way to find good potential projects is through process entitlement. If a process achieves a higher level of performance at more than three points over time, it demonstrates what is possible, what you should be entitled to expect from that process. This gap to entitlement marks this as a must-select project.

If a process has demonstrated a higher level of achievement than it averages, this is your internal benchmark. External benchmarks might show that your level of entitlement is even higher than the process has demonstrated.

As a step toward prioritizing projects, the executive team might find it useful to quantify and prioritize issues within potential projects by creating Pareto charts.

Then, for each potential project on the list, the executive team needs to make the business case. This means initially defining or scoping the project. The team also quantifies the benefits of potential projects and prioritizes them based on financial metrics. What is the process to be considered as a project? What are the boundaries? What is to be included in the process and what is to be excluded? Where does the process start and where does the process end? What is the impact? Who would be affected by improvements? Who are the owners, shareholders, customers, suppliers? What are the benefits?

Next, the team makes estimates about the process entitlement and examines the gap between baseline performance and entitlement. Finally, for each of those projects, the executive team makes the case and sets general objectives, with metrics.

There are numerous issues and challenges involved in selecting projects. When you take the top-down approach of Six Sigma and address your strategic objectives and customer expectations, you can get to the operational factors that have the greatest impact. When you select projects that isolate the key processes that are costing you the most—often in almost invisible ways—you can unlock that hidden revenue. Then, in the results, the benefits of implementing the disciplined, data-driven methodology speak for themselves. Like anything else worth doing, it takes time and training to learn how to find potential Six Sigma projects for the portfolio. Then comes the critical moment—selecting the projects to pursue. We'll get into that next and show how to plan for the DMAIC model of Six Sigma implementation.

CASE STUDY

The focus in Six Sigma, as we have noted many times, is on finding and fixing sources of variation. That's true, but I don't want you to think that you should stop all variation in all your processes. You want to reduce and control the variation that results in adverse financial results. There are a lot of people in corporate America spending a lot of time and effort working on the wrong stuff because they don't know the financial impact of the problems.

For example, I worked with a company in Batesville, Arkansas, whose managers said they had an extrusion problem. They make the rubber seal around doors. For a decade they had talked about the lumps in the extrusion as the problem. They were devoted to spending their resources to solve that problem. They had to fix it! They had held meetings to talk about it and put resources to work on it—and they did so for these 10 years. However, the problem wasn't the lumps in the extrusion process!

When I looked at the whole process as their consultant, the lump problem was about the fifth problem from the top of the list of problems. Using a Pareto chart that showed the impact of process variation problems, I asked them, "Why were we talking about lumps?" I said, "Show me the data that says we should work on lumps at all. It might be fun to talk about it, but talking costs you money. There are other processes here that account for more than half your problems—the problem of lumps is nothing by comparison. Let's fix the first problems first!"

REVIEW QUESTIONS

1. What does Six Sigma need for project selection?
   a. A solution
   b. A low-level problem to start out
   c. No financial impact
   d. A problem, a process, a financial benefit, a goal, and a customer
   e. None of the above

2. What best describes a good project?
   a. Something that pleases the boss
   b. Nonbottleneck areas
   c. A reasonable goal
   d. Something that is quantifiable with a financial impact to the business
   e. One that has a solution

3. Why is Six Sigma project selection so important?

   a. It makes it fun for the business.

   b. It helps to justify fixing problems.

   c. It's not as important as getting trained.

   d. It makes or breaks the longevity due to making money while getting problems fixed.

   e. None of the above.

4. What three things must be considered while selecting projects?

   a. Metrics, surveys, and culture

   b. Culture, expectations, and time line

   c. Training, people, and outside customers

   d. Seasonal factors, people impact, and data availability

   e. Impact, effort, and probability of success

5. How can a Pareto chart help in project selection?

   a. To point out what is not important

   b. To drill down the CTQ metrics

   c. To show the levels of drill down from the top

   d. To create a focus on the top dollars

   e. All of the above

6. Which guideline generalizes that 20 percent of the causes are responsible for 80 percent of the effects?

   a. The 80-20 rule

   b. The 20-80 rule

   c. The Pareto principle

   d. Both a and b

   e. Both a and c

   f. Both b and c

   g. None of the above

7. What is a Pareto chart?

   a. A display of the genealogy of economist Vilfredo Pareto

   b. A specialized bar chart used to display the relative importance of multiple items and track the cumulative weight of the items

   c. A diagram for counting Pareto principles

   d. A diagram for monitoring *p*rojects and *a*ny *r*esults *e*stimated at *t*ime of *out*comes (PARETO).

8. Which of the following would likely be good Six Sigma projects?

   a. Quantifying the performance of a process

   b. Reducing cycle time for an operation that is not critical

   c. Both a and b

   d. Neither a nor b

FROM PORTFOLIO TO PROJECTS AND PLANS

N OW THAT THE EXECUTIVE team has developed a strategic high-level view of potential projects, the next step is to hand off ownership to the next level of managers, the functional champions. Functional champions are responsible for taking the strategic portfolio or backlog of potential projects to a tactical level that meets the criteria that the executive team has established. It's time to select the best projects to pursue.

This can be a very difficult task, because the members of the team have proposed and examined the projects and perhaps even advocated for some of them. In my consulting, I see the same mistake over and over: the lack of reality from the boardroom that is put upon the next layer of management. In other words, executives are often far-removed from the reality of what is actually going on in their business. In fact, it is the middle manager who usually has a more realistic picture of what is really happening, which executives fail to recognize. This total disregard and disrespect for middle managers starts the barriers of Six Sigma. The executives *must* hand over the ownership by inspiring the next level of managers and soliciting input into the project selection process. I am worn out from reminding senior managers to let go of the delusion that middle managers can't think. Give them the opportunity to rise to the occasion by including middle managers in the project selection process.

Figure 6-1 shows a simple list of potential projects.

Step One: List Potential Projects

SSC
Six Sigma Consultants, inc

Business Unit:_____

Owner:_____

Black Belt:_____

Date:_____

	Potential Project	Problem Type 1. Cost/Unit 2. Defects 3. Cycle Time 4. Customer Impact 5. Employee Impact 6. Other/Strategic	Problem Definition or Goal Statement
1			
2			
3			
4			
5			
6			

FIGURE 6-1   List of potential projects

EVALUATING AND PRIORITIZING PROJECTS

The next step in the selection process is to evaluate and prioritize the potential projects. This task is easier if the executive team creates a project selection matrix. The project selection matrix, shown in Figure 6-2, provides a means of evaluating each potential project according to the importance of each criterion and comparing all of the project possibilities, in order to prioritize the projects.

Project Selection Matrix

A project selection matrix is a simple and logical decision matrix. Create the matrix as explained below; then, meet with your team to put it to use.

First, list the projects down the left side of the matrix. Second, list the evaluation criteria across the top, as column headings. Third, indicate for each criterion a significance factor, the weight assigned to it by relative importance, as determined earlier, from 1 (low) to 5 or 10 (high). Figure 6-2 shows an example.

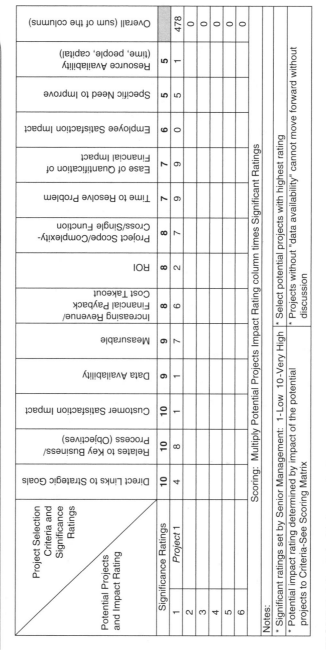

FIGURE 6-2 Prioritizing projects

In the matrix, identify each project only briefly; team members should have copies of the details—business case, preliminary problem statement, and so on, as determined by the executive team.

Determine a rating scale and provide guidelines for using the scale, general or specific, with an explanation of the ratings for each criterion and every number in the scale. What you do should depend on your situation and your needs: The purpose is for every member of the team to have a common understanding of what each rating means, just as they understand the meaning of each criterion on the matrix and the parameters of each project being considered. Figure 6-3 shows an example of scoring criteria for the prioritization matrix.

Clearly, hard data (such as cost or process performance impact) are preferable to subjective rating criteria as developed by teams. Sometimes, at the point when projects are under consideration, little data are available, so the best available method is to use a prioritization matrix to remove the inherent subjectivity as much as possible.Finally, meet with the members of your Six Sigma team. Display the project selection matrix, explain how it works, and then solicit input from each member.

It's probably most efficient and objective to use the multivote technique to rate each project, in which each member of the group is allowed to cast a number of votes, such as 5 or 7 or 10, choosing among several options or using them all for a single option. For each project on the matrix, ask the team members to assess it in terms of each selection criterion, using the ratings. Each option is attributed whichever rating receives the most votes. After counting the votes for each option, add the numbers and record the total in the appropriate cell. Then, after recording the votes for every project in terms of every criterion, multiply the votes by the weight indicated for each criterion and enter it in the cell. Finally, total the scores for each project. The result is the priority ratings for the projects.

As an example, take the option "Reduce downtime of X production line." You ask for votes on the first criterion, "alignment with strategic goals." "How many votes for a rating of 5? How many votes for 4? How many for 3? For 2? And for 1?" Then you write the "winning" rating in the cell where the option row and the first criterion column intersect. Next, you do the same with the second criterion, then the third, and so on. After that, you take the second option and go through each of the criteria again. Then, after the group has assigned each option a rating on each criterion, you do the math, multiplying the rating in each cell by the weight of the criterion and putting the result in the cell. If option 1 received a rating of 4 for the first criterion, the cell would contain a 4 and then a 32 (rating times weight). Finally, after calculating the result for all of the cells, you total the scores for each option.

Sometimes the reasons for choosing one project over another at this point are pragmatic: One criterion that will often be implicit, especially at

Document the Scoring Criteria

SSC
Six Sigma Consultants, Inc

Category Scoring Criteria

Scoring Category	0–2	3–4	5–7	8–10
Direct Links to Strategic Goals	Indirect Alignment	Some Direct Alignment	Strong Alignment	Very Strong and Direct Alignment
Relates to Key Business/Process (Objectives)	Indirect Relationship	Some Direct Relationship	Strong Relationship	Very Strong and Direct Relationship
Customer Satisfaction Impact	Customer may notice	Customer will appreciate	Major Customer Concern	Customer demands improvement
Data Availability	Does Not Exist	Attribute Data Available	Large Data Base Available	Strong Variable Data
Measurable	Complicated and Expensive Measurement	Moderate Complexity and Cost	Low Complexity and Moderate Cost	Easy Measurement at Low Cost
Financial Payback-Increasing Revenue/Cost Takeout	0–150K	150K–250K	250K–500K	500K+
ROI (Payback Period)	2+ years	1–2 Years	1 Year	6 Months
Project Scope/Complexity- Cross/Single Function	Across 4 or More Functions	Across 3 Functions	Across 2 Functions	One Single Function
Time to Resolve Problem	+180 days	91–180 days	31–90 days	30 days
Ease of Quantification	Highly Difficult	Moderately Difficult	Some Analysis Required	Straightforward
Employee Satisfaction Impact	Employees May Notice	Employees Will Appreciate	Major Employee Concern	Employees Demands Improvement
Specific Need to Improve	Infrequent Problem	Sporadic Problem	Annoying Problem	Chronic Problem
Resource Availability (time, people, capital)	None	Low	Moderate Amounts	Committed Amounts

FIGURE 6-3 Scoring criteria

this point in the project selection process, although perhaps not always explicit in lists of criteria, is resources.

For each project under consideration, you will need to ask this key question: Does the organization have the money, time, and black belts and green belts to make this project successful?

As mentioned in Chapter 5, it's also crucial to determine the entitlement of a process. What level of performance are you entitled to expect from the process? This sets the baseline and shows you the potential for savings.

Here's an example of a situation that happens all too often. A client was considering doing a project. We measured the Y (CTQ) over the past six months. The graph clearly showed that the financial benefit of obtaining the level of entitlement would have been less than $1,000 a year because the variation was so limited. This happens all the time and companies and consultants waste time when they don't check the entitlement of a process up front. In other words, they fail to measure the entitlement gap and pick projects that will not result in any financial benefit.

STATUS OF THE INITIATIVE

Up to this point of the Six Sigma initiative, the executive team has developed a portfolio of projects that it has evaluated and prioritized. For each there is a description of the opportunity, a quantification of the potential benefits, and broad objectives. This information provides direction for the champion who will be assigned to the selected project so that he can more effectively and efficiently choose people for the project team and develop a plan for the project, and it provides the basis for the project charter that the team will create.

Once the executive team has evaluated and prioritized the projects in the portfolio (backlog list of projects), it can select one or more of them and assign a member of the team to each project as champion.

As mentioned earlier, there are many criteria for selecting projects, and some of the factors depend more on timing and training and available resources than on the relative merits of the projects. Projects that are selected for implementation at this point are not necessarily the best—and projects that don't make it are not necessarily worse. The selected project or projects are simply those that best meet the immediate needs of the organization. The executive team keeps the remaining project ideas in the portfolio for the future. It continually adds project ideas to the portfolio, based on new customer issues or other issues that surface, and reformulates the list continuously. In fact, the team should develop a system for identifying potential projects and ranking them, so that there are always good project ideas in the portfolio.

At the end of the project selection process, also know as the Define phase, we are ready to move into the remaining elements of DMAIC and the true core of Six Sigma.

DMAIC: AN OVERVIEW

As mentioned in Chapter 1, there are various Six Sigma improvement models. In this book we are using the standard, DMAIC (Define-Measure-Analyze-Improve-Control).

Sometimes the methodology is applied without a formal Define phase: The steps that are usually part of the Define phase flow so smoothly from the project selection process that they could all be considered preliminary to the core of the model, the MAIC sequence, which we will show later in this chapter. However, because the five-phase DMAIC model is more commonly used, it's the model we will outline briefly here and discuss in the following five chapters.

For the DMAIC methodology to be most effective, the team must use the tools that are most appropriate for the tasks. However, the team does not always need to use all or even most of the tools. And, as mentioned in Chapter 1 and reiterated in Chapter 5, the methodology of Six Sigma is rigorous but not rigid. The five phases of DMAIC are not rigid, in principle; there is no sharp delineation separating one phase from the preceding and/or the following. The phases of a specific project are shaped and determined by the project champion.

Along the same lines, there are no rules that dictate the use of the tools. The black belt chooses the tools she feels are appropriate to the project. There are a handful of tools that are useful in virtually all projects and still others that are used very often. We will discuss those later in the chapters on the DMAIC phases. To cover all of the tools used in Six Sigma projects, however, would take a much larger book—and there are a few books out there that are very comprehensive (*Implementing Six Sigma—Smart Solutions Using Statistical Methods,* by Forrest W. Breyfogle III; *Statistical Quality Control,* by Eugene L. Grant and Richard S. Leavenworth).

For each project, the project champion creates and coordinates a deployment plan. In this project plan, he states the goals of the project, identifies the tasks necessary to complete the project, and outlines the five phases. With each phase, the champion schedules the steps, indicates milestones at which the black belt is to report on progress and any problems, and specifies the deliverables.

PROJECT REVIEW

To end each phase, the champion schedules a project review, also known as a *phase-gate review*, a *Six Sigma report-out*, a *Six Sigma project review*, a *stage-gate review*, a *tollgate review*, a *checkpoint review*, or a *milestone review*. They all mean the same thing: These reviews serve as status checks that the project sponsors and/or the executive team conduct in order to monitor and support the project deliverables. During this review, the project sponsors and/or the members of the executive team evaluate progress according to the plan set forth in the project charter, ask about any obstacles and ways to overcome them, discuss lessons learned during the phase, allocate resources as necessary, review time lines and deliverables, ensure that the project team is achieving the project goals according to schedule, and recognize the accomplishments of the team.

There are many objectives for the review, but the critical ones are the following:

- It serves as a safe, open environment to present the reality of what the black belt has found and to remove any barriers right then and there.

I was in a review at Navistar where one project with a cost savings of $270,000 was being held up by the 12-signature approval process for a required $20,000 capital appropriation request. This was a barrier! I spoke with Don DeFosset, who was president at the time, and told him that a lead-by-example message needed to be sent to the troops. As the barrier was presented by the black belt, Don stopped the meeting and announced that he'd had enough of these excuses and proceeded to sign the capital appropriation request. This action sent a shockwave throughout the company: silly, non-value-added barriers are not allowed.

- It is a learning environment for the champion, but it also an opportunity for black belts to be learning from each other. Black belts are expected to not be timid and to ask questions.
- It is an overall measure of commitment from executives, champions, and black belts for the program. It is not a dog-and-pony show for the executives, but a forum to show the realities of what the company is doing and the costs associated with it.

Here's what the project sponsors and/or the members of the executive team do in a review:

- Evaluate progress according to the plan set forth in the project charter.
- Ask about any obstacles and ways to overcome them.
- Discuss lessons learned during the phase.
- Allocate resources as necessary.
- Review time lines and deliverables.
- Ensure that the project team is achieving the project goals according to schedule.

- Recognize the accomplishments of the team. It's not the Rambo project, heroic feats by a black belt, but a collaborative effort by the team members. One of my best black belts was not only working the project, but also teaching the method to his team. At the third review, John was not able to make it—an absolute requirement for a black belt. In his absence, his team members presented the findings—and they were able to answer the questions flawlessly. That is a benchmark in team confidence and ownership of the process.

DMAIC: A BRIEF OUTLINE OF THE PHASES

The presentation of the DMAIC phases here is only a brief outline, an overview to prepare you for the chapters that present the phases more fully.

Define Phase

The purpose of the Define phase is to determine the objectives and the scope of the project, collect information on the process and the customers, and specify the deliverables to customers (internal and external). This phase consists of the following basic steps:

- Start with a high-level financial plan. What are the largest functional areas of cost? Create a high probability of success by going into core functions first; it's more of a surgical approach with high returns and a high profile to set the tone for the culture. Most of the time, these areas are the lead-by-example functions willing to get better. It forces a cultural pull system to success. In other words, by creating highly visible results that are recognized by core functions, a domino effect is also created in other core functions throughout the business. This creates an incentive for other core functions in the business—they want to succeed, too! Identify the champion and the process owner in those specific areas and form the project team.
- Develop the project charter (including business case, problem statement, objectives, scope, milestones, roles and responsibilities, and communication plan).
- Identify the customers.
- Collect data from the customers.
- Define the customer CTQ requirements.
- Define the core business process on which the project will focus.
- Determine the scope of the project and set the boundaries and the start and stop points.
- Create a high-level map of the current state of the process.

- Identify the important problems in the process.
- Define the deliverables.
- Determine the resources needed, including support.
- Develop a detailed process chart.
- Work out a project plan with milestones and a project status form/time line.
- Conduct a Define phase-gate review.

The basic deliverables for the Define phase include the following:

- Project charter
- Project status form/timeline
- List of customer CTQs
- Metrics graphs
- Process map with points at which to gather data
- Pareto charts of CTQs and of problems in the process
- List of project deliverables
- High-level process chart (SIPOC)
- Project plan: next steps
- Local project review with the direct champion
- Phase-gate review

Measure Phase

The purpose of the Measure phase is to identify one or more product or service characteristics, map the process, start the basic understanding of the potential X's, validate the measurement systems, assess the current level of process performance, estimate baseline capability, and quantify the problem. This phase consists of the following basic steps:

- Define defects for the black belt project core business process.
- Determine the key metrics for the black belt project process.
- Ensure that the metrics are valid and reliable.
- Assess the current data on this process to decide if it is adequate.
- Set a baseline for measuring progress—both defects and financial.
- Develop a detailed data-collection plan.
- Validate the measurement system.
- Collect data to determine types of defects and metrics.
- Use exploratory, descriptive, and graphical data analysis to understand the data.
- Start developing the $Y = f(X)$ relationship.
- Determine any special causes, to narrow the range of potential causes to analyze. (Warning: special causes are sometimes not

recognized because the time frame is not long enough. Some special causes have a pattern of repeating in the two- to four-month time frame. If you are looking at only a month, you will not see the pattern.)
- Evaluate the current capability of the process and the current sigma level.
- Conduct a Measure phase-gate review.

The basic deliverables for the Measure phase include the following:

- Project status form/timeline
- Metrics graphs
- Detailed process map with points at which to gather data
- Pareto charts of defects and causes
- Measurement tools, including gauge R&R studies
- Data on the process
- Process capability and sigma level
- Project plan: next steps
- Local project review with the direct champion
- Phase-gate review

Analyze Phase

The purpose of the Analyze phase is to evaluate and reduce the variables with graphical analysis and hypothesis testing and to identify the vital few factors out of the list of the trivial many for process improvement to arrive at the root cause(s) of the defects. We need to get down to the vital few X's, as shown in Figure 6-4.

A = All of the variation
P = Part of the variation
R = Rest of the variation
A = P + R is a Dorian Shanin equation.

This phase consists of the following basic steps:

- Analyze the data and the process map to determine the current state of the process, the root causes of defects, and opportunities for improvement.
- Assess the potential process capability.
- Compare the current state and the potential to identify and quantify any gaps.

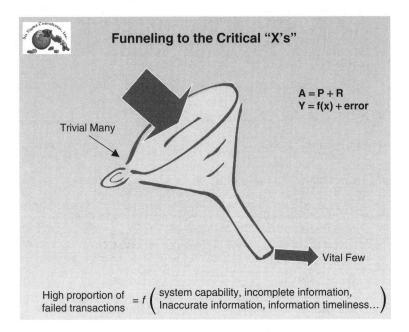

FIGURE 6-4   The critical X's

- Identify sources of variation.
- Confirm statistically significant factors/root causes.
- Identify ways to reduce or close the gap.
- Identify any non-value-added activities.
- Prioritize opportunities to improve the process.
- Confirm the benefits in terms of ROI or a cost/benefit analysis.
- Decide on the people and the resources necessary to improve the process.
- Identify potential problems and obstacles to improving the process.
- Conduct an Analyze phase-gate review.

The basic deliverables for the Analyze phase include the following:

- Project status form/time line
- Metrics graphs
- List of significant factors/root causes
- Testing hypothesis X's for the solution (root cause)
- Project plan: next steps
- Quantification of the expected results
- Local project review with the direct champion
- Phase-gate review

Improve Phase

The purpose of the Improve phase is to discover variable relationships among the vital few, establish operating tolerances, and validate measurements. You are creating the $Y = f(X)$ relationship. This phase consists of the following basic steps:

- Form the possible design of experiments (DOE) that will establish and create the $Y = f(X)$ equation for the project.
- Generate ways to improve the process and achieve the project goals.
- Test the potential improvements with a DOE.
- Plan and map the future state of the process.
- Make the changes that were validated with the DOE to improve the process.
- Use statistical methods to validate the results.
- Develop an implementation plan, which will include how to transition the solution from the team to make it operational.
- Conduct an Improve phase-gate review.

The basic deliverables for the Improve phase include the following:

- Project status form/time line
- Metrics graphs
- List of significant factors/root causes
- Solution equation (the list of X's and their percentage contribution)
- Project plan: next steps
- Quantification of the expected results
- Local review with the direct champion
- Phase-gate review

Control Phase

The purpose of the Control phase is to determine the ability to control the vital few factors and implement process control systems. This phase consists of the following basic steps:

- Verify the improvement metrics and benefits.
- Establish control over risk, quality, cost, schedule, scope, and changes to the plan.
- Ensure that the business goals of the project were achieved and the quality levels are maintained.
- Monitor the results for sustainability.
- Write progress reports.
- Develop a transition plan to the functional area.

- Institutionalize the improvements by modifying systems, procedures, policies, instructions, and budgets.
- Hand off the improved process to the process owners.
- Conduct a Control phase-gate review. This is where the team starts to get approvals and sign off with the appropriate managers to ensure ownership of the solution.

The basic deliverables for the Control phase include the following:

- Project status form/time line
- Metrics graphs
- Specific control/validation plans (with signatures)
- Verification of improvement results (metrics and savings)
- Significant lessons learned
- Final report with financial audit and signoff by controller
- Phase-gate review (potential replication)

Four-Phase Breakthrough Strategy (MAIC)

Figure 6-5 shows the steps of the Six Sigma process, including the focus tools and concentration on the Xs and the Ys of the process.

Phase	Step	Focus
	The Breakthrough Cookbook:	
	Measure, Analyze, Improve, Control	
Measure	1–Select Product or Process CTQ Characteristic(s); e.g., CTQ y	y
	2–Define Performance Standards For y	y
	3–Validate Measurement System for y	y
	4–Establish Process Capability of Creating y	y
Analyze	5–Define Improvement Objectives For y	y
	6–Identify Variation Sources In y	$x_1, x_2, \ldots x_n$
	7–Screen Potential Causes For Change in y & Identify Vital Few	$x_1, x_2, \ldots x_n$
Improve	8–Discover Variable Relationships Between Vital Few x_i	
	9–Establish Operating Tolerances On Vital Few x_i	Vital Few x_i
	10–Validate Measurement System For x_i	
Control	11–Determine Ability to Control Vital Few x_i	Vital Few x_i
	12–Implement Process Control System on Vital Few x_i	
SUSTAIN	Typically, a 12-step process	

FIGURE 6-5   Breakthrough strategy

THE POWER AND DISCIPLINE OF THE SEQUENCE

The DMAIC method is designed and sequenced to keep the project team on a data trail. It takes you away from a mentality of "I think," "I feel," or "I believe." The Six Sigma approach is very conservative. The members of the project team do not draw conclusions from any data unless they are at least 95 percent confident of the meaning of the data.

Once data credibility has been established, the model will take the team through a rigorous and disciplined sequence of tool selection, leading to conclusions that will narrow the field of causal factors and leading ultimately to a more robust process with less variation. (Less variation = fewer defects = less waste = less cost.)

Don't skip steps! It might be tempting to try to speed up a project by skipping steps in Six Sigma, but it won't yield the information you need to correct and eliminate the problem in question. Let the data do its job and tell the story. Stay in the realm of quantifiable facts and do not deal in assumptions. If no data exist for a potential X that has never been tried before, try it! But with trying that solution, you *must* test the hypothesis of the Y with the X. Many black belts stay inside the comfortable box of "This is what the process is" and don't question why and try other potential solutions. It's a hypothesis and it's OK to try it. It must cause a statistical and practical difference in the Y. You apply statistical measurements and metrics to analyze the issues so that you can prove with data, and not by opinion, why and how you can make lasting changes.

PROBLEMS WITH CHAMPIONS

As we finish discussing preliminary plans and prepare to move into the first phase of the DMAIC model, it seems appropriate to offer some warnings about the role of the champion.

The champion is a very important member of both the executive team and the project team. It's logical, then, that just as champions often merit much credit for project successes, they sometimes deserve blame for project failures. Here are some of the reasons cited by Six Sigma experts:

- The champion believes that the black belt should be responsible for the project. Although the black belt is responsible for leading the team in applying the Six Sigma tools and techniques to achieve the project's objectives, the champion must allow the black belt the freedom to do so and provide the necessary resources. In other words, the role of the champion during the project is to ensure that the black belt can focus completely on the project.

- The champion tells the black belt what to do and what not to do. A champion might have a lot of Six Sigma experience and feel certain that he knows the best way to manage a project. However, the black belt is responsible for the project and should have gotten sufficient training to succeed.
- The champion does not monitor the project and conduct project reviews. A champion is responsible for monitoring and reviewing the project. This means checking with the black belt regularly throughout each phase, particularly at the Six Sigma reviews conducted at the end of each phase. It might be wise for the executive team to draw up a list of questions that every champion should use to guide every project review.
- The champion believes that she should be able to use all the Six Sigma tools. This is the role of the black belt. Of course, the champion should be familiar with the concepts, tools, and techniques, in order to understand what the black belt and the others on the project team are doing and to provide appropriate support. However, the black belt is responsible for using the tools.

The champion plays a key role in a Six Sigma project. He must play this role and only this role, just as the black belts and the green belts and the other team members must know and play their roles. Otherwise, it's not really teamwork and a methodology, but chaos.

SUMMARY

After a list of potential projects has been devised, the executive team hands off ownership of the portfolio or backlog of potential projects to the functional champions. The functional champions are responsible for selecting the best projects to pursue.

The champions might use a project selection matrix. They should also be pragmatic and ask this key question: Does the organization have the money and the time and the black belts and green belts for this project? In addition, they should definitely examine the entitlement of each process.

The standard model for the Six Sigma methodology is DMAIC (Define-Measure-Analyze-Improve-Control). Sometimes, however, there is no distinct Define phase and the model is simply MAIC.

The DMAIC method is designed and sequenced to keep the project team on a data trail, away from a mentality of "I think," "I feel," or "I believe." The model will take the team through a rigorous and disciplined sequence of tool selection, leading to conclusions that will narrow the field of causal factors and leading ultimately to a more robust process with less variation.

The champion is a very important member of both the executive team and the project team. It is logical, then, that just as champions often merit much credit for project successes, they sometimes deserve blame for project failures. There are four main problems with champions: The champion believes that the black belt should be responsible for the project, the champion tells the black belt what to do and what not to do, the champion does not monitor the project and conduct project reviews, and the champion believes that she should be able to use all the Six Sigma tools.

REVIEW QUESTIONS

1. A Six Sigma project review is also known as
   a. A Six Sigma report-out
   b. A Six Sigma phase-gate review
   c. Both a and b
   d. Neither a nor b

2. What is critical about the Define phase?
   a. To define solutions for the target problem
   b. To figure out the meaning of terms used in Six Sigma
   c. To deliver a report to the executive committee explaining the primary Six Sigma tools
   d. To determine the objectives and the scope of the project and specify the deliverables to customers
   e. None of the above

3. What is critical about the Measure phase?
   a. To measure every characteristic of the product, service, or process
   b. To identify CTQs and validate the measurement system
   c. To deliver a report to the executive committee explaining the measurements to be used
   d. To measure the gains achieved through the improvements made
   e. None of the above

4. What is critical about the Analyze phase?
   a. To analyze the effects of the improvements implemented in the target process
   b. To better understand the demographics of the external customers
   c. To deliver a report to the executive committee explaining the analytical process

d. To identify the vital few factors and arrive at the root cause(s) of the defects

e. None of the above

5. What is critical about the Improve phase?

a. To validate the measurement system

b. To determine the cost of the defects

c. To set up the baseline

d. To identify the vital few factors

e. None of the above

6. What is critical about the Control phase?

a. To establish ways to control the project team members

b. To organize the DMAIC phases

c. To identify the vital few factors

d. To determine ways to control the vital few factors

e. None of the above

7

DEFINE PHASE

PURPOSES OF THE DEFINE PHASE

The purpose of the Define phase is to determine the purpose, objectives, and scope of the project, to collect information on the customers and the process involved, and to specify the project deliverables to customers (internal and external).

The Define phase starts a project out toward success by addressing the following questions:

- What is the problem that we need to focus on?
- Who are the customers affected by the problem?
- What are the factors that are critical to the customers and the processes involved?
- What are the processes involved in the problem?
- What are the factors that are critical to the process(es)?
- What is our goal?
- What is our time line for achieving our goal?

DEFINE PHASE ACTIVITIES

The Define phase consists of the following steps. This outline is generic; the first few steps depend on how an executive team chooses to start a project, and the remaining steps of this phase depend on how the champion and the black belt decide to modify the model as appropriate to the specific project.

Select the Champion and Identify the Process Owner

The first step is to identify the champion and the process owner in the specific areas affected by the project.

The champion is generally the senior manager who is closest to the process. The roles of the champion have been presented in Chapter 2 and subsequent chapters. The champion initiates and sponsors a project, ensures that the project team members understand and commit to the project, and is directly accountable for the results of that project.

The process owner is the person responsible for the performance of the process and for sustaining the gains achieved through Six Sigma and identifying future opportunities for improving the process. The champion and the process owner might be the same person.

Initiate the Project Charter

The project charter is not a one-shot document. It is dynamic: It starts when the project starts, develops during the Define phase, and then continues to evolve throughout the project.

The project charter officially establishes the project and the project team; it sets a direction and objectives.

The project charter actually starts unofficially before the Define phase, when the executive team defines the project and roughs out a business case for it, giving reasons why the project is an important investment of time and other resources.

Then, when the project is selected and the champion is appointed, he usually drafts the charter, at least listing the members of the team and their roles and responsibilities, setting the objectives for the project, and creating the project rationale or justification.

When a black belt is chosen to lead the team, she reviews and clarifies the project rationale with the champion. The project charter should also include a statement of the project objectives and link them to the objectives of the organization.

Figure 7-1 shows an example of a project charter. At this point, the charter will contain very little information. Throughout the Define phase, the team members will add information to the charter and modify it.

Most of the items in a project charter are easy to understand. We'll discuss a few of the more substantive items a little later in this chapter.

However, one point should be made here about the project title. It's important to give the project a title that describes it accurately and will allow others to understand at a glance the focus and purpose of your project. That might not seem important when the project starts or throughout the life of the project. But after it ends, others might want to know about it, to use the project reports as a guide or as a source of lessons learned. The

Project Team Charter	
Black Belt Name:	Champion Name:
Project Start Date:	Project Location:
Projected Complete Date:	
Business Case:	
Problem Statement:	
Project Objective:	
Team Members:	
Stakeholders:	
Subject Matter Experts:	
Constraints/Assumptions:	
Scope Start Point:	
Scope Ending Point:	
Preliminary Plan: (attach to this form)	
Black Belt Signoff:	
Champion Signoff:	

FIGURE 7-1   Team charter, sample format

name should make it easy for them to know what they are likely to find in the project reports.

Also, when listing the subject matter experts, it might be useful to indicate in parentheses after each name the area of expertise, especially if the team is cross-functional and the members don't know each other or if there are subject matter experts who are not members of the project team.

The project charter is the official documentation of the project and the project team; it gives the champion and the project team authority to use organizational resources for the project and forms the basis of communication with stakeholders. It should provide all of the information necessary for anyone in the organization to understand the basic facts of the project—what, who, when, how, and (especially) why.

In some organizations, it might be useful to also create a team charter. Although this term is sometimes used synonymously with project charter, a team charter is also a document that authorizes each member of a project team to work on that team. It should detail when the team will meet and how much time the members will need to be released from their jobs. The managers of the departments from which the members are selected then sign off on the team charter, acknowledging and approving the partial loan of their employees.

Form the Project Team

The formation of the team begins with the black belt who will lead the team. (As mentioned earlier, the team leader might be a green belt.) This person must have sufficient training in Six Sigma, of course, but also facilitation skills and leadership skills. This is crucial because Six Sigma teams must have leadership from two people: The champion is the *strategic leader* and the black belt (or green belt) must be the *tactical team leader*. Because of the importance of the responsibilities of this position, a black belt is required to be on a project full time. The team leader might be chosen by the champion and/or the executive team.

Then, the team leader selects or helps the champion select the other members of the project team. It is generally best if the team is formed jointly by the black belt and the champion in consultation with the line managers of the prospective members. This is especially important if the organization is new to Six Sigma or if the line managers are territorial and/or unsure about Six Sigma. The project will take the team members away from their regular jobs, so it's wise to ensure that their managers feel a sense of ownership in the project.

The team that works with the black belt should be small—four, five, or six members. There could be more if necessary, but the larger the team the more difficult it becomes to schedule meetings and to manage the efforts and actions required to complete the project.

The team should include green belts, if any are available (green belts should be able to devote at least 25 percent of their time to a project), and employees who know the process and have experience with it. The team should be cross-functional, which means that all needed aspects must be covered to effect possible changes resulting from the solution and that the team must include a representative from finance, someone to serve as a financial champion or specialist in conjunction with the operational champion. It might be appropriate to include people from other functional groups that are needed to support the project, such as information technology, human resources, purchasing, or research and development.

The people chosen for a project team must be familiar with Six Sigma and be able to commit some time to the project. A black belt will spend time educating the team members to ensure awareness. Remember: You must have the executive state the importance of the Six Sigma initiative, so that all members of the team connect to the sense of urgency. In addition, and perhaps most important, the champion and the black belt should consider the dynamics of the mix of personalities as carefully as they consider the mix of knowledge and skills that each potential member would bring to the team.

This is another lesson that the business world can learn from the world of sports: As many coaches have come to realize, bringing together the top players doesn't necessarily form a Dream Team. This does not mean that all the team members have to agree and get along. The goal of this team is to fulfill the mission to get a business result: "The boss of the team is the project goals." Getting a result is a requirement; getting along is an added benefit, but not a requirement. Action item follow-ups to complete tasks on time are the measurement of progress toward the required goal of project results. Pick the people based on talents and skills needed for the success of the project. Leverage the champion to work on personality conflicts that are causing barriers.

As mentioned in Chapter 2, in the beginning of the Six Sigma initiative, the master black belt will be provided by the implementation partner (the Six Sigma consultant working with the organization), but after black belts have been promoted within the organization, they will be the master black belts guiding the black belts.

The next step is to identify the key stakeholders. Stakeholders are people with a vested interest in the success of the project, whose support or at least cooperation is necessary for the team to succeed. This is an important activity in any organization, but it's crucial in some.

Stakeholder buy-in will make the difference in time to complete the project. In some cases, the biggest barrier to project success has been stakeholders. Why? They have been forced to engage in the process and are not willing to change. Most of these stakeholders slow the process down with reactions of "That can't be done" or simply "No." These types of stakeholders have a short life—and they can't avoid the reality that the black belt team will finally uncover. Unfortunately, this type of stakeholder delays the project. The team *must* collect data and analyze it and act on it and stay on course. The truth and the facts will finally win. It's a great lesson for the black belt—but it takes time.

Here's an example. I was working with a black belt who found that a 20-year-old welding practice was not ever needed to make a good weld, but the practice was installed 20 year ago by a person who was now the executive stakeholder and who was against taking it out—even after the black belt presented data that clearly showed non-value-added cost in excess of $300,000. I remember it like it was yesterday: The comparison graph was so obvious at the large Six Sigma review. The stakeholder argued without presenting any data—and in the end the business wanted the $300,000, not the ego fulfillment of this stakeholder. Money talks and you know the BS walks.

Next we need to build a system chart to show levels of involvement in decisions. A typical model is called RACI (pronounced ray-see), which stands for the following four levels of involvement:

- **Responsibility**—people who are expected to actively participate and contribute as much as possible
- *Accountability*—person who is ultimately responsible for the results
- *Consultation*—people who are to be consulted, either because they have some expertise relevant to specific decisions or because they exercise some authority (such as finance, which often serves in a consulting role)
- *Inform*—people whom the decision will affect and who therefore need to be notified after the decision is made

Involvement is the start of ownership and a system like a RACI chart (such as shown in Figure 7-2) helps unite the team and stakeholders into a common focus for results. This method will help balance the efforts between black belts and teams. As a rule, black belts should be facilitating a problem-solving method, using data to drive decision makers. They're trained as experts in Six Sigma problem-solving and they have an ongoing responsibility to help drive the team to solutions to the problem.

A RACI chart does not leave the assignment of responsibilities to chance. Organizations can avoid innumerable conflicts by taking the time to make deliberate choices about who will be involved in what activities and in what ways. A RACI chart helps cut across the politics and culture of your organization by creating a contract of responsibilities. It helps provide actionable information within the political and cultural context of your organization. The purpose is to identify the people affected by the project and decide how best to work with each of them.

Task	Activities							
	Identify Project	Select Project	Project Execution	Project Results	Team Support	Manage Change	Install Solution	Sustain Gain
Executive Team	R	I	I	I	I		I	
Champion	A	A	I	R	R	A	R	R
P&L Mgmt	I	R	I	I	I			A
Process Owner	C	R	R	A	R	A	R	A
Black Belt	C	A	A	A	R	A	R	R
Team Members		I	A	R		R	R	R
Controller		I	I	R		R		

FIGURE 7-2   Sample RACI chart

The last activity of this step of the Define phase is for the black belt to hold a team kickoff meeting. The meeting provides an official start to the project, as the first activity for the chosen individuals as a team.

It is mandatory to ensure that a high-level executive stakeholder attends the kick-off meeting and opens by affirming the importance of the project. That executive initiates the kick-off, states his or her commitment, and then leaves the team empowered to kick off the project.

These planning stages can be considered as the steps necessary to laying the foundation for Six Sigma. Each Six Sigma deployment follows essentially the same success model for implementation. The specifics of your particular situation, the projects you select, and the champions and black belts will determine how you create a plan and a schedule for all activities.

In case you're wondering how all of this gets done, remember that your outside consultant is there to direct, train, and execute the critical elements of the planning process. Your implementation partner can help you orchestrate all responsibilities, roles, and schedules to make a smooth transition from planning to implementation.

Let me elaborate on why you should select an outside consultant to help you start with Six Sigma and how to make the most appropriate choice. First, you need to work with someone who preaches *and* practices Six Sigma. When you're talking about implementing a strategy that's going to change not only your outcomes, but also your processes and the deployment of your people, you'd better get it right the first time. You need to choose an outside partner with a demonstrated record of being a real "money miner" for client companies. After all, you want your investment to pay off as fast and as effectively as possible. Your consultant should help you lay the groundwork and set up the required infrastructure so you can move toward self-sufficiency quickly. The consultant should be focused on knowledge transfer, on showing you how to solve problems through the most effective methods and fix process defects with the right tools, so you can transfer that knowledge throughout your organization.

A quick way to distinguish among outside consultants is to look at how they structure their own employee reward systems. We all need to make money, of course. But here's a big difference. Some consultants are rewarded for *time*, on the basis of their billable hours. Others are rewarded for *results*, on the basis of the speed and size of the client's return on investment. Both groups of consultants are committed to your success in theory, but only the latter consultants are in the same boat as you, rowing toward the same objective—financial results.

The typical agenda for a kick-off meeting includes such topics as these:

- Executive kick-off statement, ensuring that the team members know that they are empowered
- Purpose of the project
- The possible barriers to address

- Team members introductions
- Team issues on the projects (team exercise)
- Project expectations and objectives
- The definition of the defect for the project
- Why us?
- Awareness of Six Sigma
- Roles and responsibilities
- Ground rules for the team
- What do we start with?
- Review initial finding and myths
- Venting for the team
- Customer critical issues
- The importance of timely action items
- Define next steps and the date and time for the next meeting

The champion, the black belt, and the master black belt should begin the meeting by introducing themselves and summing up their roles and responsibilities in the Six Sigma project. The black belt should then introduce the members of the project team to the project, by presenting the elements that form the beginning of the project charter.

The members of the team should then introduce themselves. The champion, the black belt, and the master black belt should welcome each member and ask questions to encourage him or her to talk a little about the knowledge, skills, and experiences he is contributing to the team. They should also encourage the others to feel free to get involved. The introductions should be informal and open into discussion, rather than the stock recitation of the basics that is common at initial project meetings ("Hello, my name is Tabitha Jenkins, I'm a designer in the Widget Department, and I'm looking forward to being on this project team"), followed almost always by a few awkward seconds of silence.

This interchange among the team members starts building a spirit of collaboration that will be a vital part of their teamwork throughout the project. The members should start getting to know each other and feel comfortable working together. Because a key to success with Six Sigma is that the team members question and challenge the current performance of processes, a spirit of critical inquiry that is not alive and well in many organizations, members of a project team should feel safe to work together in that spirit.

Project teams, whether traditional or Six Sigma, can encounter problems in their meetings from the beginning. One way to make meetings more effective is to develop some ground rules in the initial meeting, to codify expectations about behavior, especially interactions among the members.

By involving all members of the project team in the first meeting, the black belt sets the tone for all meetings. By showing what is expected—that the meeting starts on time, that it follows the agenda, that the members participate actively and that they work together in a spirit of cooperation and respect, and so forth—she is truly acting as the team leader.

One matter that could be discussed at the kick-off meeting is scope. Even though the team is not ready to scope the project at this point, before gathering data from the customers, the black belt can discuss the procedures for proposing any modifications in the definition of the project, including scope, and getting approval for them. He can then prepare a formal change control document that outlines the procedures for making any modifications.

Also during the kick-off meeting, the team might start working on the next steps of the Define phase—identifying the customers and collecting customer data. This approach not only pools the members' areas of knowledge and their thinking abilities, but also promotes ownership from the start and gets the individuals working together as a team.

In addition, at this point, as the champion and the black belt begin working together and with the master black belt and the other members of the project team, decisions should be made about communications within the team. (Toward the end of the Define phase the black belt will develop a comprehensive communications plan for the executive team, stakeholders, and others in the organization who are not members of the project team.)

Communications should be appropriate for the needs of the team members and the complexity of the project and the team structure and dynamics. The black belt and the master black belt should communicate regularly with the champion and the other members of the team. In particular, they should always keep the champion apprised of any problems. The expectations and procedures should be established from the start of the project:

- The means of communicating—team meetings, champion-black belt meetings, phone conferences, e-mail, or memos
- The format for status reports
- The content to be included in status reports
- The frequency of status reports
- The length of status reports—in pages for written reports, in time for meetings and phone calls

These guidelines are for regular reporting; if there is any emergency, whoever becomes aware of it should notify the other members of the project team immediately.

Identify the Customers

Who are the customers? That question is the vital first step in any Six Sigma project. The team must begin the project by identifying all customers of the project, external and internal.

A customer is any person or organization that receives a product or service from a process. A customer is external if not a part of the organization supplying the product or service and internal if a part of the organization. In many companies the team would also distinguish between partners (e.g., distributors and retailers) and end users or consumers.

This task might be relatively simple. On the other hand, sometimes it's more complicated. It might be necessary to consult with customer service representatives, marketers, and others in the organization. The team should group the customers into categories according to their relationship to the company and the product, service, or process that is the focus of the Six Sigma project.

Collect Customer Data

Once the team has identified all of the customers of the project process(es), it must find out about the customers' needs and expectations. The team should determine what it needs to know in order to identify the critical requirements of the customers. In Six Sigma, this is called gathering the voice of the customer (VOC).

There are two basic ways to gather the VOC, reactively and actively. The team can analyze existing data, such as complaints, which is reactive data, or benchmarking data. It can then fill the gaps in its knowledge of the customers' needs and expectations with active data, using such means as the following to get the type of data indicated in parentheses:

- Customer complaints—qualitative (subjective)
- Telephone survey—quantifiable (objective)
- Mail survey—quantifiable (objective)
- Focus group, in person—qualitative (subjective)
- Focus group, online—qualitative (subjective)
- Interviews, one-on-one—qualitative (subjective)
- Intercepts (interviews on the street or in malls)—both qualitative (subjective) and quantifiable (objective)

There are a few basic guidelines for using surveys or any other sampling methods. In order to gain accurate results, the research should ensure the following:

- Survey a sampling that is representative of the entire population of customers.
- Select participants at random.
- Make the survey objective and focused in order to yield results that can be translated into quantitative requirements.

The master black belt should help the black belt develop a survey that will be most appropriate for the project and the customers. This is the base on which the team will build its improvement efforts, so it's well worth the investment of time and effort up front to construct a good survey and use it properly.

Six Sigma requires that you truly understand customer viewpoints. You must really know what customers want, not go by what you think they want. You must ask what's important to them. What are their CTQ criteria?

Define the Customer CTQ Requirements

As mentioned briefly in Chapter 1, any characteristic of a product, a service, or a process that a customer considers critical to quality is labeled a CTQ. A CTQ usually must be converted from a qualitative opinion into a quantitative specification that a project team can use to take action. So, the next step in the Define phase is for the team to take the customer data (VOC) and translate it from "customer language" into CTQs—customer requirements. It needs to identify the more important CTQs and then determine which areas of the project would have the greatest impact on those CTQs.

This activity, VOC analysis, can involve one or more of several tools.

One way to identify measures that translate CTQs is the CTQ tree. This diagram is a tree chart (Figure 7-3). The team starts with a CTQ, which it puts in a box. The team then breaks the CTQ down into components, which go into the next generation of boxes. It then breaks down each of those components into a subsequent generation of components. This procedure continues until the team arrives at things that can be measured.

| Timely processing of orders (CTQ) | Average orders received per hour | Orders received by phone
Orders received online
Orders received in person
Orders received by mail
Orders received by fax |
| | Average time to process an order | Time to enter order
Time to check inventory
Time to process payment/invoice
Time to arrange shipment |

The team can also use a cause-and-effect diagram to help identify the causes (X's) that lead to the results (Y's) that satisfy or dissatisfy. To use the cause-and-effect diagram to represent the transfer function, $Y = f(X)$, the head of the fish is the effect (Y) and the bones are the possible causes (X's).

To prioritize CTQs, the team can use a CTQ matrix. This is a YX diagram or cause-and-effect matrix that can be used to link customer CTQs to

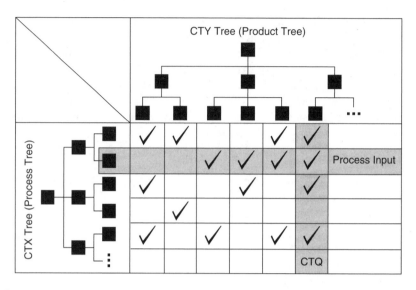

FIGURE 7-3   Critical to Quality tree

process inputs and to identify an area of focus for a failure modes and effects analysis (FMEA) or the initial factors for a designed experiment (DOE). The matrix is a grid of rows and columns, with output variables (Y's) along one axis and input variables (X's) along the other axis, with each output variable assigned a weight for its relative importance to the customers. Each X is compared with each Y and rated with a number. The number for each X is then multiplied by the weighting for each Y to produce a series of scores and percentages.

This is a good way to identify the areas that the team needs to improve in order to better satisfy the most CTQs or the most important CTQs.

If the CTQs are very subjective and fuzzy, the team can do a CTQ flowdown. This is a diagramming technique for identifying the transfer functions (dependencies) between Y's and X's. A CTQ flowdown can be done using the House of Quality, a matrix for mapping the voice of the customer into the voice of the engineer. (It can also be done using quality function deployment—QFD—but this tool seems more complicated than necessary for a CTQ flowdown in DMAIC.)

The House of Quality is the first matrix in QFD, which consists of four phases that link four matrices. The purpose is to allow the team to assess the importance of relationships between CTQs (Y's) and features of the process (X's). The House of Quality shows the strength of the $Y = f(X)$

Y's	Customer Priority Rank #	Taste	Aroma	Price	Acidity				Rank	% Rank
		10	10	10	2					
X's						Association Table				
Key Process Input Variable										
Coffee Type		10	10	10	10				320	24.43%
Amt. of Coffee		9	7	10	10				280	21.37%
Grind Time		9	6	2	3				176	13.44%
Water Temp.		9	3	2	2				144	10.99%
Cup Type		2	4	4	2				104	7.94%
Cup Size		2	4	5	1				112	8.55%
Brew Time		9	6	2	2				174	13.28%

FIGURE 7-4 Example of a *YX* diagram for making coffee

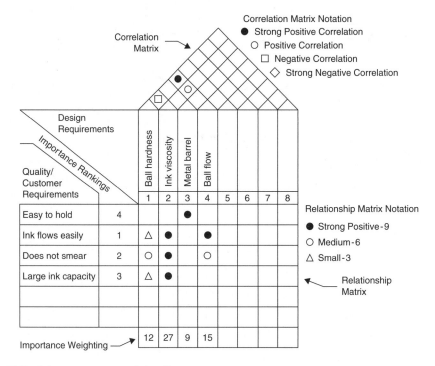

FIGURE 7-5   House of Quality

transfer function relationship between every CTQ and every process requirement and the interrelationship among the process requirements.

The House is a matrix with a triangular matrix on top, like a rectangular house with a peaked roof. The main matrix works much like the project selection matrix in Chapter 6. The matrix on top is for correlation, so the team can evaluate how the specifications defined in the main matrix work together or in conflict. That might seem confusing, but Figure 7-5 and step-by-step instructions will show how it works. (It can be more complicated than shown in this example, but this degree of complexity is sufficient for translating CTQs into project requirements.)

Down the left side of the main matrix, the team lists what the customers need or want—the whats, AKA the Y's. Next to each is a ranking of the importance of that item to the customers (e.g., 1 to 5). Across the top of the main matrix, the team lists the project requirements—the hows, AKA the X's. In the cells the team indicates the strength of the relationship between the connected need/want and requirement with a rating (e.g., 1 to 10).

After each Y-X possibility has been rated, the team multiplies the ranking of each need or want by the rating of each requirement. The products of all the cells in each column are summed at the bottom, to give a score for technical importance to each requirement (How important is that requirement in terms of all of the CTQs?). The products of all the cells in each row are summed at the right, to give a score for completeness to each need/want (How completely can that CTQ be satisfied by all of the requirements?).

Next, at the top of each column heading, the team puts an indication of how that feature should be changed to improve the process in terms of the CTQs: An arrow up means "more is better," an arrow down means "less is better," and a circle means a specific amount or level is best (neither more nor less). At the bottom of each column, above the scores for technical importance, the team puts the target value for that requirement.

Finally, the team uses the roof of the House of Quality—the correlation matrix. In each cell the team puts an indication of the impact of the two requirements that intersect in that cell: an O for a positive, a bold O for a strong positive, an X for a negative, and a bold X for a strong negative.

By using the House of Quality, the team knows the strength of the $Y = f(X)$ transfer function relationship between every CTQ and every project requirement, so it knows which project requirements (Xs) are the most important to the CTQs (Ys) and how the requirements are interrelated.

Another way for a team to translate customer CTQs into requirements is failure modes and effects analysis (FMEA), which is a disciplined methodology for identifying and examining the ways in which a process can fail, assessing the effects of each mode of failure, and planning to prevent the failures. FMEA is more commonly used in the Measure, Analyze, and Improve phases of Six Sigma, so it's presented in Chapter 8. However, it can be used in the Define phase to determine which CTQs have the greatest effect on the output of a process and which are the hardest to detect, so the team can target the most important.

Determine the Scope of the Project

Project scope refers to the boundaries within which the Six Sigma team works. The black belt and the champion, with the help of the master black belt, decide on what the team should be doing and what it should not be doing. In a way, "project scope" is synonymous with "project definition."

Scoping ensures that the team will be focusing on the biggest problem, the best opportunity for improvement. When scoping a project, those involved should understand where they could gain the greatest financial benefits.

One way to do this is by using a Pareto chart. As explained in Chapter 5, a Pareto chart is a bar chart that is used to display the relative importance of items—in this case, problem areas and the impact of each—and track the cumulative effect of the items. The team can use the chart to identify the areas where the project could achieve the greatest impact. It then must decide how much it can handle within its project. It might not be able to attack all of the most important areas, but it could hit four of the seven greatest problems, for example, which could amount to 70 percent of the cost of the problem. It's better to scope properly and achieve 70 percent of the benefits than to scope too widely or too vaguely in order to chase after 100 percent of the benefits and then fail.

It must set the boundaries and the start and stop points for the project. This is an important part of the charter because it sets limits by specifying what will be included and what will be excluded. The team should seek a balance between being ambitious and being realistic: It's great to want to take make the biggest gains possible but it's necessary to finish the project within six months or so.

Determining the scope from the start helps the team avoid "scope creep"—the all too natural phenomenon when a team feels drawn to attempt a little more, to change direction slightly, or to avoid a situation that turns out to be more problematic than expected. Scope creep can undermine a project and even cause it to fail.

"The secret of success is constancy of purpose."

—BENJAMIN DISRAELI (1804–1881)

If the scope of a project seems too large, the team should recommend a plan for splitting it into two or more smaller projects, of realistic scope, to be worked simultaneously or in succession. It might be possible, for example, to break a large project into a black belt project and one or more smaller projects to be led by green belts.

Scoping also allows the black belt and the champion to identify the resources and the skills that the project will require and to sketch out a time frame for completing the project.

Here are some suggestions for scoping Six Sigma projects:

- Know about what other projects or activities might affect the project area and specifically the project being scoped.
- Clarify project expectations. If there is more than one expectation, make sure that they are in alignment, so that the expectations do not pull the team in more than one direction.
- Focus on finances. The chances of a project succeeding are better if the financial benefits are carefully quantified from the start.
- Differentiate between soft (subjective) and hard (objective) metrics.
- Keep the project from crossing boundaries: If a project has two or more owners, it can create conflicts and problems later.
- Keep time in mind: Even if a project can be easily delimited in terms of start and stop points, if it cannot be delimited sufficiently to fit into the four- to six-month time frame, the scope might not be

right. It might be necessary to break the project down into smaller projects.

■ Create a scope statement that expresses the project scope precisely and concisely—an "elevator speech." The more easily project team members can grasp the scope, the easier it will be for them to focus on the project and to communicate about it with each other and with people outside the project.

Define and Map the Core Business Process—the Project Focus

Next, the black belt should define and map the core business process on which the project will focus. This is a natural and logical extension of scoping the project. This is an activity that might involve the champion and that can and often should involve the other members of the project team.

They create a high-level map that documents the current state of the process. This is a simple flow chart that names and defines the process. They set start and stop points for the process and sketch the basic (high-level) steps (usually four to seven) in sequence. It can be useful to label each step in process as critical, major, or minor in terms of the output of the process.

The fundamental building block for the process map is the step (Figure 7-6).

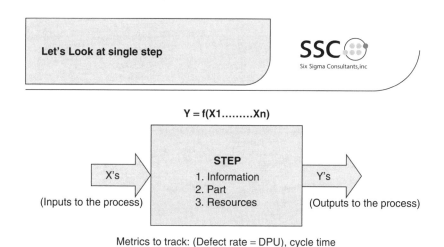

FIGURE 7-6   Process mapping: step

They also indicate the supplier(s), the inputs and the outputs of the process and of every step, and the customer(s). For this reason, this process map is generally called *a SIPOC diagram* (suppliers, inputs, process, outputs, and customers) and the activity is a SIPOC analysis. Figure 7-7 shows an example.

SIPOC diagrams are simple, although not necessarily easy. It's generally a good idea to use a blackboard or flipchart pages or sticky notes rather than to start with a sheet of paper.

In putting the customers and the outputs on the map, the team might also want to identify the preliminary requirements of the customers for those outputs. This addition will help transition into a key activity later in the Define phase.

When the team has finished mapping the process, they should discuss it with stakeholders in order to make sure that it is complete, that they understand the process.

A process map can help the team determine initial measurement goals. Then it can examine the subprocesses within the SIPOC diagram in order to better understand the process flow. It can determine which subprocess steps to map by evaluating which of the major steps in the SIPOC have the biggest impact on the output. The team might decide that the initial focus area should become several Six Sigma projects.

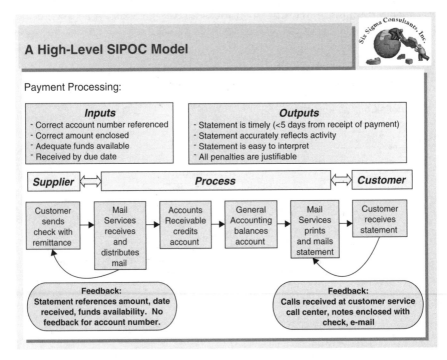

FIGURE 7-7   SIPOC diagram: example for processing payments

A process map should also reveal the true cost of goods or services sold. Study every aspect of your processes to understand where money is going. By separating value-added activities from non-value-added activities, you can isolate the hidden waste streams.

Establish the Project Metrics

After the team has translated the VOC data from "customer language" into CTQs—customer requirements—it must choose the measures by which it will be assessing its progress toward meeting those requirements, throughout the project and, ultimately, at the end of the project. It should be relatively easy to derive the metrics from the CTQs. The project metrics (distinct from process metrics, which will be determined in the Measure phase) are basically specifications for the CTQs.

The selection of project metrics is one of the crucial elements of the project charter. Project metrics should reflect the VOC, of course, but they should also reflect the voice of the business—the stated mission, goals, and objectives and unstated needs or requirements of the organization. This is how the project is aligned with business strategies and objectives. When selecting metrics, the project team should consider how the metrics relate to key business metrics.

The members should specify all the metrics that they think might be relevant, but the metrics must be within the scope of the project. Metrics are generally according to any of three basic dimensions—quality, time (cycle time or delivery), and money (cost or price). In Six Sigma terminology, these are critical to quality (CTQ), critical to delivery (CTD), and critical to price (CTP).

The metrics should be simple, straightforward, and meaningful—they must help understand how the process is performing. Also, the metrics should be commonly understood by all members of the project team, whatever their functional areas. Good examples would be cost of poor quality (COPQ) and rolled throughput yield (RTY).

The team should review its metrics with the executive team to ensure that they align with the strategies and objectives of the organization.

Identify the Important Problems in the Process

The team has defined the customer CTQ requirements, determined the scope of the project, mapped the core business process, and established metrics for the project. Now it must figure out why the process is failing to meet the customer requirements.

Problems are often identified very qualitatively at first. The team should work to define each problem more specifically, with quantitative data, when possible. The more specific the definition, the better.

Develop the Problem Statement(s) and the Business Case

After identifying the problem(s), the team develops a statement for each problem (or opportunity for improvement) in the process. Creating a good problem statement, also known as a project statement, can take a lot of thought and work. It must be specific in defining the problem and it must quantify it; otherwise, it's difficult to set meaningful goals, establish good metrics, focus the efforts, measure progress, and show the results of the project in terms that matter. The experience of Six Sigma practitioners suggests that about 80 percent of the projects that fail are doomed from the beginning because they are not defined properly.

The problem statement should define the problem area objectively, specifically, and concisely. It should include the basic facts, such as the circumstances in which the problem occurs and the extent of the impact of the problem. It should focus on observable symptoms and not suggest any possible causes or, certainly, imply any blame.

Developing a good problem statement is critical to communicating and directing your project mission.

Here's an example of a good problem statement: "Product returns are 5 percent of sales, resulting in a profit impact of $5 million and customer dissatisfaction rates in excess of 50 percent." The statement is specific: It presents defined numbers illustrating the problem, and indicates the core cost and customer satisfaction issues.

In contrast, a poor problem statement would be "Our product return levels are too high due to product A and will be reduced by analyzing first- and second-level Pareto charts." This problem statement is poor for two reasons. First, there are no numbers, so there's no quantifying the scope or scale of the problem. Second, it states only what you're going to do, instead of precisely and accurately addressing the problem.

The problem statement should also provide a baseline, set improvement goals, indicate the approach for resolving the problem, sketch a time frame for the project, and give an estimate of the benefits and financial savings for the organization—the opportunity in resolving the problem.

This is also known as making the business case for the project, developing the case made by the executive team when it generated and evaluated project ideas. The purpose of developing the business case is to identify and quantify all of the potential benefits of committing time and other resources to the project and modifying the problematic processes. The business case should be compelling to the executive managers. Otherwise, the project might be dropped before it gets through the Define phase.

The business case communicates the need for the project in terms of meeting business objectives. It consists of the following:

- Output unit (product/service) for external customer
- Primary business measure of output unit for project

- Baseline performance of primary business measure
- Gap in baseline performance of primary business measure from business objective

Know your business case type:

- No. 1 projects directly impact the income statement or cash flow statement.
- No. 2 projects impact the balance sheet (working capital).
- No. 3 projects avoid expense (or investment) due to known or expected events in the future.
- No. 4 projects are risk management/insurance projects that prevent unpredictable events or reduce their severity. Creating the ability to capitalize on market opportunities might also fall into this category.

You might have a combination of types.

A baseline is simply a measurement of the current status of the process using one or more key metrics. The most basic would be to calculate how much it costs for the process to produce a certain product or provide a certain service. Another basic measurement would be the sigma. Other standard baselines might be calculations of cycle time and rolled throughput yield. The baseline can be simple at this point; the team will calculate more specific baselines during the Measure phase.

The improvement goals should address those metrics, estimating improvement in terms of percentages and dollars saved. The team should calculate the performance gap, the difference between the baseline and the entitlement (defined as the best performance that can be reasonably expected from the process). A goal is the portion of that gap that the project team is trying to capture.

What results does the team anticipate from this project? To reduce defects by at least 85 percent? To reduce cycle time by 45 percent? To identify variable costs and limit them to $75 per transaction? The team should set goals that are challenging but realistic goals. It should also indicate what it plans to do to achieve those goals and when it expects to achieve them, in a preliminary project plan that the black belt will develop further after the executive team approves the project and allocates the resources.

In order to give an estimate of the benefits and financial savings for the organization, the team should perform a cost-benefit analysis. To do so, the team must ascertain the cost of poor quality. It's as easy or as difficult as quantifying the waste in the process. If it's producing scrap, quantify it. If it's causing rework, quantify it. If employees are spending time in non-value-added activities in the process or because of it, quantify it. After estimating the cost of poor quality, the team should estimate the cost of resources to do the project. Then it can make the business case by calculating return on investment.

The problem statement has two purposes:

- To focus the team on the problem(s) in the process
- To communicate the purpose of the project to the executive team

The problem statement should answer the following questions for the executive team:

- What's the problem?
- What is the status of this process?
- What do we need to do to change the process?
- How long will it take to make the changes?
- How much money will it save?

The problem statement should be objective, specific, and concise, as stated above, but it should also be compelling. The project team should keep in mind that it is answering this pair of related questions:

- Why are we doing this project now?
- What negative consequences will there be if we do not do this project now?

In other words, the problem statement should make a case for the importance and urgency of the project.

The problem statement(s) and the business case should be included with the project charter.

From the problem statement, the black belt can further develop the preliminary project plan. In consultation with the master black belt and the champion, the black belt adds to the preliminary plan the training that she and the other members of the team will need throughout the project.

Focus on the Vital Few Factors

It's rare that a Six Sigma team can or should attack all of the root causes of a problem. It's usually necessary to focus on the most important to measure, analyze, improve, and control. In terms that have descended into Six Sigma use from the work of Vilfredo Pareto, father of the 80/20 principle that holds that 20 percent of the causes are responsible for 80 percent of the effects, the team must distinguish between the "vital few" factors that contribute most to the problems and the "trivial many."

The usual way to identify the "vital few" is through a Pareto analysis. As described in Chapter 5, this is a technique that uses data to assess the relationships between causes and a specific effect and then creates a graphic display of the causes in order of importance and tracks the cumulative effects.

The team begins with its definition of the problem and lists the causes of a specified effect, such as a defect or an error. It's usually best to limit the list to 8 or 10, so it might be necessary to group causes into categories.

The team then uses data to determine the importance of each of the causes or categories of causes in terms of the specified effect. If there is no data available or the data is insufficient, the team will have to gather data on the occurrence of that effect. (Pareto analysis is more reliable if there are at least 50 data points across all categories.)

The team groups the data points for each cause or category of causes. Then it totals the points for each.

The next step is to create a table with four columns, with headings for the problem, the data count, the percentage, and the cumulative percentage, and to insert the calculations (Figure 7-8).

The team then creates a graph, with the horizontal axis to represent the problems, the vertical axis on the left to represent the percentage for each problem, and a vertical axis on the right to represent the cumulative percentage. The team plots a bar for each of the problems on its list, from left to right in descending order of importance, with a narrow space between bars, and labels each bar with the name of the problem.

If there is any data that doesn't fit into the table and the chart, the team should do what comes naturally to most of us—create a "miscellaneous" category for this data and put it in a bar on the far right of the chart.

Finally, the team plots a line above the bars for the cumulative percentage, using the vertical axis on the right. It determines the break point, the point on the cumulative percentage line at which the slope decreases significantly. The causes to the left of the break point are the vital few; the causes to the right are the trivial many. If there's no obvious break point, the causes that account for the first 60 to 80 percent of the problems would be the trivial few. This is a general guideline to help the team decide on which of the causes it should focus in the Measure, Analyze, Improve, and Control phases.

Figure 7-9 shows a completed Pareto chart.

Problem	Count	Percentage	Cumulative Percentage
Late Delivery	54	45%	45%
Wrong Product	30	25%	70%
Incorrect Price	18	15%	85%
Incomplete Order	12	10%	95%
Damage	6	5%	100%
TOTAL	**120**	**100%**	**100%**

FIGURE 7-8 Table with results of Pareto analysis

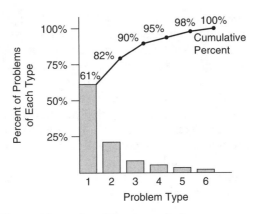

FIGURE 7-9   Chart with results of Pareto analysis

Define the Deliverables for Each Phase

The project team determines what it will be responsible for delivering by
the end of each of the five phases. Here are the basic deliverables for the
phases, as outlined in Chapter 6. The items as listed here are generic; for
each project, they could be made specific. Also, a project team might decide
to add deliverables, as appropriate to its project.

Define

- Project charter
- Project status form/time line
- List of customer CTQs
- Metrics graphs
- Process map with points at which to gather data
- Pareto charts of CTQs and of problems in the process
- List of project deliverables
- High-level process chart (SIPOC)
- Project plan: next steps
- Phase-gate review

Measure

- Project status form/time line
- Metrics graphs
- Detailed process map with points at which to gather data
- Pareto charts of defects and causes
- Measurement tools, including gauge R&R studies
- Data on the process
- Process capability and sigma level

- Project plan: next steps
- Phase-gate review

Analyze

- Project status form/time line
- Metrics graphs
- List of significant factors/root causes
- Solution (root cause)
- Project plan: next steps
- Quantification of the expected results
- Phase-gate review

Improve

- Project status form/time line
- Metrics graphs
- List of significant factors/root causes
- Solution
- Project plan: next steps
- Quantification of the expected results
- Phase-gate review

Control

- Project status form/time line
- Metrics graphs
- Specific control/validation plans
- Verification of improvement results (metrics and savings)
- Significant lessons learned
- Final report
- Phase-gate review

Determine the Resources Necessary

Based on the preliminary project plan, the list of deliverables, and the scope of the project, the black belt—in consultation with the master black belt, the team member from financial, and the champion—can determine the resources needed for the project. These resources would be financial, of course, and organizational and administrative support, including ongoing training for the black belt, any green belts, and the other members of the team, as appropriate and specified in the preliminary project plan.

The black belt should take these figures generated in this step and update the calculations for the earlier cost-benefit analysis and/or ROI for the business case.

Obtain Approval for the Project

At this point, the black belt and the champion should be ready to present the project charter (with the business case), the preliminary project plan, and the request for financial and other support to the executive team for review and approval. The procedure is similar to the procedure for reviewing and approving or denying other types of projects.

If the project is approved and the resources are allocated, then the team continues through the Define phase. If not, the executive team might ask the black belt and the champion to rework the charter, the plan, and/or the request. It's also possible that the executive will decide that the estimated gains of the project make it a questionable investment and end the project at this point and disband the team.

Whether or not the executive team approves the project charter and allocates the requested resources, the implementation partner should meet afterwards with the executive team. The focus of the meeting should be to help the members of the executive team learn from the findings reported by the project team. Knowing about certain difficulties or certain advantages at this point can help the executives adjust their expectations and goals for other Six Sigma projects. The implementation partner can help them understand that they can learn from each project just as the project teams are learning as they work on their projects. The project team will prepare a final report on lessons learned when it completes a project, but it's wise for the executive team to learn lessons as soon as they emerge so they can be applied to other projects, current and future, throughout the organization.

Start Training the Team Members

As soon as possible after the executive team approves the project charter and allocates the resources requested, training should begin. The training is provided as needed and just in time for the steps outlined in the plan. The training focuses on the tools and techniques that will be necessary for the steps planned for that specific project.

In the beginning of the Six Sigma initiative, the training will be provided by the master black belts supplied by the implementation partner. As black belts within the organization earn certification and then move up to become master black belts, they will be able to provide the training.

Form a Project Plan

The black belt, the master black belt, and the champion develop the preliminary project plan into a detailed project plan. This plan structures the project into steps and schedules milestones, deliverables, and goals for the five phases.

The milestones indicate when and where the team should be in the project. At each milestone, the black belt is to report to the champion on the progress of the team and any problems.

For each task, the project plan should specify the person with primary responsibility for each task and indicate the start and finish times and duration for each task. When the steps overlap, it might be useful to create a Gantt chart to represent the sequencing and timing.

The plan should include a checklist of the tools to be used for each task. The black belt and the master black belt should indicate which of the Six Sigma tools are to be used in each of the steps scheduled. They should then review this tool check-off list regularly and update it throughout the project. Before each phase-gate review, they should ensure that the team has used the tools as planned.

The black belt, the master black belt, and the champion should also specify and schedule the training needed by each member of the team. The master black belt can recommend the training that the team members will need for the techniques and tools identified in the plan.

The black belt and the champion should also schedule the five phase-gate reviews, as mentioned in Chapter 6, to provide a checkpoint and closure at the end of each phase.

Finally, the project plan will include a communications plan. It might be most practical for the black belt to create a table to show the following:

- *What* is to be communicated—e.g., minutes of team meetings, project status reports, project time line, project reviews/tollgates, etc.
- *Who* will be communicating it—e.g., black belt, champion, master black belt, a green belt, a team member, etc.
- *To whom* it will be communicated—e.g., team members, champion, master black belt, executive team, subject matter experts, stakeholders, financial department, quality department, etc.
- *When* it will be communicated—e.g., specific dates, frequency (such as "every Friday by 3:00"), timing (such as "within 24 hours of the milestone report"), etc.
- *How* it will be communicated— e.g., memo, e-mail, voice mail, conference call, presentation, etc.
- *Where* the information will be kept for later reference—e.g., file cabinet, intranet, etc.

The table might also indicate *why* it is to be communicated—although it might not be necessary to specify the reasons that are behind the decisions that go into the communications plan.

Conduct the Define Phase-Gate Review

The black belt holds a review at the end of the Define phase. The black belt reports to the executive team on the status of the project. The review provides the members of the executive team an opportunity to ask questions about the project, make comments, discuss any obstacles, allocate resources as necessary, ensure that the project team is achieving the project goals according to schedule, and provide positive reinforcement for the project team. Phase-gate reviews are not technical; it is assumed that the master black belt and the black belt have worked out any technical problems. They are primarily to ensure that the project is proceeding according to the plan, that the team is meeting the deliverables by the milestones, and that the project is on time and on budget.

To prepare for the review the black belt, and the champion should meet to discuss questions such as the following, with or without the other members of the project team:

- Have we completed the project charter?
- Have we described the project clearly and stated it concisely and compellingly?
- How much have we estimated that we can save by improving the process?
- What potential barriers and risks do we face? What have we done to minimize these? What else should be done?
- Does our process map delimit the scope of the project and represent the basic steps in the process?
- What metrics will we use in the project?
- What tools and techniques will we use?
- What training do we need in order to use those tools and techniques?
- Have we developed a project plan that shows how we will produce the specified deliverables by the milestone dates and achieve its goals on schedule?

Also, there are good, basic checklists and worksheets to help a team prepare for the phase-gate review in *The Six Sigma Way Team Fieldbook*, by Peter S. Pande, Robert P. Neuman, and Roland R. Cavanagh.

After the phase-gate meeting, the implementation partner should meet with the executive team to review the lessons learned as presented by the project team. He should facilitate a discussion of how the executives can apply what was learned to other projects.

DEFINE DELIVERABLES

The basic deliverables for the Define phase include the following:

- A project team is formed and receiving training according to a schedule for each of the five phases of the DMAIC model
- Project charter
  - Problem statement
  - Goal statement
  - Business case (financial impact and a clear link to business strategy)
  - Project scope
  - Team members and roles
  - Stakeholders—project stakeholder analysis sheet
  - Project plan (at least at a high level)
  - Resources required
- Project status form/time line
- List of customers and their validated CTQs
- Metrics graphs
- Process map with points at which to gather data
- Pareto charts of CTQs and of problems in the process
- List of project deliverables
- High-level process map (SIPOC)
- Project plan: next steps
- Phase-gate review

SUMMARY

The purpose of the Define phase is to determine the purpose, objectives, and scope of the project, to collect information on the customers and the process involved, and to specify the project deliverables to customers (internal and external).

The Define phase consists of the following steps:

- Select the champion and identify the process owner.
- Initiate the project charter.
- Form the project team.
- Identify the customers.
- Collect customer data.
- Define the customer CTQ requirements.
- Determine the scope of the project.
- Define and map the core business process—the project focus.
- Establish the project metrics.
- Identify the important problems in the process.
- Develop the problem statement(s) and the business case.
- Focus on the vital few factors.
- Define the deliverables for each phase.

- Determine the resources necessary.
- Obtain approval for the project.
- Start training the team members.
- Form a project plan.
- Conduct the Define phase-gate review.

REVIEW QUESTIONS

1. A RACI chart shows the following:
   a. Reaction, Action, Control, and Improvement
   b. A breakthrough strategy developed by Hector Raci
   c. Responsibility, Accountability, Consultation, and Inform
   d. Both a and b
   e. Both c and b
   f. None of the above

2. A CTQ is
   a. Usually derived through VOC analysis
   b. Any characteristic of a product, a service, or a process that a customer considers critical to quality
   c. Both a and b
   d. None of the above

3. To prioritize CTQs and link customer CTQs to process inputs, a team can use the following:
   a. A cause-and-effect matrix
   b. A CTQ matrix
   c. Both a and b
   d. None of the above

4. What is a diagramming technique for identifying the transfer functions (dependencies) between Y's and X's?
   a. An YX switch
   b. A VOC
   c. An XY transfer maneuver
   d. A CTQ flowdown

5. What is the House of Quality?
   a The first matrix in QFD
   b. A structure for assessing the importance of relationships between CTQs (Y's) and features of the process (X's)

    c. A means of showing the strength of the $Y = f(X)$ transfer function relationship between every CTQ and every process requirement and the interrelationship among the process requirements

    d. Both a and b

    e. Both b and c

    f. Both a and c

    g. a, b, and c

    h. None of the above

CASE STUDY QUESTION

The business case should lead you to a business process to examine. Let's look at the payment processing example (Figures 7-10 to 7-12.).

    Notice the structure of the problem statement:

- It has defined a specific process-related defect.
- It has quantified an objective.
- It has expressed in business terms the results of achieving that objective.

The Business Case Template

Six Sigma Consultants,inc

Fill in the Blanks for Your Project:

During _____ , the _____ for
    (Period of time for baseline performance)   *(Primary business measure)*

_____ was _____ . This gap of _____
(A key business process) *(Baseline performance)*   *(Business objective target vs. baseline)*

from _____ represents _____ of cost impact.
   (Business objective)   *(Cost impact of gap)*

FIGURE 7-10   Template for the business case

Start with the Business Case

- The Business Case should lead you to a Business Process to examine

- Let's look at the Payment Processing example:

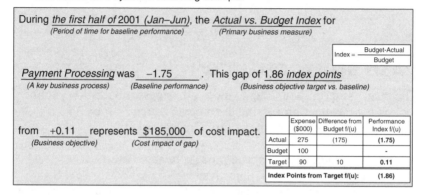

FIGURE 7-11   The business case

The challenge comes as organizations try to estimate the financial impact of projects. Any financial analyst will tell you that a dollar saved has varying degrees of importance depending on how it affects the financial statements. For example, $100,000 in savings achieved from the reduction of an FTE might be viewed differently from $100,000 that is saved from the reduction of inventory or from $100,000 that is saved by eliminating the need to purchase capital to increase capacity. And the savings calculations and prioritizations get *really* tricky when project teams start talking in terms of an estimated savings due to customer satisfaction or reduced employee turnover.

Because there is no magic technique for calculating project savings—Six Sigma projects are no different in this regard from any other strategic project—good old-fashioned project cost-benefit analysis discipline must be applied to at least estimate the anticipated returns for the Six Sigma efforts. Once this foundation of effective financial discipline is applied to projects, the savings can then be categorized based on the impact to the financial statements.

So, let's get back to our case of payment processing.

Issue

The purchase order placement cycle is too long and will not effectively support a high-volume and repetitive manufacturing program. Current PO

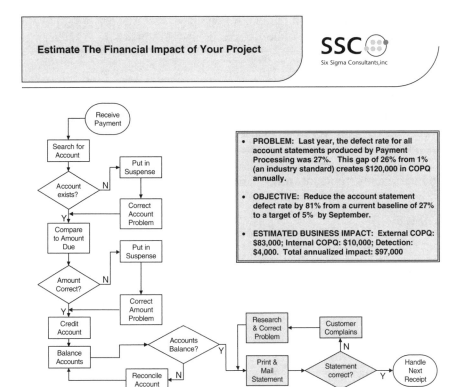

Estimate The Financial Impact of Your Project

SSC
Six Sigma Consultants,inc

- **PROBLEM:** Last year, the defect rate for all account statements produced by Payment Processing was 27%. This gap of 26% from 1% (an industry standard) creates $120,000 in COPQ annually.

- **OBJECTIVE:** Reduce the account statement defect rate by 81% from a current baseline of 27% to a target of 5% by September.

- **ESTIMATED BUSINESS IMPACT: External COPQ: $83,000; Internal COPQ: $10,000; Detection: $4,000. Total annualized impact: $97,000**

FIGURE 7-12   Financial impact

placement cycle times often result in inefficient purchasing, incorrect staffing allocations, and material deliveries insufficient to support planned stock dates.

Here's what happens when we apply the four-phase Breakthrough Strategy (MAIC) mentioned in Chapter 6.

Measure

Because there was no effective data-collection system, the first step was to collect detailed historic records on POs from the previous business year. PO placement cycle time specs were created. Process capability indicated that material was late 23 percent of the time.

Analyze

Pareto charts by dollar threshold values were created. A common problem area among all four categories was the process span time from supplier selection to actual entry of the PO. A hypothesis test was performed to alleviate concern that dollar value thresholds had an impact on PO placement cycle time drivers.

Improve

Review of data and brainstorming pointed to three problems causing long cycle times: Buyer workload distribution, lack of a preferred supplier base, and inadequate purchasing software. Work teams were organized to manage buyer workload issues. A preferred/certified supplier program was started and on-line procurement forms have been made available.

Control

A management report series has been developed to report monthly on departmental and individual metrics. Performance goals were introduced to buyer annual performance plans.

Results

Overall process capability improved. Average cycle time dropped from 17 days to 11 days. Material deliveries improved from an average of 23 percent late to 16 percent late. The company saved $105,000 annually in decreased buyer staffing requirements.

8

MEASURE PHASE

WHEN WE START APPROACHING what we don't know, that is the beginning of the Six Sigma journey. The measure is that beginning or the start on the game board to that journey.

After the Define phase, the team has a project charter, an overview of the process to be improved, information the customers consider critical to quality, and a statement of the problem. Now the team members must decide what additional measurements they need to take to quantify the problem.

The main objective is to ensure that the data that is being used for the project is validated using specific tools. Concurrently they are selecting one or more metrics in the process (i.e., dependent variables—Y's), mapping the process, making the necessary measurements, and recording the results to establish the current capability, the baseline. The focus is on getting accurate and sufficient measurements of the process. Sample plans are created to ensure sufficient size, frequency of collection, and a rational subgroup that represents the process reality.

Remember this question: What does Six Sigma need?

1. It needs a problem.
2. It needs a process.
3. It needs a financial benefit.
4. It needs a metric and a goal.
5. It needs a customer metric.

The Measure phase is now going to quantify, qualify, and validate those Six Sigma needs. We normally do *not* find solutions, but discover more opportunities and lay a foundation for the culture to follow. It is the pioneer stage of the settlers, when struggles occur and barriers emerge.

In the Measure phase, it is worth mentioning that the black belts and their efforts will invariably run up against cultural resistance. Although our strategy and deployment prime the pump for the cultural change, it is in the Measure phase that "the rubber meets the road." It would be naïve to expect the culture of an organization to jump for joy to be asked to install a system that will inevitably reveal detailed information that will be used to attack core practices or undermine people's beliefs and authorities and change the definition of success and failure. After all of the stress of downsizing, TQM'ing, reorganizing, and reengineering, managers and employees alike will often view Six Sigma as the latest threat to their "illusory meaning of job security."

During the Measure phase, the true reality of the process will be revealed and in some cases the defects will go up as the real levels of the defect rates are uncovered. Once these new opportunities are no longer hiding, the team members will have to redefine the problem to reflect the defect level and also the true cost of the adverse defect. They search for root causes, by measuring the process to determine the focus and extent of the problem and using data to identify the major factors or vital few root causes.

PURPOSES OF THE MEASURE PHASE

The primary purpose of the Measure phase is to focus the improvement effort by gathering information about the current situation. This will help the team narrow the range of potential causes it needs to investigate in the Analyze phase. More specifically, the purpose of this phase is to define one or more CTQ characteristics (dependent variables), map the process in detail, evaluate the measurement systems, assess the current level of process performance to establish a baseline capability, the short- and long-term process sigma capabilities, and quantify the problem.

Figure 8-1 shows a detailed map of the activity in the Measure phase. Note the extent of the involvement of the team in this phase. This is where the team facilitation tools learned in the Define phase will become especially important.

You might notice that the sequence of the tools presented in this flowchart is different from the sequence of the topics in the training material for this phase. There are three reasons for this:

1. The sequence presented on this flowchart is what one would expect to see in a "perfect" world. The flowchart shows the sequence for using the tools, as a general guide. There are times when the sequence is not followed and the black belt is to seek out a master black belt to clarify the purpose of deviating. The usual sequence is process map, cause-and-effect (fishbone) diagram, *YX* matrix, and

FMEA, in that order. In a perfect world, we would also expect measurement system analysis (MSA) to precede capability.

2. From a training perspective, process mapping is a fairly intuitive topic and experience indicates that a topic like this is best presented prior to the more difficult concepts of capability. The foundation of the DMAIC training is a layer of the typical tools needed to transition to the next phase of training, thereby allowing the black belt to apply the tools as the team develops a project solution, until achieving the final goal.

3. In many cases, however (and this is especially true for transactional projects), the black belt must first establish a data collection system, and while enough data are being compiled to perform a capability study, then the black belt can begin to execute the sequence of tools— process map, cause-and-effect (fishbone) diagram, *XY* matrix, and FMEA.

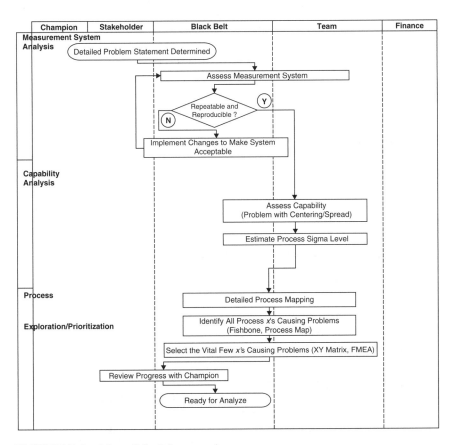

FIGURE 8-1   Map of the Measure phase

MEASURE PHASE ACTIVITIES

This is the detailed description of the activities in the Measure phase. Note the extent of the involvement of the team in this phase. This is where the team facilitation tools learned in the Define phase will become especially important.

You might notice that the sequence of the tools presented in this flow-chart is different from the sequence of the topics in the training material for this phase. There are two reasons for this:

1. The sequence presented on this flowchart is what one would expect to see in a "perfect" world. The flowchart shows the sequence for using the tools, as a general guide. There are times when the sequence is not followed and the black belt is to seek out a master black belt to clarify the purpose of deviating. The usual sequence is process map, cause-and-effect (fishbone) diagram, YX matrix, and FMEA, in that order. In a perfect world, we would also expect measurement system analysis (MSA) to precede capability.
2. From a training perspective, process mapping is a fairly intuitive topic and experience indicates that a topic like this is best presented prior to the more difficult concepts of capability. The foundation of the DMAIC training is a layer of the typical tools needed to transition to the next phase of training, thereby allowing the black belt to apply the tools as the team develops a project solution, until achieving the final goal.

An objective of this phase is to collect all the qualitative and experiential information possible and then objectively categorize and rank its importance through a few different tools. Additionally, some quantitative and statistical tools will be employed to derive a list of possible process inputs (X's) that will be statistically characterized in the Analyze phase.

One group of tools, the measurement system analysis (MSA) tools, will ensure that the data the black belt is using is appropriate for its intended purpose. The MSA will assess the measurement error.

One of the objectives of training black belts for the Measure phase should be to inspire them with a sense of curiosity and desire to learn as much as possible about their processes. This sense of curiosity, particularly applied with the intent of controlling the environment and making the process perform better, is contagious. When the team adopts this desire to constantly learn, then the black belt has made an important first step as a change agent. A team that demonstrates a desire to learn and a sense of curiosity will help to disseminate the Six Sigma culture and make it become a way of life for the organization.

Being able to synthesize what is learned is such an important aspect of the Six Sigma approach. The best black belts will take the tools learned in class and apply them appropriately to drive change in their processes. Many of the tools, especially the ranking and prioritizing tools of the Measure phase, can be applied creatively. This is less true for the Analyze phase tools, because they are limited by the requirements of statistical models and assumptions.

These are the most important tools used by the project team in the Measure phase:

- Process mapping
- *YX* diagrams
- Failure modes and effects analysis (FMEA)
- Measurement systems analysis (MSA)
- Capability analysis

Map the Process in Detail

One of the most important tools is the process map. It can be used to document how a process actually works, with several levels of detail.

Detailed process mapping, going beyond the high-level SIPOC map from the Define phase, helps the team think about the process and identify forms of waste. Flowcharting software comes in handy when creating process maps, but it is not necessary. PowerPoint is effective.

Process mapping will help a project team do the following:

- Describe how activities are being done.
- Understand the big picture.
- Identify how, when, or where a process should be measured.
- Investigate where problems might occur.
- Identify where modifications might best be made.

A process map is an illustration of how a process works. It consists of flowcharts of the steps in a process—operations, decision points, delays, movements, handoffs, rework loops, and controls or inspections. Process maps are living documents and must be changed as the process is changed.

Keep in mind that some of the data required for a detailed process map might not be available to a team beginning the Measure phase, but documenting what data are available and determining what data are still needed will help the team as it moves into the Analyze phase. It should quickly set up a system for collecting data wherever it determines that data is necessary.

Mapping a process in detail should be an iterative process, as the team learns more about the process. The mapping begins at a high level, with what the team created in the Define phase. With this information, the team can determine the most appropriate area to focus its investigation to determine more about the process.

These are typical symbols used in a detailed process map.

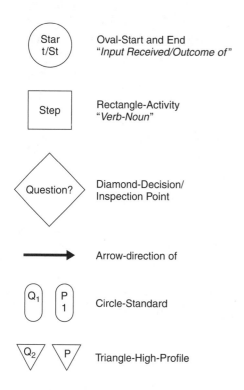

Oval-Start and End
"Input Received/Outcome of"

Rectangle-Activity
"Verb-Noun"

Diamond-Decision/
Inspection Point

Arrow-direction of

Circle-Standard

Triangle-High-Profile

These are not the only symbols used in process maps.

The most important symbols to use in problem solving are the first four: oval, rectangle, diamond, and arrow.

Occasionally some confusion surrounds the use of the ovals (start and end points). The following should remove any confusion:

Start point. The receipt of an input from a previous process supplier, either internal or external.

Stop point. The point at which an interim product or service is delivered to the next process customer.

The circle and triangle symbols are basically optional for the problem-solving process and become more useful when the process map is used as a perpetual documentation tool in process management. Here are some definitions for these indicators:

- Quality indicators (Q's) measure output performance against specified requirements.

- Process indicators (P's) are upstream measurements that are considered predictive of the quality indicator performance.
- Standard indicators monitor defect rates, cycle times, and costs per unit or transaction against specifications.
- High-profile indicators monitor risk, compliance, safety, or other regulatory requirements.

Multiple P's and Q's in a given process are differentiated by the subscript number, which indicates the order in which they occur in the process. This is purely for indexing and reference purposes. In the process management environment, each process will have at least one Q indicator. P indicators are optional but encouraged, depending on their importance.

Every rectangle should have at least one arrow coming in and one arrow going out. Incoming arrows represent the introduction of resources into the process; outgoing arrows represent process deliverables for that activity. Consider the types of meaningful data that can be acquired for this activity. Also consider how the output is evaluated as good or bad.

Note that, in many service environments, the "product in" is information. In this case, we distinguished between information that is required to manage the account in the future ("product in") and information that is a necessary input for this step but not required to manage the account once it is approved ("information in").

Process maps must identify forms of waste, as borrowed from the lean enterprise management systems. It is a great way to evaluate and classify the contribution that process activities make to the desired value-added output, according to the specified requirements. All of these wastes are influenced by and related to process bottlenecks and the inability of the process to flow smoothly. Flow is interrupted by decision points—places where the process can flow in two or more directions. When a process is mapped, any diamond (the symbol for a decision point) indicates waste.

In a manufacturing environment, each of the seven elements of waste is simple to understand; making the connections in a service application can be less intuitive, but there are relationships.

Waste of correction includes the waste of handling and fixing mistakes. This is common in both manufacturing and transactional settings.

Waste of processing relates to overprocessing that might not be adding value in the eyes of the customer. For example, in a transactional environment, excessive signature authority for a $1,000 purchase can delay the acquisition of critical software, thereby slowing the value-delivery process. In a manufacturing setting, overengineering of a product can be an example of this. And how often have you seen an employee spend way too much time formatting a presentation to make it look nice when all the audience cares about is the content?

Waste of conveyance is the movement of material. It is intuitively understood in manufacturing: The customer is not willing to pay extra money for material that travels farther. In the transactional setting, the definition is less clear but just as relevant, with information instead of materials. In most transactional processes, information is acquired from a customer, manipulated or transformed in some way, then returned to the customer in a desired, value-added format. A lot of money is spent to manage information (movement and storage, communication infrastructure, server capacity, and even the cost to carry a contract from the second floor to the seventh floor); these costs do not typically add value to the customer. The customer is willing to pay only for the transformation of information into its value-added output according to specified requirements.

Waste of motion examines how people move to ensure that value is added. This is closely related to ergonomics and workstation layout in a manufacturing setting; in a transactional world it relates to the distance required, for example, to access last month's general ledger or to copy the new vacation policy for distribution.

The next three types of waste could be considered "meta waste," in that they are the result of the previous four types of waste. Waste in these last categories is an insurance policy that the process owners purchase in order to compensate for problems (defects) in the way the process flows.

Waste of waiting is the cost of an idle resource. This is typically the result of either a bottleneck in the process upstream or defects in capacity planning and utilization. This should be intuitive in both manufacturing and transactional situations, although because in a transactional process most resources are on salaries, the cost of waiting can be difficult to quantify.

Waste of overproduction relates to the excessive accumulation of work-in-process (WIP) or finished goods inventory. Most transactional processes, while they might have significant stocks of WIP due to failures in the process flow, have little if any finished goods because services cannot be stored for delivery later; they must be delivered as they are executed. In the lean systems design world, any inventory is waste. But just because inventory is not given a financial value in a cost accounting sense doesn't mean that it doesn't exist and that it doesn't use significant resources.

Waste of inventory is identical to overproduction except that it refers to acquiring raw material before it is needed. In service processes, the biggest problem with acquiring information too soon is that it often becomes obsolete very quickly. There is typically no carrying cost or additional facilities cost associated with raw material in a service process. Again, just because it is difficult to quantify the financial value doesn't mean that it doesn't exist.

Now we see (Figure 8-2) how the process map can be truly detailed. This is the level of information you should strive to achieve.

The steps described here represent greater detail of a portion of the process maps shown earlier, the "Accounts Receivable Credits Account" block in the SIPOC. Note also that the DPU and cycle time numbers tie out

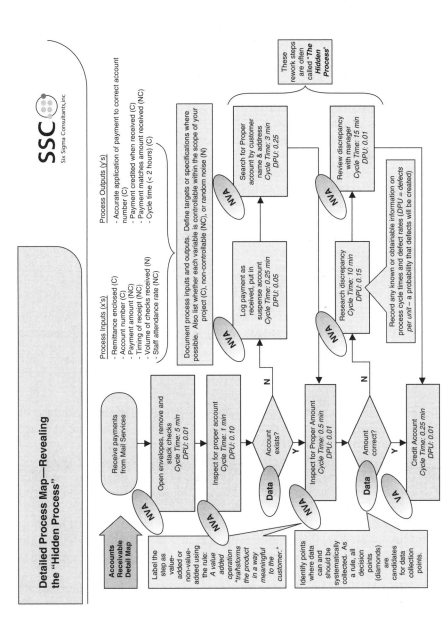

FIGURE 8-2 The hidden process

169

to the numbers shown on the SIPOC. This should serve to demonstrate to the black belts that their numbers should be consistent as they segment and drill down in their processes.

In summary, a process map is a graphical representation of a process that is used to identify the following:

- All steps as value-added and non-value-added
- Key process inputs (X's)
- Key process outputs (Y's)
- Data-collection points
- First X's to put into a FMEA
- Cycle time per step

Through mapping the process, the project team should be able to identify:

- Systems for which measurement studies are needed
- Y's for capability studies
- Holes in the control plan
- Opportunities for eliminating steps

The importance of process mapping can't be emphasized enough. The SIPOC, the cross-functional process map, and the detailed process map are required deliverables.

Create a *YX* Matrix

The *YX* matrix—also known as a cause-and-effect diagram or a house of quality—takes information first identified in the process-mapping exercise and then documented through brainstorming methods like the cause-and-effect (fishbone) diagram. The *YX* diagram is a method for quantifying and prioritizing the strength of the relationships between the input variables (X's) and the output variables (Y's). It is very similar in function and structure to the project prioritization matrix.

The *YX* matrix is a very important team tool. The team will use it to start thinking analytically about the process and it will help facilitate buy-in for the solutions later. The matrix is used to collect data for failure modes and effects analysis (FMEA).

While the *YX* matrix helps make the analysis of critical inputs and outputs as objective as possible, the source of its information is still team experience and collective wisdom. The results are not necessarily tied to hard data.

To summarize, the *YX* is a team-based prioritization tool for the potential X's. This is not real data; this is organized brainstorming! The key success factor in the use of the tool is the team makeup. Because this tool addresses characteristics from a variety of functional areas, it is wise for the black belt to consider organizing a cross-functional team for this exercise.

Here are the steps for creating a *YX* diagram:

Step 1: Call a team meeting and introduce the concepts of the *YX* diagram and indicate why they are important. Assemble the list of potential *X*'s from the three sources:
- Process mapping (standard, cross-functional, VA/NVA)
- Brainstorming (cause-and-effect/fishbone, affinity analysis)
- Preliminary data analysis (graphical and statistical)

Step 2: Enter the process name and revision date in the matrix information section.

Step 3: Enter the *Y*'s (primary or secondary) deemed important by the team and/or customer. (Use the outputs identified on the process map.)

Step 4: Score each *Y* from 1 to 10, as viewed by the customer, ranking the most important as highest and the least important as lowest.

Step 5: Enter all potential *X*'s felt to impact *Y*. (Use all the *X*'s identified in Step 1 on the process map, brainstorming, and the basic data analysis.) This should be a full list, leave nothing off the list.

Step 6: Score the impact of each *X* on each *Y*, with 1 having the least impact and 10 the greatest impact. This is a "best guess" estimate at this point, because no numerical relationships have yet been established.

Step 7: Analyze the results.

We revisit our Accounts Receivable process and we are focusing directly on the tasks associated with Cash Application. The *Y*'s that go in the *YX* diagram should be the *Y*'s that relate to your metrics. Some people mistakenly enter the *Y*'s for each process step (off the process map), which are just the *X*'s on the next step. The team should start out at a high level. Later it might create a new *YX* diagram focused on just a single step.

The scoring step can be very tedious for the team. Make sure that the experts are available who live with the process everyday. Consensus is the best decision method to use when scoring these inputs. When the matrix is complete, the team should check for reasonableness.

The black belt should budget enough time in the team meetings to allow for this tool, which takes a lot of time. Don't plan to execute a *YX* diagram in less than 30 minutes; it is not uncommon for this tool to require two hours or more.

Again, this is simply a quantification of what the team thinks is most important. It is not based on hard data. This just means that the results should be treated with some skepticism and they should be verified for

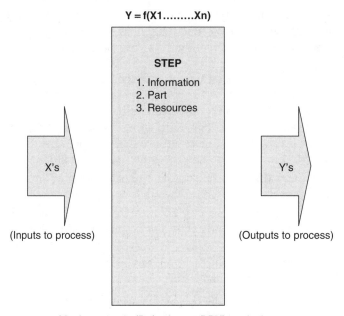

Y = f(X1.........Xn)

Metrics to track: (Defect rate = DPU), cycle time

KEY QUESTIONS THAT *MUST* BE ANSWERED:

1. Why do you do this step?
2. How do you know it's good?

FIGURE 8-3   *YX* diagram

logic and reasonableness. The *YX* diagram will challenge current status of what is believed and will bring out healthy disagreements.

The *YX* diagram summary (Figure 8-4) is used as a priority compass to indicate where to start looking for the practical factors causing the defect. The tool creates a common dialogue for the team, resulting in a natural team bond to resolve the defect. The enemy is the defect!

Do a Failure Modes and Effects Analysis (FMEA)

A failure modes and effects analysis (FMEA) is a technique that the project team should use to study all possible problems in a process, the potential impact of each problem, and how to deal with each problem.

The failure modes and effects analysis (FMEA) addresses the following question: What do you want to know about a defect? It is the knowledge about the product, process, or service. It forces questions to collect the knowledge in a systematic process and in a specific format.

YX Diagram

Name:		Process:	Cash Application
Department:		Date:	

	Output Variables (Ys)	Description	Payment applied to correct account	Payment matches amount received	Correct Interest Applied	Available Credit Calculation	Payment Posted on time	Ranking
			1	2	3	4	5	
	Weight=>		10	9	6	4	9	
Input Variables (Xs)								
1	Remittance enclosed		8	7	10	10	8	315
2	Correct account setup		10	0	9	10	10	284
3	Legibility of remittance		7	9	7	7	6	275
4	Correct send-to address		7		9	8	10	246
5	Staff attendance		5	5	5	5	8	217
6	Daily volumes		5	5	5	5	8	217
7	Data entry errors		8	10	10	10	8	342
8	Recon report accuracy		2	4	2	2	9	157
9	Recon report availability		2	4	2	2	9	157
10	System uptime		6	5	2	2	10	215
11	Batch processing		6	5				105
12								
13								

FIGURE 8-4 *YX* diagram summary

173

The FMEA is a tool that derived from the scientific world. It was used in the 1960s in the aerospace industry during the Apollo missions. In 1974 the Navy developed MIL-STD-1629 regarding the use of FMEA. In the late 1970s, automotive applications, driven by liability costs, began to incorporate FMEA into managing their processes. Companies in the automotive industry currently use FMEA extensively. However, FMEA is becoming much more common in the service sector, especially as companies begin to adopt management system standards like ISO and enterprise risk. It is especially effective at evaluating operational risk.

The FMEA starts with tribal knowledge (unwritten information known by people close to a particular process), known defects, and current data collection. Later the FMEA can be updated using data so that better estimates of detection and occurrence can be obtained. The FMEA is not a tool to resolve the X's that cause Y's and eliminate X's. It is a useful tool to identify potential X's and prioritize the order in which the X's should be evaluated.

However, it is not a great problem-solving tool and it is tremendously painful to execute in a team environment. (If you thought the YX matrix was tough, try this one!) Performed correctly, however, it is the single most powerful to get the team to think about their process in ways they have never considered. They will never see processes the same way again. It is a living document used as you start to improve: It drives a systematic record keeping of the process and drives change through priorities.

There are several types of FMEA, including the following:

- *System FMEA.* Used to analyze systems and subsystems in the early concept and design stages, focusing on potential failure modes associated with the *functions* of a system caused by *design.*
- *Design FMEA.* Used to analyze products before they are released to production.
- *Process FMEA.* Used to analyze manufacturing and transactional processes.
- *Equipment FMEA.* Used to analyze failure modes in the equipment used in a process.

Here are the steps for conducting an FMEAa:

Step 1. Assign an FMEA number.
Step 2. Assign a title to your process.
Step 3. Identify the department responsible for the process.
Step 4. Identify the person preparing the FMEA.
Step 5. Enter end customer product name(s).
Step 6. Assign FMEA key date.
Step 7. Assign FMEA origination date.

Step 8. List of core team members.

Step 9. List process functions (steps).

Step 10. List potential failure modes.

Step 11. List potential failure effects.

Step 12. Assign *severity* of each effect.

Step 13. List potential *failure causes.*

Step 14. Assign *occurrence* level to each cause.

Step 15. List current process controls for the prevention/detection of failure modes.

Step 16. Assign *detection* level to failure modes.

Step 17. Calculate the *risk priority number.*

Step 18. Specify recommended actions.

Step 19. Assign responsibility.

Step 20. Assign actions to be taken.

Step 21. Recalculate the risk priority number.

(The steps here correspond to those in *Potential Failure Mode and Effects Analysis (FMEA) Reference Manual,* developed by the Automotive Industry Action Group, Chrysler Corporation, Ford Motor Company, and General Motors Corporation (1995, pp. 29–45), excluding step 13, which is omitted here, and with a renumbering of the sequence.)

To explain this tool, it is better to view the entire form. Some the terms and titles are self-explanatory, but others are not, which are described below.

- *Process Function (Step).* The description and purpose of each process step.
- *Potential Failure Modes.* The ways in which the process could fail to meet customer requirements, the actual defects.
- *Potential Failure Effects.* The possible effects of the failure mode on the customers.
- *SEV.* Rating (1–10) for severity, the seriousness of the failure mode.
- *Cause of Failure.* How the failure could have occurred (X). Refers to the failure mode.

#	Process Function (Step)	Potential Failure Modes (process defects) (Y's)	Potential Failure Effects (Y's)	SEV	Potential Causes of Failure (X's)	OCC	Current Process Controls	DET	RPN
1									
2									

FIGURE 8-5   FMEA 1

- *OCC.* Rating (1–10) for occurrence, the probability that the failure mode will occur.
- *DET.* Rating (1–10) for detection, the ability of controls to find the failure mode.
- *RPN.* Risk Priority Number, an overall rating calculated by multiplying the three ratings: SEV X OCC X DET. The RPN is used to rank-order the concerns needing attention.

Here are some practical rules for using an FMEA:

- An RPN greater than 80 is an indicator of a critical need for immediate action.
- A severity rating greater than 5 starts into safety-related defects.
- A high RPN with a low probability of detection—P(DET)—is likely to result in defects escaping internal tests and reaching customers.
- A high probability of occurrence—P(OCC)—is an indicator of poor capability.

The following charts (Figures 8-6 through 8-9) provide guidance for rating severity, occurrence, and detection.

Because the FMEA is not specifically intended to be an ongoing process documentation tool in the context of DMAIC, the team should execute it only on a *part* of the process under consideration, not the entire process. The part of the process to which the FMEA is applied is determined by the process map and the *YX* matrix. The part of the process with the highest-scoring *X* variables from the *YX* matrix is where the FMEA should be focused. In a perfect world, this might be a small part of the entire process. In reality, however, it is often several parts of the process that might not be adjacent. The black belt should use sound judgment in applying the FMEA, as it is necessary but time-consuming.

(The black belt might find that the FMEA will be an important part of the control plan in the Control phase. In that case it might actually become an ongoing documentation tool. In the Measure phase, however, FMEA should not be performed on the entire process, just on the parts of the process that are of greatest interest as indicated by the results of the *YX* matrix.)

Once the elements of the process that will be documented with the FMEA are determined, these process steps should be listed in the appropriate column. Leave some space under each process step to allow for multiple-line entries related to the various failure modes and effects at each step. Keep in mind that each step can have several failure modes, each failure mode can have several causes, and each cause of a given failure mode can have a unique effect with different severities.

Here's an example. Say the failure mode is a damaged check. Now assume that the check could be damaged due to causes like water from that pesky leak in the mailroom roof or by a rushed operator ripping the check

Effect	Criteria: Severity of Effect Defined	Rating
Hazardous: without Warning	May endanger operator. Failure mode affects safe vehicle operation and/ or involves noncompliance with government regulation. Failure will occur *without warning.*	10
Hazardous: with Warning	May endanger operator. Failure mode affects safe vehicle operation and/ or involves noncompliance with government regulation. Failure will occur *with warning.*	9
Very High	Major disruption to production line. 100% of product may have to be scrapped. Vehicle/item inoperable, loss of primary function. Customer very dissatisfied.	8
High	Minor disruption to production line. Product may have to be sorted and a portion (less than 100%) scrapped. Vehicle operable, but at a reduced level of performance. Customer dissatisfied.	7
Moderate	Minor disruption to production line. A portion (less than 100%) may need to be scrapped (no sorting). Vehicle/item operable, but some comfort/convenience item(s) inoperable. Customer experiences some dissatisfaction.	6
Low	Minor disruption to production line. 100% of product may have to be reworked. Vehicle/item operable, but some comfort/convenience item(s) operable at reduced level of performance. Customer experiences some dissatisfaction.	5
Very Low	Minor disruption to production line. The product may have to be sorted and a portion (less than 100%) reworked. Fit/finish/squeak/rattle item does not conform. Defect noticed by most customers.	4
Minor	Minor disruption to production line. A portion (less than 100%) of the product may have to be reworked on-line but out-of-station. Fit/finish/squeak/rattle item does not conform. Defect noticed by average customers.	3
Very Minor	Minor disruption to production line. A portion (less than 100%) of the product may have to be reworked on-line but out-of-station. Fit/finish/squeak/rattle item does not conform. Defect noticed by discriminating customers.	2
None	No effect.	1

FIGURE 8-6 Severity Rating Chart: Example (automotive industry). *Source:* FMEA, from AIAG, *Potential Failure Mode and Effects Analysis Reference Guide*, SAE J 1739 (February 1993), p. 35.

Effect	Criteria: Impact of Effect Defined	Rating
Critical Business Unitwide	May endanger company's ability to do business. Failure mode affects process operation and/or involves noncompliance with government regulation.	10
Critical Loss: Customer-Specific	May endanger relationship with customer. Failure mode affects product delivered and/or customer relationship due to process failure and/or noncompliance with government regulation.	9
High	Major disruption to process/production down situation. Results in near 100% rework or an inability to process.	7
Moderate	Moderate disruption to process. Results in some rework or an inability to process. Process is operable, but some workarounds are required. Customers experience dissatisfaction.	5
Low	Minor disruption to process. Process can be completed with workarounds or rework at the back end. Results in reduced level of performance. Defect is noticed and commented upon by customers.	3
Minor	Minor disruption to process. Process can be completed with workarounds or rework at the back end. Results in reduced level of performance. Defect noticed internally, but not externally.	2
None	No effect.	1

FIGURE 8-7 Severity Rating Chart: Example (production). Copyright Six Sigma Consultants, Inc.

Probability of Failure	Possible Failure Rates	Cpk	Rating
	≥1 in 2	<0.33	10
Very High: Failure is almost inevitable.	1 in 3	≥0.33	9
	1 in 8	≥0.51	8
High: Generally associated with processes similar to previous processes that have often failed.	1 in 20	≥0.67	7
	1 in 80	≥0.83	6
	1 in 400	≥1.00	5
Moderate: Generally associated with processes similar to previous processes that have experienced occasional failures, but not in major proportions.	1 in 2,000	≥1.17	4
Low: Isolated failures associated with similar processes.	1 in 15,000	≥1.33	3
Very Low: Only isolated failures associated with almost identical processes.	1 in 150,000	≥1.5	2
Remote: Failure is unlikely. No failures ever associated with almost identical processes.	<1 in 1,500,000	≥1.67	1

FIGURE 8-8 Occurrence Rating Chart: Example. *Source:* FMEA, from AIAG, *Potential Failure Mode and Effects Analysis Reference Guide*, SAE J 1739 (February 1993), p. 39.

while opening the envelope. The water damage might render the check totally useless (high severity), whereas the ripped check might be salvageable (medium severity). One failure mode, different causes, different effects.

When we analyze the data collected during the Measure phase, it is vital to understand how the failure modes affect critical-to-quality characteristics. FMEA is a disciplined procedure that allows you to anticipate failures and prevent them. Identify ways in which the product or process can fail. Then plan to prevent those failures.

Conduct a Measurement System Analysis (MSA)

Any time you measure the results of a process you will see some variation. This observed variation might result for either of two reasons. First, there

Detection	Criteria: Likelihood that a defect will be detected by test content before product advances to next or subsequent process	Rating
Almost Impossible	Test content detects <80% of failures	10
Very Remote	Test content must detect 80% of failures	9
Remote	Test content must detect 82.5% of failures	8
Very Low	Test content must detect 85% of failures	7
Low	Test content must detect 87.5% of failures	6
Moderate	Test content must detect 90% of failures	5
Moderately High	Test content must detect 92.5% of failures	4
High	Test content must detect 95% of failures	3
Very High	Test content must detect 97.5% of failures	2
Almost Certain	Test content must detect 99.5% of failures	1

FIGURE 8-9   Detection Rating Chart: Example. *Source:* FMEA, from AIAG, *Potential Failure Mode and Effects Analysis Reference Guide*, SAE J 1739 (February 1993), p. 41.

are always variations in any process. Second, any method of taking measurements is imperfect; thus, there are always variations in any measurement system. The project team must determine whether any variation they note in measurements is due to causes to identify and address or is the effect of the measurement system.

If variation is due to the process, the team will use statistical process control to identify the sources and reducing that variation as much as possible. But before doing any SPC analyses, it should determine to what extent the variation observed might be due to the measurement system.

Measurement system errors can be classified into two categories: *accuracy* and *precision. Accuracy* refers to the difference between recorded measurements and the actual values for the parts measured. *Precision* refers to the variation in measurements when a device is used to measure the same part repeatedly. Problems of either type can occur within any measurement system. For example, it's possible to have a device that measures parts very precisely (little variation in the measurements) but not accurately or a device that is accurate (the average of the measurements is very close to the correct value), but not precise, i.e., the measurements have large variance. It's also possible to have a device that is neither accurate nor precise.

Imagine a dartboard. Imagine that you're tossing a dozen darts. If they all end up clustered together away from the center, your tosses are precise but not accurate. If they all end up scattered around the center, your tosses are accurate but not precise. If they all end up scattered all over the board and maybe onto the wall, your tosses are neither precise nor accurate. If they all end up crowded at the center, then your tosses are both precise and accurate.

These two concepts, precision and accuracy, are a little more complicated than this simple example. As a champion, you should understand the basics, although you don't need to know as much as your black belts.

Accuracy

The concept of accuracy consists of three components: stability, bias, and linearity.

> *Stability* is freedom from special cause variation over time. A team can measure process stability with statistical process control (SPC), scatter plots, or other forms of statistical analysis.
>
> *Bias* is the influence of any factor that causes that causes the sample data to appear different from what it actually is. A team can measure process measurement bias by comparing the data average with a reference value.
>
> *Linearity* is statistical consistency in measurements over the full range of expected values. A team can measure linearity using measurement standards calibrated to higher authorities, such as the National Institute of Standards and Technology.

Precision

The concept of precision consists of two components: reproducibility and repeatability.

> *Reproducibility* is variation due to the measurement system. It's the variation observed when different operators measure different parts using the same device.
>
> *Repeatability* is variation due to the measuring device, when the same operator measures the same part with the same device repeatedly.

Measurement error could be reported as probable error, a reasonable estimate of typical uncertainty of any single measurement. Probable error defines the effective resolution of a given measurement. In essence, the probable error defines the confidence interval within which actual measurements exist. This becomes critical when making pass/fail decisions based on measurements.

Ideally, measurement system analysis (MSA) should take place at the outset of the Measure phase, to ensure that the data that is used to track process performance and to reveal the nature of the defects is appropriately accurate, precise, and sensitive. The reality of time constraints dictates (as we have mentioned before) that other project work, such as the process map—*YX* matrix—FMEA sequence, be initiated before MSA is complete. In some cases, the MSA process can continue into the Analyze phase, but team members should understand that there is some risk in making bad decisions on bad data until the measurement system is assessed and improved.

The project team must collect measurement data on the "critical to" characteristics. When there is variation in this data, it can be attributed either to the characteristic that is being measured or to the way that measurements are being taken, which is known as measurement error. When there is a large measurement error, it affects the data and might lead to inaccurate decisions.

The primary contributors to measurement system error, however, affect the spread of the distribution and describe the measuring system's precision—repeatability and reproducibility. Repeatability is the variation in measurements obtained by one operator measuring the same characteristic on the same parts with the same measuring instrument. Reproducibility refers to the variation in the average of measurements of an identical characteristic taken by different operators using the same instrument.

Given that reproducibility and repeatability are important types of error, they are the object of a specific study called a *gauge (gage) repeatability* and *reproducibility* study (*gauge R&R*). This study can be performed on both attribute-based and variable-based measurement systems.

Attributes data are data that fit into categories that can be described in terms of words (attributes)—such as "good" or "bad," "go" or "no-go," "pass" or "fail," "correct" or "incorrect," and "yes" or "no"—and counted.

An attribute study can be used on most transactional process. For example, an invoice is filled out either correctly or incorrectly. It enables the evaluation of the consistency in measurements among operators, clerks, bookkeeper, or agents after having at least two people measure several parts or evaluate a transactional process step at random on a few trials. If there is no consistency, the measurement system must be improved.

Variables data are quantitative data, consisting of two types: discrete, data that are counted, and continuous, data that are on a continuum, usually in decimal form.

Here are the basic steps for performing an MSA or a gauge R&R:

Step 1. Calibrate the gauge or ensure that it has been calibrated.

Step 2. Have each operator measure all the samples once in random order.

Step 3. Repeat step 2 for the required number of trials.

Step 4. Use a spreadsheet or software to determine the statistics of the R&R study.

Step 5. Analyze the results and determine follow-up action, if any.

Figure 8-10 shows the layout of the study.

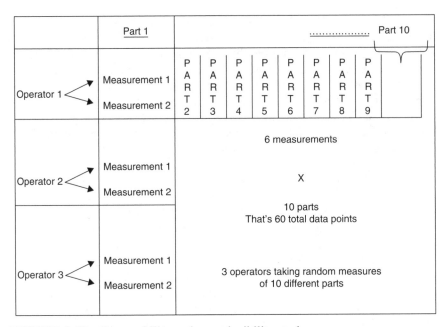

FIGURE 8-10   Repeatability and reproducibility study

Here's an example of a bad gauge R&R, from a graphical point of view (Figure 8-11). This is Minitab software output using a gauge run chart. You can use this chart to quickly assess the differences in measurements between or among different operators and parts. A stable process would give you a random horizontal scattering of points. With an operator or part effect, you would see some kind of pattern(s) in the plot.

Let's look at Part number 3 and Operator 1, for example. The two black dots clearly show a large variation in that operator's measurement of this part.

Let's contrast those results with a good MSA or gauge R&R (Figure 8-12).

As you can see every operator is consistent within and between each other and each part is not causing variation. This is how good your system needs to work to ensure that the data you will be analyzing is good. This is the goal to achieve!

REAL CASE STUDY: RIVETS AND AIRCRAFT, GAUGE R&R STUDY

Rivet height is a critical-to-quality characteristic in manufacturing aircraft. The rivets attach the skin of the aircraft and prevent it from coming off in flight. Also, rivets that are not flush affect the aerodynamics in terms of

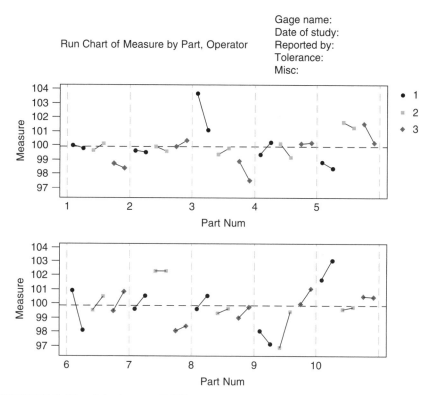

FIGURE 8-11   A bad gauge R&R

performance and fuel economy. The critical-to-quality characteristic of the rivets is height, which directly affects the attachment.

Here's an example of an attribute gauge study of an Assembly Process with Excel. The black belt is describing the procedure to the team members.

> I select 20 rivets that have been installed on my sample parts. Referring to the specifications of these parts, I know which ones that have been installed slightly below or above limits. I take note of the rivets that are good and bad and enter them into my data spreadsheet in Excel, in the "attribute" column. This will enable me to then determine how consistently operators evaluate a set of samples against a known standard, which we refer to as "attribute."

A team member asks, "But how do you evaluate the consistency between them?"

The black belt explains:

> Well, I am going to work with both the day and night shift operators of this machine. They will both measure the 20 rivets of this sample, which are

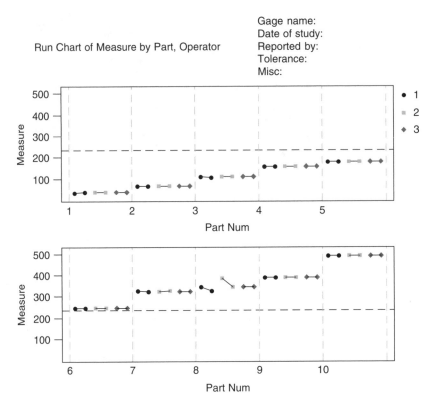

FIGURE 8-12   A good gauge R&R

provided to them in a random order, two different times. Meanwhile, I will record all of their measurements for both trials in my Excel spreadsheet so that we will be able to compare these scores with the standard scores that I have already entered. This will provide us with the data that is necessary to evaluate the measurement system.

The black belt presents the results to his team.

On the spreadsheet, the appraiser's score shows us how consistently the operators are able to repeat their own measurements. This score is obtained by comparing the operator's trials for all samples to determine the proportion of consistent scores. The "score vs. attribute" value shows us how consistent the operators' measurements are with the known standard, in the 'attribute' column.

Here, we take the attribute, trial 1 and trial 2, and calculate the proportion of scores that are consistent across the samples. The results of the first operator reveal a score of 95 percent (19/20) between the two trials and 90 percent (18/20) for the "score vs. attribute" value. For operator 2, the appraiser score is 100 percent and the "score vs. attribute" is 95 percent.

Attribute Gage Study with Excel

SCORING REPORT

Attribute Legend	
1 G	
2 NG	

DATE: 4/8/97

NAME: Dep. 282 Boeing

PRODUCT: Rivets

SBU: 148T2610-238

TEST CONDITIONS: GT996645-GTOOO1 (Mod)

Known Population		Operator #1		Operator #2		Y/N	Y/N
Sample #	Attribute	Try #1	Try #2	Try #1	Try #2	Agree	Agree
1	G	G	G	G	G	Y	Y
2	G	G	G	G	G	Y	Y
3	G	G	G	G	G	Y	Y
4	G	G	G	G	G	Y	Y
5	G	G	G	G	G	Y	Y
6	G	NG	G	G	G	N	N
7	G	G	G	G	G	Y	Y
8	G	G	G	G	G	Y	Y
9	NG	G	G	NG	NG	N	N
10	NG	NG	NG	G	G	N	N
11	G	G	G	G	G	Y	Y
12	G	G	G	G	G	Y	Y
13	NG	NG	NG	NG	NG	Y	Y
14	G	G	G	G	G	Y	Y
15	G	G	G	G	G	Y	Y
16	G	G	G	G	G	Y	Y
17	NG	NG	NG	NG	NG	Y	Y
18	G	G	G	G	G	Y	Y
19	G	G	G	G	G	Y	Y
20	G	G	G	G	G	Y	Y

% APPRAISER SCORE [1] ->	95.00%	100.00%
% SCORE VS. ATTRIBUTE [2] ->	90.00%	95.00%

SCREEN % EFFECTIVE SCORE [3] ->	85.00%
SCREEN % EFFECTIVE SCORE vs. ATTRIBUTE [4] ->	85.00%

FIGURE 8-13   Attribute study

We also want to know how consistent our measurement decisions are over-all. In this case, we want to know the effective scores for both operators. And, then, we want to compare the effective score with the standard score. The target value is 100 percent , meaning that all measurement decisions are consistent.

In our case, both scores are 85 percent . We obtain these numbers by com-paring all of the operators' scores for both trials in all 20 samples and deter-mining the proportion of consistent samples. When measurement decisions are not consistent, it means that we should improve our measurement system by improving the measuring method and/or the gauge itself or by providing better training to the operators.

Determine the Process Capability

The project team assesses process capability to determine whether a process, given its natural short-term variation, has the potential long-term capability to meet established customer requirements or specifications.

What's the difference between short-term capability and long-term capability? A short-term capability study covers a relatively short period of time (days or weeks) and consists of 30 to 50 data points. It measures the potential (short-term) capability of the process. This method of estimating sigma considers the variation within a subgroup; it does not consider the shift and drift between or among subgroups.

A long-term capability study covers a relatively long period of time (weeks or months) and consists of 100–200 data points. It measures the actual (long-term) capability of the process. Total standard deviation says to estimate sigma considering the variation both within and between or among subgroups.

A subgroup is a logical grouping of objects or events that displays only random event-to-event variations: The objects or events are grouped to create homogenous groups free of assignable or special causes. By virtue of the minimum within-group variability, any change in the central tendency or variance of the universe will be reflected in the subgroup-to-subgroup variability.

The team can make a sampling window small enough to exclude systematic nonrandom influences by creating rational subgroups. These are subsets of data that the team defines by a specific stratifying factor, e.g., shift, time, operator, customer type, etc. By identifying factors and stratifying accordingly, the team can exclude variation from special causes. If it does not use rational subgroups, it could end up overstating the problem or, worse, underestimating the effects.

Indices of Capability

As mentioned in Chapter 3, there are various measures of process capability. The two most widely used are *Cp* and *Cpk*. *Cpk* is sometimes called *process performance,* to distinguish it from *Cp, process capability.*

Cp is a ratio of the tolerance width to the short-term spread of the process. *Cp* does not consider the center of the process. It estimates the "instantaneous capability" of the process.

Cp indicates the short-term level of performance that a process can potentially achieve. Tolerance width is the distance between the upper specification limit (USL) and the lower specification limit (LSL). Short-term process spread represents six times the short-term standard deviation ($\pm 3\sigma$ ST).

What do the results mean?

- If $Cp < 1$, the process output exceeds specifications: the process is incapable.
- If $Cp = 1$, the process barely meets specifications: there is a probability that at least 0.3 percent defects will be produced—and even more if the process is not centered.
- If $Cp > 1$, the process output falls within specifications, but defects might be produced if the process is not centered on the target value.
- $Cp = 2$ represents the short-term objective for process capability. Because Zst (short-term process capability) $= 3 \times Cp,$ we achieve 6 sigma when $Cp = 2$.

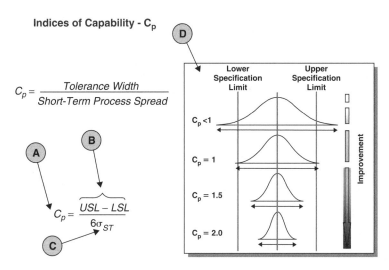

FIGURE 8-14 Capability index *Cp*. *Source:* Joseph M. Juran and A. Blanton Godfrey, *Juran's Quality Control Handbook,* 4th ed., Chap. 16, pp. 19–35.

Z is a measure of process capability corresponding to the process sigma value. *Zst* is the short-term process capability when special factors are removed and the process is centered properly. *Zst* is the metric by which processes are compared. For example, if a process is 3 sigma, it means that three standard deviations lie between the mean and the nearer of the specification limits, $Z = 3$.

Cp is used for continuous data and is based on several assumptions. *Cp* assumes that the process is statistically stable and that the data are approximately normally distributed. Because *Cp* does not consider process centering, it should not be used alone to describe process performance. It should be used in conjunction with *Cpk,* which considers process centering. If the data are non-normal, performing a capability on the process that is producing many parts is still a relevant tool. The nonnormal shape of the data is the problem to solve and with the analysis it gives a great baseline of the problem.

Cpk is a measure of the capability of a process to meets established customer requirements or specifications, given its short-term variation. *Cpk* considers process centering. *Cpk* is a ratio of the distance measured between the process mean and the specification/tolerance limit closer to half of the total process spread.

Cpk indicates the level of performance that a process can achieve, taking into account the location of the process mean. It is equal to the smaller of either *Cpl*—the process capability index using the lower specification limit—or *Cpu*—the process capability index using the upper specification limit. When the process is centered, $Cpu = Cpl = Cpk = Cp$.

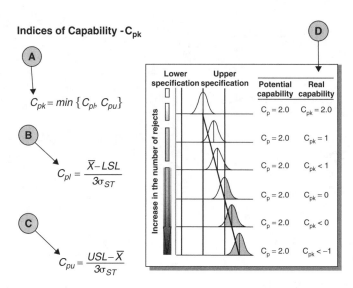

FIGURE 8-15   Capability index *Cpk.* Source: Joseph M. Juran and A. Blanton Godfrey, *Juran's Quality Control Handbook,* 4th ed., Chap. 16, pp. 19–35.

What do the results mean?

- If *Cpk* = *Cp,* the process mean is on target.
- If *Cpk* = 0, the process mean falls on one of the specification limits; therefore, 50 percent of the process output falls beyond the specification limits.
- If *Cpk* < –1, the process mean is completely out of the specification limits; therefore, 100 percent of the process output is out of specification limits.

Cpk is used for continuous data and is based on several assumptions. *Cpk* assumes that the process is statistically stable and that its data is approximately normally distributed. *Cpk* assumes that data are approximately normally distributed. If the distribution of the data is very skewed, *Cpk* considers process centering and the short-term variation in the process. However, it should not be used alone to describe process capability. It should be used in conjunction with *Cp,* which is the short-term process capability index.

When the data are nonnormal, don't panic. Nonnormality is a way of life, because no characteristic (height, weight, etc.) will produce a distribution that's exactly normal.

However, most technical statistical gurus will drive you to transform the data. Transformation is one strategy for making nonnormal data resemble normal data is by using a transformation. Data transformations are commonly used tools that can serve many functions in quantitative analysis of data.

Data transformations are the application of a mathematical modification to the values of a variable. There are a great variety of possible data transformations, from adding constants to multiplying, squaring, or raising to a power, converting to logarithmic scales, inverting and reflecting, taking the square root of the values, and even applying trigonometric transformations such as sine wave transformations. The transformations most commonly discussed in statistics texts for improving the normality of variables are square root, log, and inverse. While these are important options for analysts, they do fundamentally transform the nature of the variable, making the interpretation of the results somewhat more complex.

There could be a chapter on transforming data, but to make a long story short, non-normal data are okay. It is a valid request to transform the data, but the bottom line is that when you have a process that is repetitive in producing many (>100) parts or transactions per hour, the real question is why? Why is this process nonnormal data? What is the nonnormality a function of? Is it caused by different people, different shifts, materials, adjustments, or techniques and what are the factors? That is the problem to solve.

By the way, you could transform the data into a more normal looking set of the data, but the problem still exists. Contrary to mathematical theory, it is illegal to use a "normal analysis" tool on nonnormal data. True! However the picture of capability is real, given the specs, so let's show a practical example.

REAL CASE STUDY: RIVETS AND AIRCRAFT, PROCESS CAPABILITY

Let's return to our case of the rivets, with a look at rivet height capability at Bombardier (Figure 8-16).

The rivets supplied to Bombardier had a high defect rate. They called us in to help solve the problem.

We first did a gauge study of the measurement system to ensure that the data we used was valid. Next, we collected data, using a rational data collection plan. The logical sampling of the data needed to cover the batch-to-batch variation of the rivets, shift-to-shift variation, operator-to-operator variation, tool-to-tool variation, and variation over different products over time.

Figure 8-16 shows the capability of the rivet height at Bombardier, with the lower specification limit (LSL) at 4 mm and the upper specification limit (USL) at 5 mm. (The data presented is coded to protect the confidentiality of the product.)

Pp is overall capability of 0.39, translating to a sigma value of $3 \times 0.39 = 1.17$ sigma. Cp is potential within-part variation, 1.42, resulting in a 4.26 sigma. This Cp is clearly showing you why the numbers don't work, and it would cause you to come to the wrong conclusion. You must always look at both long term and short term to ensure the entire picture.

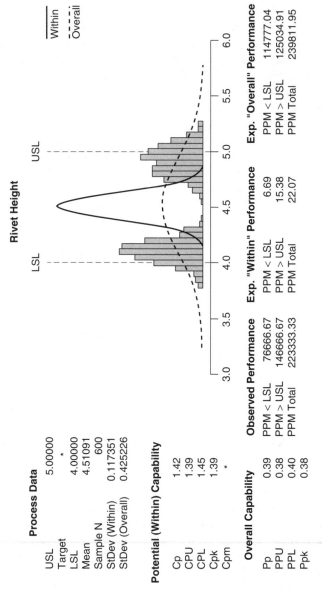

Process Data

USL	5.00000
Target	*
LSL	4.00000
Mean	4.51091
Sample N	600
StDev (Within)	0.117351
StDev (Overall)	0.425226

Potential (Within) Capability

Cp	1.42
CPU	1.39
CPL	1.45
Cpk	1.39
Cpm	*

Overall Capability

Pp	0.39
PPU	0.38
PPL	0.40
Ppk	0.38

Observed Performance

PPM < LSL	76666.67
PPM > USL	146666.67
PPM Total	223333.33

Exp. "Within" Performance

PPM < LSL	6.69
PPM > USL	15.38
PPM Total	22.07

Exp. "Overall" Performance

PPM < LSL	114777.04
PPM > USL	125034.91
PPM Total	239811.95

FIGURE 8-16 Rivet height, Bombardier

Bombardier did not look at this measurement because it's the supplier is self-certified. However, a supplier could in fact send samples from this above distribution to satisfy its capability to the spec. But that's not the real issue!

What's happening here? This graph is showing some important information. This is a non-normal data set. Specifically, it's a bimodal distribution: It shows two clear distributions.

Now contrast this Bombardier data with the Boeing data for rivet height (Figure 8-17).

First, look at the specification limits for Boeing: LSL = 4.3 mm and USL = 4.7 mm—closer than the 4.0 mm and 5.0 mm for Bombardier.

Next, look at the distribution: Their data is normal and the tools work!

Now, can you figure out why the Bombardier distribution from the same supplier is bimodal?

This is a classic supplier quality problem! The supplier is sorting through the rivets, giving the good rivets to Boeing and the leftovers to Bombardier. Distributions like this real happen. If you were to transform it, as some gurus would advise, you would lose the problem focus.

Be careful about these gurus—and be sure to focus on the problem, not the manipulation of data!

Conduct the Measure Phase-Gate Review

The black belt holds a review at the end of the Measure phase. The black belt reports to the executive team on the status of the project. The review provides the members of the executive team an opportunity to ask questions about the project, make comments, discuss any obstacles, allocate resources as necessary, ensure that the project team is achieving the project goals according to schedule, and provide positive reinforcement for the project team. Phase-gate reviews are not technical; it is assumed that the master black belt and the black belt have worked out any technical problems. They are primarily to ensure that the project is proceeding according to the plan, that the team is meeting the deliverables by the milestones, and that the project is on time and on budget.

To prepare for the review, the black belt and the champion should meet to discuss questions such as the following, with or without the other members of the project team:

- What is/are the main problem(s)?
- How have you selected critical measures?
- In what ways have you validated the measurement system?
- What is the current process capability?

Also, there are good, basic checklists and worksheets to help a team prepare for the phase-gate review in *The Six Sigma Way Team Fieldbook,* by Peter S. Pande, Robert P. Neuman, and Roland R. Cavanagh.

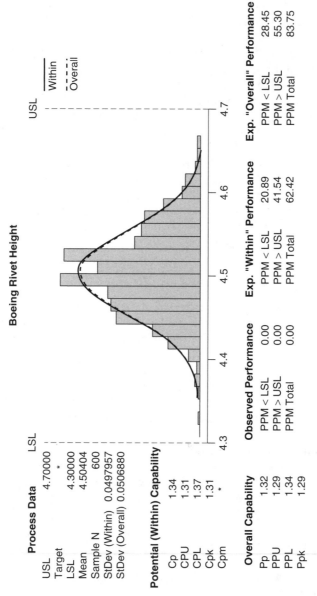

FIGURE 8-17 Rivet height, Boeing

After the phase-gate meeting, the implementation partner should meet with the executive team to review the lessons learned as presented by the project team. She should facilitate a discussion of how the executives can apply what was learned to other projects.

TYPICAL BARRIERS AND COUNTERMEASURES

The potential problem areas in the Measure phase relate to lack of participation from the team and inadequate data for making decisions and monitoring the process.

It should be noted that, if the current data on the process is inadequate, there is generally no quick cure for the problem. Black belts should be prepared to spend time either researching old records or collecting new information as it happens in the process. This can be tedious and time-consuming, but it's important for making good decisions based on fact. It might be necessary to enlist the help of the champion to make the appropriate resources available. In any case, make sure that the data collected is for a purpose, not simply for the sake of collecting data or to satisfy an undefined insecurity about the information provided by the process.

Have the team members provide input as to their own assessment of the roadblocks they have encountered so far and expect to encounter.

MEASURE PHASE DELIVERABLES

The basic deliverables for the Measure phase include the following:

- Project status form/time line
- Metrics graphs
- Detailed process map with points at which to gather data
- Pareto charts of defects and causes
- Measurement tools, including gauge R&R studies
- Data on the process
- Process capability and sigma level
- Project plan: next steps
- Local project review with the direct champion
- Phase-gate review

SUMMARY

In the Measure phase, the team members must decide what additional measurements they need to take to quantify the problem identified in the Define phase. The main objective is to ensure that the data that they will be using is validated. Concurrently they are selecting one or more metrics (dependent variables), mapping the process, taking the necessary measurements, and recording the results to establish the current capability, the baseline. The team focuses on getting sufficient and accurate measurements. It creates sample plans in order to ensure that the sample size is sufficient, that samples are collected frequently enough, and that it is sampling from a rational subgroup that represents the process reality.

Six Sigma needs a problem, a process, a financial benefit, a metric and a goal, and a customer metric. In the Measure phase, the team must quantify, qualify, and validate those needs. The most important tools in this phase are the process map, the cause-and-effect (fishbone) diagram, the YX matrix, and the failure modes and effects analysis (FMEA), usually in that order. Teams normally do not find solutions; they discover more opportunities and encounter barriers.

REVIEW QUESTIONS

1. In the Measure phase of DMAIC, what are the items needed?

   a. A solution to the problem

   b. Data for doing a Design of Experiments

   c. Data to help break down the problem

   d. A problem, a process, a financial benefit, a metric and a goal, and a customer metric

   e. A valid measurement system

2. In the Measure phase, we are going to establish a defect rate, but black belts typically see the defect rate go down.

   a. True

   b. False

3. What is one of the first important milestones that indicate that a black belt is on track?

   a. Lack of buy-in from the team members.

   b. No data are available.

   c. The champion does not know the project benefit.

   d. The process map is complete.

   e. When the team adopts a desire to constantly learn.

4. How many data points do you need to have a short-term capability?

   a. Two data points.

   b. Over 100 data points.

      c. Fewer than five data points.

      d. Between 30 and 50 data points.

5. Process mapping is a

      a. A one-time event

      b. A tool used for statistical validation

      c. A tool used at the end of the DMAIC process

      d. An ongoing living document used throughout the DMAIC process

6. In process mapping, which are the two key questions to ask for each single step?

      Q-1. How many inputs are in this step?
      Q-2. What happened prior to this step?
      Q-3. What are the outputs of this step?
      Q-4. Why do we do this step?
      Q-5. How do we know that this step is good?

      a. Q-1 and Q-2

      b. Q-1 and Q-3

      c. Q-1 and Q-4

      d. Q-1 and Q-5

      e. Q-2 and Q-3

      f. Q-2 and Q-4

      g. Q-2 and Q-5

      h. Q-3 and Q-4

      i. Q-3 and Q-5

      j. Q-4 and Q-5

7. A *YX* diagram is a statistical tool.

      a. True

      b. False

8. A *YX* diagram helps point the black belt into a direction with factual evidence.

      a. True

      b. False

9. A failure modes and effects analysis (FMEA) describes which of the following?

      a. Potential defects

      b. The risk of the problem

      c. Capability of the process

d. Root cause

e. What you want to know about a type of defect

10. An FMEA is complete during the Measure phase.

   a. False

   b. True

11. In an FMEA, what is the RPN if P(OCC) is 5, P(DET) is 4, and the P(SEV) is 9?

   a. 0

   b. 20

   c. 9

   d. 180

   e. None of the above

12. Measurement system analysis (MSA) is used

   a. To assess capability.

   b. To validate the data used for analysis.

   c. As an optional tool during the DMAIC process.

   d. A nonstatistical assessment of the process.

13. MSA is a tool that can be omitted in the DMAIC model.

   a. True

   b. False

14. *Cp* is a capability index with the units measured in

   a. Meters

   b. Gallons

   c. Yards

   d. Productivity

   e. Defect rate or yield

   f. No units

15. If the *Cp* is 1.0, what is the sigma value?

   a. 1.

   b. 2.

   c. 3.

   d. 6.

   e. None of above.

16. Can Cp be greater than Cpk?

    a. Yes.

    b. No.

    c. Sometimes.

17. What is the Cp and Cpk index number when you have a six-sigma capability?

    a. $Cp = 1.0$ and $Cpk = 0.5$.

    b. $Cp = 1.5$ and $Cpk = 2.0$.

    c. $Cp = 3.0$ and $Cpk = 6.0$.

    d. $Cp = 2.0$, and $Cpk = 1.5$.

    e. None of the above

18. What is the purpose for gauge R&R?

    a. Statistical analysis to evaluate measure error

    b To understand repeatability and reproducibility of your MSA

    c. To help validate what is a defect and what is not

    d. Look for variation within operator and between operators

    e. To gauge the rest and relaxation needed for a black belt

    f. a through d

    g. None of the above

19. If your data are nonnormal, you are stuck in the Measure phase.

    a. True

    b. False

C H A P T E R

ANALYZE PHASE

PURPOSES OF THE ANALYZE PHASE

The purpose of the Analyze phase is to sort through all the potential X's that are causing the costly defects. It's like inputting all the X's through a funnel so that the resulting output is the vital few X's that are causing the defects.

In Figure 9-1 you recognize, of course, the transfer function, $Y = f(X)$. The $A = P + R$ is an expression coined by Dorian Shainin, a problem-solving guru who died in 2000. It means All the variation = Part of the variation plus all the Rest. Unfortunately, most companies are working on the wrong thing— the rest of the problems and not the real issues that are right in front of them.

A plant in Batesville, Arkansas, where they made vehicle sealing for the automotive industry serves as a good example of this issue. The "biggest problem" they believed was "lumps in the extrusion" in the rubber that was being used as the sealant. After basic analysis using simple tools such as Pareto charts and comparing other defect types, we discovered that "lumps in the extrusion" was not the biggest problem. It was only #6 in terms of defect level and #10 in terms of cost. When the facts showed that what everybody believed was wrong, the company was able to work at solving more important problems and saving more money than if it had focused on "lumps in the extrusion."

In the Analyze phase, we will start breaking the problem into its vital few factors. The last thing your company needs is to fix a political or mythical problem that will not gain a financial result.

The Analyze phase is the portion of the project where the black belt will work closely with the team to review the data that has been collected and to form hypotheses that the team will test. We'll discuss hypothesis testing later in this chapter, but we should touch upon it briefly here.

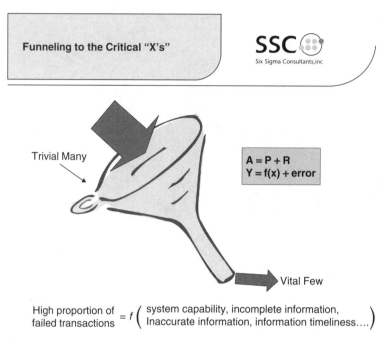

FIGURE 9-1   The critical X's

A hypothesis, in its simple form, is just a question. For example, if I change a setting from level A to level B, will the defect go away? Or if this person does the service rather than this other person, will there be a difference in the service call rates?

You are simply going to prove or disprove the question you state in your hypothesis, but you will state the risk of being right in terms of a percent of confidence. Typically in Six Sigma, we would aim at a 95 percent confidence in our answer. This is the phase where many of the trivial X's will be eliminated and the vital few X's will be analyzed more closely.

ANALYZE PHASE ACTIVITIES

Figure 9-2 shows the typical activities in the Analyze phase.

The potential problem areas in the Analyze phase relate to lack of participation from the team members and inadequate data for making decisions and monitoring the process.

It should be noted that if the data that already exist for the process are not adequate, there is generally no quick cure for the problem. Black belts should be prepared to spend time either researching old records or collecting new information on the process. In some cases they might have to install a data collection process if one does not exist. This can be tedious and time-

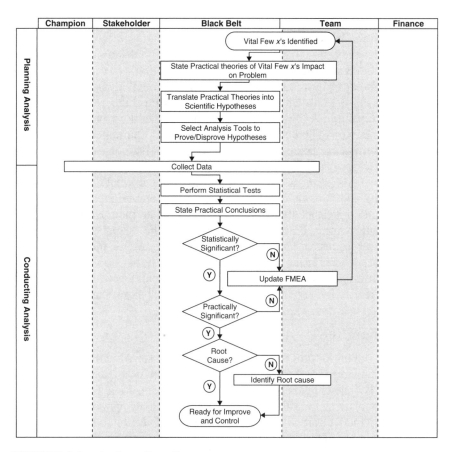

FIGURE 9-2   Analyze flow diagram

consuming, but it's required to ensure a successful Six Sigma project: Without valid data the team will not progress! It might be necessary to enlist the help of the champion to make the appropriate resources available. In any case, the black belt should sure that the data collected has a purpose—the team should not be not collecting data simply for the sake of collecting data or to satisfy an undefined insecurity or a non-value-added political purpose.

The purpose of the Analyze phase is to evaluate and reduce the variables, using graphical analysis and hypothesis testing, and to identify the vital few factors in order to identify the root cause(s) of the defects. The team members examine the processes that affect the CTQs and decide which X's are the vital few that must be controlled to result in the desired improvement in the Y's.

The Analyze phase helps to quantify the performance gap and the benefits of improving the process and to generate ideas for improvement. In some cases during the Analyze phase, one factor might prove to be the largest contributor to the defect levels. Once the factor has proven the hypothesis and the defect rate can be switched on and off, the project is complete, with no need to go through the Improve and Control phases.

Consider the following example: The AlliedSignal Automotive plant in Clearfield, Utah, was producing an oil filter end cap that was very defective— 200,000 parts per million. One of the hypotheses was that end cap warpage was causing the defects. The hypothesis test proved there was a statistical and practical difference in the defect rate when the end warpage was below a certain dimension. The defect rate dropped to 100 parts per million. The black belt in this case fixed the problem in the Analyze phase and went on to a second project.

When we talk about statistical difference , it means that there is a confidence or a risk of not being different. For example, one might state that there is a 95 percent confidence that women are shorter than men, with a 5 percent chance of being wrong. Practical significance, on the other hand, relates the difference to a business or financial benefit. In our example, the practical difference is that men can reach for higher objects with a step stool. You can have a practical difference but not a statistical difference and, conversely, you can have a statistical difference that results in no practical significance.

Analyze Phase Tools

Let's look at the basic tools used in the Analyze phase. We will be reviewing some graphical tools with examples that will help us to set up statistical hypotheses. By viewing the data graphically, we can look for critical X's. Graphical analysis or data demographics shows where opportunities are in determining which X's are affecting the desired Y's. Data demographics in this context is the study of the data population and its vital factors. Remember that non-normality is a reality of a black belt's life and the challenge is to break down the vital factors that cause the distribution to be non-normal (refer to Chapter 8). We should be happy when the data sets aren't normal, because that non-normality gives us a path to search for sources of variation (X's).

Figure 9-3 outlines guidelines for the Analyze phase. It includes the basic tools typically used in this phase.

These are the basic tools of the Analyze phase:

1. Histograms
2. Box plots
3. Dot plots
4. Interval plots
5. Scatter plots
6. Regression
7. Time series plots
8. Multivari analysis
9. Hypothesis testing
10. Analysis of variance (ANOVA)

Scope	Activities	Tools
Define performance objectives.	Develop analysis plan. Do graphical data analysis.	Histogram Box plots Multivari analysis
Document potential X's.	Identify root causes. Perform statistical tests.	Cause-and-effect (fishbone) diagram Hypothesis tests (Minitab)
Analyze source of variability.	Identify primary factors.	Multivari analysis Hypothesis tests (Minitab) ANOVA Regression

FIGURE 9-3   Analyze phase guidelines

Data demographics come from Measure phase tools, namely the process map, YX diagram, FMEA, and cause-and-effect (fishbone) diagrams. Focus on the top X's from the YX diagram. Variability in Y's happens for a reason and data demographics are other process characteristics (potential X's) that might have changed when Y changed.

Here are some examples of data demographics:

- Time: shift, hourly events, day of the week, week of the month, or season of the year
- Location/position: facility, region, branch, division, office, pod
- Operator/Clerk: training, experience, skill, technique, name

What are your data demographics?

1. Histograms

A histogram is a bar graph that displays the relative frequency of continuous data values. This is why it's also known as a *frequency plot chart*. The data values are classed in incremental bins: e.g., if machine bolts are measured, the lengths might be grouped in increments of 1 millimeter: 10–11, 11–12, 12–13, and so on. The widths of the bars are proportional to the increments into which the continuous data has been divided (bins) and the heights of the bars are proportional to the frequencies (counts), showing the shape, centering, and spread of the data distribution. Figure 9-4 shows a histogram that displays the heights of 50 men.

2. Box Plots

A box plot (also known as a *box-and-whisker plot*) is a basic graphing tool that displays five points that represent the centering, spread, and distribution of a set of continuous data. The plot consists of a box, whiskers, and outliers and shows the maximum value, the minimum value, the median, the 75th percentile (third quartile), and the 25th percentile (first quartile).

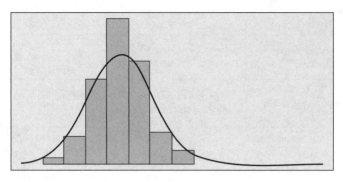

FIGURE 9-4   Histogram, heights of men

It might sound complicated, but it's a handy way to show five points of information in one graphic. A box is drawn (vertically or horizontally) such that one end indicates the third quartile (Q3) and the other end indicates the first quartile (Q1). Typically a line across the box shows the median of the distribution. From each end of the box is drawn a line (a whisker); the lines extend to the maximum and minimum values. Outliers—points outside the upper and lower limits—are plotted with dots and sometimes asterisks, as shown in Figure 9-5.

Figure 9-6 shows a simple box plot and the histogram from Figure 9-4 displaying the heights of 50 men.

Consider this real-life example of using box plots. A company with two customer service call centers was studying the potential X's that influenced performance (call times in seconds—faster is better). The X's here were location, method, and time of day.

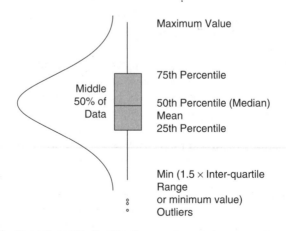

FIGURE 9-5   Box plot with distribution curve

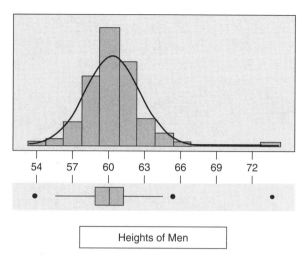

FIGURE 9-6   A simple box plot

Always check the scale to make sure you are looking at the same range and that it is practically significant. Always draw specification limits or desired targets on the box plot to show the relative capability or lack of capability. The box plots (Figure 9-7) don't have targets, but perhaps at least you can start establishing the desired targets and specifications.

The box plot for location shows that the GA location has a slightly higher performance than the NV location, the box plot for method graph shows no difference in performance between expert and team, and the box plot for time of day shows the largest variation at 1,300 hours. We would need to dig deeper into the time of day.

Figure 9-8 has a big difference in variation. As you can see, location one has a low variation or spread of the data set and the spread for location two is almost five times greater than the spread for location one. The median for location two is 10 percent lower than for location one. Let's assume for this example that the target specification is 97 to 102 for a good unit of measure. What would you conclude? If you see that the focus of the problem is on location 2, but we can learn from location 1 which X's are making the data Y's defective, you are getting the concept of the box plot. The power of the box plot is in showing the entire data set, multiple distributions, on a single graph.

3. Dot Plots
A dot plot is a simple graphical display of data points of a noncontinuous variable, with each observation represented by a dot placed above a horizontal line marked with a range of values. The display is similar to a histogram (with a horizontal axis), but the axis is divided into more classes; ideally, each distinct observation would have its own plotting position.

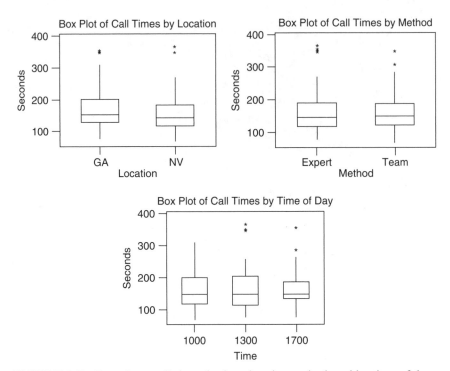

FIGURE 9-7   Box plots, call times by location, by method, and by time of day

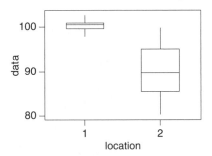

FIGURE 9-8   Box plot, call times by location

In Figure 9-9, some dots are overlapping, which causes a concentration that is much darker than other areas.

The dot plot is an excellent tool to ensure that the box plot is confirming a conclusion by ensuring that outlier or specific individual data points are not skewing the conclusion leading to the wrong decision. For example, if a data set is bimodal (two distinct distributions), the resulting box plot would be symmetrical, meaning that the data is approximately identical on both sides of the median, and the distribution would seem to be normal. A dot plot of the data would reveal that the distribution is bimodal.

The box plot in Figure 9-10 shows a data set that is bimodal and symmetrical. As you can see, the dot plot in Figure 9-11 serves as a check for the box plot.

In the dot plot shown in Figure 9-11, there are clearly two distributions being shown by the concentration of dots in the 70 units and another in the 50 units.

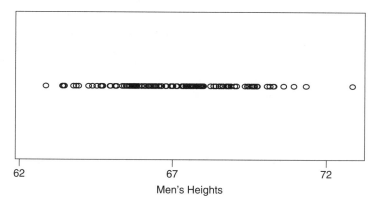

FIGURE 9-9   Dot plot, heights of men

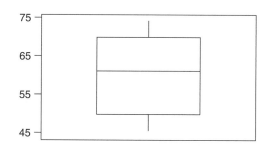

FIGURE 9-10   Box plot of a bimodal data set

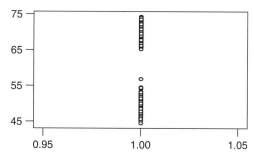

FIGURE 9-11   Dot plot showing the bimodal distribution not shown by the box plot

It's always a good idea to perform checks and balances on data sets by looking at individual data as well as the overall total distribution. Dot plots are especially useful for comparing distributions.

Figure 9-12 shows one more example of the dot plot. A manufacturer needs to ensure that the caps on the ketchup bottles are being fastened properly. If fastened too loosely, they might fall off during shipping. If fastened too tightly, they might be difficult for customers to open.

You collect a random sample of bottles and measure the amount of torque required to remove the caps. The specification for good torque is between 16 to 23 pounds. So let's interpret the results. The majority of the ketchup caps were fastened with a torque of 17 to 22 pounds. There were 12 caps that are too loose, with a torque of less than 16, and 17 caps that are too tight, with a torque greater than 23.

4. Interval Plots
The interval plot is a great graphical tool to compare two factors. The graph shows the spread of data around the means of groups by plotting confidence intervals (Figure 9-13). In some cases it is easier to interpret than the box

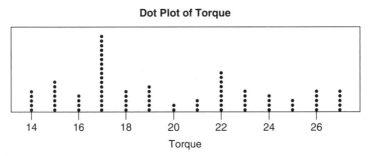

FIGURE 9-12   Dot plot

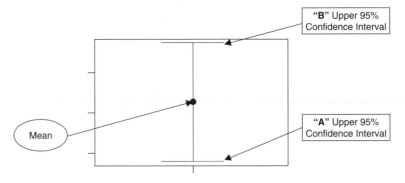

FIGURE 9-13   Interval plot

plot and the dot plot. However, it must be used with care, due to the fact that it is graphing the 95 percent confidence end points by calculating them.

A confidence interval for specific statistics gives us a range of values around the statistic where the "true" (population) statistic can be expected to be located with a given level of certainty. Most of the confidence is based on one minus the probability value (*p*-value), typically 5 percent , making the confidence 95 percent . It is stated that you can conclude that there is a 95 percent probability that the population mean is greater than *A* and lower than *B*. If you set a lower *p*-value, then the interval would become wider, thereby increasing the "certainty" of the estimate; if you set a higher *p*-value, the interval becomes narrower and the "certainty" decreases. It's like with a weather forecast: the more vague the prediction, that is, the wider the confidence interval, the more likely it will materialize. Note that the width of the confidence interval depends on the sample size and on the variation of data values.

The calculation of confidence intervals is based on the assumption that the variable is normally distributed in the population. This estimate might not be valid if this assumption is not valid, unless the sample size is large, say, $n = 100$ or more. The calculation is based on the total distribution. Although it's similar to the layout of a box plot, the representation is *not* of the data set, but of the data set mean and standard deviation, which are used to calculate the confidence interval.

The following is a real example from GE back in 1994. The weight of the agitator in a washing machine is a function of each of 10 mold cavities. If an agitator is incorrectly weighted, this defect can cause leaks; the correct weight is therefore a critical-to-quality characteristic for the customer. A correct weight means no warranty costs for repair. Also, a correct weight means easier installation: no carpal tunnel syndrome in the operator and only one person per shift required to install the agitator.

The interval plot is the start of making statements about a hypothesis and percentage of risk or the confidence in your conclusion. For example, I am 95 percent confident that if I sample a weight from mold cavity one it will be between 30.0 and 30.1 units, based on data that has been validated. This statement is contrasted with "I think that cavity one is okay and much better than cavity two."

As you can see all mold cavities are not created equal. The specification for a good agitator weight is between 29.5 and 30.5 pounds. A correct agitator weight means no warranty costs for repair, no carpal tunnel syndrome in the operator, only one person per shift required to install the agitator, and no adverse effect at the customer's home. Controlling these costs would result in $1 million in additional cash for GE. We were 95 percent confident that the first four molding cavities (represented on the graph, Figure 9-14) were going to produce properly weighted agitators. The other six were producing problems.

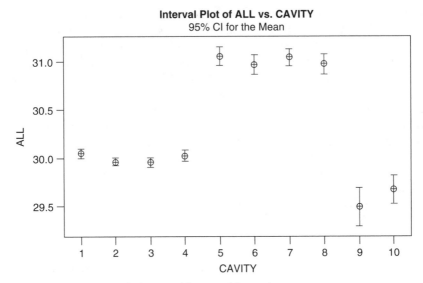

FIGURE 9-14   Interval plot, washing machine agitators

This basic interval plot graphically proved that hypothesis of weight and contained the problem at the supplier's location. It was enough proof to save the $1 million for GE. Containment is not root cause, but was enough to sort the good and know what else needed to be addressed.

5. Scatter Plot
The scatter plot reveals relationships or association between two variables. It shows a relation (correlation) between two variables, X and Y (e.g., weight and height). Individual data points are represented in two-dimensional space, where axes represent the variables (X on the horizontal axis and Y on the vertical axis). The scatter plot is the first step toward doing a correlation and regression analysis; the graph shows a graphical relationship between the the dependent variable and the independent factor. To illustrate the scatter plot, the graph below (Figure 9-15) shows an independent knob A that might have a relationship on Y, the dependent variable. As you can see, there is some sort of a relationship: The plot shows that there is a trend, as there's an increase in Y when there's an increase in knob A.

There is a warning to the scatter plot and correlation and regression tools: Just because there is a relationship does *not* mean there is causation. It's okay to repeat what causation is in this context: It's a cause-and-effect relationship, not a coincidence.

Scatter plots are great for investigating the influence of one factor at a time over the output or CTQ you suspect to be vital. It helps prove or disprove a hypothesis you might have formulated about the problem. By the way, disproving a hypothesis is proving a null hypothesis. Another example is in a claim resolution department: Volume and productivity were graphed

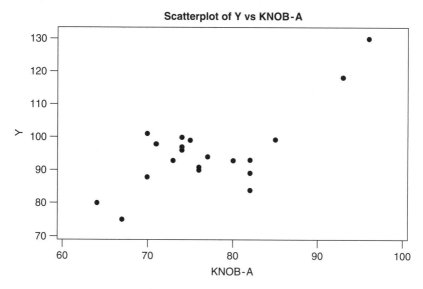

FIGURE 9-15 *Y* versus knob A

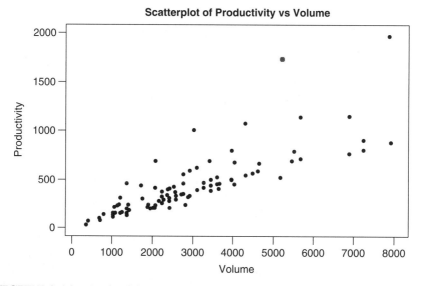

FIGURE 9-16 Productivity versus volume

to determine whether volume had an impact on productivity (Figure 9-16). What do you think?

It definitely looks like there is a relationship. It also looks like there is something going on with the variation as the volume increases. Notice that productivity was chosen as the *Y* variable because it is considered to be

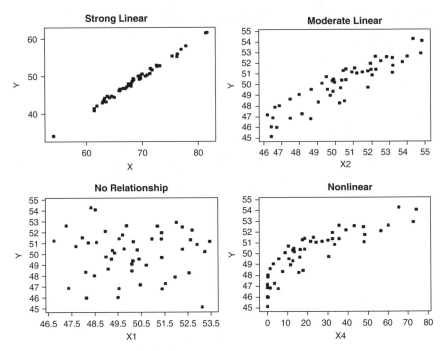

FIGURE 9-17   Scatter plots showing types of relationships

the dependent variable, that is, the variable that is expected to be influenced by changes in the independent variable, volume.

Figure 9-17 presents some graphs to guide you in interpreting the scatter plots.

10. Regression

Although we are not covering regression yet, it's good to show the same graph of a regression in the data set for Y and knob A early. It will show you that the transition into regression is simple.

Figure 9-18 clearly shows the scatter-plot relationship between Y and knob A. The $Y = 11.0277 + 1.09503X$ is the simple linear equation for the relationship. The $R^2 = 0.532$ is stated as the "R-squared value," which is defined as the strength of the YX relationship. It also shows the equation and the R^2 value that shows the percent contribution that knob A describes Y, or 53 percent of Y can be explained by the factor called knob A. There will be more on regression in Chapter 10, but this quick peek into the regression plot will serve as a jumping point.

7. Time Series Plots

A *time series* is a sequence of measurements, taken at successive points in time. It includes a wide range of exploratory and hypothesis-testing methods that have two main goals: to understand the phenomenon represented by the

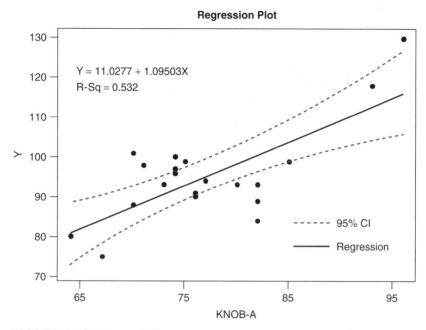

FIGURE 9-18 Interval plot

measurements and to predict future values of the variable tracked in the time series. Both of these goals require that we identify and describe more or less formally the pattern of time series data. We are looking for a pattern in the data that we can interpret and integrate with other data, so that we can use it in our hypothesis. We can validate our hypothesis by identifying and examining before-and-after trends. We can also extrapolate from any pattern we identify to predict future events.

Most time series patterns can be described in terms of two basic categories—trend and seasonality. Trend analysis is a time series plot that shows the data, the fitted trend line, and forecasts. However, the understanding of your model is critical to the analysis. A model of the trend can be covered by four main categories: linear, quadratic, exponential, and S-curve, where the trend starts slowly and moves up quickly to finally reach a plateau or flat line. Seasonality (seasonal dependency) is a time series pattern that shows a basic repetitive pattern over a long period of time, such as annual holiday sales for retailers. For the Analyze phase, the main concept to grasp is the defect rate over time, as Figure 9-19 shows.

The plot clearly shows that as of the 60th day something changed that caused a reduction in defects. It clearly shows proof of a before-and-after trend.

Another simple example is displayed in Figure 9-20, which shows a repetitive pattern. The goal was to understand the cause of the pattern and solve a $450,000 defect problem through a time series analysis.

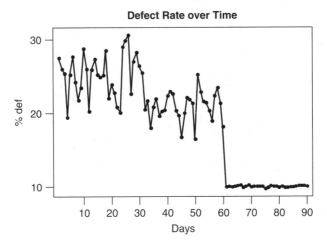

FIGURE 9-19   Times series plot: defect rate over time

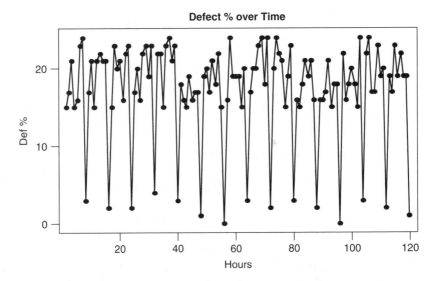

FIGURE 9-20   Times series plot: defect percentage over time

This time series spikes every eight hours and then the defect rate drops to less than 3 percent . But what is the cause? We focused on the eighth-hour time events—and found that the factor was what was not happening during that time frame. There was a break for the material handles that would deliver materials to the machine using a large forklift. The machine was not mechanically isolated from the floor, causing vibration to falsely fail parts and inflate the defect rate. Figure 9-21 shows the time series plot after mechanical isolation was installed to resolve the problem and reduce the defect rate.

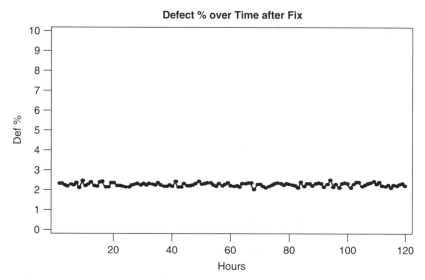

FIGURE 9-21   Times series plot: defect percentage over time, after fix

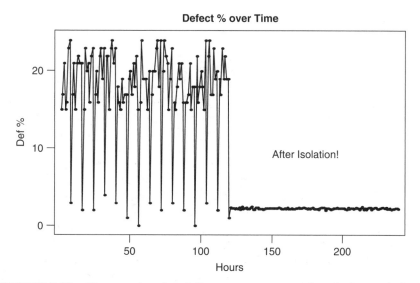

FIGURE 9-22   Times series plot: defect percentage over time, before and after

To really show the benefit of the problem resolution, a before-and-after time series can dramatically validate the changes, as shown in Figure 9-22.

You could also show the same data with an interval plot (Figure 9-23) to show that there is a statistical difference in using isolation as a corrective action to resolve the problem.

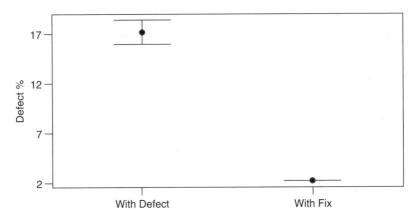

FIGURE 9-23   Interval plot: defect percentage over time, before and after

The basic tools of the Analyze phase are used to break down the components of variation and can be used to validate or send the problem-solving process into a data-driven direction. Combinations of the basics can be used to help clarify direction as well as progress.

8. Multivari Analysis

Multivari analysis is a graphical analysis technique used to identify and quantify dominant sources of variation in a process when the Y's are continuous and the X's under investigation are discrete. Data collection is passive in that the process is monitored in its natural, unchanged state. The tool can be used to assess capability, stability, and graphical relationships between X's and Y's. You are evaluating the effects of inputs on the process outputs and examine the data for any trends or interactions by creating a multivari chart.

It is very important that the team members understand that this is not a means to do an experiment on the process. It is a passive study: Data are gathered and plotted with the objective of finding the largest source of variation. Multivari analysis was originally used in manufacturing to separate out the three primary sources of variation: within a unit, between units, and temporal or over time. It can be used effectively in transactional processes, but the sources of variation are not so tightly defined.

When we understand where the largest source of variation is occurring, it allows us to focus our energies on causes that could be contributing to that source.

Multivari studies should continue until the full range of the output variable is observed and all treatment combinations have been captured. (A treatment is a property or characteristic that allows us to distinguish one population from another.) If all treatment combinations have been observed and Y has not varied through its normal range, the X's are not critical to Y. The goal of multivari is to reduce the large number of possible causes of variation to a smaller family of variation. This will allow the team to focus on that family of variation.

You cannot know in advance how long it will take or exactly how many samples will be necessary to perform an appropriate multivari study. Typically, we start with a data collection sheet that makes sense based on our knowledge of the process. Then, after the data are collected, we check to see if the variation in the study is similar to the variation that has been observed from the process. If we see only minor variation in the sample, we go back and collect additional data. For a multivari to work, the output must be continuous and the sources of variation must be discrete.

For example, Figure 9-24 shows data for the sales of three styles of china recorded at five locations over four time periods. Red circles are the five locations, red squares are average sales per style, and blue diamonds are average sales for a time period.

We look for patterns in the data. We are trying to see how location, style, and time affect sales. Where is the largest source of variation? Within locations? Between styles? Over time? Does the variation in the plot represent what we are used to seeing in the process?

Here are the basic steps in multvari analysis:

Step 1: Call a team meeting and introduce the concepts of multivari analysis. Explain the purpose and the procedure in collecting and analyzing the data.

Step 2: Select the potential *X*'s to include in the study. Potential *X*'s should come from the process map, the *YX* diagram, and/or the FMEA.

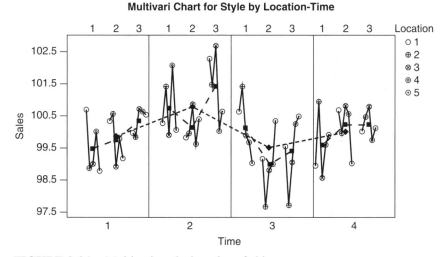

FIGURE 9-24 Multivari analysis: sales of china

Step 3: Establish a sampling plan. Sampling plans should be designed to capture all relevant sources of variation. Multivari studies should continue until the full range of the output variable is observed and all treatment combinations have been captured. (Factors or X's are referred to as treatments and the level of the X is the treatment level.)

Step 4: Plan the method for collecting data. Determine what fields of a database need to be queried to capture the appropriate information for each record. If it is manual, the data collection should be formatted such that associates can easily log the data. A column is set up for each X being evaluated. The data sheet should include a column for each of the following:

- Process X's being evaluated
- Uncontrolled noise variables
- ID information, such as the product type, employee, time, location, etc.

Each level of a factor must include all the levels of the remaining factors. Provide a means to document unusual observations.

Step 5: Collect the data.

Step 6: Analyze the results.

9. Hypothesis Testing

The central activity of the Analyze phase is hypothesis testing. There are many types of hypothesis tests, tests for comparison of both variable data and attribute data sets. It's always best to start with the types of risks that can be studied.

There are two types of hypothesis. A null hypothesis (H0) states the assumption that there is no difference in parameters for two or more populations, that any observed difference in samples is due to chance or a sampling error. It states, basically, "There is no difference in _____."

A null hypothesis is used to check whether the new process mean differs from the old process mean. The test is to determine if any change in mean is simply due to random variation or whether the process has changed and the new mean is significantly different from the old one. The null hypothesis is assumed true until sufficient evidence is presented against it. The null hypothesis will state that all the data belongs to the same underlying population, with the new process essentially equivalent to the old one.

The *beta risk* (,) is the probability of accepting the null hypothesis (H0) as true when it is actually false. It is the risk of not discovering a difference in the sample characteristic of interest (e.g., the mean), when in reality such a difference does exist. An alternate hypothesis (Ha or H1) is any hypothesis that differs from a given null hypothesis. It states that the observed difference or relationship between two populations is real, that it is not the result of chance or a sampling error. While the null hypothesis is a statement of "no effect" or "no difference," an alternative hypothesis will state that a difference or effect exists.

This is the statistical way of keeping track—and it's also the way to start hating statistics. Don't get lost by the designations; it all boils down to comparisons! Are they the same or not? If it's the same, then you fail to reject the null hypothesis. A statistical hypothesis test is done by establishing two hypotheses, the "null" and the "alternate" hypotheses and then deciding which one to accept. Somewhat akin to the concept of "innocent until proven guilty," the null hypothesis assumes that the process parameter in question is unaffected by what we did to change the process. In other words, any differences between the two distributions initially are presumed to be due to random variation from one sampling of the process to another. Continuing the analogy, the alternate hypothesis bears the "burden of proof" that manipulating the process has led to a detectable change in its distribution. The computations must lead to a high probability (rarely less than 90 percent and often much higher) that the change is real, before we will accept the alternative hypothesis.

The decisions in a hypothesis test can be based on the probability value (p-value) for the given test. If the p-value is less than or equal to a predetermined level of significance (α-level), then you reject the null hypothesis and go with the alternative hypothesis.

If your p-value is greater than the α-level, then you cannot reject the null hypothesis: There's no support for the alternative hypothesis. When you perform a hypothesis test, there are four possible outcomes, as summarized in Figure 9-25). The outcomes depend on whether the null hypothesis is true or false and whether you reject or fail to reject the null hypothesis.

When the null hypothesis is true and you reject it, you make a type I error. The probability of making a type I error is called alpha (α) and is sometimes referred to as the level of significance. When the null hypothesis is false and you fail to reject it, you make a type II error. The probability of making a type II error is called beta (β).

Decision	True	False
Fail to reject null hypothesis	Correct decision	Type II error
Reject the null hypothesis	Type I error	Correct decision

FIGURE 9-25   Null hypothesis: four possible outcomes

Let's go back to the GE example that we examined with the interval plot, but now let's use hypothesis testing. Remember: We are comparing weight of washing machine agitators from different mold cavities.

10. Analysis of Variance (ANOVA)

We are going to use an *analysis of variance* (ANOVA) method to illustrate the simple tool. The purpose of ANOVA is to test for significant differences between or among two or more means by comparing variances within groups and variances between and among groups. We use ANOVA to calculate the amount of variation in a process and determine if it is significant or if it is caused by random noise—input that consistently causes random and expected variation in the output. More specifically, by partitioning the total variation into different sources (associated with the different effects in the design), we are able to compare the variance due to variability between or among groups or treatments with the variance due to variability within a group or treatment. (As mentioned earlier, a treatment is a property or characteristic that allows us to distinguish one population from another.) Under the null hypothesis that there are no mean differences between or among groups or treatments in the population, the variance estimated from the variability within the group or treatment should be about the same as the variance estimated from the variability between or among groups or treatments.

There are two types of analysis of variance. One-way ANOVA allows comparison of several groups of observations, all of which are independent but possibly with a different mean for each group. Two-way ANOVA is a way of studying the main effects of two factors separately and, sometimes, together (the effects of their interaction).

Before we go too far, we need to explain *statistical significance* (*p*-level), which we mentioned earlier, in the context of interval plots and confidence intervals. The statistical significance of a result is an estimated measure of the degree to which it is "true"—representative of the population. More technically, the value of the *p*-level represents a decreasing index of the reliability of a result. The higher the *p*-level, the less we can believe that the relation between variables observed in the sample is a reliable indicator of the relation between the respective variables in the population. Specifically, the *p*-level represents the probability of error involved in accepting our observed result as valid, that is, as representative of the population.

For example, the *p*-level of .05 (i.e., 1/20) indicates that there is a 5 percent probability that the relation between the variables found in our sample is a fluke. In other words, assuming that in the population there was no relation at all between those variables and we repeated our experiment again and again, we could expect that in every 20 replications of the experiment, approximately, there would be one in which the relation between the variables in question would be equal to or stronger than the relation found in the first test. In many areas of research, the *p*-level of .05 is customarily treated as a borderline acceptable error level.

One-Way Analysis of Variance for the Agitator Problem
Analysis of Variance for Weight

Source	DF	SS	MS	F	P
CAVITY	9	346.409	38.490	137.10	0.000
Error	990	277.934	0.281		
Total	999	624.343			

Source: The source of the variation (or X's)

DF: Degrees of freedom associated with each SS (sums of squares, a measure of the variation between the samples). In general, DF measures how much "independent" information is available to calculate each SS.

SS: Sum of squares (SS) or amount of variability in the data due to different sources.

MS: Mean squares (MS), an estimate of variance, the sum of squares divided by their respective degrees of freedom. MS takes into account the fact that different sources have different numbers of levels or possible values.

F: Determines if the effects of Operator, Part, or Operator $\times$ Part significantly impact the measurement.

P: *p*-value associated with F. P Part, for example, is the probability of seeing an F statistic as large as or larger than the calculated one, assuming that all parts share the same mean. So as F gets larger, P gets smaller. A small P implies that the assumption that all parts have the same mean is probably not true.

If a factor is a common cause and it contributes significantly to variability in the output, the team has an opportunity to improve the process by controlling the factor.

If the primary sources of variation are special causes, uncontrollable, and they are significant, the team might decide to recommend redesigning the process to withstand that variability to the degree possible (Chapter 13 discusses this alternative) or that the project be abandoned.

If any sources of variation are uncontrollable, but the team assesses their effect as minor, it might continue with the project but adjust its goals correspondingly.

Ascertain and Prioritize the Vital Few Causes of Variation

After identifying any causes of variation as common and controllable or special and uncontrollable, the team narrows its focus. At this point, it screens potential causes for change in the target *Y* and identifies the vital few *X*'s.

The vital few factors are the inputs that have the greatest effect on variation in the output being measured in relation. Typically, data shows that in most processes there are six or fewer factors that most affect the quality of outputs in that process, even if there are hundreds of steps in which a defect could occur. These are the vital few. When you isolate these factors, you know what basic adjustments you need to make to markedly improve the process.

The team begins with the insights gained in its initial analysis to identify the root causes, the fundamental relationships of KPIVs to the KPOVs under study. To identify the critical factors that have the greatest influence on performance, the team uses the five whys, cause-and-effect diagrams, and Pareto charts. Then, to confirm that it will be focusing on the vital few root causes of variation, the team uses hypothesis testing and Design of Experiments.

To estimate the impact of each X on Y and prioritize the causes, the black belt will develop theories about possible causes and the use data to confirm or disprove those theories. The tools used provide insights into the relationships between the key process input variables and the key process output variables.

To verify its findings, the team then gathers additional data and might conduct experiments on the process, making certain changes to see if the problems disappear, or use pilot testing, trying the changes on a small scale to see if they improve the results.

To determine the key input variables that cause the target output variables to vary and then to prioritize those inputs, the team can use ANOVA, analysis of means (ANOM), F-test, t-test, chi square test, and/or Design of Experiments.

What are these tools?

ANOM is a statistical procedure for analyzing the results of experimental designs with factors at fixed levels and providing a graphical display of data. It was developed as an alternative to ANOVA, easier to use because it's an extension of the control chart.

An F-test is used to determine whether two samples drawn from different populations have the same standard deviation, with a specified confidence level.

A t-test is used to determine whether the averages of normally distributed population samples differ from each other with statistical confidence.

The chi square test, which is the most popular hypothesis testing method for discrete (count) data, uses a matrix to look for statistical differences among populations. The test consists of three types of analysis:

- Test for goodness of fit, which determines if the sample being analyzed was drawn from a population that follows some specified distribution.
- Test for homogeneity, which shows that the populations being analyzed are homogeneous in terms of some characteristic.
- Test for independence, which tests the null hypothesis that two criteria of classification are independent when applied to a population of subjects.

The team might check its findings by using an association matrix. $Y = f(X)$ relationships that the team identifies, verifies, and quantifies as the vital few will form the basis for the solutions in the Improve phase.

The root causes can be checked against the critical outputs using an association matrix. This matrix helps the team prioritize possible solutions to develop for the root causes associated with the highest-priority outputs. List the root causes across the top and the possible solutions down the left side; then mark in each cell the potential of each solution to reduce or eliminate the effects of each root cause.

In this step a project team can also use multivari analysis and failure modes and effects analysis (FMEA).

To know how the inputs affect the output capabilities of the process, the team uses multivari analysis to identify the significant inputs and characterize the process. Multivari studies allow a team to identify the inherent capabilities and limitations of a process.

First, the team gets samples, using one or more of several types of representative sampling—random, systematic, subgroup, and cluster or stratified sampling. Then the analysis generates a chart that presents an analysis of the variation in the process in its normal state by differentiating three main sources:

- Intrapiece (variation within a piece, batch, or lot)
- Interpiece (variation from piece to piece)
- Temporal (variation related to time)

Then the team graphs the interrelationship of multiple variables in a process to determine which one contributes the most to that variation, using a multivari plot, a box plot, a main effects plot, or a regression plot.

The studies allow the team to compare input variables and output variables. It can also quantify basic correlation, by using regression—the relationship between the mean value of a random variable and the corresponding values of one or more independent variables—with the data from the multivari analysis to determine the formula that correlates input variables and output variables. Sometimes a multivari analysis will reveal the causes of variations; in other cases, the outputs of a multivari analysis become the inputs for a factorial experiment.

A failure modes and effects analysis (FMEA) is a disciplined procedure that enables you to anticipate failures, identify them, and prevent them. It's a method for making a process more reliable while minimizing causes of failure.

The team first defines the processes to be analyzed and agrees on the level of FMEA and the scope. From its maps of the processes and its SIPOC (suppliers, inputs, process, outputs, customers) analysis, the team then defines every potential failure mode for each process step and the possible effects, both immediate and eventual. Next, it evaluates each failure mode from three perspectives:

In terms of the worst potential results, rating it from 1 to 10 for severity (SEV)

In terms of the likelihood of it occurring, rating it from 1 to 10 for occurrence (OCC)

In terms of the detection methods, rating it from 1 to 10 for detectability (DET)

The team then multiplies the three ratings—SEV, OCC, and DET—to calculate the risk priority number (RPN). It uses the RPNs as a guide in determining how to correct failure modes or compensate for their effects. After taking measures to correct or compensate, the team again rates severity, occurrence, and detectability and calculates new RPNs. Finally, it documents the FMEA and any problems that it could not correct and any special controls necessary.

At this point the team might assess current control plans. What is being done now to control the X's that affect the targeted Y's?

Transform the Gaps into Improvement Projects

Now the team identifies ways to reduce or close the gap between the current performance and the potential, to improve the process. First, team members prioritize the opportunities to improve the process. Which problems should they solve to achieve the greatest gains? Then, they generate alternatives, evaluate those alternatives, and then select the best solutions.

Next, they identify any potential problems and obstacles they might encounter in implementing those solutions.

Once they've mapped out what they want to do and any problems and obstacles, they decide on the people and the resources that will be necessary to improve the process.

Finally, the team translates the improvement opportunity into financial terms. There are three basic questions to answer:

- What is the cost of poor quality that they intend to save by implementing their solutions?
- What is the investment in people and resources that the improvement will require?
- What will be the financial gain, in terms of ROI or a cost-benefit analysis?

Review the Project with the Champion

The black belt meets with the champion to discuss the Analyze phase of the project, to prepare for the phase-gate review that will conclude this phase. These are some of the questions they might discuss:

- Did the team identify possible causes for variation in the targeted outputs?
- Did the team formulate hypotheses concerning the suspected causes of variation? How did it and test those hypotheses?
- What conclusions did the team draw from the hypothesis tests? Did it then test those conclusions?
- Has the team planned to analyze the key metrics data?
- Did the team identify any nonvalue activities? If so, how has it eliminated those activities?
- Did the team use any statistical tests? If so, which ones and for what purposes?
- Does the team understand the root causes of variation and verified them?
- Are there any significant factors to be further investigated in the Improve phase?
- Are the project and financial statements still valid or has it changed them?
- Have the problem and goal statements been updated to reflect the additional knowledge gained from the Analyze phase?
- Have any additional benefits been identified that will result from closing all or most of the gaps?
- What were the financial benefits resulting from any "ground fruit" or "low-hanging fruit" (quick fixes)?

There are good, basic checklists and worksheets to help a team prepare for the phase-gate review in *The Six Sigma Way Team Fieldbook*, by Peter S. Pande, Robert P. Neuman, and Roland R. Cavanagh.

Conduct an Analyze Phase-Gate Review

The black belt holds a review at the end of the Analyze phase and reports to the executive team on the status of the project. The review provides the members of the executive team an opportunity to ask questions about the project, make comments, discuss any obstacles, allocate resources as necessary, ensure that the project team is achieving the project goals according to schedule, and provide positive reinforcement for the project team. Phase-gate reviews are not technical; it is assumed that the master black belt and the black belt have worked out any technical problems. They are primarily to ensure that the project is proceeding according to the plan, that the team is meeting the deliverables by the milestones, and that the project is on time and on budget.

After the phase-gate meeting, the implementation partner should meet with the executive team and review the lessons learned as presented by the project team. She should facilitate a discussion of how the executives can apply what was learned to other projects.

TYPICAL BARRIERS AND COUNTERMEASURES

Typically a repetitive barrier in the Analyze phase is that the black belt was not able to complete the Measure phase. The team and the champion must help the black belt be successful by removing barriers to getting or collecting data. The champion *must* remove barriers that the black belt has tried to remove in a first attempt. Having no valid data going into the Analyze phase is unacceptable, not only for the black belt, but also for the champion for not being aware of the problem. In the Analyze phase all the barriers have been listed and a plan has been installed to remove them. Having no data at this point is a failure and an excuse.

A rule of thumb is that the black belt has 24 hours to remove the barrier. (This teaches the black belt to develop negotiation skills and techniques.) If the barrier is still there, then the champion *must* step in and remove it. Any barrier must be identified with facts and data. For example, a barrier can be a request for MIS to generate a report in four days, but the report is now late by two days.

Consider this example from Nokia: There was a Six Sigma review on a Monday for the Analyze phase. The reviews typically take an entire day and the black belt presents his or her deliverables for the phase. That day at Nokia a black belt started his presentation with only a cup of coffee in his hand, without a computer and with no data to present to the class and the executives who took time out of their busy schedules to attend the Six Sigma review. It was embarrassing. He started his "story" and about two minutes later I stopped him and asked him to sit down. I then arranged for an off-line discussion with his champion about his current status. It's not a good message to the organization if the deliverables are not taken seriously.

ANALYZE DELIVERABLES

The basic deliverables for the Analyze phase include the following:

- Project status form/time line
- Metrics graphs
- List of significant factors/root causes
- Statement of practical theories
- Translation of practical theory into scientific hypothesis
- Analysis plan for proving/disproving hypothesis
- Hypothesis tests for X's as root causes
- Data collection for hypothesis testing
- Conclusions of hypothesis tests
- Project plan: next steps

- Quantification of the expected results and financial benefits
- Local project review with the champion
- Phase-gate review

SUMMARY

The purpose of the Analyze phase is to sort through all the potential X's that are causing the costly defects. In the Analyze phase, the black belt works closely with the team to review the data that has been collected, using graphical analysis, and to form hypotheses that the team will test.

The basic tools used in the Analyze phase are histograms, box plots, dot plots, interval plots, scatter plots, regression, time series plots, multivari analysis, hypothesis testing, and analysis of variance (ANOVA). A team might also use failure modes and effects analysis (FMEA).

After identifying and studying the vital few X's that are causing the greatest variations in the most significant Y's, the team identifies ways to improve the process to reduce or close the gap between the current performance and the potential. First, team members prioritize the opportunities to improve the process. Then, they generate alternatives, evaluate those alternatives, and select the best solutions. Next, they identify any potential problems and obstacles they might encounter in implementing those solutions. After that, they decide on the people and the resources that will be necessary to improve the process. Finally, the team translates the improvement opportunity into financial terms.

The Analyze phase concludes with a review of the project between the black belt and the champion and with the phase-gate review.

REVIEW QUESTIONS

1. What is the lay description of a hypothesis test?

    a. Helping to solve problems

    b. Breaking the problem up

    c. Dissecting the data

    d. There is no way to make it simple

    e. A tool for comparing stuff

2. What are the reasons for nonnormality?

    a. All data has that pattern

    b. Due to abnormal conditions

   c. Bimodal conditions exist

   d. Different normal distributions are within the data set

   e. Both *a* and *d*

   f. Both *c* and *d*

   g. None of the above

3. If you have a nonnormal data set, does transforming the data fix the nonnormal causes of the problem?

   a. Yes

   b. No

   c. Neither a nor b

4. What would best describe a bimodal distribution?

   a. A manufacturing process

   b. Material variance

   c. Transactional defects

   d. Multivari chart

   e. Within-part variation

   f. An *X*-factor that has two different *Y*-output distributions

   g. Both d and f

5. How does comparing factors help solve the problem?

   a. It breaks down the problem into the vital *X*'s.

   b. It contrasts between the trivial many and the vital few.

   c. It helps answer the hypothesis question.

   d. It deals with data, facts that can be proven.

   e. It focuses the team on data, not opinion.

   f. All of the above.

6. Tool wear can cause nonnormal distributions.

   a. True

   b. False

7. Which plot describes the many distributions in one graph in quartiles?

   a. Interval plot

   b. Capability plot

   c. Probability plot

   d. Median plot

   e. Box plot

8. Is it okay to remove outliers in a data set that cause an increase in standard deviation?

   a. Yes

   b. No

   c. Yes, but only if you know the cause of stopping it

   d. *b* and *c*

9. What is the best way to show multimode distributions?

   a. Bimodal graph

   b. Interval plot

   c. Dot plot

   d. One-way ANOVA

   e. Box plot

   f. Both *a* and *b*

   g. *b*, *c*, and *d*

10. Lowess analysis fits a robust line through the data to display a relationship between X and Y.

    a. True

    b. False

11. In a multivari analysis, the X levels are randomly selected levels during the study.

    a. True

    b. False

12. Different operators producing the same Y cannot cause asymmetric (nonsymmetric) distributions.

    a. True

    b. False

13. A two-way interaction cannot cause asymmetric distributions.

    a. True

    b. False

    c. Sometimes

    d. None of the above

14. In simple terms, what is meant by a p-value of less than 0.05?

    a. That there are no significant differences.

    b. The variance terms are equal.

    c. The mean has a shift of 1.5 sigma.

    d. You're 95 percent confident that there is a statistical difference.

    e. All of the above.

15. The 95 percent confidence interval increases as the standard deviation decreases.

    a. True

    b. False

16. A multivari analysis is an active form of comparing within- and between-part variations over time.

    a. True

    b. False

17. You do not need a capable measurement system for multivari analysis.

    a. True

    b. False

18. Shift-to-shift variation can be measured on one shift.

    a. True

    b. False

19. A hypothesis test can show the interaction of the factors.

    a. True

    b. False

20. Sample size has no effect on the width of a distribution.

    a. True

    b. False

21. If an *X* has been identified as statistically significant, do you disregard it if an expert tells you to ignore it?

    a. No

    b. Yes

    c. Ask what data the expert can show to ignore it.

    d. None of the above

    e. Both *a* and *c*

22. If you were told to purchase new technology for over $2 million to make the business more productive, but the hypothesis of the new technology shows no statistical difference in productivity. Do you purchase it?

    a. No

    b. Yes

23. What does hypothesis testing fundamentally change?

    a. It's the departure from "I think" and "I feel" culture.

    b. Destroys the emotions of the problem.

    c. Turns the problem into a fact-based process.

    d. Data are now used to drive decisions.

    e. All of the above

24. If you changed an X that was proven to be statistically significant and the Y was given to you within three months prior to the change and one month after, could you show a before-and-after hypothesis to validate the change?

    a. Yes

    b. No

25. Using an Anderson-Darling normality test, normal data has a p-value less than 0.5.

    a. True

    b. False

10

IMPROVE PHASE

PURPOSES OF THE IMPROVE PHASE

This phase is usually initiated by selecting those product or process performance characteristics that must be improved to achieve the goal. Then, those characteristics are diagnosed to reveal the major sources of variation. Next, the key process input variables (X's) are identified through statistically designed experiments. Proven process variables that have been filtered through the Analyze phase that are identified as the vital few X's will be included in the experiment. The goal is to now form the $Y = f(X)$ relationship that will be leveraged and to establish performance specifications.

The role of a statistically designed experiment is to identify the most influential factors (vital few) associated with a particular CTQ characteristic and to define their relationships using analytical quantities. Because interactions between and among various factors are also defined, a single design of experiment (DOE) can yield many revealing facts, allowing the experimenters to quickly improve their process.

In the Improve phase, the team should be ready to develop, test, and implement solutions to improve the process by reducing the variation in the critical output variables caused by the vital few input variables. The team must demonstrate, with data, that its solutions work. In this phase, the team members generate ideas for improving the process, analyze and evaluate those ideas, select and test the best potential solutions, plan and implement the solutions, and then validate the results with data and statistical analysis.

Thomas Pyzdek makes an important point in *The Six Sigma Project Planner: A Step-by-Step Guide to Leading a Six Sigma Project Through DMAIC* (p. 139):

To some extent, the Analyze and Improve phases are conducted simultaneously. In fact, there is Improvement in every phase of the project. The work done in the Define, Measure, and Analyze phases all help better determine what the customer wants, how to measure it, and what the existing process can do to provide it.

So, he states, a team might make enough improvement in the first three phases that it meets the project goals before reaching the Improve phase. If that happens, the decision might be made to end the project. However, this situation is rare. Generally, teams follow the steps outlined below.

IMPROVE PHASE ACTIVITIES

This phase consists of the following basic steps. This outline is generic; the champion and the black belt will modify these steps as appropriate to the specific project.

The team continues to check for relationships among the vital few X's and between the X's and the Y, as in the Analyze phase. It might be necessary to run tests to understand any interactions among the input variables and analyze the variation contributed by each component to see if one component is causing most of the variation in the target outputs. The team uses design of experiments (DOE), analysis of variance (ANOVA), and regression analysis.

Improve Phase Tools

In the Improve phase, the project team uses the following major tools that will be covered in this chapter:

- Correlation and regression analysis
- DOE planning
- DOE, both full factorial and fractional factorial

There are many more topics to be covered, but the heart of the Improve phase will demonstrate the power of Six Sigma and the main thrust of this phase.

CORRELATION AND REGRESSION ANALYSIS

How do correlation and regression fit within the overall Six Sigma methodology?

When we analyze the data collected during the Measure phase, it is important to be able to reliably determine if there is a relationship between process/product inputs and process/product outputs and measure the strength of that relationship. This is the goal of the Improve phase.

Correlation is a measure of the relation between two or more variables. Correlation coefficients can range from −1.00 to +1.00. A value of −1.00 represents a perfect negative correlation, a value of +1.00 represents a perfect positive correlation, and a value of 0.00 represents a lack of correlation. The basics:

1. Correlation aids in establishing $Y = f(X)$.
2. Correlation is a measure of strength of association between two quantitative variables (e.g., pressure and yield).
3. Correlation measures the degree of linearity between two variables.
4. Correlation lies between −1 and +1.
5. Rule: correlation > .80 is important and correlation < .20 is not significant. However, be careful with sample size.
6. The coefficient of linear correlation r is the measure of the strength.

See Figure 10-1 and Table 10-1.

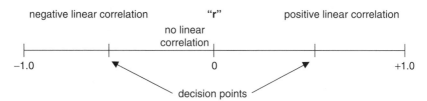

FIGURE 10-1   Correlation continuum

TABLE 10-1   Decision Point Table

n	Decision point	n	Decision point
5	0.878	18	0.468
6	0.811	19	0.456
7	0.754	20	0.444
8	0.707	22	0.423
9	0.666	24	0.404
10	0.632	26	0.388
11	0.602	28	0.374
12	0.576	30	0.361
13	0.553	40	0.312
14	0.532	50	0.279
15	0.514	60	0.254
16	0.497	80	0.22
17	0.482	100	0.196

The type of data that needs to be collected to do a correlation must be bivariate. Bivariate data describe two pieces of data that are variable. Expressed mathematically, bivariate data comprise ordered pairs; let's call them X and Y (X, Y). It is customary to call the input variable (independent) X and the output variable (dependent) Y.

Sample size to guide for correlation decision points:

For example, if $n = 17$, the decision point to state that there is correlation would be .482.

This is Bivariate data pairs, where "$Y = f(x)$," Y is Y, and the X's are $X1$ = knob A, $X2$ = knob B, and $X3$ = knob C. The Bivariate data pair is $Y/X1$, $Y/X2$, and $Y/X3$.

Y	Knob A	Knob B	Knob C
99	85	76	44
93	82	78	42
99	75	73	42
97	74	72	44
90	76	73	43
96	74	69	46
93	73	69	46
130	96	80	36
118	93	78	36
88	70	73	37
89	82	71	46
93	80	72	45
94	77	76	42
75	67	76	50
84	82	70	48
91	76	76	41
100	74	78	31
98	71	80	29
101	70	83	39
80	64	79	38

The usual measure of linear correlation is the *Pearson correlation coefficient* (*Pearson r*, also called the *product-moment correlation*). In lay terms, you can say that the correlation coefficient determines the extent to which values of two variables are "proportional" (related linearly) to each other.

Pearson r:

$$r = \frac{\sum (x - \bar{x})(y - \bar{y})}{(n - 1)s_1 s_2}$$

	Y	Knob A	Knob B
Knob A	0.729		
Knob B	0.367	0.041	
Knob C	−0.487	−0.035	−0.666

$N = 20$, so the decision point is .444 to state the strength.
Knob A $= 0.729$ has the highest correlation to Y.

The interpretation is r is the correlation coefficient which was previous defined, and show to be a number between −1 to 1. The .729 means that "Knob A" explains 73 percent of the output called "Y."

Regression analysis is used to construct relationships between a dependent or response variable (Y) and one or more independent or predictor variables (X's). The goal is to determine the values of parameters for a function that cause that function to best fit a set of data observations. Regression analysis is one of the more widely used methods of data analysis, a technique for investigating and modeling the relationship between variables.

The approach consists of two steps. First, the team identifies the dependent variable Y it wants to predict. Then, it carries out multiple regression analysis that focuses on the independent variables it wants to use as predictors or explanatory variables, the X's. The analysis identifies the relationship between the Y and the X's as a mathematical formula, a model.

There are regression tools to examine both linear and nonlinear (curvilinear) relationships. In linear regression, the function is a straight-line equation. In other words, regression analysis fits a straight line to data points so they are distributed evenly along the line; this creates a simplified but often accurate representation of the relationships. A curvilinear relationship is one that is described by a curve, not a straight line.

The analysis output that will be reviewed fit a regression model using a least-squares approach. The least-squares fit is the line or curve that comes closest to going through all the points plotted on a graph; technically, the line minimizes the sum of the squares of the distances of the points from the curve. A line in a two-dimensional or two-variable space is defined by the equation $Y = a + b \times X$. In full text, the Y variable can be expressed in terms of a constant (a)—also known as the *intercept*—and a slope (b)—also known as the *regression coefficient* or B *coefficient*—times the X variable. This two dimensional fits a simple linear or polynomial (second or third order) regression model and plots a regression line through the actual data

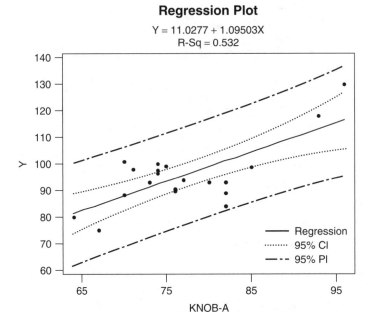

FIGURE 10-2   Regression plot, with confidence interval (CI) and (PI)

Polynomial. This fits to the data, a polynomial function of the form: $y = b_0 + b_1x + b_2x^2 + b_3x^3 + \ldots + b_nx^n$ where n is the order of the polynomial. The polynomial is much more complex, and might represent such things as chemical The fitted line plot shows you how closely the data lie to the fitted regression line.

The output from the fitted line plot contains an equation that the input (predictor) variable to the output (response) variable. The R^2 is the square of the correlation coefficient. It is also the *fraction of the variation in the output (response) variable that is explained by the equation.* What is a good value for the correlation coefficient? It depends on the situation. For example, a chemist might require an R^2 of .99. However, the fact that one input variable might account for 65 percent of the variation in your final product might be phenomenal. The cost and financial impact is the primary criterion.

DOE PLANNING

Planning is the most important process of the DOE process. The analysis is straightforward and takes about 10 percent to 20 percent of the time for the entire experiment. The purpose of the DOE is simply to cause an informative event that can be observed. Here are the basics of this method and some of the essential terms.

Experiments are designed to be more efficient than the traditional method of running a series of experiments, each testing just a single factor (the one-factor-at-a-time [OFAT] approach). In DOE, a *full factorial design* combines the levels for each factor with all the levels for every other factor. The number of experimental runs can be reduced by fractioning the design. In a *fractional factorial design*, the team excludes some of the possibilities.

A level is a value or a setting for a factor, an assignment of high or low for the different states of the X's being used in the DOE. For example, a voltage might be 3.2 V (low) or 5.4 V (high), a transactional cycle time might be high for checkout clerk 1 and low for checkout clerk 2, or a clean unit might be a low level and a dirty unit might be a high level.

The runs are calculated through the use of a design matrix (also known as an *array*), the table of treatment combinations that will be used to set the X's for the levels (values) that are defined and collect the Y's that will be analyzed.

Treatment combinations are the different combinations of X's and their levels (values) that are producing a single Y. In a design matrix, treatment combinations are only one row of X's and its corresponding levels that are directly on the Y in the same row.

When the design calls for an experiment to be run more than once, the subsequent run might be either a repetition or a replication. For a *repetition,* the factors are not reset. For a *replication,* the factors are reset. *Replicates* tend to provide a better estimate of experimental error, but they cost more. Be sure to not overlook the economics.

Along those lines we should mention *randomization*: This is a decision to order the runs randomly, when there are concerns about the possibility of unknown external factors affecting variation. A team might randomize its runs to spread out variation that might be induced by run setup, different operators, etc. or to counter any unidentified factors. However, this too is a question of time and money. Do you have the resources to possibly change all of your factor settings after every run?

Here are typical barriers that a project team should avoid:

- Problem not clear
- Objectives not clear
- Inadequate brainstorming
- No verification of significant factors in the Analyze phase
- Levels of the factors are too low
- Results of the experiment unclear
- DOE is costly due to not narrowing the factors (X?s)
- DOE is time-consuming
- Lack of understanding of DOE strategies
- Lack of understanding of DOE tools
- Not confident during the early stages
- Lack of management support

- Need for instant results
- Lack of adequate coaching and support

In a DOE the team creates treatment combinations that cause defects that it needs to understand the equation and the space. The fact that defects will be created causes apprehension from management, but the upside is the knowledge gained to reduce or eliminate the problem. It should be considered an investment in knowledge, not a cost—or, put a different way, it could be the continued cost of *not* knowing.

"The purpose of an experiment is to better understand the real world, not to understand the experimental data."

—WILLIAM DIAMOND,
IBM, RETIRED STATISTICIAN

There are two components to a DOE: experimental design and analytical procedure. In order to produce the best result, it's best to think these out carefully before conducting the DOE. Depending on how well a process is understood, there are various types of DOE that can be used. DOEs are generally classified in three ways. *Screening* designs are typically used early in the process where many factors are involved (typically, more than five factors), to identify which factors are the vital few on which to focus. *Characterization* designs narrow the number of factors down to only a few and allow for some quantitative understanding of the relationships among the factors, including interactions. *Optimization* designs focus on only one or two factors, but in much more depth, to gain a precise understanding of the relationships.

To ensure that a DOE is designed correctly, the black belt must consider such topics as Yates order (the standard order for a two-level factorial design, explained later), factor levels using the -1, 1 notation, balance orthogonality (a mathematical property of a matrix, indicative in DOE of a very good design, explained later), confounding, and interactions between and among factors. Also, there are design factors that influence the time and cost of the DOE, such as replications and the design type.

The two-level, two-factor design is relatively common and makes a good starting point for most problems. When replications are taken into account, very meaningful results can be achieved with as few as eight to 16 runs. When you don't know which factor has a substantial effect on a response variable and you want to verify several factors, then the fractional factorial design is preferred. It is common practice to do a fractional factorial experiment when there are five factors or more, because a fractional factorial experiment requires fewer runs. For example, a six-factor two-level experiment with no replications would involve 64 runs. This number can be reduced if the team runs experiments that represent only a portion of the matrix.

To analyze the data from a DOE, the team must first evaluate the statistical significance, which it does by computing the *one-way ANOVA* or, for more than one factor, the *N-way ANOVA*. The practical significance can be evaluated through the study of sums of squares, pie charts, Pareto diagrams, main effects plots, and normal probability plots. There are situations in which factors are statistically significant, but not practically significant. In any analysis, it is important to analyze every residual (the difference between a prediction and an observation) prior to drawing any conclusions. The team must adopt a step-by-step approach to designing and conducting a DOE. It's essential for a cross-functional team to select the factors to study, design the experiment, conduct the experiment, analyze the data, make recommendations, and implement the results. It all requires careful planning and attention to detail to achieve success.

Some quality gurus contend that bigger DOE are better. That's wrong! It not the size of the DOE, but what you do with it. Experimental design is a smart way to test relationships among factors efficiently, with less time and resources and better results than through traditional, one-factor-at-a-time experimentation.

EXAMPLES OF DOE

The generic figure below show the process with multiple outputs "*Y*" with corresponding inputs "*X*'s" The equation for Thickness of the molded part is a function of what factors? How do you set the factors to obtain the "*Y*" you desire? How do you make the "*Y*" stable? The DOE and the improve phase is to establish the answers to these questions (see Figures 10-3 to 10-5).

Note: Avoid guru worshiping. Learn from all sources! The reason for this mention is that there are a lot of different methods in the DOE, and not one methods is the guiding law. It's important to learn key concept and methods from gurus, but do not become a groupie of any one guru. Learn by taking the best from each. There are a few more concepts that are important in DOE.

Inference space is the area within which conclusions can be drawn; it's basically the span or focus of a study. Inference space is classified as either narrow or broad. In a narrow-inference study, the experiment is focused on specific subset of overall operation, such as only one shift, one operator, one machine, one batch, one line, etc. Narrow-inference studies are not as affected by noise variables, because the focus is narrowed. A broad-inference study usually addresses an entire process (all machines, all shifts, all operators, etc.) and generally more data must be taken over a longer period of time. Broad-inference studies are affected by noise variables.

As mentioned earlier, DOE designs can be either *full factorial,* combining the levels for each factor with all the levels for every other factor, or *fractional factorial*, excluding some of the possible combinations.

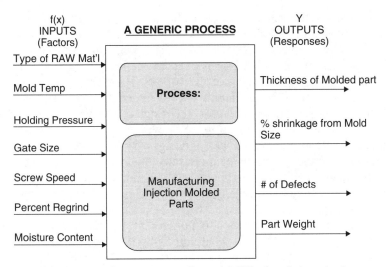

The DOE will approximate a true math model of the inputs to outputs.

FIGURE 10-3   DOE

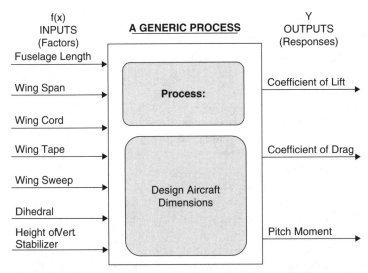

The DOE will approximate a true math model of the inputs to outputs.

FIGURE 10-4   DOE

Full factorial would be best, theoretically, because it would cover all of the combinations and provide the best data. However, it also takes the most time and resources. It might be decided that a full factorial requires too many resources or that a slightly non-orthogonal array is acceptable. Then, the team would use a fractional factorial. These designs are also referred to as 2-k factorials: The 2 is the number of levels and the k is the

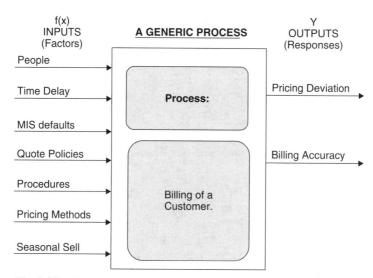

The DOE will approximate a true math model of the inputs to outputs.

FIGURE 10-5 DOE

1	−1	−1	−1
2	−1	−1	1
3	−1	1	−1
4	−1	1	1
5	1	−1	−1
6	1	−1	1
7	1	1	−1
8	1	1	1

FIGURE 10-6 Design array for a 2^3 full factorial experiment

number of factors. The mathematical representation for a full factorial is 2^k and for a fractional factorial it is 2^{k-1}. Here is how these factorial items work.

For example, a 2^3 (two to the third) experiment is an experiment involving three separate variables, each at two levels. There are $2^3 = 8$ possible combinations or total runs. Figure 10-6 shows the design array for this full factorial.

A 2^4 (two to the fourth) experiment is an experiment involving four separate variables, each at two levels. There are $2^4 = 16$ possible combinations.

For a fractional factorial experiment, the mathematical expression is 2^{k-1}. For example, if we use three factors, it would be 2^{3-1}, or 2^2, and there would be four runs, not eight. This is half the number of the full factorial, so it's called a *half fractional factorial experiment*.

Figure 10-7 shows the design array for this fractional factorial.

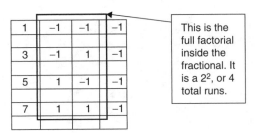

FIGURE 10-7   Design array for a 2^{3-1} (2^2) fractional factorial experiment

The combinations are half the total eight combinations. The design is nicely balanced; that is, each factor is studied the same number of times at each level (equal number of + and −).The design collapses into a full factorial. Should any factor turn out not to matter, the result is a full factorial in the other factors.The design covers much of the region of interest with only half the runs. If the experiment uses expensive experiment or takes a long time, the team can reduce the cost by almost half. If it's possible to get the same information from fewer runs, it is worth considering a fractional factorial experiment.

The design matrix is generally organized according to Yates order, which is the standard. Here's how it works. With k as the number of factors, as explained above, the kth column consists of 2^{k-1} minus signs (the low level of the factor) followed by 2^{k-1} plus signs (the high level of the factor). This order gives us, for a full factorial design with three factors, the following design matrix:

```
−  −  −
+  −  −
−  +  −
+  +  −
−  −  +
+  −  +
−  +  +
+  +  +
```

For a fractional factorial design, determining the Yates order requires knowledge of the confounding structure of the design.

The term *orthogonality* was used a little earlier, as a mathematical property of a matrix, indicative in DOE of a very good design. Generally, orthogonality describes independence among factors. One of the objectives in a DOE is to determine the effect of each of the factors on the response variable and on the total variation of that variable, independent of the effects of the other factors.

The design matrix below (Figure 10-8) is orthogonal. It is balanced both vertically and horizontally. For each factor, there are equal numbers of high and low values (vertical balance). For each level within each factor, there are equal numbers of high and low values (horizontal balance).

As mentioned earlier, one advantage of DOE over traditional, one-factor-at-a-time experimentation is that DOE tests for interactions between or among factors (known as *interaction effects*) and not just single-factor effects (known as *main effects*).

Interpretation of this main effects plot (Figure 10-9) is straightforward. It clearly shows that if you want to increase yield you should use the X called "temp."

An interaction plot is similar to the main effects plot, but the interaction can be interpreted by how the lines cross between factors, as shown in Figure 10-10.

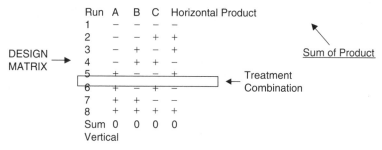

FIGURE 10-8   Design matrix, showing orthogonality

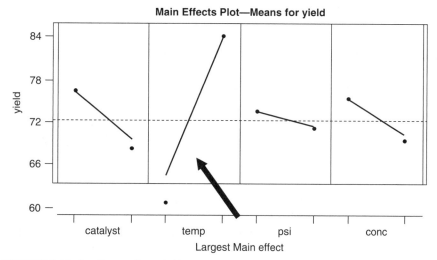

FIGURE 10–9   Increasing yield

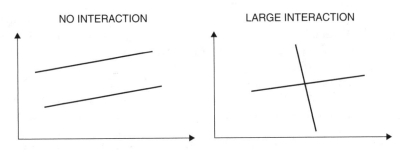

FIGURE 10-10   Interaction plots

Fractional factorial designs are useful for screening factors, because they reduce the number of runs. However, there are disadvantages. When you do not run all factor-level combinations, some of the effects of those factors might be confounded, mixed together so that the effects cannot be estimated separately. In DOE terms, the effects are *aliased*: It's impossible to determine which factor is causing which effect.

One method of measuring aliasing in two-level designs is called *resolution*. The resolution of a design indicates how the effects are confounded. Resolution is typically measured as III or higher, with a higher number indicating less significant aliasing. Here are some common design resolutions:

- *Resolution III.* No main effect is aliased with any other main effect, but main effects are aliased with two-factor interactions and two-factor interactions are aliased with each other.
- *Resolution IV.* No main effect is aliased with any other main effect or two-factor interaction, but two-factor interactions are aliased with each other.
- *Resolution V.* No main effect or two-factor interaction is aliased with any other main effect or two-factor interaction, but two-factor interactions are aliased with three-factor interactions.

Finally, here are some common errors with DOE:

Errors in conducting the experiment. Operators/technicians are often given flexibility to change settings to prevent defects. You must teach them why you're conducting the experiment and share the goal.

Measurement error. I can't stress this common error enough!

Too much variation in the response. Too much variation is a result of poor hypothesis testing, and not working through the X's driving the variation of the output "Y." The DOE will find this "too much variation" in the error term of the BALANCED ANOVA. It is better to go into the DOE with the leveraging factors, and not spend time doing DOE after DOE as a method to reduce the factors to the Vital Few.

Wrong assumptions on interactions. Lack of knowledge about process or a poor design. The team might have aliased the wrong factors or interactions or made an incorrect assumption of linearity. In either case, the predictive model the team develops might not confirm the response

Something changed. Shift, material, weather changes, or other noise factors are driving the error. Look to monitoring noise factors

Extrapolation. The team is unable to find the optimum because it's not experimenting in the right ranges of the factor. Perhaps a linear relationship within the domain of interest is nonlinear outside of the experimental applied region.

Not identifying the right factors for DOE. The error term (percent contribution) will tell.

SIMPLE EXAMPLE OF USING DESIGN OF EXPERIMENTS

To demonstrate DOE, we'll use a break session that we used at GE and walk you through the process from beginning to end.

Figure 10-11 shows an electromagnet. How many BB's can you lift? Which variables have the greatest effect on results? What is the cost of the best design?

Planning Steps

1. Define the problem.
Design a satisfactory electromagnet.

2. Establish the objective or hypothesis.
Maximize the number of BB's picked up. Keep costs in line.

3. Select the response variable(s), the Y's.
Number of BB's lifted.

4. Select the independent variable(s), the X's.
Build on facts learned during preliminary investigations.

Number of wire turns	Nail size
Number of batteries	Others....Wire type

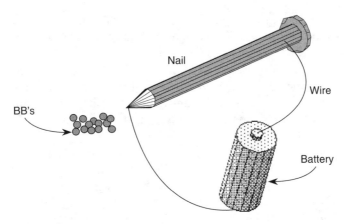

FIGURE 10-11   Nail figure

Battery arrangement
Nail head type

Experience shows that only two to six variables will end up being the vital few. The challenge is to find the influential ones and the test range that will illuminate these vital X's. Test the most likely candidates first. Keep the design simple unless little is known and you need to test many variables to narrow in on a likely candidate. It is a judgment call: Sometimes you will be wrong. By the way, it is not a failure when the experiment doesn't prove your hypothesis. It provides you with more information to move to the next experiment. It took over 4000 experiments to create the light bulb, so you're in good company.

5. Choose the variable levels, the settings of the X's to be studied.
Build on facts learned during preliminary investigations. Capability data can be used to know the natural levels, and the extreme levels. Do not go beyond the safety level, or physics of the problem. Usually two levels are used in initial experiments that are set wide enough to detect effects. The two levels (low and high) are designated as -1 and $+1$.

For the magnet problem, we might choose two types of nails:

Low level (-1): 12-penny nail
High level ($+1$): 20-penny nail

The range must be wide enough to show a difference. Some combinations in the test will produce unacceptable units; these results are expected and accepted.

	Variable Level	Code
Nail	12 Penney	−1
Nail	20 Penney	1
Batteries	one	−1
Batteries	two	1
Wire Turns	45	−1
Wire Turns	55	1

Let's construct the array for the magnet experiment. There are three factors that will be set at two levels. Therefore, we will use a two to the three: 2^3A "two to the three" experiment equals 8 runs or treatment combination that will cover all combinations of the different settings. Below show the design matrix with all combinations of levels for these factors. These are the setting that will used to collect and analyze the DOE output.

Run #	# Turns	# Batt	Nail Size
1	−1	−1	−1
2	1	−1	−1
3	−1	1	−1
4	1	1	−1
5	−1	−1	1
6	1	−1	1
7	−1	1	1
8	1	1	1

Should we replicate the experiment? Replications take more time and cost more, but they reduce variability and increase your ability to estimate error. Replications in a DOE depends on what the statistical and practical problem is trying to solve. For example if you have a spread or variation problem beyond the specification (let's say it is a $Cpk = Cp = 0.3$) you must replicate to analyze the cause of the variation, not just the centering or mean of the problem. If you replicate once the only way you can analyze the variation is by the measure of spread using range. Remember range is taking the "Y" of the treatment combination by taking the difference. More replication is better when trying to solve the a spread or dispersion problem. If you had replication of the DOE to be 5 then we could analyze the standard deviation of the "Y." The replication of 5 would be able to show not only the factors causing the centering problem, but also the dispersion factors. Sometime it is the economics of the DOE that prevent the replication; for example, if you are wrecking cars into a cement wall and are looking at 5 factors with 5 replications to get the problem solved (of course, if there is a safety problem, the business needs to do the right thing), this would be 25 (5^2) times 5 if you wanted all combinations, resulting in 125 cars to be totaled at a possible cost of $30,000 per car, which equals $3,750,000. Wow! It makes you want to do good hypothesis test during the analyze phase.

For our example, we'll use a two-level, three-factor (2^3) design with one replication:

- Number of turns (windings): low spec (−1), high spec (1)
- Number of batteries: one battery (−1), two batteries (1)
- Nail size 12-penny (−1), 20 penny (1)

7. Run the experiment and collect the data.
Running the experiment is straightforward. However, there are some fundamentals to follow.

- Plan the DOE by anticipating potential problems with the trial.
- Adjust the test plan to minimize the effects human error. Don't assume that everyone understands the DOE plan, so review it with all the players on the team that will be participating.
- Randomize the runs to reduce confounding. Confounding means that the factor being studied is being blurred or blended with the interaction effect of two or more factors, resulting in an inability to evaluated the single factor separately.
- It is a method of conducting the design of experiments with levels that were not deliberately arranged by the experimenter.
- Prepare the run sequence considering the following:
  - Difficulty of setup change
  - Effect of time trends
  - Changes of test equipment
  - Changes of ambient conditions
- Prepare logical, clear data sheets to match run sequence.
- Be present during the DOE! *This is a requirement!* As a champion you need to be aware of the DOE plan, and the milestones be around to ensure the Black Belt is getting the proper support. The Black Belt must be present during the DOE.
- Document conditions or unplanned events.

Collecting the data is a critical step. They say that there is no such thing as a poor experiment, only one that's poorly designed or poorly executed. Poor planning leads to poor execution. It is vital that the person or persons who will be carrying out the DOE and setting the factor levels understand(s) the need for rigor and attention to detail throughout the experimental sequence. One way to ensure this rigor and attention to detail is to do a dry run, to verify and improve the data-collection procedures, before starting the experimental sequence.

The operators running the process are a key component for a successful experiment. Not only will they have to run the experiment in the randomized sequence, but they will also need to record in detail any unusual occurrences during the experiment. They will need to reset the control variables, then hold them constant, and usually measure the output from each experimental run.

I cannot overemphasize the need for highly capable measurement equipment, as the results of the experiment can be greatly affected by a large degree of measurement error. So, setting controllable factor levels accurately is another aspect in successful experimentation that needs to be carefully monitored throughout the experimental cycles.

8. Analyze the data.

9. Draw conclusions.
Once we have analyzed the data and have determined the practical significance of each factor and interaction, we determine the combination of factors and interactions that optimize our process to meet our CT (critical to) objectives. It is good practice to replicate the optimum setup and ensure that the results can be reproduced. When we have proven our findings, we have to draw our conclusions and make our recommendations to senior management.

Check that you have considered all the observed data. As the Black belt confine all initial conclusions and deductions to the experimental evidence at hand. Make sure that you as the champion understand the meaning , and business aspects of the DOE conclusion. The champion will need to explain the results of the study and gain buy-in with the executives depending upon what the changes will be to the business,and the owners of the process, always try to explain the analysis in both graphical as well as numerical terms.

10. Achieve the objective.
What do you do if you find that you have not optimized the process from your experiment? Use what you have learned to input into planning the next DOE. It is impossible to fully optimize a process based on one experimental sequence.

When you have proven that the process is improved and is set at the optimum operating configuration, what comes next?

If you have reached this stage in your experimental process, then you are ready to implement conducting a good experiment. You are now ready to institutionalize the changes, to ensure that entropy does not affect the optimized process over time. Entropy is the fact that everything in nature decays. We can improve and optimize the process, but if we do not institutionalize the recommended changes formulated by the DOEs and put controls on the key aspects of the process, the process will revert back to less than perfect over time.

This is the main reason for the Control phase, using control techniques such as SPC to control the critical-to-process parameters (CTPs). This is in the next chapter.

So what does all of this mean regarding our magnet experiment? Consider a 2^3 design on the magnet (Figure 10-12).

The analysis shows that the turns and the nail size matter (see Figures 10-13 and 10-14).

Analysis of Variance for BB's Lift

Source	DF	SS	MS	F	P
N turns	1	8064.5	8064.5	8.10	0.047
N batteries	1	288.0	288.0	0.29	0.619
Nails, size	1	3784.5	3784.5	3.80	0.123
Error	4	3981.0	995.3		
Total	7	16,118.0			

	A	B	C	Response
Run #	N_Turns	N_Batt	Nail_Siz	BBs_Lft
1	−1	−1	−1	14
2	1	−1	−1	40
3	−1	1	−1	21
4	1	1	−1	38
5	−1	−1	1	34
6	1	−1	1	136
7	−1	1	1	4
8	1	1	1	113

FIGURE 10-12   Design matrix for 2^3 experiment

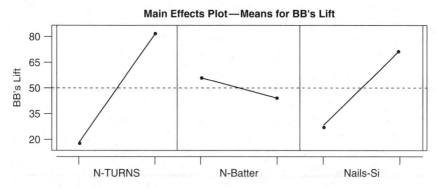

FIGURE 10-13   Lifting the BB's

Analyzing the Data (ANOVA)

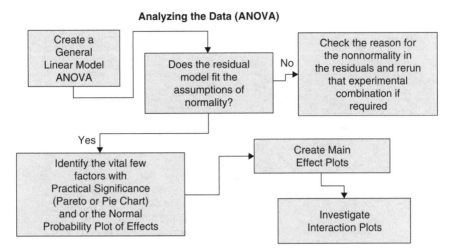

FIGURE 10-14   Analysis of data using ANOVA

Factors	SS	% Contribution
N-Turns	8064.5	**50.0%**
N-Batteries	288	1.8%
Nails-Size	3784.5	23.5%
Error	3981	24.7%
Total	16118	

FIGURE 10-15   Practical significance table

The ANOVA table shows that all the effects are statistically significant at an alpha level of 0.05. *P*-values that are less than 0.05 are statistically significant. The only one less than .05 is the *N*-turns factor. Although they are all statistically significant, they are not all practically significant, as demonstrated when we consider the magnitude of each sum-of-squares compared with the total sum-of-squares (Figure 10-15).

Fifty percent of the *Y* can be explained by the *N*-turns factor (Figures 10-15 and 10-16).

The Pareto chart is a great way to illustrate the percent contribution of each factor and the practical percentage of the cumulative effect of the *X*'s on the *Y*.

Lessons Learned from the Improve Phase

In order to design an experiment, we must first clearly understand the process and decide which feature we want to investigate. Once the experiment is

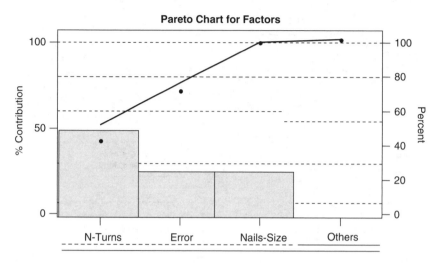

FIGURE 10-16   Pareto chart showing results of the experiment

completed, we will better understand what is important and we can design another experiment. We do this until we obtain the desired result.

Each DOE has two elements: the experimental design and the analytical approach. We must think through the two elements in order to collect appropriate data that can be analyzed meaningfully.

Compared with the traditional one-factor-at-a-time approach to experimentation, a DOE can provide a wealth of knowledge about several factors and their interactions in a very cost-effective manner, because several factors can be varied at the same time, all within one experiment.

The most common way to design an experiment to consider all combinations is to use the Yates standard order. This notation (−1, 1) is used to set factor levels and coefficients. The ANOVA table is used to assess statistical significance initially and then practical significance of factor effects and interaction effects on the output. A factor might be statistically significant, but practically insignificant.

We use pie charts and Pareto diagrams to visually display the relative effects of several factors. We then often plot the main effects on a graph in order to visualize the difference in the response output between the low and high settings of each important factor. Graphs are also useful to visualize interaction effects between factors and to find the optimal settings for both factors.

Even if the main effect is not statistically significant, it might affect the output through an interaction with another factor. We should consider both the main effects and interaction plots prior to specifying optimal settings. Two-factor interactions are common, but three-factor and higher interactions are rarely seen in our industry.

It is common practice to do a fractional factorial experiment when there are five factors or more. In general, factor levels should be set wide, but not so much so that they extend beyond the operational range of the factor.

The general steps for conducting a statistical analysis are ANOVA (with residual analysis), practical significance (sum of squares, pie chart, etc.), and main effect plots (with interactions considered).

A successful experiment does not happen by chance; it takes careful planning and attention to detail to ensure that a designed experiment produces meaningful results. There is no such thing as a poor experiment, only an experiment that is poorly designed or executed.

Actively communicate your plan with all those concerned. This is vital to the success of an experiment.

Review the Project with the Champion

The black belt meets with the champion to discuss the Improve phase of the project, to prepare for the phase-gate review that will conclude this phase. These are some of the questions they might discuss:

- What solutions to the problem did the team consider?
- What criteria did the team use to decide on a solution?
- What solution did the team choose?
- How did the other solutions compare in terms of the criteria?
- How is the solution linked to the causes identified and verified in the Analyze phase?
- What plans has the team developed to implement the solution?
- Did the DOE surprise the team? If so, how?
- What level will be used to solve the problem? Is it the most economical?
- Was the cost of the DOE worth doing?
- What new knowledge do we have as compared to not doing the DOE?

There are good, basic checklists and worksheets to help a team prepare for the phase-gate review in *The Six Sigma Way Team Fieldbook*, by Peter S. Pande, Robert P. Neuman, and Roland R. Cavanagh.

Conduct an Improve Phase-Gate Review

The black belt holds a review at the end of the Improve phase. The black belt reports to the executive team on the status of the project. The review provides the members of the executive team an opportunity to ask questions about the project, make comments, discuss any obstacles, allocate resources as necessary, ensure that the project team is achieving the project goals according to schedule, and provide positive reinforcement for the project team. Phase-gate reviews are not technical; it is assumed that the master black belt and the black belt have worked out any technical problems. They are primarily to ensure that the project is proceeding according to the plan, that the team is meeting the deliverables by the milestones, and that the project is on time and on budget.

After the phase-gate meeting, the implementation partner should meet with the executive team and review the lessons learned as presented by the project team. She should facilitate a discussion of how the executives can apply what was learned to other projects.

TYPICAL BARRIERS AND COUNTERMEASURES

Not wanting to create a problem or defect during the DOE. To find out the solution we have to sometimes create failure, defects, scrap, time delays. The countermeasure to this reluctance to the disruption is looking at for what is real is "an investment in knowledge" and reducing the problem for the overall business results. What is the business cost of *not* knowing?

IMPROVE PHASE DELIVERABLES

The basic deliverables for the Improve phase include the following:

1. Project status form
2. Metric graph
3. Tool use as applicable
   - DOE plan, gauge R&R, three-level Pareto
   - Contingency table, update FMEA, etc.
4. Solution (root cause)
5. Improvement plans/next steps
6. Quantification of improvement plans
7. Complete local project review

SUMMARY

The team begins the Improve phase by selecting the performance characteristics that must be improved to achieve its goal. It then diagnoses those characteristics to reveal the major sources of variation, using correlation and regression analysis. Next, it uses statistically designed experiments (DOE) to identify the key process input variables (X's).

The team tests variables that have been filtered through the Analyze phase and identified as the vital few X's. The objective is to form the $Y =$

$f(X)$ relationships that will be leveraged and to establish performance specifications.

Designed experiments enable the team to identify the most influential factors associated with a particular CTQ characteristic and to define their relationships. Because a designed experiment defines interactions between and among various factors, it can yield many revealing facts, allowing the team to quickly improve its process.

The Analyze phase concludes with a review of the project between the black belt and the champion and with the phase-gate review.

REVIEW QUESTIONS

1. How many runs does a 2^3 full factorial experiment consist of?

   a. 6

   b. 5

   c. 8

   d. 12

2 In an experiment, inputs are allowed to vary randomly throughout the specification range.

   a. True

   b. False

3. One-factor-at-a-time experiments generate more powerful data than a full factorial experiment.

   a. True

   b. False

4. What is an experimental factor?

   a. The input variables for the experiment

   b. The metrics of the process

   c. A covariant

   d. The largest standard deviation

5. What does orthogonal mean?

   a. One or more effects that cannot unambiguously be attributed to a single factor or factor interaction

   b. Involves running the experimental runs in random order

   c. A property that ensures that all experimental factors are independent of each other. No correlation exists between X's.

6. What is a "Balanced Design?"

   a. A design in which each of the variables has a different number of runs at the high and low levels

   b. A design in which each of the variables or factors has the same number of runs at the high and low levels.

   c. A design in which two of the variables have a different number of runs at the high and low levels

   d. All of the above

7. Standard order is the same as run order.

   a. True

   b. False

8. Why use factorial plots? Answer: e.

   a. Allows you to see the plots of the main effects

   b. Allows you to see the interaction plots

   c. Allows you to see the cube plots

   d. Shows how to set each factor to either maximize or minimize the response

   e. All of the above

9. What tools can be used to determine if factors have interaction?

   a. Balanced ANOVA

   b. Standardized effects

   c. Interaction plots

   d. Fractional factorial fits

   e. All of the above

10. What does it mean when no p-values are presented in the ANOVA output?

   a. Means the factors are statistically significant

   b. Means the factors are not different

   c. Only one repetition was run at each treatment combination.

   d. Had no center points

   e. All of the above

11. Why do we replicate our experimental runs?

   a. So we can look for special causes

   b. To obtain a better estimate of the error and look at interactions

   c. To determine the factor levels

   d. So we can look at the same thing run again

12. To use a center point in your experimental design, at least one factor must be able to be set at it's midpoint coded value = 0.

   a. True

   b. False

13. Why use center points in your experimental design?

   a. To check for linearity

   b. To check for interactions

   c. To detect curvature

14. If a center point is significant, its *p*-value in the ANOVA table will be greater than 0.05.

   a. True

   b. False

15. Fractional factorial designs require more runs than full factorial designs given the same number of factors.

   a. True

   b. False

16. What is the main reason for using a fractional factorial design?

   a. Allows you to test and screen a large number of factors in fewer runs

   b. Gives you good estimates of low order interactions

   c. Gives you relative significance of the factors

   d. All of the above

17. Given three factors, A, B, and C, the highest-order interaction would be ABC.

   a. True

   b. False

18. In a four-factor 1/2 fractionated design, the AB interaction is confounded with the CD interaction.

   a. True

   b. False

19. What does it mean when A is confounded with BC?

   a. A is contributing to the result.

   b. BC is contributing to the result.

   c. The computed coefficients are related to the sum of the two individual effects.

   d. The sums of squares are related to the sum of the two individual effects.

20. In a resolution IV design, two-factor interactions are aliased with three-factor interactions.

    a. True

    b. False

21. In a resolution III design, single factors are not aliased with any other factors.

    a. True

    b. False

22. The identity expression I + ABCD is used to generate the confounding pattern.

    a. True

    b. False

23. Why are resolution V designs preferred over resolution III and resolution IV designs?

    a. No main effect is confounded with any other main effect or second-order interactions.

    b. No second-order interactions are confounded with any other second-order interaction, and second-order interactions are confounded with third-order interactions.

    c. Allows for the differentiation of the effects down to the second order, assuming that the effects of third-=order interactions are negligible.

    d. All of the above.

24. Why should you do a hypothesis test before running a DOE?

    a. Statistically test for the correct factors

    b. Find the trivial many

    c. To ensure that your measurement system is good

    d. To ensure that you have all the process steps identified

    e. To identify as many the vital few factors prior to DOE

25. What is the mission of the Improve phase?

    a. Find the relationships between X and Y

    b. Validate hypothesis tests

    c. Which inputs to control in the next phase

    d. Run a pilot to validate experiment

    e. All of the above

26. Can you calculate epsilon-square percent contribution for the DOE given that the degree of freedom for each factor is different in the ANOVA?

    a. Yes

    b. No

11

CONTROL PHASE

PURPOSES OF THE CONTROL PHASE

As the project team went through the first four phases of the DMAIC process, it picked a project, measured where it was in the project, identified the vital few X's that caused the defects, and defined the relationship for the CTQ or Y of the project and the vital few X's. Now it *must* control the X's to ensure a sustained Y—that is the sole purpose of the Control phase.

During the Improve phase, the project team tested the solution and planned for implementation. The purpose of the Control phase is to maintain the changes that the team made in the X's in the transfer function equation in order to sustain the improvements in the Y's. The team must document and monitor the process using the metrics defined earlier in DMAIC, evaluate the solution, assess the capability of the process over time, establish control systems to ensure that the solution works for the long term, standardize procedures, hand over the process to the process owners, and then calculate and document the gains.

The objective of the Control phase is to establish the required action plan that reflects the finding from the Improve phase and to drive controls to sustain the improved performance. The team must ensure that the new process conditions are documented and then monitored via statistical process control methods. After a "settling in" period, the process capability should be reassessed. Depending upon the outcomes of such a follow-on analysis, it might be necessary to revisit one or more of the preceding phases.

CONTROL PHASE STEPS

Figure 11-1 shows the steps of the Control phase.

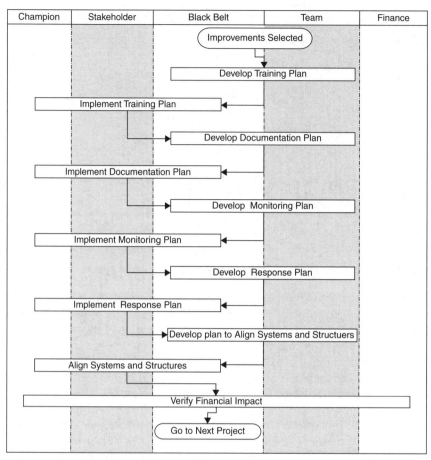

FIGURE 11-1   Control phase steps

1. Process Improvements

The team assesses the results of the implementation according to the implementation plan developed in the Improve phase.

The most important thing is to ensure that the improvements have enabled the process to achieve the business goals of the project. How effective is the solution? Did the team achieve the results it expected? Do the targeted outputs of the process now meet the customers' requirements?

At this point, the team might find it necessary or wise to make minor adjustments, to tweak the process a little.

2. Stability

Is the process stable?

3. Capability

If the team verifies that the process is stable, it then can determine process capability/process sigma.

In the Control phase, the process of evaluating capability is repeated to ensure that improvement occurred. What is the most recent process yield (or sigma calculation)? Calculate and document improved process capability:

- Capability analysis (*Cpk*) study
- Confidence intervals (review)

4. Sustainability

Monitor the process for sustainability to sustain the gains, maintain the quality levels, and prevent the recurrence of problems. Validate the measuring system: In the Control phase, the process of validating the measurement system is repeated to ensure that improvement occurred.

5. Calculate, Verify, and Document the Improvement Metrics and Financial Benefits

- ROI (or CBA)
- Cost/benefit analysis
- Before and after analysis
- Verify benefits, cost savings/avoidance, profit growth

The finance department can assist in investment calculations, profits, ROI, etc.

These are the major Control phase tools used in the Control phase steps that will be covered in this chapter:

- Statistical process control (SPC)
- Mistakeproofing
- Control plans

There are many other topics in this phase, such as more DOE methods. However, the main purpose of the Control phase will be covered to ensure a deeper understanding without additional advanced topics that are not the core of the Control phase.

Control Plan

The *control plan* is one of the marquee tools of the DMAIC process. It is one of the important elements that differentiate Six Sigma projects from traditional projects.

The control plan should extend well beyond control charts. It should include procedures for process setup, monitoring, control, and troubleshooting. The plans need to be complete enough to ensure that the process owners and operators can maintain over time the gains achieved by the Six Sigma team.

The control plan is a management tool to ensure that the process changes are maintained. Control plans provide a written description of the actions that are required at each phase of the process to ensure that all process inputs and outputs will be in a state of control.

Control plans are living documents maintained and updated throughout the life cycle of a process. Updates are made as measurement and processing systems are improved. Control plans do not replace detailed operator instructions, but only describe how the process will be controlled.Control plans ensure that improvements are sustained over time and that plans are in place that will continue to identify opportunities within the process.

These are the five elements of a complete control plan:

- Training plan (as discussed below, under "Training")
- Documentation plan (as discussed below, under "Documentation")
- Monitoring plan (as discussed below, under "Monitoring")
- Response plan (as discussed below, under "Contingency Plans")
- Institutionalization plan, to align systems and structures (as discussed below, as institutionalization, under "Documentation")

The team working on the project is responsible for creating the control plan. Anyone who has a role in defining, executing, or changing the process could be involved—operators, clerks, bookkeepers, managers, MIS personnel, maintenance technicians, engineers, supervisors, etc.

The team develops the control plan using all available information from the following:

- Results from the Measure, Analyze, and Improve phases
- Lessons learned from similar products and processes
- Team's knowledge of the process
- Design FMEAs
- Design reviews

Here's an example of a control plan and the steps for completing it, as developed by the Automotive Industry Action Group (*Advanced Product Quality Planning and Control Plan Document Number, Reference Manual,* 1994, pp. 32–45):

Step 1: Indicate the appropriate category: Prototype, Pre-Launch, Production.

Step 2: Part name and description.

Step 3: List primary contact responsible for the control plan.

Step 4: Indicate ID# specified by customer.

Step 5: Enter original date.

Step 6: Date of last revision.

Step 7: List of core team members.

Step 8: Gauge R&R legend.

Step 9: Obtain customer approval (if required).

Step 10: Assign the document number.

Step 11: Document date of latest updates.

Step 12: Characteristic class and legend.

Step 13: Part/process number.

Step 14: Process description/operation.

Step 15: Identify processing equipment.

Step 16: List process output variable (Y).

Step 17: List process input variable (X).

Step 18: List numbers from FMEA.

Step 19: List product specifications/tolerance.

Step 20: List process specifications/tolerance.

Step 21: List measurement technique.

Step 22: List gauge number.

Step 23: List R&R of measurement system.

Step 24: List capability indices.

Step 25: Document sampling plan.

Step 26: Describe the control method.

Step 27: Describe reaction plan.

Step 28: List name of division, plant, department.

Step 29: Obtain necessary approvals.

See Figure 11-2.

Training

The black belt, the champion, and the master black belt should develop a training plan for the owners and operators of the process. It should include instructions for reading and interpreting control charts, guidance in understanding and using all the documentation on the improved process, and knowing the contingency response plan and how to implement it, if necessary.

Another aspect of the training is the responsibility of the champion and members of the executive team, in consultation with the master black belt: lessons learned. Each project will add to what the organization knows

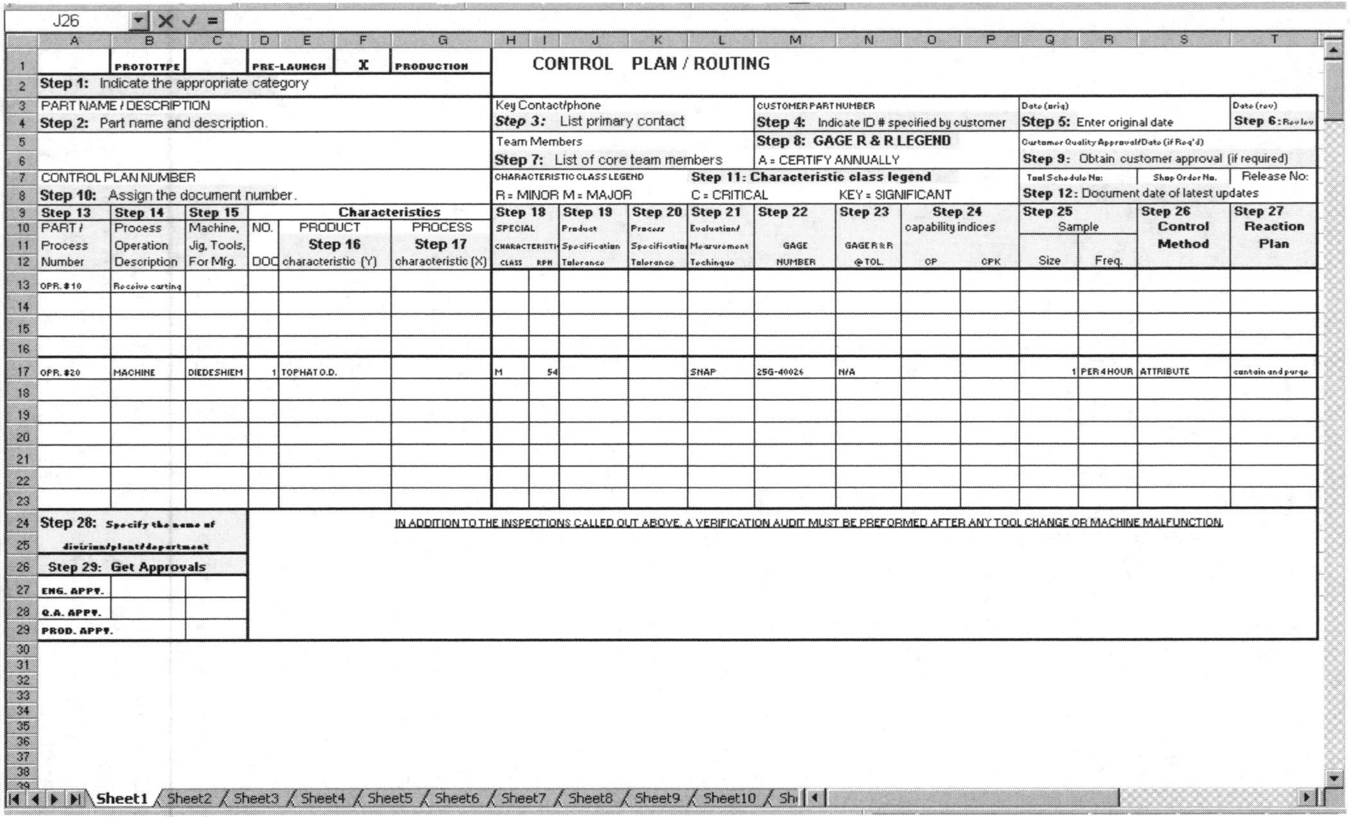

FIGURE 11-2 Control plan

about its processes and Six Sigma—but that knowledge will be power only if it's shared throughout the organization through training. This is an important part of change management, essential for transforming and maintaining an organizational culture that embraces change and improvement.

Documentation

The project team should ensure that its improvements are institutionalized—that all new process steps, standards, and documentation are integrated into normal operations and that systems, procedures, policies, instructions, and budgets are modified to sustain the gains achieved through Six Sigma.

We must stress two points here. One is the reality behind the sigma shift: process performance naturally tends to decline over the long term. The other point is expressed in this quote:

> It's not a single, great, heroic deed that defines who you really are. It's the little things you do day by day that count.

It's often easier to change a process than to change the people who are responsible for operating that process and sustaining the gains. That's why institutionalization is critical to Six Sigma—and why it's as much about psychology as about processes.

Essential to this institutionalization of improvement is that the team develop standards and procedures and that it document and communicate them to all stakeholders, particularly to the owners and operators of the process.

The documentation should include the following:

- A detailed description of the process to be controlled
- Detailed maps of the improved process
- Updated operating procedures—for both routine and unusual situations
- A list of all variables to be measured and controlled
- Description of methods, techniques, and tools to be used to obtain data
- Instructions for monitoring the process, analyzing the data, and interpreting the control charts
- Checklists
- Flowcharts

All this documentation should be developed to make it easy for the process owners and operators to understand and to use. The language should be simple and clear. Use short sentences. Illustrate with flowcharts. Provide checklists.

Effective documentation requires some of the same wisdom and ingenuity as mistake proofing: How can you remove any reasons that the owners and operators might have for not accepting and supporting the improvements in their process?

Monitoring

The project team should develop a plan for monitoring the improved process, to ensure that the process owner will be able to detect any significant changes that will reflect a degradation of performance.

The plan should be based on statistical process control, which is the heart of this chapter, centered on measuring and analyzing key process inputs and outputs. The plan should establish a "process dashboard"—the ongoing measures that matter. That dashboard should help management focus on appropriate metrics for getting information on the process and its inputs and outputs. The plan should include checkpoints: What data will be considered indicative of changes that should be investigated? It should also include, as mentioned earlier, training for any process owners and operators responsible for monitoring the process.

Statistical Process Control (SPC)

Statistical process control was developed by Walter Shewhart in 1924. SPC is very similar to hypothesis testing. It's a statistically based graphing technique that compares current process data with a set of stable control limits established from normal process variation. Those control limits are statistically based limits to detect a shift in the process in terms of the critical statistic of interest (e.g., mean, variance, etc).

The state of statistical control is considered the null hypothesis and an out-of-control situation is the alternate hypothesis. Type I and type II errors exist in control charts. (A type I or alpha error occurs when a point falls outside the control limits even though no special cause is operating. A type II or beta error occurs a special cause is missed because the chart isn't sensitive enough to detect it.)

Control performance is measured by average run length statistics, which are the average number of samples taken until the average number of samples taken before detecting a one-sigma shift. A process is in *statistical control* if there is no uncontrolled or special cause variation present. Attentive use of control charts can identify assignable causes. Control charts only detect processes that are out of control; they don't show why.

Control charts to track process statistics over time and to detect the presence of special causes. A control chart plots a process statistic, such as a subgroup mean, individual observation, weighted statistic, or number of defects, versus sample number or time.

- Center line at the average of the statistic by default

- Upper control limit, 3s above the center line by default
- Lower control limit, 3s below the center line by default

Special causes result in variation that can be detected and controlled. Examples include differences in supplier, shift, or day of the week. Common cause variation, on the other hand, is inherent in the process. A process is in control when only common causes—not special causes—affect the process output. A process is in control when points fall within the bounds of the control limits, and the points do not display any nonrandom patterns.

We should reiterate here the distinction made in Chapter 3 between the two types of variation.

Controlled or *common cause variation* occurs naturally and is inherent and expected in a stable process. This type of variation can be attributed to "chance" or random causes. *Uncontrolled* or *special cause variation* occurs when an abnormal action enters a process and produces unexpected and unpredictable results.

Control Charts

SPC refers to a group of graphical tools called control charts, which display process input or output continuous characteristics over time—with points plotted to represent statistical values of subgroup measurements (X, X-bar, R, S, etc.) through time. The charts can serve three different purposes. They are used to control the CTP (critical-to-process) characteristic; in that case, we call this *statistical process control.* They can also be used to monitor CTQ, CTC (critical-to-cost), or CTD (critical-to-delivery) characteristics; then we call it *statistical process monitoring* (SPM). Finally, they are also used as diagnostic tools for any CT characteristics.

Control charts form data into patterns that can be statistically tested and, as a result, lead to information about the behavior of product and/or process characteristics. In order to evaluate this behavior, we use historical statistics of the process such as the mean, the standard deviation, statistical control limits, and different tests of out-of-control situations. Control charts enable the project team to detect assignable causes that affect the central tendency and/or the variability of the cause system and identify when action is needed on the process. To sustain the use of SPC, the charts have to be reviewed, changes must be made as indicated (such as adjusting the sampling interval, combining charts, and eliminating charts found unnecessary), and the team or the process owners must act on the information provided by the charts.

Basic Components of a Control Chart

The vertical axis of a control chart represents the scale of statistics associated with the CT characteristic. The horizontal axis represents the numbers of the subgroup samples in chronological order.

Each subgroup is characterized by its conditional distribution, which corresponds to the short-term variation (i.e., white noise only or within-subgroup variation). Each subgroup statistic (e.g., mean, range, standard deviation) is represented by a dot in the chart; these points form a marginal distribution (i.e., black noise or between-subgroup variation). It is customary to connect the sample points on the control chart with straight line segments, to make it easier to visualize how the sequence of points evolves over time.

The control chart is divided horizontally by the centerline, representing the average of subgroup statistical values for the process. The centerline always is the average of the plotted points, regardless of what statistic is plotted on a control chart.

There are two more horizontal lines, drawn at a conventional distance of three standard deviations ($\pm 3\sigma$) from the centerline. These are the upper control limit (UCL) and the lower control limit (LCL). The control limits are set so that if the process is in control, nearly all the points (99.7 percent) will fall between them. These limits have nothing to do with specification limits; they represent the voice of the process. The CT characteristic distribution mean reflects the centering with respect to a target and standard deviation reflects its spread.

The control limits delimit three major zones. The zone between the control limits represents random variation; the two zones below and above the control limits represent nonrandom variation. With the control limits, we can judge the variation of a CT characteristic. We consider that a CT characteristic is in control when all the points fall inside the control limits and they display only random variation, i.e., no specific patterns.

Figure 11-3 shows a control chart, with the ideal distribution curve superimposed on the right, for comparison.

When we begin to create a control chart, we must wait to have at least 20 initial points to calculate the control limits, which are called *trial control limits*. They allow us to determine whether the process was in control when

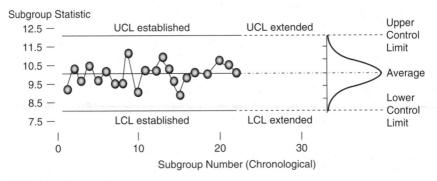

FIGURE 11-3   Control chart

the initial samples were selected. If all points fall within the control limits and no systematic behavior is evident, then we conclude that the process was in control in the past and the trial control limits are suitable for controlling current and future performance.

Once the control limits are established, they are maintained for any future samples taken from the same process, running under the same conditions. The limits are essential for evaluating whether the process remains in control and stable. As long as the new point plots are within the control limits, the process is assumed to be in control and no action is necessary. Because these control limits make it possible to distinguish between intrinsic and special cause variation, they should keep us from reacting to variation that is expected, to avoid false alarms, and when the process variation is simply random, to avoid "chasing the variation."

Generally, the effective use of any control chart will require periodic revision of the control limits and centerlines. Some practitioners set regular periodic reviews and revisions of control chart limits, such as every week, every month, or every 25, 50, or 100 samples

Out of Control

When a process is normally distributed, stable, and under control, only 0.135 percent of the points are beyond either control limit, so we expect the plotted points to be within this zone and randomly distributed. On the other hand, if a process is out of control, the control chart will show points either above the UCL or below the LCL and/or distributed systematically, in patterns. An out-of-control condition indicates that process behavior has changed significantly, so it should be investigated and a corrective action should be taken.

There are several types of patterns that indicate that a process is out of control, such as cycles, shifts, trends etc. One set of guidelines is to be found in *Statistical Quality Control Handbook,* published by Western Electric in 1956. The Western Electric rules are based on industrial experience and have been observed to work for most processes. They also have a basis in probability theory.

- At least one point is outside the three-sigma control limits.
- Two out of three consecutive points are more than two sigma away from the centerline, on the same side of the centerline (in either zone A, Figure 11-4).
- Four out of five consecutive points are more than one sigma away from the centerline, on the same side of the centerline (in either zone B, Figure 11-4).
- Eight consecutive points are on the same side of the centerline.

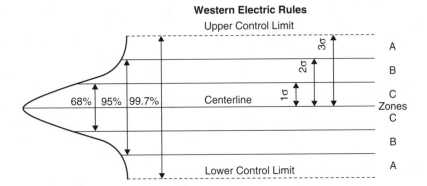

Western Electric Rules

Western Electric rules are triggered when:

- One point falls beyond zone A
- Two out of the three consecutive points fall in zone A or beyond
- Four out of five consecutive points fall in zone B or beyond
- Eight consecutive points fall on one side of the centerline

FIGURE 11-4   Control chart showing zones for interpreting Western Electric rules

The Behavior of Processes

A process behavior is the result of superimposing random variation (due only to "white noise") and variation due to special or assignable causes ("black noise"). White noise is mainly due to the level of technology in the process and is related to process entitlement—the level of performance a process should be able to achieve. Black noise is the main object of Six Sigma improvements. We must eliminate it so our processes can achieve Six Sigma performances.

The five process conditions in Figure 11-5 exhibit different problems with the mean and/or the standard deviation. However, in all cases we should strive to decrease the standard deviation (process variation) and to center the mean on the target value.

SPC must enable us to control both process centering and spread in order to sustain the improvements. To avoid any "false alarm," SPC enables the operator to know if the process is behaving "normally" (showing random variation only) or if it is exhibiting variation due to special causes.

Planning and Managing SPC and SPM

It's important to plan and manage SPC and SPM implementation. The team should consider such issues as availability of resources (money, people, etc.), time constraints, risk and confidence requirements, impact on specific parties, potential benefits to be derived, and potential for successful implementation. The general step-by-step approach for the implementation is as follows:

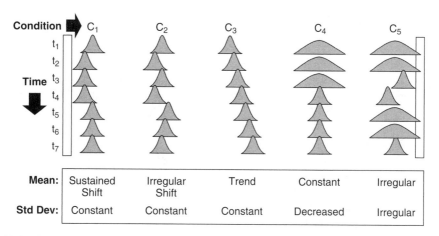

FIGURE 11-5 Process behaviors

- Define the problem.
- Establish the measurement system.
- Determine the control charts.
- Prepare for data collection.
- Implement the control charts.
- Use the control charts and continuous improvement.

When selecting control charts for practical application, the team should consider criteria such as the sample size, the desired sensitivity level for detecting small shifts in the process, and the allowable complexity level of the charts are considered.

Types of Charts

Statisticians distinguish between *attributes* data—data that fit into categories that can be described in terms of words (attributes), such as "good" or "bad" or "pass" or "fail"—and *variables* data—data that are either discrete (counted) or continuous (on a continuum, usually in decimal form). Within each of the two categories there are several types of charts often used:
Attributes Charts:

- *U chart.* Number of defects per unit. The subgroups need not be of equal size.
- *C chart.* Number of defects. The subgroups must be of equal size.
- *P chart.* Proportion of defective units. The subgroups need not be of equal size.
- *NP chart.* Number of defective units. The subgroups must be of equal size.

Variables Charts:

- *Xi–MR chart (individuals and moving-range chart).* Can be used for tracking both X and Y. The method incorporates two separate charts: The individuals chart tracks individual measurements, and the moving-range chart tracks the moving range between individual measurements.
- *X-bar–R chart (average and range chart).* Used for tracking X and/or Y. The method incorporates two separate charts: The average chart tracks the subgroup average, and the range chart tracks the range within each subgroup.
- *Precontrol chart.* Used mainly during setup to make run or no-run decisions on the production line. The output Y is the variable of interest.
- *EWMA chart (exponentially weighted moving average).* Can be used to monitor both X and Y. Used to detect small shifts and drifts in the process: WWMA is a statistic that averages data in a way that gives progressively less weight to data as they become further removed in time.

The possibilities might seem overwhelming! The control chart roadmap (Figure 11-6) should help you through any confusion.

USING CONTROL CHARTS

Here are the basic steps for using control charts:

1. Select the appropriate variable to chart. Ideally, this should be a critical X.
2. Select the type of control chart to use.
3. Determine rational subgroup size and sampling interval/frequency.
4. Determine measurement method and criteria.
5. Do a gage capability study if necessary.
6. Calculate the parameters of the control chart.
7. Gather the data.
8. Calculate the control limits.
9. Train the necessary people.
10. Implement and analyze the charts.

The following pages describe two control charts, the P chart and the *X-bar* chart, and explain how they are used.

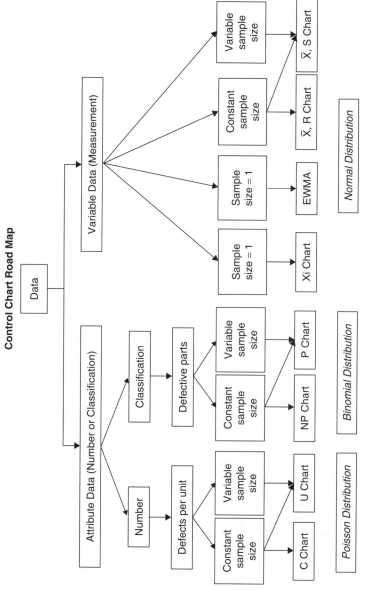

FIGURE 11-6 A Poisson distribution is a probability distribution that characterizes discrete events occurring independently of one another in time. A binomial distribution is a probability distribution for the number of times that an outcome with a constant probability will occur in a succession of repetitions of a statistical experiment.

P CHART

Figure 11-7 is an example of a *P chart*, widely used for attributes data. The purpose is to observe and evaluate the behavior of a process over time and against control limits and to take corrective action if necessary.

The P chart plots the proportion of defective units collected from subgroups of equal or unequal size. The "P" stands for *proportion* of defective units in a subgroup. (P charts differ from NP charts in that they plot the proportion of defective units rather than the number of defective units.)

Terminology

Proportion—Proportion of defective units observed, obtained by dividing the number of defective units observed in the sample by the number of units sampled.

Sample number—The chronological index number for the sample or subgroup whose proportion of defective units is being referenced.

Lower control limit (LCL)—Represents the lower limit of the variation that could be expected if the process were in a state of statistical control, by convention equal to the man minus three standard deviations. Because the sample size varies, the lower control limit is recalculated each time, resulting in a "staircase" effect.

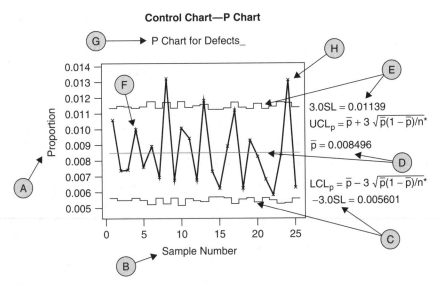

FIGURE 11-7   P chart. *Source:* Automotive Industry Action Group, *Statistical Process Control Reference Manual* (1991), pp. 91–110.

Process average proportion nonconforming (p)—Average value of the proportion of defective units in each subgroup, over the period of inspection being referenced.

Upper control limit (UCL)—Represents the upper limit of the variation that could be expected if the process were in a state of statistical control, by convention equal to the mean plus three standard deviations. Because the sample size varies, the upper control limit is recalculated each time, resulting in a "staircase" effect.

Plot of proportion nonconforming versus sample number—Any point in this plot above the UCL or below the LCL represents an out-of-control condition to be investigated.

Out-of-control point—By definition, any point that exceeds either the UCL or the LCL is out of control. Minitab has a number of tests available for out-of-control conditions and normally labels each point with a number corresponding to the test that the point fails. If the sample size is not constant, however, the tests are not applied.

Major Considerations

The P chart plots the proportion of units defective, not the proportion of defects. A P chart is preferred over an NP chart if using the rate of defective units is more meaningful than using the actual number of defective units and if the subgroup or sample size varies from period to period.

Large subgroup sizes should always be selected ($n > 50$ is considered normal), and the *np* value should always be greater than 5.

Application

1. Determine the purpose of the chart.
2. Select the data-collection point.
3. Establish the basis for subgrouping.
4. Establish the sampling interval and determine the sample size.
5. Set up forms for recording and charting data and write specific instructions on use of the chart.
6. Collect and record data. It is recommended that at least 20 samples be used to calculate the control limits.
7. Compute *p,* the proportion nonconforming for each of the *i* subgroups.
8. Compute the process average proportion nonconforming *p*.
9. Compute the upper control limit UCL*p*.
10. Compute the lower control limit LCL*p*.
11. Plot the data points.

$$UCL_p = \bar{p} + 3\sqrt{\bar{p}(1 - \bar{p})/n^*}$$

$$\bar{p} = (\Sigma_{i=1}^{k} (np)_i)/(\Sigma_{i=1}^{k} n_i)$$

$$LCL_p = \bar{p} - 3\sqrt{\bar{p}(1 - \bar{p})/n^*}$$

FIGURE 11-8 Equations for calculating the control limits and the centerline. Note: as the subgroup size n changes, the UCL and LCL must be recalculated for each subgroup.

12. Interpret the chart, together with other pertinent sources of information on the process, and take corrective action if necessary.
See Figure 11-8.

X-BAR CHART

Figure 11-9 is an example of an *X-bar chart,* widely used for variables data. The purpose is to observe and evaluate the behavior of a process over time and take corrective action if necessary. The *X*-bar chart plots the average values of each of a number of small sampled subgroups. The "*X*-bar" refers to the sample average value (*X*) being plotted. (An *x* with a bar or macron over it is the standard statistical symbol for "mean of all values *x*.") The *X*-bar chart is usually plotted in conjunction with the R (range) chart or the S (standard deviation) chart.

Terminology

Sample mean—The means of the process subgroups as collected in sequential, or chronological, order from the process.

Sample number—The chronological index number for the sample or subgroup whose average value is being referenced.

Lower control limit (LCL)—Line and numerical value representing the lower limit of the variation that could be expected if the process were in a state of statistical control, equal to the overall mean minus the average moving range multiplied by a conversion factor.

Process average—Overall average value of the individual process readings, over the period of inspection being referenced.

Upper control limit (UCL)—Line and numerical value representing the upper limit of the variation that could be expected if the process were in a state of statistical control, equal to the overall mean plus the average moving range multiplied by a conversion factor.

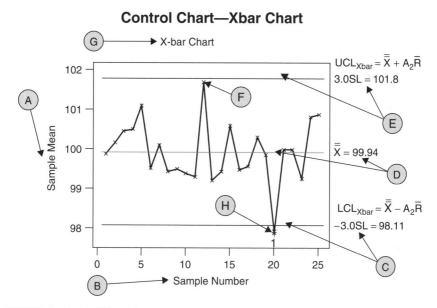

FIGURE 11-9 *X*-bar chart. *Source*: Automotive Industry Action Group, *Statistical Process Control Reference Manual* (1991), pp. 29–68.

Plot of the individual sample means versus sample number—Any excursion in this plot above the UCL or below the LCL represents an out-of-control condition and should be investigated.

Out-of-control point—By definition, any point that exceeds either the UCL or the LCL is out of control. Minitab has a number of tests available for out-of-control conditions and labels each point with a number corresponding to the test that the point fails.

Major Considerations

The *X*-bar chart, together with the R chart, is a sensitive control chart for identifying assignable causes of product and process variation and gives great insight into short-term variations.

The control limits for the *X*-bar chart differ depending on whether it is being plotted for use with the R chart or with the S chart.

Application

1. Determine the purpose of the chart.
2. Select the data-collection point.
3. Establish the basis for subgrouping.
4. Establish the sampling interval and determine sample size *n*.

5. Set up forms for recording and charting data, and write specific instructions on use of the chart.
6. Collect and record data. A minimum of 25 subgroups or samples of size n should be measured.
7. Compute the process average X.
8. If using the R chart, compute the average moving range R.
9. If using the S chart, compute the average standard deviation S.
10. Compute the upper control limit UCLX-bar.
11. Compute the lower control limit LCLX-bar.
12. Plot the data points.
13. Interpret the chart, together with other pertinent sources of information on the process, and take corrective action if necessary.

CONTINGENCY PLANS

What happens if process measures indicate an out-of-control condition? The project team should plan for that possibility, by developing, communicating, explaining, and deploying response plans. The basis for good contingency plans is any FMEA conducted during the earlier phases of the project. The results show the potential problems, the likely effects, and the best ways of handling each problem.

The team should establish the critical parameters to monitor. That might be all the variables for which there are control charts or it might be selected variables. The response plan should include a instructions on specific corrective actions to take when identified factors cause the process to go out of control. It should also include a troubleshooting guide if possible.

CONTROL CHARTS: LESSONS LEARNED

- With Six Sigma, control charts for continuous data are used for controlling CTP characteristics, monitoring CTQ, CTC, and CTD characteristics, or diagnosing any CT characteristics.
- Control charts enable us to control both process centering and variation simultaneously. They are a practical tool for detecting changes in product and/or process performance in relation to historical performance.
- The control limits are essential to evaluate whether the process remains in control and stable. The zone between the control limits represents random variation; the zone outside the limits is the area of nonrandom variation.
- The control limits are set at a distance of plus or minus three standard deviations of the centerline ($\pm 3\sigma$). The conservative nature of

these three-sigma limits is strong enough to absorb the effects of non-normality.

■ At least 20 points must be used to calculate the control limits.

■ Out-of-control conditions send a clear message that process behavior has changed, so it should be investigated and corrective action should be taken.

■ The principal types of control charts for continuous data used in Six Sigma are X-MR, X-bar–R, X-bar–S, and EWMA.

■ The success of control charts depends on the proper selection of subgroups.

■ There are several types of out-of-control conditions, such as cycles, shifts, trends, stratification, etc.

■ The Western Electric Rules can help us to detect out-of-control situations.

■ X-bar–R charts are powerful tools and the most common type of charts used.

MISTAKEPROOFING

Mistakeproofing (or *poka-yoke* as it is known in Japan) is one of several control concepts where the solution is not dynamic, as is the case with a closed loop feedback control system. It should be noted that *poka-yoke* is very consistent with the fundamental aims and philosophy of Six Sigma and widely applied in manufacturing, engineering, and transactional processes. It involves actions designed to eliminate errors, mistakes, or defects in activities and processes.

Mistakeproofing is the use of experience, wisdom, and ingenuity to remove opportunities for errors. The methodology involves complete understanding of the cause-and-effect relationship and identification of the simplest remedy that can be applied to eliminate that particular error in the future. Sometimes this involves adding a simple feature, changing the sequence of an operation, programming a software message that reminds the operator—anything to help to totally eliminate or substantially reduce mistakes.

The traditional application of mistakeproofing is in a production environment. Here are some examples:

■ A stop is added to a drill press.
■ A hydraulic ram is added to align a component during assembly.
■ A lever is designed into an assembly fixture to index the part.
■ A pin is added so the part cannot be installed backwards.

Mistakeproofing is the primary form of control for transactional procedures. Here are some examples:

- Fields on a data entry form are highlighted as being critical.
- An authorization procedure is introduced to control spending.
- A checklist is created to ensure that all items are taken into account when planning a training session.
- A new policy is developed to ensure that expense claims are completed properly.

Often, mistakeproofing focuses on errors produced by humans, whether it is the machine operator, the person filling out a form, someone packing materials, and so forth. While this source of error can be large, it is also possible to apply mistakeproofing methodology in many other aspects of our business. The emphasis should be put on modifying processes so those mistakes are impossible to make, instead of blaming employees for making mistakes.

The mistakeproofing planning sheet (Figure 11-10) provides an organized, logical tool for reducing the opportunities for errors.

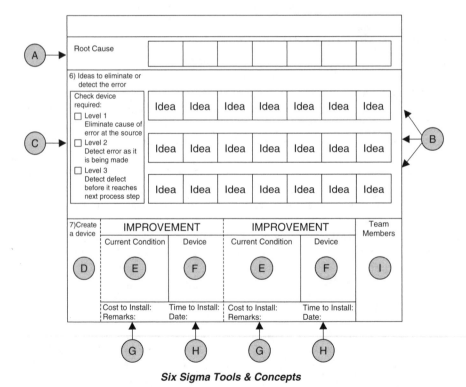

Six Sigma Tools & Concepts

FIGURE 11-10 Mistakeproofing planning sheet. *Source:* J.M. Juran and Frank M. Gryna, *Quality Planning and Analysis: From Product Development Through Use,* 4th ed. (McGraw-Hill, 1999), p. 347.

Identify the root cause of the error or defect. For each defect-producing process step, brainstorm and list ideas for ways to eliminate the errors that occur at the specific step. Indicate where in the process the defect or error should be detected or prevented—before it occurs, as it is occurring, or after it has occurred. Describe the improvement(s), devices, or methods for eliminating the defect or error. Give the cost of implementing the improvement and the length of time needed to install it. Finally, identify the team members involved in the mistakeproofing exercise.

MISTAKEPROOFING: LESSONS LEARNED

Mistakeproofing is a methodology for avoiding mistakes in any process. It can be very helpful in eliminating errors or defects when other, more analytical methods cannot be applied or do not produce results. The technique involves the use of wisdom and ingenuity to create devices that will reduce opportunities for errors. Because mistakeproofing applies in such a wide range of areas, it is possible only to provide general guidelines: There are no rules and no structure fits all situations.

An error does not necessarily cause a defect unless it escapes detection and reaches the customer. However, even errors that are caught and corrected are undesirable because they contribute to the hidden factory of activity and increase costs.

We must avoid blaming humans for defects. Most processes, even ones prone to human error, can be redesigned to be robust to operator differences, boredom, lack of experience, etc.

- Mistakeproofing does not apply just to human error; it can be applied to automated machines, computer software, or any process that contains variation.
- Mistakeproofing is the primary means of control for transactional processes, through standard operating procedures, forms, checklists, etc.
- Mistakeproofing is applied in the engineering environment by the use of FMEAs that document all possible failure modes of every component and system associated with the product.

There are many examples of mistakeproofing all around us. Many people do not realize that so much thought has gone into designing products and services to ensure that they are as user-friendly as possible.

There are various levels of control imposed by mistakeproofing. It might be possible to only announce that a mistake has been made or it might be possible to completely eliminate the possibility of making the mistake. Obviously, whenever possible, prevention is better than detection.

Mistakeproofing can be applied in the Improve and Control phases of Six Sigma with respect to DOE: Mistakeproofing can be used to control the CTPs identified through a DOE or simulation.

HAND OFF THE PROCESS

- Develop a transition plan to the functional area.
- Build a process management plan/process management chart.
- Develop a transfer plan, and hand off to process owner.
- Evolve a transfer plan to the client.
- Hand off solution to process owners/accountability and ownership.
- Hand off responsibilities to day-to-day operations staff.
- Hand off solution(s) to appropriate stakeholders. This usually takes place in a formal ceremony with the Six Sigma team, process owner(s), and stakeholders.
- Hand off solution to process owners.
- Ownership of the project is finally transferred to a *finance* partner who tracks the financial benefits for a specified period, typically 12 months.

Transfer of Ownership (Project Closure)

Transfer ownership and knowledge to process owner and process team tasked with the responsibilities.

- Who is the process owner?
- How will the day-to-day responsibilities for monitoring and continual improvement be transferred from the improvement team to the process owner?
- How will the process owner verify improvement in present and future sigma levels, process capabilities?
- Is there a recommended audit plan for routine surveillance inspections of the DMAIC project's gains?
- What is the recommended frequency of auditing?
- What should the next improvement project be that is related to the process?
- What quality tools were useful in the control phase?

Communication

Communication in the Control phase should cover four purposes:

- To describe and explain the improvements and the new process—for the process owners and operators

- To summarize the project and share all lessons learned—for other current and future champions and black belts as well as for anybody responsible for training
- To list the improvements and report on all the benefits achieved and expect, particularly financial—for management
- To spread the word about Six Sigma and the success achieved on this project—for the entire organization

The first type of communication was outlined above, under "Documentation." It's part of the control plan, essential to transferring the process back to the owners.

The second type of communication—project summary and lessons learned—should be already almost complete at this point. The project team has been documenting its activities from the start of the project and reporting on its findings at the phase-gate reviews that end each phase of the DMAIC model. Responsibility for drafting a report from the documentation maintained throughout the project could be delegated to members of the team, by phases. The black belt and the champion can then compile the reports for each phase and finalize the full report.

This report should be a comprehensive statement of what the team did and what it learned from the project. It should state each project objective and outline the steps taken in each phase toward the objectives. It should indicate where the team found defects and problems, what statistical tools it used to identify them, what corrective actions the black belt decided to take and the reasons for that decision, and the results of the action.

Each project report becomes part of the knowledge base accessible to the executive team and Six Sigma for future projects. They show how a team has proceeded, explain why, and describe the results. Make sure, as champion, that you get all lessons learned into whatever system the executive team has set up for sharing Six Sigma knowledge.

The third type of communication—reporting on the benefits, particularly financial, to management—should be relatively easy, because that's been the focus of the project from the very start, when the executive team listed and prioritized potential projects. It's even easier if the team has worked with a representative of the financial department in the Define phase, at least. At this point, the black belt and the champion should have all the facts and figures they need to prepare a report on the benefits of the project

The second and third types of communication might be combined, depending on the organization and the means of reporting and disseminating information. If the black belt and the champion prepare a report that will summarize the project, share lessons learned, and present the benefits of the project, here's some guidance, from *Six Sigma for Managers* (pp. 161–162):

> To be effective, final reports need to include certain key elements that present and quantify a given project's objectives. While each one is unique to the

problem addressed, there are seven basic sections that you need to incorporate in each report. Within each, you can get as specific as necessary about a given project in terms of how you went about measuring, analyzing, improving, and controlling the problem. These are the seven main sections to develop:

1. Executive Summary summarizing the main problem, project goals, and project results
2. Problem Statement
    2.1. Customer Requirements
    2.2. Project Objectives
    2.3. Outline of Project Strategy
    2.4. Project Schedule
    2.5. Final Project Description
3. Experimental Data (Actions Taken)
    3.1. Gauge Studies
    3.2. Materials Characterization (if appropriate)
    3.3. Process Specifications
    3.4. Capability Studies (short and long term)
    3.5. Design of Experiments
4. Implementation
    4.1. Operating Specification
    4.2. Process FMEA
    4.3. Performance Tracking Systems
    4.4. Performance Data
    4.5. Support Systems
    4.6. Control Plans
5. Conclusions
    5.1. Discussion of Results
    5.2. Lessons Learned/Recommendations
6. Team Member Listing
7. Data Storage

Each final report must address the unique concerns and conclusions—one within these main sections and their subsections. The main headings are a place to start understanding the basics of a final report. As you conduct each project, you can include the critical information that you and the project team have gathered to justify the project's goals and demonstrate how and why you reached your conclusions.

Finally, the fourth type of communication—to spread the word about Six Sigma and the success achieved on this project to the entire organization—began when the team was formed and will continue indefinitely, in various ways. When people are doing something that promises to provide significant returns, they tend to talk about it. When people are learning, when they're confronting challenges and resolving problems, they tend to talk about it. As the project champion, you should encourage the members of your team to share their experiences with their coworkers. Also, you should take advantage of any opportunities to discuss the project and Six Sigma. This is especially important when the organization is beginning its Six Sigma initiative, because successful projects should convince the skeptics and even make enthusiastic advocates out of at least some of them. They can't easily or logically argue with the financial results. As the saying goes, "Money talks and BxxxShxx walks"

Talk about what you and the team are doing and what you've accomplished—and emphasize what it could mean to the rest of the organization. What are you and the team learning that might help others? What knowledge could be leveraged elsewhere? What other areas of the organization might benefit from the ongoing improvements and the lessons you're learning? Because they're your colleagues, other managers might be interested in what you're doing—but they'll pay much better attention if they know there are benefits in it for them.

Promote your project, promote the system through which project knowledge and lessons learned can be shared, and promote Six Sigma.

Review the Project with the Champion

The black belt meets with the champion to discuss the Improve phase of the project, to prepare for the phase-gate review that will conclude this phase. These are some of the questions they might discuss:

- Did the solution achieve the project objectives?
- What are the vital few X's? What key inputs and outputs will be measured and monitored on an ongoing basis?
- What is the plan for monitoring and controlling the inputs and outputs? How will the process owners and operators be able to sustain the gains and detect for out-of-control conditions?
- Which control charts are being used? How will the control charts me checked and interpreted to monitor performance?
- What is the plan for training the process owners and operators?
- How has the team documented the improvements and the new process?
- What mistakeproofing ideas have been implemented in the process?
- Are there other areas of the organization where the improvements could be replicated? If so, how?
- What lessons have been learned that could benefit other areas of the organization?
- Are the black belt and the champion ready for the project signoff?

There are good, basic checklists and worksheets to help a team prepare for the phase-gate review in *The Six Sigma Way Team Fieldbook*, by Peter S. Pande, Robert P. Neuman, and Roland R. Cavanagh.

Conduct a Control Phase-Gate Review

The black belt holds a review at the end of the Control phase. The black belt reports to the executive team on the status of the project. The review provides the members of the executive team an opportunity to ask questions about the project and the reports submitted by the black belt and the champion.

At this final phase-gate review, the black belt and the champion finalize the project with a signoff with the controller, after a financial audit, and with the appropriate managers, as a formality of turning over ownership of the improved process.

Celebrate

Now, as the project is officially ended and the paperwork is completed, it's time to celebrate the success. It's important for Six Sigma teams to celebrate their projects. Celebrating should be part of the Six Sigma culture. When you celebrate the completion of a project, it's not just about celebrating success and financial benefits, but also about celebrating the teamwork and enthusiasm and persistence that achieved that success.

Of course, if your organization has a system for rewarding members of Six Sigma teams for their contributions, as we strongly recommended in Chapter 2, that puts a little more punch into the celebration. But whether the team members share a little in the financial benefits they've achieved or not, as the champion you should do whatever you can to make sure they receive some recognition for their work.

TYPICAL BARRIERS AND COUNTERMEASURES

Roadblocks can occur during each phase. Three specific roadblocks are most critical. Solutions rely on training; there could be problems if the control plan does not ensure the effectiveness of training in the long term. It's also possible that the process owners are willing to accept solutions but not control plan requirements to document and monitor the process. Consequently, the problem returns. Last but not least, the Control phase could end with no systems/structures in place to ensure that the process owners are accountable for the new level of process performance in the long term. There must be an owner!

CONTROL PHASE DELIVERABLES

The basic deliverables for the Control phase include the following:

- Project status form/time line
- Statement of practical solutions

- Cost-benefit analysis of potential solutions
- Justification of selected solutions
- Verification of improvement results (metrics and savings)
- Implementation plan for solutions
- Control plan:
  - Training plan
  - Documentation plan
  - Monitoring plan
  - Response plan
  - Institutionalization to align systems and structures
- Implementation of solutions and control plan
- Capability analysis
- Project summary and lessons learned
- Final report
- Phase-gate review and signoff, including verification of financial impact and transfer of ownership (project closure)

SUMMARY

In the Control phase, the team works to maintain the changes that it made in the X's in order to sustain the improvements in the Y's. The team must first develop a control plan, which consists of five basic parts: training plan, documentation plan, monitoring plan, response plan, and institutionalization plan.

With the training plan, the black belt, the champion, and the master black belt should develop a training plan for the owners and operators of the process. It should include instructions for reading and interpreting control charts, guidance in understanding and using all the documentation on the improved process, and knowing the contingency response plan and how to implement it, if necessary.

With the documentation plan, the project team should ensure that its improvements are institutionalized—that all new process steps, standards, and documentation are integrated into normal operations and that systems, procedures, policies, instructions, and budgets are modified to sustain the gains it has achieved.

With the monitoring plan, the team must document and monitor the process using the metrics defined earlier in DMAIC, evaluate the solution, assess the capability of the process over time, and establish control systems to ensure that the solution works for the long term.

With the response plan, the team establishes checkpoints that will signal out-of-control conditions and defines the actions to be taken.

With the institutionalization plan, the team tries to align systems and structures in order to ensure that the changes will continue. It develops standards and procedures and documents and communicates them to all stakeholders, particularly to the owners and operators of the process.

Finally, the team, with the controller, calculates, verifies, and documents the financial gains of the project. Then, the black belt and the champion close the Control phase and formally end the project with the final phase-gate review, handing over the process to the process owners. And, last of all, the team celebrates its success and the teamwork that made it possible.

REVIEW QUESTIONS

1. The WECO (Western Electric Company) rules are based on probability. We know that for a normal distribution, the probability of encountering a point outside $\pm2.5\sigma$ is 0.3 percent. This is a rare event. Therefore, if we observe a point outside the control limits, we conclude the process has shifted and is unstable? Answer: a, because it should be outside $\pm3\sigma$.

   a. True

   b. False

2. Outliers usually have a significant affect on an equation derived with regression analysis.

   a. True

   b. False

3. Using $Y = f(X)$, do we set tolerance limits for Y?

   a. True

   b. False

4. What is the residual?

   a. It is the equation from the data.

   b. It is the standard error of the equation.

   c. It indicates how well the equation fits.

   d. It is a calculation of the expected value minus the observed value.

   e. c and d

5. What are control charts?

   a. Design of experiment (DOE)

   b. A plot showing Y over time

   c. Charts showing average control

   d. Charts are used to routinely monitor quality

   e. None of the above

6. What does a P-chart track?

   a. Process chart showing the main factors

    b. Sample size of the process over time

    c. Simple chart used to track the number of nonconforming units, percentage of defective parts, assuming sample size is *not* necessarily constant

    d. None of the above

7. A DOE is always needed to solve process issues.

    a. True

    b. False

8. The purpose of performing a designed experiment is to determine what?

    a. The mathematical relationship $Y = F(x1, x2, x3, \ldots)$

    b. Which X's most impact Y and therefore need to be controlled

    c. The level of each X to achieve the desired mean Y

    d. The level of each X to minimize the variability of Y

    e. All of the above

9. Within the DOE, the easiest way to test for curvature is to include center points.

    a. True

    b. False

10. The most common response surface design is called the central composite design.

    a. True

    b. False

11. Control plans provide a written description of the actions that are required at each phase of the process to ensure that all process inputs and outputs will be in a state of control.

    a. True

    b. False

12. Control plans are only generated at the start of the life cycle of a product.

    a. True

    b. False

13. SPC is a statistically based graphing technique that compares current process data to a set of stable control limits established from normal process variation.

    a. True

    b. False

14. Control limits and specification limits are the same thing.

    a. True

    b. False

15. Control limits are typically set at plus or minus 2 standard deviations from the target of the control chart.

    a. True

    b. False

16. Regular residuals are the actual values of the residuals calculated by subtracting the expected value from the observed value?

    a. True

    b. False

17. What is the best description of a data transform?

    a. A transformation of the data using a power table to treat linearity in the data

    b. A transformation of the data using a power table to treat nonlinearity in the data

    c. Improves the variance within the data

    d. A transformation of the data using a power table to treat the units of the data

    e. It transforms data into a more approximate normal distribution.

18. Outliers usually have a significant affect on an equation derived with regression analysis.

    a. True

    b. False

19. When an "out of control" situation is signaled on a control chart, the person using the chart will know why the data are giving the signal.

    a. True

    b. False

20. Once the special causes of variation in a process have been discovered and eliminated, the long-term goal of anyone managing a process will be to reduce common cause variation by improving the process or system itself.

    a. True

    b. False

21. An "out of control" situation in a production process may be signaled by a sample f output, which generates a data point outside the control limits on either the *Xbar–R* range chart.

    a. True

    b. False

22. Mistakeproofing seeks to gain permanency by eliminating or rigidly controlling human intervention in a process.

a. True

b. False

23. Six Sigma product and process design or process changes made to the product or process that eliminate the error condition from occurring are called what?

    a. TQM

    b. Mistakeproofing

    c. Mistake elimination

    d. Foolproofing

    e. All of the above

24. Systems that monitor the process and automatically adjust critical X's to correct settings are called what?

    a. Full automation

    b. Process interruption

    c. Mechanism

    d. SPC

25. In order for mistakeproofing systems to operate effectively, the following rules must not be observed.

    a. The systems must be installed and properly adjusted before process startup.

    b. The systems must be periodically audited and maintained.

    c. Systems are periodically disabled.

    d. Inoperative or missing systems must be repaired or replaced before operating the process.

    e. System overrides must not be used except in an emergency.

26. The EWMA or Exponentially Weighted Moving Average chart is a variable data control chart:

    a. True

    b. False

12

SUSTAINING SIX SIGMA AND SPREADING THE SUCCESS

L
ET'S IMAGINE THAT your initial Six Sigma projects have achieved their goals and even that you're achieved process capability. Now what?

Six Sigma is dedicated to making permanent changes to realign your processes through the implementation of metrics. It enables you to know what you can expect from your people and processes. By maintaining and controlling that performance, you keep the value and purpose of your Six Sigma efforts in the forefront of all your activities, both today and into the future.

Six Sigma helps you identify what you don't know, indicates what you should know, and helps you reduce defects that cost time, money, opportunities, and customers. Will you achieve a six-sigma level of quality, only 3.4 million defects per million opportunities—99.9997 percent perfect? That's really not the question. The question is "How much are process variations and defects costing you?" If you don't have that knowledge, you don't have the power to reduce or eliminate those problems and achieve significant savings.

This chapter is about how to follow up on your first Six Sigma successes, how to build upon those results, how to keep the energy level high, and how to spread Six Sigma throughout the organization—and beyond.

CONTINUE THE CONQUESTS

As part of your Six Sigma commitment, you need to initiate new projects, find more dollars, raise your quality levels, and maintain the momentum of your initiative. While Six Sigma might be initiated from the top, it works because of the employees on the project teams. Thus, managers at all levels should be focused on this big question—"How can we keep employees energized on Six Sigma?"

To get the best return on your investment and keep customers competitive and content, you need to *move with the momentum* and *sustain the gain.* After all, you don't make the investment in Six Sigma and take the time to train people, to select projects, and then to drill down to your costs of poor quality *once.* Six Sigma is ongoing; it's a constant, "living" methodology that needs to continue as long as your business does. After all, to quote Aristotle, "We are what we repeatedly do. Excellence, then, is not an act, but a habit." Or, as an unknown philosopher has put it, "It's not a single, great, heroic deed that defines who you really are. It's the little things you do day by day that count."

It's helpful to break up the basic infrastructure required for successful Six Sigma into a two-year context. In the first year, you lay a foundation for success. In the second year, you follow up on your successful start and build on that foundation.

In the first year, you need to do the following:

- Train the best of the best for black belt projects.
- Limit dropout rates to 5 percent or less.
- Develop your ongoing project list to register projected and actual savings.
- Set up your database to capture lessons learned.
- Get green belt training under way.
- Establish your ongoing communication plan, both externally and internally.
- Break even within approximately eight months after the initial training.
- Create compensation plans and progression plans for a full two years.
- Develop a common metric and reporting/review system that evaluates and updates the status of all projects monthly.
- Begin the backlog of projects and actively manage the reviews.
- Establish process metrics and set baseline data into strategic plans for the next year.
- Discover two to four master black belts upon the completion of training.

In the second year, you need to do the following:

- Transition all training from your outside consultant to your own resources.
- Have your internal master black belts train black belts.

- Promote training such that 10 percent of the people in your organization become green belts.
- Increase dollar savings by 300 percent over the first year's targets.
- Engage your key suppliers in the Six Sigma methodology.
- Build Six Sigma goals into companywide strategic plans.
- Hold quarterly reviews with senior management.
- Host certification events that reward and recognize black belt achievements.
- Develop compensation/incentive plans, not just for black belts and team members, but also for upper managers, to ensure continued support.
- Get each black belt to work on four to six projects a year.
- Promote at least some of your black belts.
- Create a "pull" system for the Six Sigma initiative. Publicize the benefits so widely that there's more interest in becoming black belt than space in your classes.
- Determine the next year's goals in the number of black belts, green belts, master black belts, project selection, and savings projections.

As you make progress with Six Sigma, all of these elements will become routine and obvious aspects of the overall scope. However, this is where it's most important to recognize that there's no room for complacency or easing off on Six Sigma projects—sustaining their gains is critical to the continual success of your initiative. All of the items listed point in one direction: Keep it focused, keep it moving forward, and keep it in the forefront of everything you do.

Lessons Learned

It's possible to contribute to sustaining the gains obtained through Six Sigma by knowledge transfer. An organization's prosperity depends on being able to learn at a faster rate than its competitors and to transfer and apply that learning to its operations to sustain its competitive advantage. So it's crucial to build and maintain a database of "lessons learned."

That means documenting what you've learned and achieved with projects to date and then relying on and sharing that information. Once you've fixed something, you need to be able to share what you know about it. It's important to share the lessons far and wide, not only to tout your success, but also to address similar issues elsewhere in the organization. There's not much value in eliminating defects and keeping it to yourself—knowledge transfer needs to happen continually, both inside and outside of the project at hand.

It's important to provide coaching and training to ensure that the members of the project team transfer their knowledge to others and share information throughout the Six Sigma phases. The difficult process of managing information during Six Sigma projects can be made easier through Web-based software applications that maximize knowledge transfer and access for all members of the design project team.

Not all knowledge transfer requires technology, however. Because members of Six Sigma project team come from various areas of the organization, they can spread the word and share the knowledge more widely, taking it back home into their functions and to their coworkers. Nobody keeps success a secret. Those who have learned and applied the approach and the tools are going to be sharing them.

Communication Plan

A communication plan is essential for sharing lessons learned and sustaining your Six Sigma success. Whether it's press releases, monthly newsletters, company intranet updates, video presentations, or quarterly company meetings, you need to get the message out regularly and conspicuously to people inside and outside the organization.

You can report on the progress of projects, itemize actual dollar savings to date, explain Six Sigma acronyms, or focus in on the key tools. What's essential is to keep getting the word out on the benefits of Six Sigma.

As you know, all levels of personnel should be familiar with the basics of your Six Sigma mission, including terminology, roles, and metrics. This is to ensure that people can "link" between the big picture and actionable items in their different areas. Again, it's all about communicating, in real terms, the powerful implications of each and every project.

Keep Focused on the Customers

Continue to focus on the customers. Keep getting input, using means such as those cited in Chapter 7:

- *Customer complaints.* Encourage them and review them regularly.
- *Surveys.* Target specifically the new product or service.
- *Focus groups.* Arrange sessions to discuss the new product or service.
- One-on-one interviews.
- *Contextual inquiry.* Test the product or service with customers.

Find better ways to get input—and ways to discover the customers' latent needs and expectations.

Build Support for Six Sigma

It's essential to grow Six Sigma throughout the organization. One way is through recognition and rewards. Rewards can take the form of advancement.

For example, choose master black belt and black belt candidates from among your top performers and make Six Sigma a path to promotion for managers. Another reward to offer is a compensation plan. To cover the full scope of Six Sigma activities, create compensation plans and progression plans for a full two years. Make Six Sigma, in the words of Jack Welch, "part of the genetic code" of your organization.

Transform the Organizational Culture

Much of the success of any Six Sigma initiative will depend on the culture of the organization.

Six Sigma is more than an approach and a set of tools. It generates a cultural change within an organization. It transforms attitudes and mentalities.

You cannot change the culture of your organization by mandate. You start bringing about changes through the results of your projects. When your projects deliver results, everyone who participates in the projects or benefits from the results will appreciate the power of Six Sigma. As your organization experiences success after success, the culture will change.

Success on Six Sigma projects should convince most people in your organization of the advantages of Six Sigma for all. However, acceptance of Six Sigma, which George Eckes calls "the ignored element in implementation," might take more effort. If this is the case in your organization, you might benefit from reading his book, *Making Six Sigma Last: Managing the Balance Between Cultural and Technical Change*.

How important is organizational culture? Consider the situation at GE under Welch—commonly cited as one of the top success stories for Six Sigma.

Success did not come quickly—and it did not come from simply implementing Six Sigma. It came through preparation and initiatives that transformed thinking and attitudes.

Welch went through several stages at GE:

- In the 1980s, he focused on eliminating variety in GE's portfolio of businesses, which meant reducing the business units that were not meeting performance expectations, in a push to either be tops in every market or not compete in it.
- From the late 1980s to the mid-1990s, he focused on simplifying and eliminating activities that were not adding value, through Work-Outs and the Change Action Process, in a push to find better ways to do everything and to break down functional boundaries within the company.
- It wasn't until 1995 that he started using Six Sigma to focus on eliminating variation from business operations.

So GE was prepared, operationally and culturally, for Six Sigma.

Training for Six Sigma

When you start Six Sigma, you focus on training black belts, because they're the tactical leaders of each and every project. When you start out, the ratio of black belts to green belts is about one to three. However, by the time you start the second year, green belts generally increase to about 10 percent of your company's population.

That increase comes through training, to some extent, of course. But it also comes through expanding projects and providing opportunities to develop expertise on projects. In addition, as noted above, knowledge transfer, both structured and informal, promotes the spread of information throughout the organization. As black belts and green belts become more proficient, they reach out to train others. The exponential benefit is impressive; you must keep the momentum alive by fully recognizing and maximizing the power of this new resource by putting the black belts and green belts to work on new projects.

As you assign black belts and green belts to design projects, you will be involving other managers and employees in the Six Sigma initiative. It's natural, then, to provide green belt and black belt training to more and more employees.

You can also take this one step further by requiring that all your staff members be trained as green belts; in this way, you are assured that the majority will not only understand, but also participate in the entire Six Sigma initiative. In fact, this training in and of itself can be a project for black belts, as they take on the training responsibility for green belts in their areas.

Finally, who should be trained in Six Sigma? According to GE, every employee:

> All GE employees are trained in the strategy, statistical tools, and techniques of Six Sigma quality. People create results. Involving all employees is essential to GE's quality approach. GE is committed to providing opportunities and incentives for employees to focus their talents and energies on satisfying customers.
>
> —General Electric Web site

GE's experience and results would indicate it's worth striving for more training for employees, more black belts and green belts, and more employees on project teams.

Black Belts: Certification

At least 70 percent of your black belts should be certified in the first year of your initiative. How are they certified? By completing a minimum of two projects with financial benefits that are independently confirmed by the company controller. (You might remember that in Chapter 2 we discussed the importance of including and informing the controller's department. This becomes even more evident when you seek certification.) Black belts also undergo a tool assessment, an investigation into whether or not they're using the tools correctly. It looks at how they're interpreting the data and whether or not they're getting the maximum financial results from it.

Certification basically translates to a confirmation that your black belts are doing what they're supposed to, that they're following the DMAIC method and using the key tools to unearth defects and dollars. Black belts also need to demonstrate a complete list of backlog projects. Simple as it sounds, if you don't have a list of your backlog projects, you're going to have trouble sustaining the gain. Why? Because of the Six Sigma discipline of documenting and quantifying what you're going to work on, why you're going to work on it, and when. It's essential that this be communicated.

On top of this, you need to keep at least 75 percent of your black belts focused and working on Six Sigma projects. You want to aim for a dropout rate of no more than 5 percent and have a structured plan to replace dropouts. Given the scope of the investment in every aspect, it's critical that you maintain and grow what you've started. Your success in this area can best be measured by filling black belt training classes. Remember that Six Sigma is an ongoing process: You need to keep spreading the message and methodology throughout the organization to keep retrieving those hidden dollars.

Black Belts: Recognition

Because black belts are the primary players in a Six Sigma initiative, it makes good business sense to recognize their accomplishments formally and properly. As they meet or exceed their individual objectives, you must celebrate their successes, along with the results for the organization.

By hosting certification events, you send a clear signal that black belts and their efforts are highly valued. It's essential to do so—no matter what the individual rank, the project scope, or the dollar value realized, you must show that you appreciate their work and their successes. This recognition fosters a positive and supportive atmosphere, of course, but it also shows how seriously you take the Six Sigma initiative.

When you publicly acknowledge the successful performance of black belts and their team members, you acknowledge that the investment in Six Sigma has paid off for all parties—company and individuals. Recognition events signal the impact and relevance of Six Sigma projects and indicate just how positive and profitable they are. They certify that black belts have mastered the necessary skills required for eliminating defects in any given process.

Depending on the size of your organization and the culture, these certification events can take the form of awards, percentage bonuses, or other incentive packages. They can range from lavish and elaborate banquets to more simple incentive programs. But whatever the form of recognition, when you emphasize the results achieved, the black belt reward structure inspires others to attain black belt status. Certification events are highly motivating public relations tools that really promote each individual success.

Black Belts: Retention

In addition to rewarding your black belts, it's important to retain them, especially because what they've been doing for your organization might attract the attention of other organizations.

As an aid to retaining black belts, consider hosting certification events that reward and recognize black belt achievements. To ensure continued support, develop compensation/incentive plans that include not just black belts and team members but also upper management.

If at all possible, you want to avoid a "brain drain" of your Six Sigma personnel. Obviously, people's circumstances can change as they get promoted or leave the company. However, you can minimize the losses through recognition programs. Rewarding master black belts, black belts, and green belts can generate sustained interest and energy. Consider implementing an incentive-based compensation plan for all those involved in Six Sigma. From executives to line workers, managers to support staff, the compensation plan is a proven tool for retention.

Linking all of your recognition of Six Sigma contributors to the structure of your compensation plans gives you a powerful motivator at the employee level to sustain the gain! Rewarding master black belts, black belts, and green belts for their efforts virtually guarantees sustained interest and energy. You need to establish compensation plans to keep the skill and expertise you've invested so much to develop.

Think about it: How can you avoid a "brain drain," where you lose the entire investment in Six Sigma personnel? Obviously, there's going to be some attrition as people's circumstances change, as they get promoted or they leave the company. You can minimize the losses, however, by clearly communicating and committing to a specifically structured, incentive-based compensation plan for all those involved in Six Sigma at any level.

From executives to line workers, managers to support staff, the compensation plan is a proven tool for keeping the Six Sigma fire burning brightly in the organization. When you measure individual performance and tie bonuses to outcomes, you can be assured that your projects will continue to turn in the results you want.

THE PROBLEM WITH SUCCESS

All of the successes of Six Sigma and all of the emphasis on six-sigma levels of quality and customer satisfaction might make some managers confident about the future and complacent. After all, as you use Six Sigma to improve your products and services and processes, you should be gaining great competitive advantages, right? Absolutely! This would be a tremendous accomplishment and you need to celebrate this accomplishment. But you must not let complacency set in around the organization. That would be dangerous.

We need only think back to Chapter 3 and the 1.5 sigma shift—or, more properly, the *long-term dynamic mean variation.* This shift of the process average, the degradation from the short-term capability to the long-term performance, seems inevitable.

As we mentioned, what this means, in simple terms, is that the performance of the product, service, or process that a project team improves to meet the rigorous six-sigma level will decline over time. Small declines will likely not prevent your products from meeting a high level of acceptability, but that might generally not be good enough—especially after you've set your goal as six sigma and achieved it.

So how do you do it? How do you avoid the seemingly inevitable outcome of decreasing momentum and declining participation?

Well, the honest answer is that it's not easy. In fact, it's the hardest thing to do—even harder than learning how to use all the statistical tools! However, it's essential. No matter how difficult it might be, you must strive to keep Six Sigma alive. Otherwise, your customers will eventually feel the negative effects of its disappearance and, therefore, so will you.

SUSTAIN THE GAINS

It's crucial to keep your demonstrated entitlement—the capability of the processes that you improve through Six Sigma. For each process improved through a Six Sigma project, ask the following questions:

- What capability does your target process demonstrate in terms of your metrics?
- What are the factors affecting that capability?
- How do you keep and control that capability?

Once you know that, you can maintain the optimum and consistent performance of the process. It doesn't matter whether you're delivering goods or services, once you know what you can achieve, you can retain it for sustained productivity and profitability.

Leadership

Leadership is required to sustain the gains of Six Sigma initiatives. We all know that change generally makes people uncomfortable. CEOs should expect some resistance and more than a little anxiety when implementing

Six Sigma. If CEOs and champions do not prepare to recognize and address all of the following conditions from the beginning, any of them can impede Six Sigma initiatives:

- Senior managers are ambivalent about the initiative or even reluctant to get involved.
- Managers and employees do not understand the principles of Six Sigma.
- Senior managers, champions, and master black belts plan initiatives that are either too broad or too narrow in scope.
- Managers and employees do not participate or even cooperate with the project teams.
- Managers fail to resolve cultural issues that stand in the way of Six Sigma methods and objectives.

The move to change the culture of the organization must start at the top. The CEO must provide vision and must lead the move in such a way that all of the managers accept and embrace the business imperative as a key strategy for the organization, the way of the future. Being good is not good enough. Improvements should not lead to complacency, but to greater zeal to make more improvements.

Reinforcement and Control

It's an executive responsibility, as noted earlier, to make sure that Six Sigma becomes intrinsic to all business operations and the culture of the organization, part of the "genetic code" of the company, by inspiring and promoting a Six Sigma culture throughout the organization. It's also necessary for executive management to regularly review and oversee the entire Six Sigma initiative. This ownership from the top is important to reinforce the depth of the Six Sigma commitment and to keep senior leaders involved and engaged in the process. At least quarterly, senior executives should know and understand the progress of all current projects, the financial results achieved, and the projects ahead.

Six Sigma planning should be built into the business plan; it should be considered an integral element of any strategic planning. As goals are set, Six Sigma personnel and projects should be included as key to achieving them. Six Sigma, over time, must become part of the "genetic code" of the business, an integral part of every tactic and strategy.

Here are some ways that leaders can structure the organization to promote and sustain Six Sigma:

- Build Six Sigma goals into companywide strategic plans.
- Host quarterly reviews with senior management.

- Develop an ongoing project list that registers both projected and actual savings.
- Develop a common metric and reporting/review system that evaluates and updates the status of all projects monthly.
- Determine the next year's goals in the number of black belts, green belts, master black belts, project selection, and savings projections.

Sustainability Checklist

One way to ensure that you're sustaining Six Sigma properly is to use a "sustainability checklist." That's a methodical, clear approach to knowing whether or not you're managing to keep the fire burning.

We recommend the following 21 questions as an excellent guide to assessing the sustained performance of your Six Sigma initiative. By routinely examining and reinforcing your mission with this status check, you minimize the potential for slipping or slacking in company-wide projects. Keep asking and keep answering these fundamentally important questions and you'll keep your initiative on track:

1. Do you think the Six Sigma process is self-sustaining in your group?
2. What is the status of your master black belts?
3. What is the status of your green belts?
4. How many reviews do your senior executives attend?
5. What are the dropout rates?
6. How many projects are officially completed?
7. How many black belts are ready for certification?
8. Has the finance department been an active part of the process?
9. Have you and the finance department agreed on the guidelines that define true savings?
10. Do you currently have a manual system for tracking the backlog list of black belt projects by plant?
11. Have you identified the next set of black belts? Are the upper managers supportive?
12. Do you think you are focusing on implementing project completions?
13. Are you attempting to change the program or are you staying with the black belts' focus?
14. Should you stop doing Six Sigma?
15. What is the status report you are giving to senior managers?
16. Are the controllers signing off on your projects?
17. Are the controllers aware of the savings?
18. If you were to spot-check the controllers, what defect rate would you find? (In other words, how many do not know about the savings achieved by the projects?)

19. What database are you going to use through the life of tracking your Six Sigma projects?
20. What is the status of the black belt incentive program discussed at the beginning of the Six Sigma initiative?
21. What are the consequences for champions if they do not help and drive black belts?

All these questions are highly relevant and thought-provoking. And all your answers must be true and backed up by proof, not assumptions, to keep the momentum going.

The last question is directed at you, specifically, as a manager. You need to honestly examine whether or not you're removing barriers and supporting black belts in their efforts to achieve financial results. If you're not, then you need to take the necessary steps to do so. Remember: Black belts and project teams see you as the motivating force, the initiator of the culture change required to identify and remove defects!

Here's a real case study in using the 21-question survey, with the answers from a major automotive company eight months into the deployment of Six Sigma.

October 18, 2001

To: Corporate Director
From: Corporate Six Sigma Champion
Subject: Response to Six Sigma Self-Assessment Questions Distributed 10/12/01

Please find below the response to your six-sigma self-assessment questions that were distributed on Friday, October 12, 2001:

1. **Do you think the Six Sigma process is self-sustaining in your group?**
   No, the senior management team has recognized that the six sigma tools are not be utilized to their fullest potential and as a result are in the process of making some fundamental changes in our approach in order to be successful in achieving this in 2002.

2. **What is the status of your master black belts?**
   We are currently defining which of our Black Belt candidates should proceed forward for Master Black Belt certification. Our plan is to define a core group at each operation, supporting them with black belts and green belts in the appropriate functional areas.

3. **What is the status of the green belts?**
   We are in the process of nominating candidates and finalizing our training strategies for green belts. We have an internal review by the

champions scheduled for 10/25/01 and plan to finalize our direction by our mid November senior management review. Black Belt candidates from both our XXX and ABC facilities participated in the train the trainer session held the week of 10/9/01 by the training team.

4. How many reviews do the senior executives attend?
President has chaired quarterly reviews since the initial black belt training began in February of this year. In addition, he has reviewed the program status and barriers on a frequent basis to determine how effectively the organization is embracing and implementing these tools. The status is also reviewed monthly at the QOS reviews.

5. What are the dropout rates?
Twenty-five of 33 original Black Belt candidates are still actively involved in obtaining their certification. Four candidates were lost to attrition, with the remainder being returned to their operational activity. We are currently reviewing the competencies of all of our black belts and may choose to certify some as green belts only. Others may be certified and returned to their functional areas to execute specific cost reduction initiatives that include the use of the six-sigma tools. The remaining core group will be nominated for master black belt certification and continue to focus on initiatives that require the skills developed in training focusing on the challenging high dollar opportunities.

6. How many projects are officially completed?
None are officially closed, assuming the benchmark is sign off from Six Sigma Corporation [implementation partner]. Final reports have been submitted for 15 of the 35 projects completed to date and are under review. We have requested that SSC wait until a few additional projects are complete before they visit our facility to discuss these activities. I expect this to happen by the end of November2001.

7. How many black belts are ready for certification?
None of the black belts have completed two projects with final reports. I expect that our certifications will begin in December 2001 with the final black belts being certified in the early quarter two 2002.

8. Has the finance department been an active part of the process and do we have agreed-upon guidelines for what is true savings?
The finance activities have been an integral part of our process. The opportunity for us is to be more consistent across divisions in how we define hard and soft savings. Our CFO has recently joined the organization to focus 100 percent on the six-sigma activity to further enhance our financial analysis and focus the black belts on high potential projects. He will be assisting us in developing best practices to promote the most accurate definition of the financial benefits of a project. We will ensure this complies with the corpo-

rate guidelines you plan to share with us. Our objective is to enter 2002 documenting our savings under the best practice format.

9. **Do you currently have a manual system for tracking the backlog list of black belt projects by plant?**
Yes, Mr. Smith developed the format and it has been implemented division wide.

10. **Do we have the next black belts identified and are the GMs and management supportive?**
We are proposing to adapt a slightly different strategy based on our lessons learned from wave 1. First, we are in the process of identifying some additional candidates at our XXX facility to ensure we have a sufficient critical mass to drive the program. We expect this will consist of 3–4 people. We are proposing to proceed next with a wave of green belts, assess their skills and commitment and determine the qualified candidates to submit for Black Belt certification at the appropriate time in the future. We plan to submit this proposal to the management team in November.

11. **How do we combine DFSS into one program and get the presidents and VPs to buy in?**
I believe the strategy we discussed during our review of DFSS program on 10/4/01 is the most effective approach. Integrating the DFSS activity into our Product Development Process will clarify our commitment to the organization. PDP is already a culture and the DFSS tools clearly supplement our design tool kit. The PDP best practices review to be led by Interiors will help us do this effectively. We can then focus our training activities on understanding how to use and apply the tools. The culture of following a systemic process already exists and I do not believe we need to purchase training to reinforce it. We can focus the training on the tools, which I believe will allow us to obtain savings at a faster rate.

12. **Do you think we are focusing on cost of the contract or implementing project completions?**
I believe we are clearly focused on project completions. The issues with the contract focus on services received verses costs incurred. From our perspective, we have learned through the process that the SSC recipe was adaptable to customization for automotive applications. This is resulted in the strategic decision to develop a program that provides the best value to the organization. We also believe that SSC should be an integral part of this strategy. This is what we plan to do over the next four weeks.

13. **Are you changing the program to help you obtain a cost reduction on the contract vs. the black belt project focus?**
A cost reduction on the contract has never been discussed. As I stated above, our focus has been strategic.

14. **Should we stop doing Six Sigma?**
    Absolutely NOT, the six-sigma tools are imperative for the success of our cost reduction initiatives.

15. **What is the status report you give to the champions and the presidents?**
    We provide a detailed project list including backlog, savings, and status to the champions on a weekly basis. The GM's and Presidents see the savings status to plan in the monthly QOS review. Quarterly, we do a high level breakdown by operation for the Presidents. This shows savings to date and forecasts for a 2 year planning cycle, number of projects in the backlog, and how many have been closed. We are in the process of developing a monthly summary report for the GMs and VPs.

16. **Are the controllers signing off on the projects?**
    Yes, without exception.

17. **Are the controllers aware of the savings?**
    Absolutely; it does not get booked without their concurrence.

18. **If you were to spot check the controllers, what defect rate would you find?**
    The defect rate would be fairly significant. This relates the previous question relative to the definition of savings both hard and soft. We are addressing the definition of the transactional process in order to establish the guidelines necessary to ensure the quality of the event.

19. **What database are we going to use?**
    We have already developed a database at that integrates to a series of databases that support our overall cost reduction structure. We would like to propose that we continue to use our database and upload the appropriate information to the global database through an automated link. This would allow us to share the information with the least amount of re-work internally.

20. **Where is the status of the incentive program for the black belts that was discussed over six months ago?**
    We are 50 percent through the review process and plan to have it complete by the end of the year.

21. **What are the consequences for champions who are not getting the help and push for the black belts?**
    This is one of the fundamental reasons we are re-evaluating and re-focusing our activities. We are going to put the responsibility back in the hands of the AGMs and functional managers whose compensation is directly related to the success of their cost reduction activities.

Six Sigma is a powerful methodology. It works if it's constant and consistent and conspicuous throughout the organization. Keeping Six Sigma at the forefront keeps your tangible financial gains at the forefront too.

The proof that Six Sigma works is its financial impact on the bottom line—you can't misread the dollar savings! Sustaining Six Sigma takes commitment and leadership; you must be constantly striving to reinforce its value while introducing it further and further down the line to other employees. By making sure that your results are broadcast, that your black belt team is solid, and that your executive staff promotes the methodology, you will be well positioned to *sustain the gain*. It's about taking ownership!

Here's an example of a memo to achieve change and action due to lack of ownership and focus:

Sample Memo to Address Lack of Ownership

FAX MEMO
Thursday, October 11, 2001

To: President of an Automotive Company
Subject: Should we finish the current 1st wave of projects and then stop doing Six Sigma within the Interior Group? We have a problem that requires immediate corrective action.

May 2001 was our average completion of 6 waves of BBs. The start of the breakeven analysis for payback is now in its 4-month period (half of the 8 months prediction). I have attached a breakeven analysis with this memo. The problem with this analysis is it assumes that you will be doing only one project per black belt and stop the entire program at the end of 2001. The current direction shows that we need to decide on whether to focus on the completion of projects and stop doing Six Sigma or start making a resource commitment to the program. Every company we have worked with except for GE wanted instantaneous gratification (short term results with no long term strategy). The ABC Group is no different. I was hoping I would find another benchmark deployment, but this is not the case at the ABC Group. The champion has focused on the cost of the program (attempting to change the training system to save consultant days) rather than right business metrics and the return on the program. This deviates from a known success model. Your sister business unit is currently the benchmark and is focused on the right elements. This type of cost control is the easy part, the challenge to the leadership is to get projects identified and completed by the black belts. Your Group is not at a self-sustaining program as of yet (please refer to my internal consultant comments which is attached). The current focus of the program must stop. You should know the savings projections and actual cost savings per Black Belt. I've been very patient in trying to work and adjust our deployment models, but we are not going to deviate so as not have confidence in the outcome. Not knowing the program leads to the typical excuses of blaming the consultants, or lack of a database, or not enough projects. It is a failure on leadership's interest and commitment to the program. This "not knowing" is an active demonstration due to lack of ownership. The champions of the projects should not be allowed to wait until this "program of the month" fails for lack of participation as other initiatives in the past have done.

Leadership needs to know and track the following key metrics every 2 weeks.

1. A confirmation (controller approval) of completed projects and 100 percent backlog list of Projects by BB.
2. Obtain 70 percent Black Belt certification of the 1st wave of BBs within 1st year

Minimum Requirements for Certification

   a. Two projects completed with financial benefit confirmed.
   b. Master Black Belt approval.
   c. Tool assessment (which is built into the on-site support documentation)
3. 75 percent retention on all Black Belts.
4. A dropout rate of less than 5 percent with backfills to counteract dropout rate.
5. Their should be Green Belts plans that reflect selected Black Belts to populate GB in all business units, a minimum initial plan of 3 GB per major business unit worldwide. A project is required for each GB.

If you want instantaneous gratification (a magic cost reduction program), you will fail to sustain Six Sigma! The ABC Group doesn't calculate ROI for every employee; what if we didn't do Six Sigma, would you have been better off with your current cost savings method? Would you have done an ROI by each cost savings project by person? Would you have spent unneeded capital expenditures? You are now starting to think different, so stop asking for instantaneous gratification, stay the course and get focused on the real issues. **GET BLACK BELTS TO COMPLETE PROJECTS AND CHAMPIONS TO TAKE RESPONSIBILTIY OF GETTING BLACK BELTS TO COMPLETION. DEVELOP A REWARD SYSTEM FOR CHAMPIONS (put your money where your commitment will be).** Get the masses in the culture shift of Six Sigma by providing them green belt training ASAP. Main point: Let's get more projects completed and more BB's trained and attacking high impact projects. **STOP THE DOUBTING AND START FOCUSING!!!!!!!!!!!!!!!!!!!!!!!!!!!!!!!!!!!!!!!** The original breakeven analysis was 8 months after training and 1st project completion, so we have achieved this in 4 months!!!!!! Get behind the program and the true long term culture shift needed for managing by Measure, Analyze, Improve, and Control. The message of stopping the program is that we have no faith in our employees and believe that we should not invest in our employees as assets to the company. With stopping the program you could also save approximately $50,000US to your bottom line in addition to breakeven on the contract (that would not be a great goal, but a true failure).

SO, IS THE HYPOTHESIS ("Six Sigma was a bad investment") TRUE OR FALSE? This is the question you need to answer ASAP so we can either stop the program immediately or focus on what is needed to make the program a the repeated success it has been. We will do our part to get things back on track without changing or deviating from a known success model. If you are still interested in conducting a successful Six Sigma implementation, then we together as partners need to develop a problem statement with a corrective action a plan. The next step is conduct a one-on-one meeting with you, then meet immediately to create and implement a corrective action plan with your assigned team.

I have attached a comparison of all business units to show the basic details for your information.

Regards,

Greg Brue
President and CEO
Six Sigma Consultants

INTO EVERY AREA

To be most effective, Six Sigma should operate throughout your organization. Consultants and other experts can help with the start up, but people at every level of the organization must take ownership of Six Sigma.

It seems that people tend to think more about using Six Sigma for products than for services; similarly, they think about using Six Sigma for services more than for processes. If either of these scenarios applies to the conventional wisdom within your company, it is time to spread Six Sigma into other areas.

Any process can be represented as a set of inputs that generates a set of outputs. That process could be making a product or providing a service or connecting two areas of the organization.

Put simply, a process is a process, whatever the purpose or the function or the organization:

- Every process has inputs and outputs.
- Every process has suppliers and customers.
- Every process exhibits variation.

Because the purpose of Six Sigma is to design processes in order to make them function better, faster, and at less expense, Six Sigma can be applied to every process. That logic might seem a little idealistic to many managers—especially those who have witnessed other business ideologies pushed to extremes. Traditionally, transactional processes such as sales have benefited less than manufacturing from scientific methods. Therefore, the need for the structured and systematic methodology of Six Sigma is even greater—as is the opportunity for competitive advantages.

Consider this comment by Bob Galvin, former president and CEO of Motorola: "The lack of initial Six Sigma emphasis in the non-manufacturing areas was a mistake that cost Motorola at least $5 billion over a four-year period."

It might not be enough to achieve six sigma with your products but remain at only three or four sigma with your services. We commonly hear comments like "That company has a great product, but it's sure difficult to do business with them!"

If anybody suggests that Six Sigma is for manufacturing only, just show the following figures from the *Quality Digest* 2003 Six Sigma Survey. This is how the respondents reported that Six Sigma was used in the following functional areas of their organizations:

Manufacturing	520
Plant operations	357
Engineering	349
Customer service	311
Test/inspection	303
Administration	300
Purchasing	256
Shipping/receiving	240
Sales	207
Research/development	193
Document control	190
Pollution prevention	100

A survey by DynCorp showed the following breakdown of companies using Six Sigma:

Manufacturing companies	49.3 percent
Service companies	38.2 percent
Other companies	12.5 percent

GOING BEYOND YOUR WALLS

Organizations that are committed to improving their products and processes should involve everyone upstream and downstream in the value chain of their customers, to improve everything incorporated into their products or services. That means involving suppliers, contractors, outsource partners, and distributors.

Work with these members of the value chain to improve their products and processes. Establish a common language and standard metrics, share your expectations of quality, and help develop attitudes of excellence among all people who are linked in the value chain. If other contributors to the chain are not involved in improving quality as an extension of the Six Sigma initiatives, you cannot hope to be providing the best quality in your products and services.

Make your suppliers a part of your Six Sigma world. You want them involved in your initiative because, depending on your industry, if you're engaged in making or servicing anything, chances are good that you use their parts or processes to complete it. Obviously, they affect your defect levels and waste streams.

Basically, you want to train them and get them up to speed with Six Sigma so they can fix or eliminate defects before they reach you. You can leverage both Six Sigma standards and your supplier relationships to further effective, positive, and lasting change in this area. It's in the best interests of your top 10 suppliers to conform to your new standard of quality—not only to retain your business, but also to actually improve their own simply by embracing the core attributes of Six Sigma.

Partnering with suppliers is an excellent source of improvement and savings; by equally sharing in the techniques, tools, and dollar savings, both parties benefit tremendously. Again, it's a long-term view that yields both short- and long-term results. Look into how and where you can do the same with your primary suppliers, because it's an excellent example of how to pick low-hanging fruit.

GOING BEYOND SIX SIGMA

When a project team has achieved the goals set for its project, it establishes control measures to sustain that high level of performance. Then, the process owner should monitor performance and communicate the results. If necessary, a Six Sigma team can be formed to improve the product, service, or process, to continue the success.

Six Sigma is a methodology that needs to continue indefinitely, because there's always room for improving. And then, you can Six Sigma one big step beyond improving products and services and process—and that's the focus of the next chapter.

SUMMARY

To build on the first Six Sigma successes, it's necessary to keep the energy level high, initiate new projects, find more dollars, raise quality levels, maintain the momentum of the initiative, and spread Six Sigma throughout the organization and even beyond.

In the first year, you lay a foundation for success through training more black belts, developing the list of projects to register projected and actual savings, building the database of lessons learned, starting training green belts, continuing to communicate about Six Sigma (both externally and internally), creating compensation plans and progression plans, and developing two to four master black belts.

In the second year, you build on that success, through transition all training from the implementation partner to your own resources, making green belts out of 10 percent of the people in your organization, increasing dollar savings by 300 percent over the first year's targets, recognizing and rewarding achievements of black belts, developing compensation and incentive plans for all participants in the Six Sigma initiative, and engaging your key suppliers in Six Sigma.

It's essential to continue to focus on the customers, to keep getting input and to find better ways to discover the customers' latent needs and expectations. It's also essential to transform the culture of your organization. Six Sigma is more than an approach and a set of tools. It changes attitudes and mentalities.

All of the successes of Six Sigma might make some managers confident about the future and complacent. But it would be dangerous to let complacency set in around the organization.

Unfortunately, it's even harder to avoid a decrease in momentum and a decline in participation than to start Six Sigma.

To sustain the gains of Six Sigma initiatives requires leadership. The move to change the culture of the organization must start at the top, so that all of the managers accept and embrace the business imperative as a key strategy for the organization, the way of the future.

Six Sigma planning should be built into the business plan and considered an integral element of any strategic planning. Over time, Six Sigma must become part of the "genetic code" of the business, an integral part of every tactic and strategy.

One way to ensure that you're sustaining Six Sigma properly is to use a "sustainability checklist"—a methodical approach to assessing the sustained performance of your Six Sigma initiative. Have a clear vision of where you are and where you want to be in terms of decreasing costs and increasing bottom-line profits. Use a project-tracking system to monitor results. You can usually get one from a qualified implementation partner. Ask the hard questions like "What caused this?" and "What is this a function of?"—and then find the answers. Again, keep it under control: You want to work on the vital few factors, not the trivial many.

To be most effective, Six Sigma should operate throughout your organization. People at every level of the organization must take ownership of Six Sigma. They must apply it to products, services, and processes.

Involve every member of your value chain, upstream and downstream—suppliers, contractors, outsource partners, and distributors. Work with these members of the value chain to improve their products and processes. Partnering with suppliers is an excellent source of improvement and savings; by equally sharing in the techniques, tools, and dollar savings, both parties benefit tremendously. It's a long-term view that yields both short- and long-term results.

REVIEW QUESTIONS

1. By the end of the second year of Six Sigma, how many of the people in your organization should be trained as green belts?

    a. 5 percent

    b. 10 percent

    c. One for every black belt

    d. Anybody who wants to be a green belt

2. How many of your black belts should be certified in the first year of your initiative?

    a. 10 percent

    b. 50 percent

    c. At least 70 percent

    d. All who are found to be insane

3. How many projects should each black belt work on in a year?

    a. One or two

    b. Four to six

    c. As many as he or she wants to do

    d. All of them

4. What should be the maximum dropout rate for black belts?

    a. 1 percent

    b. 5 percent

    c. 10 percent

    d. 15 percent

5. What is a good way to recognize black belts?

    a. Special privileges, like assigned parking spaces

    b. Honorary titles

    c. Certification events

    d. Name tags

6. What's a good way to retain black belts?

    a. Flattery

    b. Compensation plans

    c. Promises of promotions

    d. Noncompete contracts

7. What is the long-term dynamic mean variation?

    a. 1.5 sigma shift

    b. Normal fluctuation in Six Sigma responsibilities

    c. An average black belt attrition rate of 5 percent

    d. Attitude changes over time

8. How can leaders promote and sustain Six Sigma?

    a. Develop an ongoing project list that registers savings.

    b. Build Six Sigma goals into companywide strategic plans.

    c. Develop a common metric and reporting/review system for projects.

    d. Both *a* and *b*

    e. Both *b* and *c*

    f. All three—*a*, *b*, and *c*

    g. None of the three—*a*, *b*, and *c*

9. Whatever the purpose or the function or the organization, the following is true.

    a. Every process has inputs and outputs.

    b. Every process has suppliers and customers.

    c. Every process exhibits variation.

    d. *a* and *b*

    e. *b* and *c*

    f. All three—*a*, *b*, and *c*

    g. None of the three—*a*, *b*, and *c*

10. Why should you work with your suppliers, contractors, outsource partners, and distributors to improve their products and processes?

    a. So they can save money through Six Sigma too

    b. So they like your organization and do more business with you

    c. So they can help your organization save more money

    d. Because it's the right thing to do

13

DESIGN FOR SIX SIGMA

YOU CAN GET THE maximum return on your Six Sigma investment by spreading it throughout your company, continuing to train employees in the Six Sigma methodology and tools to lead process improvement teams, and sustaining the gains you achieve by keeping the initiative going.

Yet there's a barrier—the point at which our efforts to improve our products and services are limited by the capability of our designs for products, services, and processes. Some call this the "5 sigma barrier" or "4.5 sigma barrier" or even "4 sigma barrier." Whatever we call it and wherever we bang against it, beyond that point the returns that we can achieve by improving our products and services and processes diminish and quality costs more than it's worth.

But there's an evolution of Six Sigma that can take companies in exciting new directions—Design for Six Sigma (DFSS).

Think about the focus of the Six Sigma DMAIC model and how we've been applying it. We have been fixing problems that exist right now. We've been dissecting and diagnosing products, services, and processes that are not performing as well as we suspect they should be performing. We're doing our best to minimize the damage and save money by removing defects with DMAIC.

Now think about this. How much could we save if our products, services, and processes were achieving six-sigma capability (only a 3.4 DPMO defect rate) from the onset? This is the reason for doing DFSS. It gives us a competitive advantage that we'd be foolish to ignore.

WHAT IS DESIGN FOR SIX SIGMA?

Design for Six Sigma is a systematic methodology for designing or redesigning products, services, or processes to meet or exceed customer requirements and expectations. Six Sigma focuses on production; DFSS starts earlier, at the beginning, in research, design, and development of products and services and the processes involved in them.

There are variations of DFSS, but they all use basically the same tools and techniques throughout the design process. Some of those tools will be familiar to you through your experiences with Six Sigma, but some are specific to DFSS. Similarly, the DFSS process, of which there are at least a half-dozen variations, is similar to the Six Sigma process of DMAIC (Define, Measure, Analyze, Improve, and Control).

Is DFSS right for your organization? To start answering that question, answer these two questions:

- How does your organization develop new products and services?
- What is the ratio of failures to successes with your products and services?

Robert G. Cooper makes some surprising points in *Winning at New Products: Accelerating the Process from Idea to Launch* (pp. 10–11), including these three:

- Between 25 and 45 percent of new products fail.
- For every seven new product ideas, only four make it to development—and then only one succeeds.
- About 45 percent of resources allocated to developing and commercializing new products go into products that are killed or fail to provide adequate financial return.

He lists the following reasons that companies gave for the failure of new products (p. 25):

- Inadequate market analysis: 24 percent
- Product problems or defects: 16 percent
- Lack of effective marketing effort: 14 percent
- Higher costs than anticipated: 10 percent
- Competitive strength or reaction: 9 percent
- Poor timing of introduction: 8 percent
- Technical or production problems: 6 percent

What's wrong with this picture? The new product cycle is definitely not operating at a six-sigma level. In fact, it's closer to the average four-sigma quality level at which many companies operate today. Plus, even as manufacturing problems are corrected by deploying Six Sigma methods, newly developed products often are the source of new problems. So, an organization practicing Six Sigma methodology and attaining a six-sigma level in various functional areas might well be far below that level in developing new products or services. It's obvious that DFSS could help companies overcome many of the problems that cause new products to fail.

Once you've mastered the essentials of Six Sigma, you might well be ready for the essentials of DFSS, to carry that improvement into the development and design of new products, services, or processes. As with Six Sigma, DFSS can be used for any types of business activities—production, assembly, transportation, retail, services, administration and support. . . . Here, as in discussing Six Sigma DMAIC, we'll refer generally to products, services, and processes for the sake of convenience. Approaches to DFSS vary in some respects, but they proceed through basically similar steps toward the same basic goals using common tools. They all fit the definition of DFSS as "a rigorous approach to designing products, services, and/or processes to reduce delivery time, development cost, increase effectiveness, and better satisfy the customers."

In terms of a basic procedure, it could be outlined as follows:

- The customer requirements are captured.
- The requirements are analyzed and prioritized.
- A design is developed.
- The requirements flow down from the system level to subsystems, components, and processes.
- The capability of the product or service and process is tracked at each step and gaps between requirements and capabilities are highlighted and made actionable.
- A control plan is established.

Ultimately, DFSS is not that different from the Six Sigma work you're undertaking. In fact, it's a natural progression to continually—and relentlessly—root out defects and route hidden dollars to the bottom line. Here are the basic differences between the Six Sigma DMAIC and DFSS:

- DMAIC is more focused on reacting, on detecting and resolving problems with current designs, while DFSS is proactive, a means of preventing problems through better designs.
- DMAIC is for products or services that the organization offers currently; DFSS is for the design of new products or services and the processes.
- Dollar benefits obtained from DMAIC can be quantified rather quickly, while the benefits from DFSS are more difficult to quantify

and tend to be much more long-term. It can take 6 to 12 months after the launch of the new product before you will obtain proper accounting on the impact of a DFSS initiative.

- DFSS involves greater cultural change than DMAIC, because for many organizations DFSS represents a huge change in roles. The DFSS team is cross-functional: It's key for the entire team to be involved in all aspects of the design process, from market research to product launch.

DESIGN FOR SIX SIGMA EXPLAINED

DFSS initiatives vary dramatically from company to company. However, they typically start with a charter (linked to the organization's strategic plan) and an assessment of customer wants and needs, pass through an identification of critical-to-quality characteristics (CTQs) into concept selection, develop a detailed design of products and processes, and finish with control plans.

One common misconception about DFSS is that it's just Six Sigma in design. The truth, simply put, is that DFSS is a complex methodology of systems engineering analysis that uses statistical methods. Also, DFSS is not a replacement for your current new product development process. If no formal process exists within your company, it could be used to guide the development process, but typically DFSS provides the tools, teamwork, and data to supplement the new product development process already in place in an organization.

DFSS is a rigorous approach to designing products, services, and processes to ensure that the products and services meet customer expectations. It also enables the organization to reduce time, improve quality, and benefit financially.

The classical or traditional approach to designing products, services, and processes generally involves several functional departments working in *series*. This approach tends to lengthen the development process and increases the opportunities for defects at each step of the process. Communication among groups has little impact on the overall design, because the process is serial and rework is the accepted norm. Each challenge must then be quickly resolved with short-term fixes, because at this point root causes are either difficult to identify or expensive to fix and are therefore not pursued.

DFSS, on the other hand, is a *parallel* (concurrent) activity and all relevant areas of the organization are represented on a cross-functional team. There's a vast psychological difference between performing a task within a functional group and performing it as a member of a cross-functional team. When people from different functional groups and with different experiences and skills work together toward goals that will affect large areas, there's a synergy that maximizes what each individual brings to the project. Furthermore, all relevant knowledge and information is made available to the teams, so they can base their decisions on data rather than on judgment, as in the traditional approach. Product and/or service designs and manufacturing and/or transactional processes can be developed together, so products or services and processes can be made optimal relative to each other.

The advantages of DFSS are numerous, whether the design is for products or services or processes:

- It provides a structure for managing development projects.
- It adds value for customers.
- It enables an organization to anticipate problems and avoid them.
- It minimizes design changes.
- It reduces development times and costs.
- It improves communication among functions, as they work together from the start of the DFSS project.

These advantages can be summed up in the following four terms: customer satisfaction, quality, time, and money.

DFSS and the Customers

Conventional design processes tend to rely on assumptions about product features and services that will sell. DFSS goes to the logical extreme, to start with the essential question—What will customers buy? It's about being the customer. You'll recognize here a concept essential to Six Sigma—the voice of the customer (VOC). (See Figures 13-1 and 13-2.)

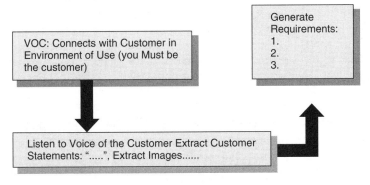

Images will provide context and insight as we develop requirements from raw customer information

VOC: Connects with Customer in Environment of Use (you Must be the customer)

Generate Requirements:
1.
2.
3.

Listen to Voice of the Customer Extract Customer Statements: ".....", Extract Images......

FIGURE 13-1   VOC

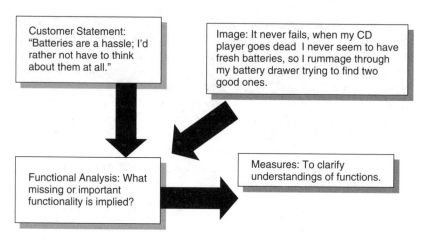

FIGURE 13-2   Example of VOC

DFSS identifies key customer needs before starting a design project and then prioritizes and translates these requirements into the design. These customer requirements (known variously as *critical-to-customer* or *critical-to-satisfaction* characteristics—*CTCs* or *CTSs*—or *critical-to-quality* characteristics—*CTQs*) are combined with cost factors (*critical-to-cost* characteristics—*CTCs*) and time factors (*critical-to-schedule* characteristics—*CTSs*), and other quality factors in making design decisions. (These characteristics are known collectively as *CTx's*.) The team can then establish specific step targets for each component and for the process.

This is a key difference between Six Sigma and DFSS. Six Sigma focuses on only one or two CTQ parameters at a time, while DFSS focuses on an entire set of CTx's for the target product, service, or process.

DFSS and Quality

DFSS improves the quality of new products and services because it focuses on determining customer requirements, expectations, and priorities from the start. This is the first type of quality, from the perspective of the customer.

It also prioritizes other quality factors in design decisions, a second type of quality, from the perspective of the organization. The project team follows these basic steps:

- It defines requirements (customer, company, and regulatory).
- It works to find creative ways to meet those requirements.
- It anticipates things that could go wrong.
- It optimizes the function of the design in terms of costs and benefits.
- It verifies that the product or service meets the requirements.

If Six Sigma defines quality as conformance to specifications, then Design for Six Sigma must establish those specifications, within the organization and even beyond, extending the expectation of Six Sigma to suppliers. (We'll discuss this aspect of DFSS toward the end of this chapter.)

DFSS and Time

For many businesses, the old axiom, "Time is money," has become "Speed is life." Companies feel more and more pressure to develop and provide products and services with greater value at lower cost in less time. DFSS allows an organization to reduce time to market—once the organization acquires some experience in applying the principles and the tools. In almost any area of business, time to develop new products and services is a critical success factor. Generally, an organization that decreases its cycle time captures a greater share of the market.

DFSS and the Bottom Line

Design for Six Sigma provides many tangible benefits to organizations. The approach results in long-term cost reductions, especially in the following areas

- Development and verification
- Manufacturing and/or transactional processes
- Service and support after the sale

When we say "long-term cost reductions," how much do we mean? It's estimated that companies performing at the current average quality level of four sigma lose 25 percent of their total revenue because of defects in processes and products.

Development and Verification
Reducing costs is a primary goal of DFSS. These costs might not be reduced, however, when first applying DFSS in the development process. While some costs will decline, others will rise because of the need to determine what the customers require or expect. But these initial costs will be recovered as the process is improved. The structured design development process focuses on getting products and services right as efficiently as possible. When there are established priorities and requirements for design and development activities, iterations and verifications are fewer, easier, and therefore less costly.

The conventional R&D approach starts from the perspective of developers and moves through designs and prototypes through iterations of building and testing. It later caused numerous design changes and wasteful rework and thus incurred losses in terms of the cost of poor quality. With DFSS, in contrast, design starts from the perspective of customers and designs are analyzed through modeling and simulation before prototypes are built and tested.

The later design errors are detected in manufacturing operations or process problems in transactional operations, the higher the cost—and the differences can be dramatic. It makes sense and saves dollars to detect problems at the earliest point and to prevent them if possible. That's the logic of Six Sigma: Reducing variations is important at any point, but the further upstream the better.

Manufacturing and/or Transactional Processes

Processes—whether manufacturing or transactional—are considered in every DFSS project. That's only logical, of course. Achieving the optimal design for a product or a service is the starting point; the project team must then work on the processes that deliver that product or service, to optimize their design as well.

This is where an organization can realize substantial savings in time and materials. By focusing on improving the design of products, services, and processes, DFSS can help reduce the time and material costs of poor quality—scrap, rework, repair, inspection, delays, customer complaints, returns, recalls, lost sales, and accounts.

Service and Support after the Sale

When you design products, services, and processes from the perspective of your customers and focus on customer CTQs, you'll have fewer problems with customer service and support.

The better the design, in terms of customer requirements, expectations, and priorities and in terms of quality, company confidence in the form of warranty terms for their product or services, the easier it is to provide service and support—maintenance, repairs, troubleshooting, and so on.

Also, because DFSS begins with the customers, employees throughout the organization are more focused on the customers, thinking more from the perspective of the customers. When employees are motivated in terms of the interests of their customers, it makes a big difference!

Even a Little Improvement at the Start

Figure 13-3 shows how DFSS in the planning stages can save in the operational stages. These rough estimates would amount to a savings of 15 percent.

Figure 13-3 shows that, although design typically represents the smallest actual cost element in products, it leverages the largest cost influence. Any incremental improvement in the design has a large direct impact on cost. For example, a 30 percent savings through design simplification would translate into over 21 percent cost savings overall, while the same 30 percent applied to labor or overhead would result in just 1.5 percent savings overall.

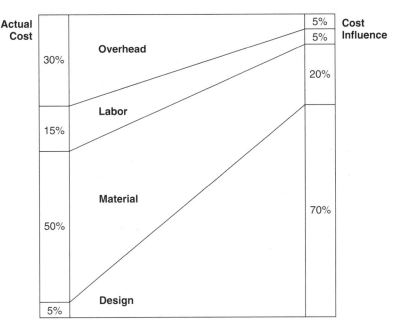

FIGURE 13-3   Impact of Design for Six Sigma in product design. *Source*: Motorola University, *Robust Design* (videotape series, 1992).

The main reason is that elemental improvement focuses on optimizing a part or process, whereas DFSS might simplify or even eliminate a part or a process. Any improvement in materials, labor, or overhead is unlikely to affect the other areas. In contrast, a simplification in design will often result in a direct reduction in material and labor cost and an indirect reduction in the cost of overhead.

Depicted simply, DFSS does not differ greatly from the generic engineering process (Figure 13-4).

However, the value of DFSS lies in the details of the approach, the attitude (focus on achieving six-sigma quality), and the tools (statistical and other).

The DFSS approach varies, of course, according to whether the design is of a product or of a process. It might also vary according to the type of product.

However a DFSS approach might be structured into phases or stages, it's important to set up a *phase-gate review,* a project review mechanism, as explained for the DMAIC model of Six Sigma. Through this mechanism, the executive team reviews and assesses the project at the end of each phase according to the plan set forth in the project charter and well-defined criteria. The managers review time lines and check key progress deliverables. They

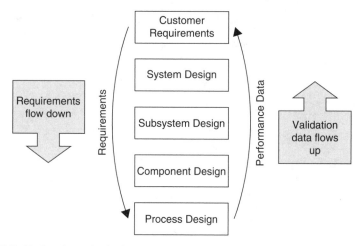

FIGURE 13-4 Generic design process

then decide whether or not the project is successful at that point and worth further expenditure of resources. DFSS adapts to the nature and needs of the organizations and differences among products and services and processes.

THE DMADV METHOD

The DFSS model is usually a five-step process, DMADV:

- *Define.* Determine the project goals and the requirements of customers (external and internal).
- *Measure.* Assess customer needs and specifications.
- *Analyze.* Examine process options to meet customer requirements.
- *Design.* Develop the process to meet the customer requirements.
- *Verify.* Check the design to ensure that it's meeting customer requirements.

However, there are also other implementation models, such as the following:

- IDOV—Identify, Design, Optimize, and Verify
- DMADOV—Design, Measure, Analyze, Design, Optimize, and Verify
- DMCDOV—Define, Measure, Characterize, Design, Optimize, and Verify
- DCOV—Define, Characterize, Optimize, and Verify
- DCCDI—Define, Customer, Concept, Design, and Implement

- DMEDI—Define, Measure, Explore, Develop, and Implement
- DMADIC—Define, Measure and Analyze, Design, Implement, and Control
- RCI—Define and Develop Requirements, Define and Develop Concepts, and Define and Develop Improvements

Design for Six Sigma is relatively new, so we can naturally expect some inconsistencies and evolution of the models as companies and consultants apply them. Even among practitioners who use the DMADV model, there are different approaches. Although we're using DMADV as the basis for our explanation of DFSS, what we say about this model applies in general to the other models.

In these five phases, you probably recognize the five phases of DMAIC, with Design being roughly like Improve and Verify being the equivalent of Control. We'll outline each of these phases. We won't get into detail for two reasons: Because the DMADV approach is similar to DMAIC and because it's just one of several models for DFSS. Also, remember that, as a champion, you are not responsible for understanding and using all of the tools outlined here: This is just an overview so you understand what the black belt, master black belt, and project team are doing.

D—DEFINE PHASE

The purpose of the Define phase is to set up the team to succeed with the project by mapping all of the vital steps, as in the Define phase of the Six Sigma DMAIC model. It entails selecting the project, providing managers to support the project, choosing people to form the team (a black belt, green belts, and others), conducting training, establishing a project charter and objectives, setting metrics and a goal, and establishing a time line.

Procedure

Select the project. It should be a highly visible development project. The selection might be made based on any of the following: customer comments, customer surveys, input from within the organization (e.g. from R&D, sales, marketing), benchmarking, and multigeneration planning (MGP).

Establish the goal.

Plan the project. Every project should have a well-defined implementation plan with responsibilities, timetables, milestones, and deliverables. The team schedules phase-gate reviews for the end of each phase of the DFSS process.

Plan and schedule the project. Every project should have a well-defined implementation plan with responsibilities, timetables, milestones, and deliverables. The team schedules phase-gate reviews for the end of each phase of the DMADV model.

Establish the project charter. As you know from Chapter 7, this is a key step in Six Sigma methodology; the project charter formalizes the DFSS initiative, captures the vision of the project, conveys enthusiasm, sets direction for the project team, and defines the parameters of the project.

Establish the project objectives. As in the Define phase of DMAIC, this step consists essentially of three parts:

- *Define the metrics.* The metrics provide a measurable, quantitative scale for assessing performance. They answer the question, How do we assess our progress?
- *Collect baseline data.* The baseline defines a starting point, based on the competition, similar products or services, etc. It answers the question, Where are we beginning?
- *Set the improvement goal.* The goal defines an improvement target. It answers the question, Where do we plan to get? This is based on entitlement, the theoretical maximum performance possible.

The project metrics should represent the voice of the customer and internal metrics selected by the organization, they should be simple and vital to the design, they should be in terms that all team members understand, and they should be connected to key business metrics.

Establish the time line. This should include major milestones.

Develop the strategic plan. The project team elaborates the plan put in place earlier by the executive team.

Select the champion or sponsor. The champion should be an upper-level manager who is responsible for the area of the project and able to handle the responsibilities of a champion part-time. Those responsibilities for a DFSS project are generally the same as for a Six Sigma project: A strong champion is vital to the success of any project.

Select the black belt. As for any Six Sigma project, a black belt appointed to lead a DFSS project should have a strong desire to do things differently and better, to be change agent. She should have outstanding people skills, communication skills, and facilitation skills.

Select green belts and team members. A DFSS project team is cross-functional: It's key for the team to include members who are involved in all aspects of the design process, from beginning to end. Choose open-minded, highly skilled people from all areas affected by the DFSS project, such as marketing, design, manufacturing, quality assurance, and vendor development. The team should represent all of the key functions that contribute to developing and testing the design and then working with the product, service, or process. The members must have functional expertise and knowledge relevant and sufficient to the project. Each member has specific duties and responsibilities. Some team members will work on the project from beginning to end; others will contribute only during certain phases.

Team members must be willing to try something new. They must understand that the DFSS initiative will require things of them that are very different.

Conduct "just-in-time" training and provide an attendance matrix. Team members should be learning only the techniques and tools they need to be applying for the project. The matrix shows which team members should attend which training sessions. For instance, the people involved in market requirements will need to attend the training sessions on VOC activities but not the sessions on tools such as FMEA or control planning.

Name the project. Be specific. Also, focus on the product, service, or process, not the people responsible.

Delimit the process. Identify the starting point and the ending point and the steps between the start and the end. As in DMAIC Six Sigma, the scope should be narrow enough to allow the team to focus and to achieve results within six months or so and broad enough to make a significant difference. If the project is too large, it can be split into phases, to be undertaken successively. This is the multi-generational approach.

Define the customers. The team might create a SIPOC (supplier-input-process-output-customer) map for the product or service to help identify and even prioritize customers. The team considers internal customers as well as external. The team might use a prioritization matrix to distinguish among the customers.

Identify and understand the customer requirements. Understanding the needs of the customer for a particular market segment is critical to success. You must get it right in this important first phase. However, far too often, organizations just review complaints and ask the customers what new features they would like to have added to a product or a service. That's valuable, of course, but it's not going far enough.

Focus groups and interviews can also provide valuable information about the customer, but respondents often offer feedback couched in terms of technical solutions. Customers offer technical solutions because they believe this is the best way to meet their needs or that it's the way the organization is thinking. The DFSS team must go beyond the suggestions and complaints to the underlying needs. Once it has determined those needs, it should consider all possible options. Then, if the team decides that a technical solution is best, the technical arm of the design team can determine the best technical solution.

As with Six Sigma, there are various means of capturing customer information; some capture expressed needs and others are used to discover latent needs. It's possible, in fact, to go too far, to become too zealous in seeking the voice of the customer. Long surveys, detailed instruments, and requests for personal information can easily try the patience of all but the most helpful customers. Think of the experience from your customers' perspective. With all VOC tools, remember: Choose and use judiciously.

To organize the customer inputs, the team might use an affinity diagram or a VOC table, a tool for recording information about customer needs that allows the team to capture the context of those needs to better understanding explicit and implicit customer requirements.

This tool is not only useful in recording information about customer needs in context, but it also serves as a preliminary exercise before the team builds a quality function deployment (QFD) house of quality.

For each customer statement, the team enters and demographic information and information about the use of the target product or service. The information is categorized to provide a context for analyzing the statements. The statements are then translated into requirements.

To categorize customer requirements in terms of levels of customer satisfaction, the Kano model is useful. This is a quadrant in which each customer requirement for a product or a service is placed in one of three classes: basic requirements or dissatisfiers, variable requirements or satisfiers, and excitement attributes or latent attributes or delighters. This simple method was devised by quality expert Noriaki Kano.

Finally, the team might benchmark comparable products, services, or processes, in order to help to create possible customer requirements. This can be a good way to challenge and inspire the team. However, benchmarking is usually less important in DFSS than in Six Sigma DMAIC. In fact, sometimes comparisons—even with the best—can hinder creativity.

Define and revise customer requirements. The team analyzes customer feedback and marketing data, as in the Define phase of Six Sigma DMAIC.

Prioritize customer requirements. The team quantifies and ranks benefits to the customers, using such tools as rank ordering, sensitivity analysis, tradeoff analysis, and analytic hierarchy process to weigh the relative importance of each requirement.

The team might use the analytical hierarchy process (AHP). This is a technique that allows us to explicitly rank tangible and intangible factors in order to establish priorities. First, decide on the relative importance of the criteria, comparing each against the others, one by one. Then, with some simple calculations, determine the weight to assign to each criterion: This weight will be between 0 and 1 and the total of all weights will be 1. Next, evaluate each factor by each criterion. All options are paired separately and compared in terms of relative merit or interest. These paired comparisons of factors and criteria are then subjected to matrix mathematics to assign a weight to each pair in order to prioritize them.

The team might use the house of quality method of QFD to identify factors that are critical to customer satisfaction and factors that are critical to quality, connected through complex $Y = f(X)$ transfer functions. The house is used to rank the importance of features that affect meeting the performance specifications.

The team might also use failure modes and effects analysis (FMEA), which can provide an excellent basis for classifying CTQs and other critical variables and to help the team direct resources toward the most promising opportunities. The team might supplement its use of FMEA at this point with quality function deployment to help plan preventive actions.

Establish other requirements—organizational, regulatory, environmental, and so forth.

Identify the CTQs and technical requirements, performance targets, and specification limits. The team translates customer and other requirements into critical-to-quality design parameters (CTQs) and their influence on the technical requirements (transfer functions), using analysis, quality function deployment (QFD), Design of Experiments (DOE, explained in Chapter 10), simulation, and/or modeling—representations of the relationships $[Y = f(X)]$ between customer requirements (*Y*'s) and design elements (*X*'s).

QFD uses a series of four grids to identify and translate customer needs and wants into technical requirements and measurable characteristics. The QFD cycle identifies factors critical to customer satisfaction and factors critical to quality, connected through complex $Y = f(X)$ transfer functions:

- The first matrix links customer wants and needs to technical requirements, connecting customer attributes down the left side of the matrix to design characteristics across the top.

- The second matrix links technical requirements to physical attributes, connecting design characteristics down the left side of the matrix to product characteristics across the top.
- The third matrix links product features to process design parameters, connecting product characteristics down the left side of the matrix to process operations across the top.
- The fourth matrix links process design parameters to requirements, connecting process operations down the left side of the matrix to a quality control plan or quality controls across the top.

To translate customer CTQs into requirements, QFD might seems unnecessarily complicated. The team might find it sufficient to use only the first matrix, to link customer wants and needs to technical requirements.

Prioritize the CTQs. The team uses QFD and FMEA to prioritize critical-to-quality features.

Document the CTQs in formal specifications. The team identifies technical requirements, performance targets, and specification limits. It sets a target and a range of acceptability for each CTQ, using benchmarking and competitive analysis. It might also decide to establish performance baselines, if designing a replacement or redesigning, in order to understand the current design well enough to ensure that it will achieve significant results by focusing on what matters to the customers, not the current design.

Benchmarking can be useful in DFSS, but it can also cause problems. It's worth studying best practices for the Define and Measure phases, but it might not help in actually developing designs. In fact, sometimes comparison—seven with the best— can hinder creativity.

Establish CTQ metrics. The team establishes ways to measure to what extent the product or service design meets the specifications, just as in the Measure phase of Six Sigma.

Create the scorecards. Throughout the project, the team uses scorecards to record design requirements, capture information, estimate performance, track results, and make any gaps obvious and actionable. The scorecards are updated at the end of each phase. Figure 13-5 shows an example of a scorecard at a subsystem level, showing the baseline and the goal in defects per million and the gap).

Populate the DFSS scorecard. At this point, the team records CTQs on the project scorecard. Scorecards typically contain CTQs, specification, process capability data, process capability calculation, and flags (for any processes for which process capability might be inadequate).

ID	Quan	Item	Sub-Item	BaseDPM	Improve%	GoalDPM	Got data?	Data source	DPM-lt	Color
Sys		Actuator/Driver system	Incidents	47303		19789.3			19655	Y
1	1	Help desk calls	Installation	15899	80%	3179.8	No		3179.8	Y
2	1	Help desk calls	Operation	2309	50%	1154.5	No		1154.5	Y
3	1	Help desk calls	Service	8049	50%	4024.5	No		4024.5	Y
4	1	Returns	NTF	10819	50%	5409.5	Yes	BB Project	4327.6	G
5	1	Trips to customer site		792	0%	792	Yes	Historical	792	G
6	1	Hardware failures	Driver	5608	75%	1402	Yes	Rel. Prediction	2350	R
7	1	Hardware failures	Actuator	396	0%	396	Yes	Historical	396	G
8	1	Hardware failures	Valve	2969	0%	2969	Yes	Historical	2969	G
9	1	Hardware failures	Resolver	132	0%	132	Yes	Historical	132	G
10	1	Other		330	0%	330	Yes	Historical	330	G

FIGURE 13-5 Scorecard at a subsystem level (example)

Quantify transfer functions. The team develops and refines transfer functions through means such as the following:
- Benchmarking historical transfer functions
- Performing analytical simulations
- Conducting designed experiments or tests

The team then applies transfer functions to develop the general layout and to approximate overall performance. It records the transfer functions on the project scorecard.

Establish target values and tolerances. The team does this with parameter and tolerance design, such as *empirical tolerance design* and *analytical tolerance design,* to create a robust design. Tolerance analysis is also a valuable tool: It enables quantitative estimation of the effects of variation on requirements in the early phases. Three common models of tolerance analysis in design are *worst case tolerance analysis, statistical tolerance analysis,* and *root-sum-square analysis* (a statistical method for establishing system capability based of the capability of the parts of that system). For tolerance prediction and analysis, the team can also use Monte Carlo simulation methods, a computerized model that approximates the operation of a process.

Assess process capability. The team should calculate process capability indices *Cp, Cpk,* and *Cr.* (*Cp* and *Cpk* are discussed in Chapter 3. *Cr* is a capability ratio used to represent the *estimated* spread of process output compared with the spread of the specification limits. It considers spread only and not process centering. The lower the *Cr* value, the smaller the spread.)

Assess process performance. The team should calculate process performance indices *Pp, Ppk,* and *Pr.* (*Pp* and *Ppk* are comparable to *Cp* and *Cpk. Pr* is a performance ratio used to represent the *actual* spread of the system compared with the spread of the specification limits. *Pp* and *Ppk* differ from *Cp* and *Cpk* in that *Cp* and *Cpk* are indices for the potential of the process, while *Pp* and *Ppk* are indices for the actual results from a specific batch of outputs. Like *Cr, Pr* considers spread only and not process centering. Also like *Cr,* the lower the *Pr* value, the smaller the spread.)

Do a gap analysis. The team tries to find any gaps in the processes that are negatively affecting the performance of the new design. To depict gaps, a spider diagram is practical.

A spider diagram (also known as a *gap analysis tool* or a *radar chart*) is a "graphic report card" that represents the performance of a number of aspects on one chart and shows the gaps between the current performance and the target. The team places the aspects on a circle and then evaluates the status of each in relation to the target, assigning each a rating, with 10 being the ideal, the target. Used alone, the spider diagram graphically depicts where and how much work remains to be done. If the team uses it with a relations diagram (aka interrelationship digraph), each aspect gets a score, so the team can prioritize areas to focus on improving.

Review lessons learned. Team members should plan to share and document what they learn throughout the project. A good time to do this is when the project passes through a phase-gate. The first project review is most important in this respect, because it sets a precedent for sharing information and communicating.

Map the process. Show how the process flows, list and categorize all the key process output variables (Ys) and the key process input variables (Xs), and begin understanding how the Xs generate the key process output variables (Ys).

Identify channels for process capability data. How will you know what results you're achieving? Process capability data is essential in allowing members of the team to contrast engineering requirements with process capability. (If the necessary process capability data does not exist, the team must flag this gap and make it actionable.)

Plan for communicating project information. Getting the word out to appropriate people in the organization, especially stakeholders, is important. The plan should specify who will communicate what to whom, why, how, and when.

Conduct the Define phase-gate project review.

M—MEASURE PHASE

The purpose of the Measure phase is to assess customer needs and set specifications for the product, service, or process, based on the voice of the customer. The team identifies the customer, the critical-to-quality specifications (CTQs), the technical requirements, and the quality targets.

Procedure

Conduct a measurement system analysis (MSA). This step is key to getting good process data.

Measure the product, service, or process to establish a baseline. Assess the current status to serve as a basis for comparison for evaluating the new design.

Formulate design concepts. The team uses a Pugh selection matrix to evaluate design concepts and refine and strengthen them, hybridizing as appropriate, to select a best solution concept for optimizing.

The purpose of this method is to narrow down the design concepts over time to one.

This matrix, developed by Stuart Pugh in the early 1980s, provides a structured way to choose among alternatives—and encourages teams to generate better ways to meet the criteria. The Pugh matrix—also known as *Pugh's method, controlled convergence matrix, decision-matrix method,* or simply *selection matrix*—structures comparisons of alternatives against selection criteria. The team uses the tool iteratively to arrive at an optimum choice.

Predict the sigma level of quality. It's important to distinguish between two types of quality—customer quality and production and/or delivery quality. The former consists of providing the features in products or services that will satisfy the customers and the latter is eliminating or minimizing the effect of problems in products or services that will dissatisfy the customers.

The team addresses customer quality primarily through VOC techniques and QFD. The team addresses production/delivery quality through tools such as FMEA and/or variants such as design failure modes and effects analysis (DFMEA) (for components and subsystems), process failure modes and effects analysis (PFMEA) (for manufacturing and assembly processes), and service failure modes and effects analysis (SFMEA) (for service functions).

Update the scorecards.

Conduct the Measure phase-gate project review.

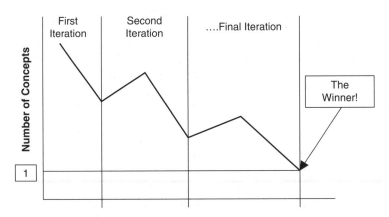

FIGURE 13-6   The next mode of evaluation is based on FMEA. Here teams will evaluate a selected design concept for potential failure modes so that they can be addressed early in the design effort.

A—ANALYZE PHASE

The purpose of the Analyze phase is to understand the product, service, or process thoroughly and to know enough about it to generate design options. The team then examines options for meeting the specifications set in the Define phase, evaluates the alternatives, and reduces the list of solutions to one, the best-fit concept.

Procedure

Use the transfer function to analyze the situation. Using the basic $Y = f(X)$ formula, the team works backwards from the Y's of the specifications established earlier to understand what X's to change and how to change them to arrive at the desired Y's.

Identify and understand X connections. The team must take into account how X's in the transfer function equation depend on external processes and people. In other words, what are the realities that surround the focus of the project? What can it change? What must it accept?

Challenge assumptions. While identifying and understanding connections might mean that the team must accept certain limitations, it should also try to remove any limitations that are based on assumptions rather than necessities.

Analyze activities in terms of adding value. Which activities are essential in terms of the specifications? Which could be eliminated with the new design?

Consider benchmarks and best practices. As mentioned earlier, benchmarking can inspire the project team or limit its creativity. At this point, the team members might benefit from studying benchmarks and best practices if they analyze not only how others do what they do but also what they do not do. This exercise can help the team challenge assumptions and eliminate activities that do not add value in terms of customer requirements and expectations.

Update the scorecards.

Conduct the Analyze phase-gate project review.

D—DESIGN PHASE

The purpose of the Design phase is to develop a new design for the product, service, or process that satisfies the requirements and achieves a balance of quality, cost, and time; to test the design to ensure that it will meet the

CTQs; to refine it as necessary; and, finally, to implement it. The steps in this phase are iterative: The team might go through the test-and-refine steps many times—and it might even implement more than one design before arriving at the best.

The team uses advanced statistical tools and modeling to predict quality level, reliability, and performance. It uses process capability information and a statistical approach to tolerancing to develop detailed design elements and optimize design and performance.

Procedure

Develop alternatives to satisfy the requirements. The team takes any concept provided for the product, service, or process earlier and develops it into a design that addresses all the key requirements.

Select the design concept. The team takes the information from the first phase of QFD and addresses potential design concepts for the various subsystems within the design. Typically, many subsystems and components can be reused or highly leveraged from previous generations of the design. For subsystems or components that will not be leveraged, the Pugh concept selection process is very useful.

DFSS teams also frequently conduct a preliminary FMEA for each design concept at this point. If designing a product, the team could also conduct a design for manufacture and assembly (DFMA) test on each alternative concept.

Move from a focus on CTQs to a focus on critical-to-process metrics (CTPs). By the end of this stage, the team will have a set of design concepts and with a set of CTPs that will constrain the formal and technical design.

Analyze the influence of the CTQs on the technical requirements. The team can use QFD I (house of quality) to translate customer CTQs into technical requirements.

The team might use any of the various tools for stimulating innovative thinking, such as brainstorming. The champion should encourage project team members to indulge in divergent thinking. Consider this comment about process redesign by Peter S. Pande, Robert P. Neuman, and Roland R. Cavanagh in *The Six Sigma Way* (p. 315):

> Envisioning, designing, and then operationalizing a new work process can be an almost schizophrenic effort. The team needs to display different "personalities" as it tries to break down accepted norms and fears, identify new workflows and procedures, and then construct a new way of doing work.

The champion should also remind the team members to challenge assumptions in developing designs as they did in the Analyze phase when working at understanding the requirements, the transfer function, and the conditions for the design. The team must focus on the required outcomes, the goals set in the Define phase.

Examine the alternatives. At this point the team members should set aside their creative hats and put on critical hats. They should focus on making each alternative as good as possible. It's natural for team members to want to move forward quickly here, but time invested in discussing alternatives now saves time testing and refining later. It's essential at this point in the Design phase to play the devil's advocate, to question answers. The champion might even need to actively discourage groupthink.

Here are two basic considerations:

- Simpler is generally better. The more steps and the more people involved in a process, the more opportunities for problems and often the more time it takes.
- Serial versus parallel. When activities in a process are sequenced successively, it's easier to coordinate, but the process takes more time. When more than one activity is happening at any point in a process, it usually saves time, but it also usually requires more attention to coordinating the activities.

Select the design. There are several techniques that a team can use to select among alternatives.

One possibility is the weighted criterion matrix, such as the project selection matrix used by the executive team, as explained in Chapter 6. The team members assign an importance to each of the requirements and then they evaluate each of the alternative designs. A team can also use the Pugh selection matrix, as explained earlier in this chapter.

The team might find that it's too difficult to select at this point. It might use one or more of the techniques below to refine the design alternatives before selecting among them.

Refine the design. There are several ways for teams to refine a design:

- They can discuss it, questioning and challenging aspects of the design, raising potential problems and offering possibilities for resolving those problems. For some designs, in some situations, and with some people, this way works well. However, there often comes a point at which the discussion is running on opinions and conjecture, not facts, so it might bog down.
- They can run simulations, to test designs virtually with computer applications and/or statistical models.

- They can conduct pilot tests—implementing a design in a limited way: on a small scale, during slow or down times, in selected sites, with certain inputs, using only some features or components, at a slower pace, and so forth.
- They can run a preliminary FMEA on the design.
- They can assess the design for X, depending upon the product or service or process and on the key requirements. There are dozens of "design for X"—DfX—methodologies (primarily for products), including design for manufacture (DfM), design for assembly (DfA), design for manufacture/manufacturing/manufacturability and assembly (DfMA), design for reliability (DfR), design for testability/testing (DfT), design for cost (DfC), design for serviceability/service (DfS), design for quality (DfQ), design for fabrication (DfF), design for disassembly (DfD), design for diagnosis (DfD), design for inspection (DfI), design for international (DfI), design for green (DfG) or for environment (DfE), design for environment, safety, and health (DfESH).

It should be mentioned here that DFSS project teams might focus on specific issues throughout the Design phase by using one or more DfX's earlier.

Identify potential failures. Perform FMEA. Use reliability data to make predictions of field failure rates. The team can also use pilot and small-scale implementations to test and evaluate performance. At this stage, testing should be to finalize the design, not to try out design ideas.

Perform risk analysis. The team uses FMEA to reduce the possibilities that things that could go wrong.

Take corrective action to mitigate or prevent those failures. The team might consider means of error proofing, such as *poka-yoke,* the first step in mistakeproofing.

Perform risk analysis. The team uses FMEA to reduce the possibilities that things that could go wrong.

Develop a robust design. The focus of the design process is to create a design that is robust, that can perform acceptably despite variations in design parameters, operating parameters, and processes. The team works to make the processes capable of meeting the design requirements, especially with critical design parameters and CTQs. It uses Design of Experiments (DOE) or Taguchi methods (a methodology based on DOE) to optimize parameter values and reduce variation. Optimization studies are performed to minimize the sensitivity of performance to CTQ design features and identify the processes most in need of improved capability.

Apply response surface methodology (RSM). Critical in optimizing process or product performance, RSM is usually applied following a set of designed experiments intended to screen out the unimportant factors. The primary purpose of RSM is to find the optimum settings for the factors that influence the response.

This statistical technique uses response surfaces to analyze quantitative data from experiments to determine and simultaneously solve multivariant equations. (A response surface is a surface that represents predicted responses to variations in factors. Depending on the number of factors, the surface can have any number of dimensions.) RSM allows the project team to predict the results of experiments without performing them.

Response surface methods can be used to answer a number of different questions:

1. How do a set of variables affect a particular response over a specified region?
2. What settings of the variables will result in a product or process that meets specifications?
3. What settings of the variables will yield a maximum (or minimum) response and what is the local geography of the response surface(s) near these maximal (minimal) values?

Apply evolutionary operations (EVOP), if appropriate. This is a continuous improvement process for optimizing the operating conditions of a process. EVOP consists of systematically making small changes in the levels of the process variables being investigated, changes small enough to minimize the risk of serious disturbances in yield, quality, or critical product characteristics, yet large enough to reveal potential improvements in performance.

Perform an engineering analysis and select materials. If it's a product that the team is designing, it can use engineering analysis such as simulation and then computer programs for material selection. It can then do preliminary work toward planning procurement and manufacturing and select equipment based on needed capability. This is especially important for products with long lead times.

Update the CTQ selection. What CTQs have emerged at the subsystem or process level?

Update capability and MSA data.

Implement the design.

Update the scorecards.

Conduct the Design phase-gate project review.

V—VERIFY PHASE

The purpose of the Verify phase is to demonstrate that the product or service satisfies the voice of the customer, to ensure that the design will meet the customer CTQs. This phase consists of testing, verifying, and validating the design, assessing performance and reliability. The team tests prototypes and the design goes through iterations as necessary.

Procedure

Validate product or service and processes. This step might include testing prototypes.

Demonstrate the process capability.

Verify tolerances.

Evaluate reliability.

Conduct an MSA. The team checks again to determine to what extent variation within the measurement process contributes to overall process variability.

Implement Statistical Process Control (SPC). Just as in Six Sigma DMAIC, the team uses statistical methods and tools—such as flow charts, run charts, Pareto charts, control charts, and process capability studies—to analyze data and monitor process capability and performance.

Define and implement the control plan. Once the design has been proven to meet the specifications of the established requirements, the team takes action to stabilize the design. It sets up a control plan, so the process owners can monitor and maintain the process.

Update and validate the scorecards.

Conduct the Verify phase-gate project review.

THE BASICS BY ANY NAME

The DFSS method—whether the DMADV approach outlined here or variants—extends the power and discipline of Six Sigma to the beginning, where it makes the most difference in terms of time and money. Now that you know the basics of DFSS, through the structure of the DMADV approach, you should be able to adapt easily to other versions—PIDOV, DMADOV, DCCDI, DMEDI, DMADIC, RCI, and so forth.

Each organization is unique and processes might vary greatly. Those responsible for DFSS projects will need to fine-tune their approach over time to make it best fit their organization.

SUSTAIN THE GAIN FROM DFSS

How can you sustain the gains achieved through DFSS? First, you continue to apply DFSS: There's always room for improving the design of products, services, and processes. Also, use Six Sigma diligently to improve the processes designed through DFSS. In other words, do what it takes to maintain the capability of the design. As mentioned in the preceding chapter, you need to guard against the long-term dynamic mean variation—the 1.5 sigma shift.

When the design of a product, a service, or a process has achieved the goals set for it, the project team establishes control measures to sustain that high level of performance. Then, the process owner should monitor performance and communicate the results. If necessary, a Six Sigma team can be formed to improve the product, service, or process, to continue the success that was built into the design.

A Process Is a Process

As stated in Chapter 12, any process can be represented as a set of inputs that generates a set of outputs. Whatever the purpose or the function or the organization, a process is a process:

- Every process has inputs and outputs.
- Every process has suppliers and customers.
- Every process exhibits variation.

Because the purpose of DFSS is to design processes in order to make them function better, faster, and at less expense, DFSS can be applied to every process.

Expanding DFSS beyond the Organization

As with DMAIC Six Sigma, you should try to involve every link in the value chain of your customers, upstream and downstream, in order to improve everything incorporated into their products or services. Work with suppliers, contractors, outsource partners, and distributors to improve their products and processes. Make them an extension of your DFSS initiative.

SUMMARY

You can maximize the return on your Six Sigma investment by expanding it through Design for Six Sigma. DFSS is a systematic methodology for designing or redesigning products, services, or processes to meet or exceed customer requirements and expectations. Whereas Six Sigma is intended to improve products, services, and processes, DFSS starts earlier, at the beginning, in research, design, and development of products and services and the processes involved in delivering them.

As with Six Sigma, DFSS can be used for any types of business activities—production, assembly, transportation, retail, services, administration and support, and so on. Approaches to DFSS vary in some respects, but they proceed through basically similar steps toward the same basic goals using common tools. They all fit the definition of DFSS as "a rigorous approach to designing products, services, and/or processes to reduce delivery time, development cost, increase effectiveness, and better satisfy the customers."

The DFSS model usually consists of five steps—Define, Measure, Analyze, Design, and Verify.

The purpose of the Define phase is to set up the team to succeed with the project by mapping all of the vital steps, as in the Define phase of the Six Sigma DMAIC model. It entails selecting the project, providing managers to support the project, choosing people to form the team (a black belt, green belts, and others), conducting training, establishing a project charter and objectives, setting metrics and a goal, and establishing a time line.

The purpose of the Measure phase is to assess customer needs and set specifications for the product, service, or process, based on the voice of the customer. The team identifies the customer, the critical-to-quality specifications (CTQs), the technical requirements, and the quality targets.

The purpose of the Analyze phase is to understand the product, service, or process thoroughly and to know enough about it to generate design options. The team then examines options for meeting the specifications set in the Define phase, evaluates the alternatives, and reduces the list of solutions to the best-fit concept.

The purpose of the Design phase is to develop a new design that satisfies the requirements and achieves a balance of quality, cost, and time; to test the design to ensure that it will meet the CTQs; to refine it as necessary; and, finally, to implement it. The team might go through the test-and-refine steps many times—and even implement more than one design before deciding on the best.

The purpose of the Verify phase is to ensure that the design will meet the customer CTQs. This phase consists of testing, verifying, and validating the design, assessing performance and reliability. The team tests prototypes and the design goes through iterations as necessary.

DFSS extends the power and discipline of Six Sigma to the beginning, where it makes the most difference in terms of time and money. Then, to sustain the gains achieved through DFSS, continue to apply DFSS to products, services, and processes and try to involve every link in the value chain of your customers by working with suppliers, contractors, outsource partners, and distributors to improve their products and processes.

REVIEW QUESTIONS

1. What are the "4 sigma barrier," the "4.5 sigma barrier," and the "5 sigma barrier"?

    a. Limitations of earlier versions of Six Sigma

    b. Points at which efforts to improve products and services are limited by the capability of the designs

    c. The progressive levels of achievement in the Measure, Analyze, and Improve phases, respectively

    d. Indications on control charts that show natural limits

2. What is Design for Six Sigma?

    a. A methodology for designing or redesigning products, services, or processes

    b. A new way to plan for a Six Sigma DMAIC initiative

    c. A master plan for marketing Six Sigma within organizations

    d. Both a and b

    e. Both b and c

    f. Both a and c

    g. None of the above

3. Design for Six Sigma is intended for the following.

    a. Manufacturers

    b. Service companies

    c. Research and development firms

    d. All companies

    e. Consultants

4. What is a CTQ flowdown?

    a. A means of getting customers to identify their critical-to-quality characteristics

    b. The passing along of critical-to-quality characteristics downstream through the value chain

    c. The diagram of a system to identify the dependencies between Y's and X's at various levels of the system

    d. None of the above

5. Which of the following is a Design for Six Sigma model?

    a. IDOV—Identify, Design, Optimize, and Verify

    b. DMADOV—Design, Measure, Analyze, Design, Optimize, and Verify

    c. DMCDOV—Define, Measure, Characterize, Design, Optimize, and Verify *d.* DCOV—Define, Characterize, Optimize, and Verify

    e. DCCDI—Define, Customer, Concept, Design, and Implement

    f. DMEDI—Define, Measure, Explore, Develop, and Implement

    g. DMADIC—Define, Measure and Analyze, Design, Implement, and Control

    h. RCI—Define and Develop Requirements, Define and Develop Concepts, and Define and Develop Improvements

    i. None of the above

    j. All of the above

6. In Design for Six Sigma, SIPOC stands for the following.

    a. Start, innovate, practice, overcome, complete

    b. Simplicity, ingenuity, patience, organization, creativity the Five Virtues.

    c. Supplier, input, process, output, customer

    d. None of the above

7. The house of quality is?

    a. A nickname for GE when Jack Welch was CEO

    b. Any organization that uses Six Sigma

    c. A tool for ranking factors that affect meeting performance specifications

    d. Jargon for a Six Sigma database

    e. None of the above

8. What are *Cp*, *Cpk*, *Cr*, *Pp*, *Ppk*, and *Pr*?

    a. Ratings assigned to a black belt for completing a DFSS project

    b. Classifications of costs and profits in DFSS

    c. Groups of characteristics that are critical or preferred

    d. Process capability indices and process performance indices

    e. None of the above

14

GROWING BEYOND SIX SIGMA

N OW YOU KNOW THE basics of Six Sigma and you're aware of the benefits, particularly the impressive financial savings possible. The purpose of this final chapter is to introduce a way of building on your Six Sigma initiative by combining it with other approaches to improving your bottom line. The additional scope of this chapter is to expose the reader to other methods of improvement, and challenge you to look at how it would accelerate the six sigma method. We present the different approaches separately and ways in which they can be integrated to result in a growth system "Beyond Six Sigma."

LEAN

Lean or lean manufacturing, according to a widely accepted definition, is "a systematic approach to identifying and eliminating waste (non-value-added activities) through continuous improvement by flowing the product at the pull of the customer in pursuit of perfection."

Charles Standard and Dale Davis offer the following definition in their book, *Running Today's Factory: A Proven Strategy for Lean Manufacturing*:

Lean manufacturing . . . is a production philosophy, a way of conceptualizing the manufacturing process from raw material to finished goods and from design concept to customer satisfaction. Lean is truly a different way of thinking about manufacturing.

The goal of lean manufacturing is to eliminate waste in every area of production—product design, production management, inventory, supplier networks, customer relations, and so on. The focus is on using less effort, less inventory, less space, less equipment, and less time to develop products in order to become more responsive to customer demand while producing better products as efficiently and economically as possible.

These are the basic principles of a lean enterprise:

- Elimination of waste
- Zero waiting time
- Zero inventory
- Just-in-time pull scheduling for materials
- Batch to flow—cut batch sizes
- Line balancing
- Short cycle times
- Quick changeover
- Make to order
- Single-piece production
- Highly flexible and responsive processes
- Highly flexible machines and equipment
- Continuous flow work cells
- Collocated machines, equipment, tools, and people
- Compressed space
- Multiskilled employees
- Empowered employees
- High first-pass yields with major reductions in defects
- Equipment reliability
- Process capability
- Continuous flow
- Material flows one part at a time
- Less inventory required throughout the production process—raw material, WIP, and finished goods
- Defect reduction
- Lead time reduction
- Error proofing
- Point-of-use storage

Lean became popular in American factories after a study by the Massachusetts Institute of Technology of the movement from mass production toward a disciplined, process-focused production. That study was described in 1990 in a book, *The Machine That Changed the World*, by James P. Womack, Daniel T. Jones, and Daniel Roos, which discusses the significant performance gap between Western and Japanese automotive industries. This

book describes the important elements accounting for superior performance as lean production.

The term "lean" was used because the emphasis in lean manufacturing
is to cut out the "fat" (waste)—anything that adds no value for the customers
or anything for which the customer is unwilling to pay.

Lean requires that we change our understanding of waste. Waste is no
longer just scrap and rework. To become truly lean and eliminate waste, we
must recognize it from the perspectives of our customers. Then we will find
many opportunities to cut waste.

These are the typical types of waste found in manufacturing systems:

Correction. Finding and reworking or repairing products. This is a big
source of waste and generally obvious. If you prevent defects, you
reduce this type of waste. You also save the time and effort of sorting
and inspecting products. Lean thinking targets inadequate process
control, poor quality, uneven inventory level, insufficient training,
poor product design, and unclear customer needs.

Overproduction. Producing more products than required by the next
process the customers or making earlier than required by the
next process or the customers. This waste is visible in the storage
of surplus products, which ties up capital and takes space. Also, if
products cannot be sold or must be discounted, the waste is obvious.
Lean thinking applies just-in-case logic, smart use of automation,
and smooth scheduling.

Inventory and Work in Process (WIP). Accumulating excess material
between operations due to producing in large lots or with long cycle
times. Excess inventory—whether in warehouses or on the floor
between processes—ties up a lot of money. Lean thinking works
at inefficiencies, product complexity, bad scheduling, unreliable
deliveries, and poor communications.

Unnecessary process steps. Doing anything that adds no value for the
customers. Lean thinking asks the same question of every step in
a process: Why is this step necessary?

Wait. Being idle between operations or while a machine is processing.
The lean principle is to maximize the efficiency of workers rather
than the use of machines. It is better for the machines to wait for
the workers than for the workers to wait for the machines. Lean
thinking scrutinizes work load, work flow, production schedules,
maintenance schedules, setup times and procedures

Transportation. Moving products or anything else during the production
process. Transportation should be minimized. It adds no value for
the customers and it can also cause damage to products, which

means more waste. Lean thinking looks at inefficient site layout and process flow and at large storage areas, big batch sizes, and long lead times.

Motion. Unnecessary, awkward, or dangerous moving of workers. A lean enterprise improves operations and locates tools and parts appropriately to minimize motion. Reducing motion reduces cycle time and stress on bodies, which can reduce injuries and worker's compensation claims. Lean thinking focuses on the efficiency of motions, appropriate workplace organization, and consistency of methods.

Underutilizing people. Not taking advantage of abilities. This waste is perhaps the least obvious, because companies and managers might be unaware of what their employees can do and therefore don't know how much they're losing by not maximizing on their potential. Lean thinking emphasizes better hiring practices, better training, higher pay, and lower turnover. It also challenges organizational politics and culture—old thinking.

Every organization has most or all of these types of waste. When you realize how much waste is in your organization, you will understand to what extent waste limits performance and profits.

Lean manufacturing eliminates waste throughout the production process, in operations within that process, and in the use of labor. Lean is a systems approach. All processes that add value for the customers must work together. Total cost is the primary performance metric. The focus is on making the entire process flow, not on improving one or more individual operations.

More about Lean

You can learn more about lean in the following books:

Feld, William M. *Lean Manufacturing: Tools, Techniques, and How to Use Them.* Boca Raton, FL: CRC Press, 2000.

Henderson, Bruce A., and Jorge L. Larco. *Lean Transformation: How to Change Your Business into a Lean Enterprise.* Oaklea Publishing, 1999.

Liker, Jeffrey K., Editor. *Becoming Lean: Inside Stories of U.S. Manufacturers.* Portland, OR: Productivity Press, 1998.

Womack, James P., and Daniel T. Jones. *Lean Thinking: Banish Waste and Create Wealth in your Corporation.* New York: Simon & Schuster, 1996.

Womack, James P., Daniel T. Jones, and Daniel Roos. *The Machine That Changed the World.* New York: Harper Perennial, 1990.

SUPPLY CHAIN MANAGEMENT

A *supply chain* is the network of companies that work together to design, produce, deliver, and service products. In recent decades, organizations have taken a greater interest in improving their supply chains, as supply chain management (SCM) has become a more important concept.

SCM is the practice of organizing, coordinating, and monitoring the flow of goods, services, and information through a series of links that work together to provide goods and services to consumers. That chain consists of suppliers, manufacturers, wholesalers, distributors, and stores. The objective of SCM is to be able to have the right products in the right quantities at the right place at the right moment at the right cost. The purpose of SCM is to increase efficiency and profitability. Managing a supply chain involves business strategy, information flow, and compatibility of systems.

In the past, companies focused primarily on improving the ways in which they operated; as they improve their operations, they are turning to extend their efforts beyond their walls to the whole supply chain. Cooperation and collaboration promise further opportunities to improve quality and cut costs.

Supply Chain Management Using Lean and Six Sigma

If you remember the rolled throughput yield, this metric alone will drive your business metrics back into the supply base. Why? Because your business processes or products are only as good as your weakest link. Do you have a supplier that's the weakest link? You want to help engage your suppliers to improve your rolled throughput yield.

Supply chain management allows an organization to extend its lean and Six Sigma initiatives through its supply chain partners. The Six Sigma focus on controlling variation and the lean emphasis on eliminating waste and reducing time can help make supply chains more efficient, to the benefit of all the linked partners.

Gerald Najarian outlines five principles of SCM in his article "Re-Conforming the Supply Chain from Supplier to Customer: Before the Software" (*Themanager.org*):

- *Elimination* of any unnecessary activities
- *Coordination* of activities, synchronizing so that no time is lost among activities
- *Cooperation*—"The essence of cooperation is subordination of maximization for the benefit of optimization."
- *Integration* of activities so that all partners are focused on the customers at the end of the chain
- *Communication*—"The mortar that holds the integrated supply chain together"

Then he concludes of these five principles, "Without any one of them, supply chain management doesn't work. The key to creating value in the supply chain is to continually subject every node in the chain to the test of these five principles."

More about Supply Chain Management

You can learn more about supply chain management in the following books:

Hugos, Michael H. *Essentials of Supply Chain Management*. New York: Wiley, 2002.

Christopher, Martin. *Logistics and Supply Chain Management: Strategies for Reducing Cost and Improving Service,* 2d ed. Upper Saddle River, NJ: Financial Times Prentice-Hall, 1998.

Simchi-Levi, David, Philip Kaminsky, and Edith Simchi-Levi. *Managing the Supply Chain: The Definitive Guide for the Business Professional*. New York: McGraw-Hill, 2003.

Chopra, Sunil, and Peter Meindl. *Supply Chain Management: Strategy, Planning and Operations,* 2d ed. Indianapolis: Pearson Education, 2003.

KNOWLEDGE MANAGEMENT

It's difficult to define knowledge management (KM) precisely and concisely. The concept of knowledge is large and encompasses so much. The concept of management seems almost too mechanical and limited for such a resource. In this context KM is not a stand alone initiative. KM requires knowledge generation of solutions to be captured, so as to replicate the gains across the applicable business areas.

Steve Barth notes in his article, "Defining Knowledge Management" (*CRM Magazine*, July 4, 2000):

There is no standard definition of knowledge management or KM. Put ten KM "experts" in a room and you are likely to get 30 definitions. Knowledge management is such a preposterous, pretentious and profoundly oxymoronic phrase that everyone who really understands KM—including many of the field's pioneers—refuses to use the term. . . . They prefer terms such as knowledge-sharing, information systems, organizational learning, intellectual asset management, performance enhancement or gardening.

Then he offers the following definition:

Knowledge management is the practice of harnessing and exploiting intellectual capital to gain competitive advantage and customer commitment through efficiency, innovation and faster and more effective decision-making.

It is the practice of identifying, mapping, accessing, and benefiting from intellectual assets. It involves generating new knowledge, making knowledge easily accessible throughout the organization, and sharing best practices. To many, KM is first and foremost the technology that enables an organization to manage its knowledge.

Barth ends his article on knowledge management with a pragmatic summation:

In the final analysis, it matters less how you define knowledge management than how you practice it. It means nothing if you don't take knowledge and turn it into customer value.

The knowledge assets to be managed would include the following tangibles: all transaction data on all processes and projects, all customers and vendors; any patents, trademarks, and research logs; marketing strategies; business plans; competitive intelligence from all information sources; the knowledge contained in every e-mail, every fax, every letter, every document, and every spreadsheet. But knowledge assets also include intangibles—what's in the heads of your employees: their experience, judgment, insights, intuition, and skills. The value of these assets is estimated to be as much as 90 percent of the value of all of your knowledge assets.

So you can gather up every piece of paper in your organization and have the most sophisticated information technology and yet miss out on most of the value of knowledge management. It's not worth much unless you value your people and their ways of gathering and sharing knowledge—what people in knowledge management call "communities of practice" (CoPs) (A CoP is a functional group of people who exchange information, face to face and virtually, and share solutions, problems, lessons, insights, techniques, applications, tools, and best practices.)

You must encourage your people to be active in learning and in sharing what they know. You must reward them for doing so. You must build trust so they do not hoard what they know, believing that knowledge is power. So, knowledge management is fundamentally a very human activity, rooted in individuals and what they believe and how they act and in the culture and politics of the organization.

Six Sigma and Knowledge Management

Some of the greatest benefits from Six Sigma do not come from the projects, at least not directly. They come from the sharing of "lessons learned" throughout the organization. They come from the information shared by black belts and champions in their phase-gate reviews. The DMAIC process is the generation of the solution. KM process is expected to replicate the best practices, but the target is to make the best practice a genetic part of the way you do your business. The goal is to have the best practice be the way you work, so the best practices are a short-term goal. They come from the thoughts that the executive managers share as they discuss and evaluate project ideas.

Six Sigma and knowledge management can work very well together. Paige Leavitt makes some interesting points in concluding her article, "Knowledge Management and Six Sigma: Exploring the Potential of Two Powerful Disciplines" (American Productivity & Quality Center, November 2002):

> Six Sigma can learn from KM how to recognize knowledge, as well as processes. . . .
>
> Six Sigma professionals also can learn from KM strategies that sustain change. For instance, communities of practice are more effective than handing off or turning over a project. . . . And with the potential duplication of projects across the enterprise, Six Sigma does not fall victim to corporate amnesia.
>
> KM can also be used as a model for the transfer of best practices. How do you capture knowledge so it will be reused? How do you transfer improved processes to other sites? "Part of the dilemma with Six Sigma without KM is what happens when the members on the team you need are outside your normal managerial sphere of influence," said Gia Preston of Sprint. And what the KM community of practice and tools like the charter do is allow us to have that ongoing Six Sigma, where it breaches divisional or departmental . . . boundaries. . . .
>
> Conversely, the KM arena can learn from Six Sigma the value of a rigorous project approach, how to use analytical and quality tools, and the benefits of maintaining a full-time staff on key projects and communities. . . .
>
> Also, Six Sigma is a model for measurement and results focus. Gain the fast financial return on easier projects in order to fund long-term capacity building. . . . .
>
> Trading such lessons learned is made possible by what KM and Six Sigma have in common. "The systems thinking is what actually drives really good implementations in Six Sigma and KM," said [APQC President Carla] O'Dell. "It is probably the defining feature. Understanding all of the stakeholders involved, understanding the intended and unintended consequences of change, and having mechanisms in place that allow the system to adjust as a result of what it's learning—that's where we believe the key is in having people who are in a position to be able to detect and to adjust to the change."

More about Knowledge Management

You can learn more about knowledge management in the following books:

Rumizen, Melissie Clemmons. *The Complete Idiot's Guide to Knowledge Management.* Indianapolis: Penguin/Alpha Books, 2001.

Sveiby, Karl Erik. *The New Organizational Wealth: Managing and Measuring Knowledge-Based Assets.* San Francisco: Berrett-Koehler, 1997.

Davenport, Thomas, and Laurence Prusak. *Working Knowledge: How Organizations Know What They Know.* Cambridge, MA: Harvard Business School Press, 2000.

GROWTH MANAGEMENT SYSTEM

What would happen if you combined Six Sigma, Design for Six Sigma, lean, supply chain management, and knowledge management? You would get Growth Management System (GMS)® (a registered trademark of Six Sigma Consultants, Inc.).

GMS is a fusion of the proven success components of Six Sigma, DFSS, lean, SCM, and KM into a total integrated solution for growth and maximum profits. GMS is a natural extension of Six Sigma, but it goes well beyond the original Six Sigma program to attack all aspects of business. It's "radical thinking" that will drive the complacent company to make sustained growth and huge profits a reality.

GMS integrates all systems that have proven their power to generate profitable growth. GMS can be compared with the famous metric of "time to *market*," but with GMS it's now "time to *profit*." GMS reduces the time it takes to realize bottom-line results by a factor of two. For example, imagine that you have $100 million in project opportunity. Using the proper Six Sigma method, it would take you two to three years to see results. With GMS, it would take only one to one and a half years.

Change Management

A brief review of change management might help you better understand GMS.

Change management is confusing. It started as an engineering system approach in the late nineteenth century. Over the years, it has evolved into an application of main core disciplines such as business, operational economics, engineering, and psychology. Changes in business happen faster and faster. Change is a necessary requirement for survival. The discipline known as change management has also changed, to encompass more skills and knowledge for global business. However, no absolute, key metric has been defined. Many change leaders are growing tired and are confused about the purpose of change management and what it really means.

To better understand change management as it is viewed today, it would be helpful to look at the two fundamental fields of thought: a systems approach to improving business performance and a psychologist's approach to managing the human side of change. These two schools of thought have evolved and have merged to become the foundation of change management. Observers of business changes have recognized that the application of only one of these two approaches, in isolation, will be unsuccessful. An exclusively "engineering" approach to business issues generates effective solutions that are seldom effectively implemented, while an exclusively "psychologist" approach makes a business receptive to new things, but without appreciating or understanding what must change in order for the business to succeed.

Contributions to change management from both engineering and psychology are producing a convergence of thought that is crucial for the successful design and implementation of business change. In other words, a business must constantly examine its performance, strategy, processes, and systems to understand what changes need to be made. Increasing external and internal factors have made this strategy essential for survival. However, an organization must also understand the implications of a new business change on its employees, given their culture, values, history, and capacity for change. It is the front-line employees who ultimately deal with the changes on a practical level and make the new processes and systems come to life.

What does this mean for change management? First, it's important to recognize that both the engineering and the psychological aspects must be considered for successful change. Second, business improvement methodologies must integrate these two disciplines into a comprehensive model for change. Finally, when you read or study change management literature, understand how the authors are using term *change management*.

Whether you are practicing TQM, BPR, Six Sigma, lean, knowledge management, or some other technique to improve business performance, change management should be viewed as an essential competency to overlay and integrate with these methods.

Change management is now an esoteric academic practice area for those who don't have the vision of leaders. You need to manage change with one purpose—to create growth. To create growth, you must create a Growth Management System to realize entitled profitability. I am not indifferent to the role that change management has played, but the concept has never had *direction*, which was the missing link and the catalyst for the Growth Management System.

Change is a given! It's what happens. Your choice is either to manage it for a purpose or to go out of business. It's a fundamental fact that we are all in business for one purpose: to *make more money*. That's it!

Peter Drucker once said that profit, if correctly perceived, must be viewed as the cost of doing business now and in the future. What Drucker meant was that business enterprises must make enough profit to continue by investing in things that perpetuate their existence. The problem with his concept of profit is that it is impossible to measure, in contrast with GMS, which is absolutely measurable. GMS is getting the entitled real cost of doing business, *not* the perceived profit. It should be illegal for a company to be unconcerned with the cost of waste and defects and *not* grow the company to its rightful profit level.

The Basic Concept of Growth Management System

Six Sigma, lean, Design for Six Sigma, supply chain management, and knowledge management programs have come of age since the late 1980s. Each approach can be successful alone, but the fusion of these approaches is even more powerful.

That's the basic concept of Growth Management System. It combines the strengths and the advantages of these approaches.

Until recently, many organizations have been implementing these methods *separately*, with disparate missions, leaders, and varying levels of management support. Certain business leaders, benchmark companies, and outside experts and specialists in these approaches have discovered that integrating a numbers-oriented structured program like Six Sigma and KM can obtain a tenfold improvement if set up correctly from the beginning.

A few organizations have realized that their process improvement programs were solving the same problems multiple times with multiple redundant resources or failing where others with similar experiences succeeded. These organizations developed effective knowledge-sharing and replication processes, such as communities of practice, knowledge-sharing databases, and best practices transfer processes to ensure that those involved in Six Sigma and/or lean initiatives would learn faster and create higher value. These organizations greatly increased the potential of their process improvement projects by capturing, sharing, and replicating the best practices and lessons learned. This realization is just the beginning of the integration toward GMS.

The initial roadmap required to implement GMS builds all of those elements of success into the integration plan and it is communicated to all levels of the organization. No element will be showcased more than another; in a sense, GMS is an alliance of approaches working together to help you succeed.

Just as Six Sigma and lean have evolved from quality programs aimed at reducing defects and waste into methodologies that help organizations embed continuous improvement in their DNA, knowledge management has evolved. We now understand how systematic KM processes impact the flow of knowledge among people and functions in organizations. Organizations have better methods and models to fill knowledge gaps in their business processes and envision how KM can improve performance. In addition, KM has become embedded into many of the software applications used in Six Sigma, lean, supply chain management, and DFSS.

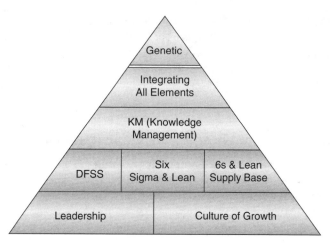

FIGURE 14-1   Fundamental building block of GMS

Figure 14-1 shows the fundamental building blocks forming the GMS pyramid for entitled maximum profit and growth. It's a system, which means it's necessary to use all of the pieces. If an organization uses only some pieces, it will succeed—but the results will be less than if it used GMS properly.

Six Sigma, Lean and Supply base are a combined block in the model due to a natural integrate pairs.It is no leap to integrate the method, nor a complicated infrastructure. The infrastructure for these methods are the same base requirements.

Review of the Basic Core Elements

Let's start at the bottom of the pyramid and cycle our way through the top. As we review the elements in the pyramid, note that each one complements the others and compensates for their weaknesses. Most of the elements have the common leadership and cultural requirements, but the big bang comes with the proper integration. While you review the basic executive summary of key elements, ask these questions: How can these elements be integrated into my company? What are the barriers? Do we have the foundation in this pyramid?

Leadership
The cornerstone of the pyramid and the very foundation is leadership. The leaders must make a decision to commit to growth. They must make promises and communicate them. Then, they must establish integrity by fulfilling their promises. Business leaders and executives play a critical sponsorship role in growth management. Sponsorship should be viewed as a legally binding contract, as it is the most important success factor.

There is confusion about the notion of sponsorship in contrast with support. The CEO of the company might support your project, but that is not the same as sponsoring your initiative. Sponsorship involves active and visible participation by senior business leaders throughout the process. Unfortunately many executives do not know what the actions of sponsorship look like. One of the roles of change agent, outside consultant, or project leader is to help senior executives do the right things to ensure successful sponsorship of the project.

Culture of Growth

The CEO sets the tone: It's a direct function of the CEO's message to the employees. The top-down approach ensures buy-in well before any approach is introduced. Education about obstacles to successful growth is provided at all levels: front-line, middle managers, and senior managers. Employees want to hear about growth from two people: the CEO or their direct supervisor.

Awareness training and intranet computer-based training (CBT) systems will be used to allow feedback to the CEO. The feedback is an anonymous email path to a suggestion box to ensure that the CEO will address issues, concerns, and potential projects that pertain to growth. This openness to feedback will establish the culture of growth. The focus of awareness is to eliminate the fear of the unknown. GMS education will present the reality options to all employees, so surprises can be minimized.

GMS involves transformation of the basic values, norms, and beliefs throughout the organization in order to transform performance. Again, this is not change management, but growth management with the goal of excessive growth.

Six Sigma

The Six Sigma approach, as you know from the rest of this book, is all about finding out what you don't know and emphasizing what you should know and taking action to reduce the errors and rework that cost you time, money, opportunities, and customers. Six Sigma translates that knowledge into opportunities for business growth.

Design for Six Sigma

As you know from Chapter 13, DFSS extends the Six Sigma methodology to the design of products, services, and processes. By incorporating DFSS, you're virtually assured that the product or service you're launching will perform dependably in the marketplace, thus setting it up for very positive acceptance.

Lean

Lean is a different way of thinking about manufacturing. As mentioned earlier in this chapter, the goal is to eliminate waste in every area of production—

product design, production management, inventory, supplier networks, customer relations, and so on. The focus is on using less effort, less inventory, less space, less equipment, and less time to develop products in order to become more responsive to customer demand while producing better products as efficiently and economically as possible.

Supply Chain Management

GMS is based on a holistic perspective. The success of your company success is in direct correlation with its supply chain. It is a critical element in the GMS integration mode.

In GMS we make the members of the supply chain effort perform Six Sigma and lean in all key processes along with partnering with all key suppliers to integrate these tools into their process, products, and services that affect the company's GMS. It's not enough to do technology solutions for supply chain management; to become an approved supplier for GMS, one must work on the same line of site goals for growth. Cost reductions and price reductions are required in a long-term partnership for GMS users.

Knowledge Management

Knowledge management, as defined earlier, is the practice of identifying, mapping, accessing, and benefiting from intellectual assets. It involves generating new knowledge, making knowledge easily accessible throughout the organization, and sharing best practices.

KM is the glue of GMS. Consider Six Sigma, DFSS, lean, and supply chain management as knowledge generation, which KM can leverage across all communities of practice to enable greater profits.

Genetic

Best practices are genetic after 85 percent replication. What is meant is that a best practice is a short condition for a solution, an idea, or knowledge because you want it to be a way of life, "the way we do things!"

It is *not* good to have a best practice to be adopted or be voluntarily accepted. The genetic element in the pyramid is for ensuring that the genetic code of the company installs best practices at a mandatory rapid rate.

Each company begins with a single belief, as each human begins with a single cell. This single belief does not contain all the functions like that single cell contains a heart, muscles, or any other tissue, but it does contain the genetic code to specify how to build all of the core beliefs and behaviors that establish a company's foundation. In the end GMS will continue to be sustained when it's embedded in the cultural DNA of the company, when it's part of the company's genetic code.

Connecting GMS to Business Functions

GMS will not succeed unless it is connected to all core business functions. GMS, like any change, needs a burning platform along with basic business assumptions to start the journey toward profitability and growth:

- Business survival is dependent upon how well we satisfy customers.
- Customer satisfaction is a function of quality, price, and delivery.
- Quality, cost, and prompt delivery are dependent upon process capability.
- Process capability is dependent upon knowledge of our process.
- People fixing problems generate process knowledge to be mined for KM.
- Knowledge can be successfully organized and transferred.
- The type of knowledge people pursue depends on leadership direction.
- The direction people are being led is established by management.

Most business leaders have not learned well enough the power of integrating successful elements and the lessons learned, often failing to be as single-minded and tenacious as others.

What Is Success through GMS?

It is designing the right product or service for which customers pay a premium competitive price, unaware that the knowledge generated by Six Sigma and lean elements along with low-cost, high-quality Six Sigma/lean suppliers are being leveraged to all required communities of practice for further study and immediate internal financial gains through KM. You are attacking the profit margin at the cost structure and the price brand equity structure simultaneously.

GMS is all about execution of growth. The basic architecture (Figure 14-2) is simple, but not to be overlooked. Each section will be explained in the section ahead. The architecture connects all core business functions with measurement.

Measurement Block

> *"When you can measure what you are speaking about, and express it in numbers, you know something about it; but when you cannot measure it, when you cannot express it in numbers, your knowledge is of a meager and unsatisfactory kind. It might be the beginning of knowledge, but you have scarcely, in your thoughts, advanced to the stage of science."*

> —WILLIAM THOMSON, LORD KELVIN (1824–1907)

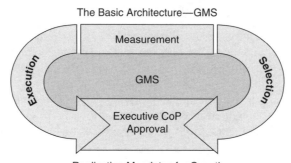

FIGURE 14-2 The basic pictorial of GMS architecture

The measurement block is the start of the process. Each core business function establishes key operating indicators (KOI) that drive activity to a strategic objective. The main assumption in the strategic planning process is that they have been validated.

In GMS we assume that the strategic plan is wrong from the start. We rebuild the metric dashboard for each business function. The business dashboard as a metaphor for critical metrics for measuring business performance originated years ago at General Electric. Just as you use the speedometer, oil gauge, battery indicator, fuel gauge, and other instruments to monitor the status of your vehicle as you drive, so you want to keep track of key indicators of the performance of your company. Like the dashboard gauges, your metrics allow you to continually assess your progress and detect any potential problems.

For each KOI we look at the level of entitlement. The entitlement level (Figure 14-3) is basically the best that you have performed on a specific dashboard metric over time. You then set that best as the specification for performance. You've used your key metrics to establish baselines for your target processes. You've gathered internal benchmark data to show how you could be performing up to your entitlement levels. Now, you compare the executive KOIs and the operational KOIs to get a realistic image of the KOIs from both sides and the difference. In technical terms, you do a gap analysis, to quantify the gaps between where you are now and where the strategy is targeting. Typically, the biggest gap revealed by this analysis is where the internal community of practice is most resistant to growth.

Selection Block
After the measurements have been validated, the company is ready to select the projects to align and allocate the resources for GMS.

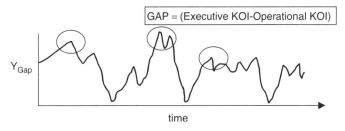

FIGURE 14-3   Entitlement level to set and validate strategic objectives and metrics

Execution and Executive Community of Practice

There will be approval for all GMS projects to ensure executive buy-in and awareness. This is not a spectator sport for executives. The problem in most best practices is that executive involvement is voluntary. In GMS, in contrast, it is mandatory to replicate project benefits across all applicable CoPs. The executive CoP is there to ensure that the CEO and corporate GMS champion are aware of the selection activities, but also to ensure that there are *no* barriers to replication. The cycle of GMS is rapidly going through measurement to execution of solution back to measurement to ensure that the company achieves its objectives of profitability and growth.

GMS is a function of knowledge generators in all CoPs actively pursuing growth. These generators of knowledge are Six Sigma, lean, supplier base, and DFSS to ensure that KM replicates the gains.

A component of GMS is an unreasonable amount of information. The company leaders in GMS view pure knowledge as intelligence, a profit lever that can be used to control a market. The brilliance behind GMS approach is that we can never be sure where the winning piece of information will come from, so we need a lot of it. The leaders sift through piles of data before a making a high-ROI decision. But with GMS, the sifting happens at light speed—and the profits and growth are worth the effort. If a little knowledge is dangerous, as the saying goes, GMS shows that a lot of knowledge can pay off big.

Growth management is the breakthrough method, using proven tools and techniques to direct communities of practice of business to achieve entitled legal profiteering for all aspects of a company including, genetic recoding for sustainability.

SUMMARY

There are several ways to build on a Six Sigma initiative, by combining it with other approaches to improving the bottom line. It can be combined with Design for Six Sigma (as shown in Chapter 13), lean manufacturing, supply chain management, and knowledge management. Each of these combinations improves the results possible through using Six Sigma alone.

If you combine all of these approaches—Six Sigma, Design for Six Sigma, lean, supply chain management, and knowledge management—you get Growth Management System (GMS) (a registered trademark of Six Sigma Consultants, Inc.). GMS is a fusion of the proven success components of all of these approaches into a total integrated solution for growth and maximum profits.

CASE STUDY QUESTION

The integration into GMS is too compelling to be overlooked, due to the overwhelming results. This can be emphasized by comparing incomplete combinations of approaches.

Question 1: What is lean without Six Sigma?

Answer 1: A single point defect reduction.

Question 2: What is Six Sigma without lean?

Answer 2: A high-speed scrap machine.

Question 3: What are continuous improvement, lean, and Six Sigma without knowledge management?

Answer 3: A whole lot less money—10 times less, very sadly—due to lack of leverage!

GMS integrates all known demonstrated systems that have derived profitable growth. GMS reduces by a factor of two the time it takes to realize bottom-line results. It's the ultimate accelerator to get the money faster! (See Figure 14-4.)

When asked about the nonfinancial benefits of knowledge capture and replication, the partner organizations listed the following three major benefits:

1. Reduction in duplication of efforts and/or projects
2. Rapid transfer of best practices and implementation
3. Achieving cultural change within the organization

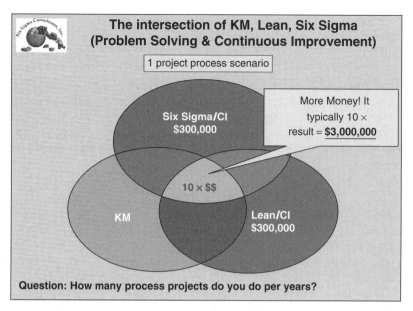

FIGURE 14-4   Proof of integrated projects that used KM, Lean, CI-continuous improvement, and Six Sigma

Brue[1] chronicled a case in which one company had two business units performing the same work, which resulted in a six-month misuse of one full-time resource and six part-time resources costing more than $60,000. Unfortunately, both teams came up with the same answer in the end. To enhance the rapid transfer of best practices and implementation, Brue writes that the cost of not replicating processes depends on the number of process points involved. In his experience, one retail company saved $25,000 on a process point, but found real value when the best practice was leveraged across 1,100 stores, which resulted in $2.75 million in savings!

To achieve those benefits, simple measurement systems can help capture the value, whereas recognition of outstanding knowledge sharing and replication behavior helps transform organizational culture. In an effort to gauge the success of replication, the partners that do measure track the percentage of completed projects implemented (leverage), average days to complete a project (cycle time), and financial savings per project per day (impact). A clear majority (75 percent) of the partners rate the effectiveness of their transfer processes as either moderate or high (only 25 percent actually track the average savings per project after leveraging knowledge of a previous implementation).

[1] Brue, Greg. *Six Sigma for Managers* (New York: McGraw Hill, 2002).

What does this say? Strong measurement of business results is a key component of the Six Sigma/Lean process, so knowledge replication goals should focus on improving the impact of the Six Sigma/Lean process. How? As discussed in Chapter 2, 75 percent of the best-practice organizations' management mandates that practitioners capture, transfer, and reuse practices from the Six Sigma/Lean process, and 63 percent include capture/transfer language in performance evaluations. The combination of business-focused goals, management mandate, performance evaluation accountability for capture/transfer, and several simple measures of replication seem to be the measurement recipe for best-practice organizations.

Case Study of Partial Integrated Programs, Not Total Growth Management System

Ford's KM program office and Six Sigma program does not launch a CoP if it cannot measure improvement. This improvement need not necessarily be demonstrated in dollars. As a matter of fact, Ford's 50+ communities have collectively identified more than 200 ways of measuring improvement. Less than 20 of those, however, are in dollars. Most state savings as percentages improved, customer satisfaction indicators, an accident rate reduction, and cycle time improvements. The program office knows these could be converted into dollars; however, it concentrates on showing the value to the users in their own metrics, which might not be expressed financially. These improvements ultimately cascade and translate as overall improvement to the bottom line. Communities show enough hard dollar savings to keep management interested. Since 1995, the most visible gains have been in manufacturing, which has seen $300 million in captured savings during banner years and now averages $100 million per year. The cost of the Best Practice Replication process itself is calculated to be less than $500,000 per year (not including the costs of implementing the transferred processes).

> *"We always ask Black Belts if a project is replicable. If it is, we ask where it might apply. It's not enough to complete a project . . . the results must be shared."*

—STAN KWIECIEN, BEST PRACTICE REPLICATION
DEPLOYMENT MANAGER, FORD MOTOR CO.

DuPont expects an increase in revenue of 3 percent per year with new hard final validated projects from each small business unit. Management has stated that increasing the numbers of new Six Sigma projects is key to meeting that goal, so each small business unit has one full-time champion work as part of the small business unit champion's network that meets quarterly. The corporate Six Sigma networks (SBU champions network and Master Black Belt network), as well as the top-line growth champions network, knowledge management collaboration network, and corporate governance network meet regularly to ensure that practices are shared throughout the enterprise. In addition, DuPont created champion network sub-teams with leaders from human resources, finance, IT, training, process management, top-line growth, communications and networking, and leveraging. Although the networks do not currently capture explicit savings from replicated projects, they recognize that approximately 20 percent of all Six Sigma projects are replicated.

Raytheon's leadership recognized that a formal KM strategy would be a key enabler to improving the benefits from the R6σ process. To that end, the leadership group established a KM champion at the enterprise level and sponsored a R6σ KM champions' network to deploy a repeatable process across the company. Additionally, Raytheon deployed communities of practice throughout the R6σ environment to ensure practitioners stay connected and continue to share practices. Each community is tasked with measuring process improvement benefits, but none have yet captured validated results.

Intuit employs communities of practice to capture and transfer knowledge, but management does not require the communities to measure their impact. However, the process excellence leaders discuss strategic high-level topics, determine how well process excellence is doing across the company, and identify areas where knowledge capture and replication makes sense. Anecdotally, Intuit feels that the networks and communities provide great value to the process excellence process.

What Does Success Look Like?
Organizations recognize the impact of an integrated approach and knowledge sharing and replication within its growth management system. Below are the following critical success factors for developing a simple, effective measurement and recognition process.

1. Embed knowledge capture, sharing, and replication in the organization's Growth Management methodology. Set the expectation that practitioners should search for projects to replicate during the Define phase and capture lessons learned during the control phase. This will drive behavior and results that can be measured and recognized.
2. Focus replication measurement on business goals. Ensure that any knowledge capture and replication processes focus on decreasing costs, diminishing errors, and improving revenue.
3. Establish a simple set of measures to capture the value of replicated projects. Capture individual project efficiency gains after each project and aggregate results two times per year.
4. Use existing database tools to allow practitioners to note where they have captured lessons, reused practices, and achieved approximate time savings or value multiples.

5. Measure the results of any networks or communities of practice by setting up activity measures, process improvement measures, and resulting outcome measures. Combining replication measures with ongoing community value can result in staggering gains.
6. Ensure that Growth Management Systems recognition and reward programs encourage knowledge sharing. Make sure sharers and those that reuse existing knowledge get credit for any results.
7. Get the organization's senior leaders involved in the recognition process by having them write thank-you notes and highlighting successes during meetings.
8. Ask the group to provide recognition, congratulations, and thanks to experts who continually take the time to share and successfully reuse practices.

FINAL EXAM

For answers to the final exam, visit the following Web site:
http://www.mcgraw-hill36-hourcourses.com
What you know could earn you a certificate of achievement from McGraw-Hill.

1. In the Measure phase of DMAIC, what are the items needed?
   a. A solution to the problem.
   b. Data for doing a Design of Experiments.
   c. Data to help break down the problem.
   d. A problem, a process, a financial benefit, a metric and a goal, and a customer metric.
   e. A valid measurement system.

2. In the Measure phase, we are going to establish a defect rate, but black belts typically see the defect rate go down.
   a. True.
   b. False.

3. What is one of the first important milestones that indicates that a black belt is on track?
   a. Lack of buy-in from the team members.
   b. No data is available.
   c. The champion does not know the project benefit.
   d. The process map is complete.
   e. When the team adopts a desire to constantly learn.

4. How many data points do you need to have a short-term capability?
   a. Two data points.
   b. Over 100 data points.
   c. Fewer than five data points.
   d. Between 30 and 50 data points.

5. Process mapping is a:
   a. A one-time event.
   b. A tool used for statistical validation.

  c. A tool used at the end of the DMAIC process.

  d. An ongoing living document used throughout the DMAIC process.

6. In process mapping, which are the two key questions to ask for each single step?
   Q-1. How many inputs are in this step?
   Q-2. What happened prior to this step?
   Q-3. What are the outputs of this step?
   Q-4. Why do we do this step?
   Q-5. How do we know that this step is good?

   a. Q-1 and Q-2

   b. Q-1 and Q-3

   c. Q-1 and Q-4

   d. Q-1 and Q-5

   e. Q-2 and Q-3

   f. Q-2 and Q-4

   g. Q-2 and Q-5

   h. Q-3 and Q-4

   i. Q-3 and Q-5

   j. Q-4 and Q-5

7. An *YX* diagram is a statistical tool.

   a. True

   b. False

8. An *YX* diagram helps point the black belt into a direction with factual evidence.

   a. True

   b. False

9. A failure modes and effects analysis FMEA describes the following.

   a. Potential defects

   b. The risk of the problem

   c. Capability of the process

   d. Root cause

   e. What you want to know about a type of defect

10. An FMEA is complete during the Measure phase.

    a. False

    b. True

11. In an FMEA, what is the RPN if POCC is 5, PDET is 4, and the PSEV is 9?

    a. 0

b. 20

c. 9

d. 180

e. None of the above

12. Measurement system analysis MSA is used:

a. To assess capability

b. To validate the data used for analysis

c. As an optional tool during the DMAIC process

d. A nonstatistical assessment of the process

13. MSA is a tool that can be omitted in the DMAIC model.

a. True

b. False

14. *Cp* is a capability index with the units measured in:

a. Meters

b. Gallons

c. Yards

d. Productivity

e. Defect rate or yield

f. No units

15. If the *Cp* is 1.0, what is the sigma value?

a. 1

b. 2

c. 3

d. 6

e. None of above

16. Can *Cp* be greater than *Cpk*?

a. Yes

b. No

c. Sometimes

17. What is the *Cp* and *Cpk* index number when you have a six-sigma capability?

a. *Cp* = 1.0 and *Cpk* = 0.5

b. *Cp* = 1.5 and *Cpk* = 2.0

c. *Cp* = 3.0 and *Cpk* = 6.0

    d. $Cp = 2.0$, and $Cpk = 1.5$

    e. None of the above

18. What is the purpose for gauge R&R?

    a. Statistical analysis to evaluate measure error

    b. To understand repeatability and reproducibility of your MSA

    c. To help validate what is a defect and what is not

    d. Look for variation within operator and between operators

    e. To gauge the rest and relaxation needed for a black belt

    f. a through d

    g. None of the above

19. If your data are nonnormal, you are stuck in the Measure phase.

    a. True

    b. False

20. What is the layperson's description of a hypothesis test?

    a. Helps to solve problems

    b. Breaking the problem up

    c. Dissecting the data

    d. There is no way to make it simple

    e. A tool to compare stuff

21. What are the reasons for nonnormality?

    a. All data have that pattern

    b. Due to abnormal conditions

    c. Bimodal conditions exist

    d. Different normal distributions are within the data set

    e. a and d

    f. None of the above

    g. c and d

22. If you have a nonnormal data set, does transforming the data fix the nonnormal causes of the problem?

    a. Yes

    b. No

    c. None of the above

23. What would best describe a bimodal distribution?

    a. A manufacturing process

    b. Material variance

    c. Transactional defects

    d. Mutlivari chart

    e. Within-part variation

    f. An *X*-factor that has two different *Y*-output distributions

    g. d and f

24. How does comparing factors help solve the problem?

    a. It breaks down the problem into the vital *X*'s.

    b. It contrasts the trivial many versus the vital few.

    c. It helps answer the hypothesis question.

    d. It deals with data facts that can be proven.

    e. It focuses the team on data, not opinion.

    f. All of the above

25. Tool wear can cause nonnormal distributions.

    a. True

    a. False

26. What plot describes the many distributions in one graph in quartiles?

    a. Interval plot

    b. Capability plot

    c. Probability plot

    d. Median plot

    e. Box plot

27. Is it okay to remove outliers in a data set that cause an increase in standard deviation?

    a. Yes

    b. No

    c. Yes, only if you know the cause of stopping it

    d. b and c

28. What is the best way to show multimode distributions?

    a. Bimodal graph

    b. Interval plot

    c. Dot plot

    d. One-way ANOVA

    e. Box plot

    f. a and b

    g. b through d

29. Lowess analysis fits a robust line through the data to display a relationship between X and Y.

   a. True

   b. False

30. In a multivari analysis, the X levels are randomly selected levels during the study.

   a. True

   b. False

31. Different operators producing the same Y cannot cause nonsymmetrical distributions:

   a. True

   b. False

32. Two-way interaction cannot cause asymmetrical distributions.

   a. True

   b. False

   c. Sometimes

   d. None of the above

33. In simple terms, what is meant by a p-value of less than 0.05?

   a. That there are no significant difference

   b. The variance terms are equal

   c. The mean has a shift of 1.5 sigma

   d. You're 95 percent confident that there is a statistical difference

   e. All the above

34. The 95 percent confidence interval increases as the standard deviation decreases.

   a. True

   b. False

35. A multvari analysis is an active form of comparing within- and between-part variation over time.

   a. True

   b. False

36. You do not need a capable measurement system for multivari analysis.

   a. True

   b. False

37. Shift-to-shift variation can be measured on one shift.

    a. True

    b. False

38. A hypothesis test can show the interaction of the factors.

    a. True

    b. False

39. Sample size has no effect on the width of a distribution.

    a. True

    b. False

40. If an *X* has been identified as statistically significant, do you disregard it owing to an expert telling you to ignore it?

    a. No

    b. Yes

    c. Ask what data does the expert have to show to ignore it

    d. None of the above

    e. a and c

41. If you were told to purchase new technology for over $2 million to make the business more productive, but the hypothesis of the new technology shows no statistical difference in productivity, do you purchase it?

    a. No

    b. Yes

42. What does hypothesis testing fundamentally change?

    a. It's a departure from the "I think" and "I feel" culture

    b. Destroys the emotions of the problem

    c. Turns the problem into a fact-based process

    d. Data are now used to drive decisions

    e. All of the above

43. If you changed an *X* that was proven to be statistically significant and the *Y* was given to you with 3 months prior to the change and 1 month after, could you show a before and after hypothesis to validate the change?

    a. No

    b. Yes

44. Using an Anderson-Darling normality test, normal data have a *p*-value of less than 0.5.

    a. True

    b. False

45. How many runs does a 2^3 full factorial experiment consist of?

    a. 6

    b. 5

    c. 8

    d. 12

46. In an experiment, inputs are allowed to vary randomly throughout the specification range.

    a. True

    b. False

47. One-factor-at-a-time experiments generate more powerful data than a full factorial experiment.

    a. True

    b. False

48. What is an experimental factor?

    a. The input variables for the experiment

    b. The metrics of the process

    c. A covariant

    d. The largest standard deviation

49. What does orthogonal mean?

    a. One or more effects that cannot unambiguously be attributed to a single factor or factor interaction

    b. Involves running the experimental runs in random order

    c. A property that ensures that all experimental factors are independent of each other; no correlation exists between X's.

50. What is a "Balanced Design?"

    a. A design in which each of the variables has a different number of runs at the high and low levels

    b. A design in which each of the variables or factors has the same number of runs at the high and low levels

    c. A design in which two of the variables has a different number of runs at the high and low levels

    d. All of the above

51. Standard order is the same as run order.

    a. True

    b. False

52. Why use factorial plots?

    a. Allow you to see the plots of the main effects

    b. Allow you to see the interaction plots

    c. Allow you to see the cube plots

    d. Show how to set each factor to either maximize or minimize the response

    e. All of the above

53. What tools can be used to determine if factors have interaction?

    a. Balanced ANOVA

    b. Standardized effects

    c. Interaction plots

    d. Fractional factorial fits

    e. All of the above

54. What does it mean when no p-values are presented in the ANOVA output?

    a. Means the factors are statistically significant

    b. Means the factors are not different

    c. Only one repetition was run at each treatment combination

    d. Had no center points

    e. All of the above

55. Why do we replicate our experimental runs?

    a. So we can look for special causes

    b. To obtain a better estimate of the error and look at interactions

    c. To determine the factor levels

    d. So we can look at the same thing run again

56. To use a center point in your experimental design, at least one factor must be able to be set at its midpoint coded value = 0.

    a. True

    b. False

57. Why use center points in your experimental design?

    a. To check for linearity

    b. To check for interactions

    c. To detect curvature

58. If a center point is significant, its p-value in the ANOVA table will be greater than 0.05.

    a. True

    b. False

59. Fractional factorial designs require more runs than full factorial designs given the same number of factors.

    a. True

    b. False

60. What is the main reason for using a fractional factorial design?

    a. Allows you to test and screen a large number of factors in fewer runs

    b. Gives you good estimates of low order interactions

    c. Gives you relative significance of the factors

    d. All of the above

61. Given three factors, A, B, and C, the highest-order interaction would be ABC.

    a. True

    b. False

62. In a four-factor 1/2 fractionated design, the AB interaction is confounded with the CD interaction.

    a. True

    b. False

63. What does it mean when A is confounded with BC?

    a. A is contributing to the result.

    b. BC is contributing to the result.

    c. The computed coefficients are related to the sum of the two individual effects.

    d. The sums of squares are related to the sum of the two individual effects.

64. In a resolution IV design, two-factor interactions are aliased with three-factor interactions.

    a. True

    b. False

65. In a resolution III design, single factors are not aliased with any other factors.

    a. True

    b. False

66. The identity expression I + ABCD is used to generate the confounding pattern.

    a. True

    b. False

67. Why are resolution V designs preferred over resolution III and resolution IV designs?

    a. No main effect is confounded with any other main effect or second-order interactions.

    b. No second-order interactions are confounded with any other second-order interaction, and second-order interactions are confounded with third-order interactions.

    c. Allows for the differentiation of the effects down to the second order, assuming that the effects of third-order interactions are negligible.

    d. All of the above

68. Why should you do a hypothesis test before running a DOE?

    a. Statistically test for the correct factors

    b. Find the trivial many

    c. To ensure that your measurement system is good

    d. To ensure that you have all the process steps identified

    e. To identify as many of the vital few factors prior to DOE

69. What is the mission of the Improve phase?

    a. Find the relationships between X and Y

    b. Validate hypothesis tests

    c. Which inputs to control in the next phase

    d. Run a pilot to validate experiment

    e. All of the above

70. Can you calculate epsilon-square percent contribution for the DOE given that the degree of freedom for each factor is different in the ANOVA?

    a. Yes

    b. No

71. The WECO (Western Electric Company) rules are based on probability. We know that for a normal distribution, the probability of encountering a point outside $\pm 2.5\sigma$ is 0.3 percent. This is a rare event. Therefore, if we observe a point outside the control limits, we conclude that the process has shifted and is unstable.

    a. True

    b. False

72. Outliers usually have a significant effect on an equation derived with regression analysis.

    a. True

    b. False

73. Using; $Y = f(X)$, do we set tolerance limits for Y?

    a. Yes

    b. No

74. What is the residual?

    a. It is the equation from the data.

    b. It is the standard error of the equation.

    c. It indicates how well the equation fits.

    d. It is a calculation of the expected value minus the observed value.

    e. c and d

75. What are control charts?

    a. Design of experiment (DOE)

    b. A plot showing the Y over time

    c. Charts showing average control

    d. Charts used to routinely monitor quality

    e. None of the above

76. What does a P-chart track?

    a. Process chart showing the main factors

    b. Sample size of the process over time

    c. Simple chart used to track the number of nonconforming units, percentage of defective parts, assuming that sample size is *not* necessarily constant

    d. None of the above

77. A DOE is always needed to solve process issues.

    a. True

    b. False

78. The purpose of performing a designed experiment is to determine what?

    a. The mathematical relationship $Y = F(x1, x2, x3, \ldots)$

    b. Which X's most impact Y and therefore need to be controlled

    c. The level of each X to achieve the desired mean Y

    d. The level of each X to minimize the variability of Y

    e. All of the above

79. Within the DOE, the easiest way to test for curvature is to include center points.

    a. True

    b. False

80. The most common response surface design is called the central composite design.

    a. True

    b. False

81. Control plans provide a written description of the actions that are required at each phase of the process to ensure that all process inputs and outputs will be in a state of control.

    a. True

    b. False

82. Control plans are only generated at the start of the life cycle of a product.

    a. True

    b. False

83. SPC is a statistically based graphing technique that compares current process data to a set of stable control limits established from normal process variation.

    a. True

    b. False

84. Control limits and specification limits are the same thing:

    a. True

    b. False

85. Control limits are typically set at plus or minus 2 standard deviations from the target of the control chart.

    a. True

    b. False

86. Regular residuals are the actual values of the residuals calculated by subtracting the expected value from the observed value.

    a. True

    b. False

87. What is the best description of a data transform?

    a. A transformation of the data using a power table to treat linearity in the data

    b. A transformation of the data using a power table to treat nonlinearity in the data

    c. Improves the variance within the data

    d. A transformation of the data using a power table to treat the units of the data

    e. It transforms data into a more approximate normal distribution

88. Outliers usually have a significant effect on an equation derived with regression analysis.

    a. True

    b. False

89. When an "out of control" situation is signaled on a control chart, the person using the chart will know why the data are giving the signal.

    a. True

    b. False

90. Once the special causes of variation in a process have been discovered and eliminated, the long-term goal of anyone managing a process will be to reduce common cause variation by improving the process or system itself.

    a. True

    b. False

91. An "out of control" situation in a production process may be signaled by a sample *f* output that generates a data point outside the control limits on either the *Xbar–R* range chart.

    a. True

    b. False

92. Mistakeproofing seeks to gain permanence by eliminating or rigidly controlling human intervention in a process.

    a. True

    b. False

93. Six Sigma product and process design or process changes made to the product or process that eliminate the error condition from occurring are called what?

    a. TQM

    b. Mistakeproofing

    c. Mistake elimination

    d. Foolproofing

    e. All of the above

94. Systems that monitor the process and automatically adjust critical *X*'s to correct settings are called what?

    a. Full automation

    b. Process interruption

    c. Mechanism

    d. SPC

95. In order for mistakeproofing systems to operate effectively, the following rules must not be observed.

    a. The systems must be installed and properly adjusted before process startup.

    b. The systems must be periodically audited and maintained.

    c. Systems are periodically disabled.

    d. Inoperative or missing systems must be repaired or replaced before operating the process.

    e. System overrides must not be used except in an emergency.

96. The EWMA or Exponentially Weighted Moving Average chart is a variable data control chart.

    a. True

    b. False

ANSWER KEYS FOR REVIEW QUESTIONS

CHAPTER 1 REVIEW QUESTIONS

1. What is Six Sigma? Answer: *d*.
   a. Problem solving
   b. Culture change
   c. Knowledge generator
   d. All the above

2. Where do you start Six Sigma? Answer: *d*.
   a. It's a bottom-up approach.
   b. From the quality director.
   c. Middle management.
   d. The CEO decides.

3. What is a defect? Answer: *d*.
   a. Something that the customer is willing to pay for
   b. A feeling that the process is causing a problem
   c. Something we should ignore if possible
   d. A measurable characteristic not conforming to a customer requirement that costs money–it's waste!

4. Achieving Six Sigma quality means your business is what? Answer: *d*.
   a. Producing 500,000 defects per million opportunities (DPMO)

    b. Producing 100,000 DPMO

    c. Producing 25,000 DPMO

    d. Producing 3.4 DPMO maximum

5. What is a process? Answer: *c.*

    a. A system used in manufacturing

    b. A Six Sigma computer application

    c. Any repetitive action in a business environment

    d. The opposite of a concess

6. What is standard deviation? Answer: *a.*

    a. A measure of variation

    b. A normal perversion

    c. A behavioral aberration that is considered typical

    d. An acceptable modification of a process

7. What is the standard model for the Six Sigma methodology? Answer: *d.*

    a. BACI

    b. CIADF

    c. DPMO

    d. DMAIC

8. What is $Y = f(X)$? Answer: *b.*

    a. A quadrilateral equation

    b. The Six Sigma transfer function

    c. One variation of $X = f(Y)$ and $Y = XF$

    d. An algorithm for controlling DMAIC

9 All of the following are phases in the Six Sigma DMAIC model except which? Answer: *b.*

    a. Measure

    b. Continue

    c. Define

    d. Analyze

CHAPTER 2 REVIEW QUESTIONS

1. A black belt works on Six Sigma projects part-time. Answer: *b.*

    a. True

    b. False

    c. Only if you have part-time problems

    d. Both *a* and *c*

    e. Both *b* and *c*

    f. None of the above

2. What is the average annual savings per black belt? Answer: *e.*

    a. We don't measure it.

    b. $10,000–$20,000

    c. $40,000

    d. $175,000

    e. $600,000 and $1 million

3. Hard dollars are? Answer: *b.*

    a. Money that's difficult to earn

    b. Savings that are tangible and quantifiable

    c. Silver coins

    d. U.S. currency in a global economy

CHAPTER 3 REVIEW QUESTIONS

1. What is variation? Answer: *d.*

    a. The fluctuation in the output of a process

    b. Something that every repeatable process exhibits

    c. Something that any improvement of any process should reduce

    d. All of the above

    e. None of the above

2. Mean is? Answer: *c.*

    a. A calculation consisting of adding the lowest and highest values in a series

    b. A representation of the sense of a Six Sigma principle

    c. The average of a series of numbers

    d. The disposition of the average Six Sigma practitioner

3. What is the midpoint in a range of data? Answer: *a.*

    a. Median

    b. Mode

    c. Discrete data

    d. Mean

4. Standard deviation is? Answer: *a.*

   a. An indicator of the degree of variation in a set of values calculated by measuring the average spread of the values around the mean

   b. The sum of the mean, median, mode, and range of a set of values divided by four

   c. A defective variation that has become accepted as inevitable

   d. The usual workaround when data is unavailable for a process

5. Which of the following statements is/are true for a normal distribution? Answer: *d.*

   a. The mean, the median, and the mode are equal.

   b. 68 percent of the values lie within one standard deviation (± 1 sigma) of the mean.

   c. It can be described in terms of its mean and its standard deviation.

   d. *a* and *b*

   e. *b* and *c*

   f. *a* and *c*

   g. *a*, *b*, and *c*

   h. None of the above

6. A common cause is? Answer: *d.*

   a. A source of variation that is found most frequently

   b. A source of variation found in all processes

   c. A source of variation that unites project team members

   d. A source of variation that is inherent in a process

7. First-time yield (FTY) is? Answer: *b.*

   a. The gain achieved from applying Six Sigma to a project initially

   b. The number of good units coming out of a process or a step divided by the number of total units going into it

   c. The gain achieved by a project team new to Six Sigma

   d. A concession by a project team in its initial efforts

8. Rolled throughput yield (RTY) is? Answer: *a.*

   a. The probability of getting through the entire process free of defects

   b. The percentage of units that finish without a defect out of the number of units started

   c. A means of calculating DPMO

   d. A means of calculating sigma level

9. What is the rolled throughout yield for a three-step process with a 90 percent yield for each step? Answer: *c.*

    a. 90 percent

    b. 81 percent

    c. 72 percent

    d. 63 percent

10. What is the cost of defects in a company with revenues of $1 million? Answer: *b.*

    a. Nothing

    b. Between $200,000 and $400,000

    c. $100,000

    d. About 10 percent

CHAPTER 4 REVIEW QUESTIONS

1. What is a business metric? Answer: *d.*

    a. A measurement of the difference between the current state of a process and the future state

    b. Any characteristic that is critical to quality for customers

    c. A means of distinguishing between processes or steps that add value for customers and those that do not

    d. Any unit of measurement that provides a way to objectively quantify a process in terms of objectives

2. In the transfer function, $Y = f(X)$, which letter represents the dependent variable? Answer: *a.*

    a. Y

    b. f

    c. X

    d. None of the above

3. This is a technique by which an organization measures the performance of a process against similar best-in-class processes in other organizations, determines how those organizations achieve their performance levels, and uses the information to improve its process. Answer: *d.*

    a. Six Sigma

    b. Cause-and-effect diagram

    c. Benchmarking

    d. Gap analysis

4. A baseline is? Answer: *b.*

    a. A Six sigma synonym for the bottom line

    b. A standard for comparisons, the current performance of a process

    c. The lowest limit in a series of data points

    d. A synonym for gap analysis

5. If we know $Y = f(X)$, then we know? Answer: *b.*

    a. Key questions to ask

    b. The function of the problem

    c. X is the dependent on Y

    d. Y is a function of the X's, which are independent

    e. None of the above

6. What is the concept of a "dashboard"? Answer: *d.*

    a. It shows what happened after the fact.

    b. It shows how to improve a metric.

    c. The metrics of the business are shown like those of a car.

    d. It shows the critical metrics to monitor.

    e. All the above

CHAPTER 5 REVIEW QUESTIONS

1. What does Six Sigma need for project selection? Answer: *d.*

    a. A solution

    b. A low-level problem to start out

    c. No financial impact

    d. A problem, a process, a financial benefit, a goal, and a customer

    e. None of the above

2. What best describes a good project? Answer: *d.*

    a. Something that pleases the boss

    b. Nonbottleneck areas

    c. A reasonable goal

    d. Something that is quantifiable with a financial impact to the business

    e. One that has a solution

3. Why is Six Sigma project selection so important? Answer: *d.*

    a. It makes it fun for the business.

    b. It helps to justify fixing problems.

    c. It's not as important as getting trained.

    d. It makes or breaks the longevity due to making money while getting problems fixed.

    e. None of the above.

4. What three things must be considered while selecting projects? Answer: *e.*

    a. Metrics, surveys, and culture

    b. Culture, expectations, and time line

    c. Training, people, and outside customers

    d. Seasonal factors, people impact, and data availability

    e. Impact, effort, and probability of success

5. How can a Pareto chart help in project selection? Answer: *e.*

    a. To point out what is not important

    b. To drill down the CTQ metrics

    c. To show the levels of drill down from the top

    d. To create a focus on the top dollars

    e. All of the above

6. What is the nominal group technique? Answer: *c.*

    a. Any technique used by a group

    b. A means of nominating people to be members of a group

    c. A method for generating ideas and then prioritizing the ideas generated.

    d. None of the above

7. What is a relations diagram? Answer: *f.*

    a. An interrelationship digraph

    b. A chart to show the dynamics among the members of a project team

    c. A diagram also used to show all of the relationships among the pieces of a situation

    d. Both *a* and *b*

    e. Both *b* and *c*

    f. Both *a* and *c*

    g. All of the above

    h. None of the above

8. What is the purpose of an affinity diagram? Answer: *c.*

   a. To display items that are not infinite

   b. To track the cumulative effect of items on a list

   c. To reveal how items in a list fit together into groups

   d. To generate ideas for a brainstorming session

   e. None of the above

9. Which guideline generalizes that 20 percent of the causes are responsible for 80 percent of the effects? Answer: *e.*

   a. The 80-20 rule

   b. The 20-80 rule

   c. The Pareto principle

   d. Both *a* and *b*

   e. Both *a* and *c*

   f. Both *b* and *c*

   g. None of the above

10. What is a Pareto chart? Answer: *b.*

   a. A display of the genealogy of economist Vilfredo Pareto

   b. A specialized bar chart used to display the relative importance of multiple items and track the cumulative weight of the items

   c. A diagram for counting Pareto principles

   d. A diagram for monitoring *p*rojects and *a*ny *r*esults *e*stimated at *t*ime of out-comes (PARETO).

11. Which of the following would likely be good Six Sigma projects? Answer: *d.*

   a. Quantifying the performance of a process

   b. Reducing cycle time for an operation that is not critical

   c. Both *a* and *b*

   d. Neither *a* nor *b*

CHAPTER 6 REVIEW QUESTIONS

1. A Six Sigma project review is also known as? Answer: *c.*

   a. A Six Sigma report-out

   b. A Six Sigma phase-gate review

   c. Both *a* and *b*

   d. Neither *a* nor *b*

2. What is critical about the Define phase? Answer: *d.*

   a. To define solutions for the target problem

   b. To figure out the meaning of terms used in Six Sigma

   c. To deliver a report to the executive committee explaining the primary Six Sigma tools

   d. To determine the objectives and the scope of the project and specify the deliverables to customers

   e. None of the above

3. What is critical about the Measure phase? Answer: *b.*

   a. To measure every characteristic of the product, service, or process

   b. To identify CTQs and validate the measurement system

   c. To deliver a report to the executive committee explaining the measurements to be used

   d. To measure the gains achieved through the improvements made

   e. None of the above

4. What is critical about the Analyze phase? Answer: *d.*

   a. To analyze the effects of the improvements implemented in the target process

   b. To better understand the demographics of the external customers

   c. To deliver a report to the executive committee explaining the analytical process

   d. To identify the vital few factors and arrive at the root cause(s) of the defects

   e. None of the above

5. What is critical about the Improve phase? Answer: *e.*

   a. To validate the measurement system

   b. To determine the cost of the defects

   c. To set up the baseline

   d. To identify the vital few factors

   e. None of the above

6. What is critical about the Control phase? Answer: *d.*

   a. To establish ways to control the project team members

   b. To organize the DMAIC phases

   c. To identify the vital few factors

   d. To determine ways to control the vital few factors

   e. None of the above

CHAPTER 8 REVIEW QUESTIONS

1. In the Measure phase of DMAIC, what are the items needed?

    a. A solution to the problem

    b. Data for doing a Design of Experiments

    c. Data to help break down the problem

    d. A problem, a process, a financial benefit, a metric and a goal, and a customer metric

    e. A valid measurement system

2. In the Measure phase, we are going to establish a defect rate, but black belts typically see the defect rate go down. Answer: *b.*

    a. True

    b. False

3. What is one of the first important milestones that indicate that a black belt is on track? Answer: *d.*

    a. Lack of buy-in from the team members.

    b. No data are available.

    c. The champion does not know the project benefit.

    d. The process map is complete.

    e. When the team adopts a desire to constantly learn.

4. How many data points do you need to have a short-term capability? Answer: *d.*

    a. Two data points.

    b. Over 100 data points.

    c. Fewer than five data points.

    d. Between 30 and 50 data points.

5. Process mapping is? Answer: *d.*

    a. A one-time event

    b. A tool used for statistical validation

    c. A tool used at the end of the DMAIC process

    d. An ongoing living document used throughout the DMAIC process

6. In process mapping, which are the two key questions to ask for each single step? Answer: *j.*

    Q-1. How many inputs are in this step?
    Q-2. What happened prior to this step?

Q-3. What are the outputs of this step?

Q-4. Why do we do this step?

Q-5. How do we know that this step is good?

a. Q-1 and Q-2

b. Q-1 and Q-3

c. Q-1 and Q-4

d. Q-1 and Q-5

e. Q-2 and Q-3

f. Q-2 and Q-4

g. Q-2 and Q-5

h. Q-3 and Q-4

i. Q-3 and Q-5

j. Q-4 and Q-5

7. A *YX* diagram is a statistical tool. Answer: *b.*

   a. True

   b. False

8. A *YX* diagram helps point the black belt into a direction with factual evidence. Answer: *b.*

   a. True

   b. False

9. A failure modes and effects analysis (FMEA) describes which of the following? Answer: *e.*

   a. Potential defects

   b. The risk of the problem

   c. Capability of the process

   d. Root cause

   e. What you want to know about a type of defect

10. An FMEA is complete during the Measure phase. Answer: *a.*

   a. False

   b. True

11. In an FMEA, what is the RPN if P(OCC) is 5, P(DET) is 4, and the P(SEV) is 9? Answer: *d.*

   a. 0

   b. 20

     c. 9

     d. 180

     e. None of the above

12. Measurement system analysis (MSA) is used? Answer: *b.*

     a. To assess capability.

     b. To validate the data used for analysis.

     c. As an optional tool during the DMAIC process.

     d. A nonstatistical assessment of the process.

13. MSA is a tool that can be omitted in the DMAIC model. Answer: *b.*

     a. True

     b. False

14. *Cp* is a capability index with the units measured in? Answer: *f.*

     a. Meters

     b. Gallons

     c. Yards

     d. Productivity

     e. Defect rate or yield

     f. No units

15. If the *Cp* is 1.0, what is the sigma value? Answer: *c.*

     a. 1.

     b. 2.

     c. 3.

     d. 6.

     e. None of above.

16. Can *Cp* be greater than *Cpk*? Answer: *a.*

     a. Yes.

     b. No.

     c. Sometimes.

17. What is the *Cp* and *Cpk* index number when you have a six-sigma capability? Answer: *d.*

     a. $Cp = 1.0$ and $Cpk = 0.5$.

     b. $Cp = 1.5$ and $Cpk = 2.0$.

     c. $Cp = 3.0$ and $Cpk = 6.0$.

    d. $Cp = 2.0$, and $Cpk = 1.5$.

    e. None of the above

18. What is the purpose for gauge R&R? Answer: *f.*

    a. Statistical analysis to evaluate measure error

    b To understand repeatability and reproducibility of your MSA

    c. To help validate what is a defect and what is not

    d. Look for variation within operator and between operators

    e. To gauge the rest and relaxation needed for a black belt

    f. *a* through *d*

    g. None of the above

19. If your data are nonnormal, you are stuck in the Measure phase. Answer: *b.*

    a. True

    b. False

CHAPTER 9 REVIEW QUESTIONS

1. What is the lay description of a hypothesis test? Answer: *e.*

    a. Helping to solve problems

    b. Breaking the problem up

    c. Dissecting the data

    d. There is no way to make it simple

    e. A tool for comparing stuff

2. What are the reasons for nonnormality? Answer: *g.*

    a. All data has that pattern

    b. Due to abnormal conditions

    c. Bimodal conditions exist

    d. Different normal distributions are within the data set

    e. Both *a* and *d*

    f. Both *c* and *d*

    g. None of the above

3. If you have a nonnormal data set, does transforming the data fix the nonnormal causes of the problem? Answer: *b.*

    a. Yes

    b. No

c. Neither a nor b

4. What would best describe a bimodal distribution? Answer: *d* and *f*.
   a. A manufacturing process
   b. Material variance
   c. Transactional defects
   d. Multivari chart
   e. Within-part variation
   f. An *X*-factor that has two different *Y*-output distributions
   g. Both d and f

5. How does comparing factors help solve the problem? Answer: *f*.
   a. It breaks down the problem into the vital *X*'s.
   b. It contrasts between the trivial many and the vital few.
   c. It helps answer the hypothesis question.
   d. It deals with data, facts that can be proven.
   e. It focuses the team on data, not opinion.
   f. All of the above.

6. Tool wear can cause nonnormal distributions. Answer: *a*.
   a. True
   b. False

7. Which plot describes the many distributions in one graph in quartiles? Answer: *e*.
   a. Interval plot
   b. Capability plot
   c. Probability plot
   d. Median plot
   e. Box plot

8. Is it okay to remove outliers in a data set that cause an increase in standard deviation? Answer: *d*.
   a. Yes
   b. No
   c. Yes, but only if you know the cause of stopping it
   d. *b* and *c*

9. What is the best way to show multimode distributions? Answer: *g*.

    a. Bimodal graph

    b. Interval plot

    c. Dot plot

    d. One-way ANOVA

    e. Box plot

    f. Both *a* and *b*

    g. *b*, *c*, and *d*

10. Lowess analysis fits a robust line through the data to display a relationship between X and Y. Answer: *a.*

    a. True

    b. False

11. In a multivari analysis, the X levels are randomly selected levels during the study. Answer: *a.*

    a. True

    b. False

12. Different operators producing the same Y cannot cause asymmetric (nonsymmetric) distributions. Answer: *b.*

    a. True

    b. False

13. A two-way interaction cannot cause asymmetric distributions. Answer: *b.*

    a. True

    b. False

    c. Sometimes

    d. None of the above

14. In simple terms, what is meant by a *p*-value of less than 0.05? Answer: *d.*

    a. That there are no significant differences.

    b. The variance terms are equal.

    c. The mean has a shift of 1.5 sigma.

    d. You're 95 percent confident that there is a statistical difference.

    e. All of the above.

15. The 95 percent confidence interval increases as the standard deviation decreases. Answer: *a.*

    a. True

    b. False

16. A multivari analysis is an active form of comparing within- and between-part variations over time. Answer: *b.*

    a. True

    b. False

17. You do not need a capable measurement system for multivari analysis. Answer: *b.*

    a. True

    b. False

18. Shift-to-shift variation can be measured on one shift. Answer: *b.*

    a. True

    b. False

19. A hypothesis test can show the interaction of the factors. Answer: *b.*

    a. True

    b. False

20. Sample size has no effect on the width of a distribution. Answer: *b.*

    a. True

    b. False

21. If an *X* has been identified as statistically significant, do you disregard it if an expert tells you to ignore it? Answer: *e.*

    a. No

    b. Yes

    c. Ask what data the expert can show to ignore it.

    d. None of the above

    e. Both *a* and *c*

22. If you were told to purchase new technology for over $2 million to make the business more productive, but the hypothesis of the new technology shows no statistical difference in productivity. Do you purchase it? Answer: *a.*

    a. No

    b. Yes

23. What does hypothesis testing fundamentally change? Answer: *e.*

    a. It's the departure from "I think" and "I feel" culture.

    b. Destroys the emotions of the problem.

    c. Turns the problem into a fact-based process.

    d. Data are now used to drive decisions.

    e. All of the above

24. If you changed an *X* that was proven to be statistically significant and the *Y* was given to you within three months prior to the change and one month after, could you show a before-and-after hypothesis to validate the change? Answer: *a*.

    a. Yes

    b. No

25. Using an Anderson-Darling normality test, normal data has a *p*-value less than 0.5. Answer: *a*.

    a. True

    b. False

CHAPTER 10 REVIEW QUESTIONS

1. How many runs does a 2^3 full factorial experiment consist of? Answer: *c*.

    a. 6

    b. 5

    c. 8

    d. 12

2 In an experiment, inputs are allowed to vary randomly throughout the specification range. Answer: *b*.

    a. True

    b. False

3. One-factor-at-a-time experiments generate more powerful data than a full factorial experiment. Answer: *b*.

    a. True

    b. False

4. What is an experimental factor? Answer: *a*.

    a. The input variables for the experiment

    b. The metrics of the process

    c. A covariant

    d. The largest standard deviation

5. What does orthogonal mean? Answer: *c*.

    a. One or more effects that cannot unambiguously be attributed to a single factor or factor interaction

    b. Involves running the experimental runs in random order

    c. A property that ensures that all experimental factors are independent of each other. No correlation exists between *X*'s.

6. What is a "Balanced Design?" Answer: *d.*

    a. A design in which each of the variables has a different number of runs at the high and low levels

    b. A design in which each of the variables or factors has the same number of runs at the high and low levels.

    c. A design in which two of the variables have a different number of runs at the high and low levels

    d. All of the above

7. Standard order is the same as run order. Answer: *b.*

    a. True

    b. False

8. Why use factorial plots? Answer: *e.*

    a. Allows you to see the plots of the main effects

    b. Allows you to see the interaction plots

    c. Allows you to see the cube plots

    d. Shows how to set each factor to either maximize or minimize the response

    e. All of the above

9. What tools can be used to determine if factors have interaction? Answer: *e.*

    a. Balanced ANOVA

    b. Standardized effects

    c. Interaction plots

    d. Fractional factorial fits

    e. All of the above

10. What does it mean when no *p*-values are presented in the ANOVA output? Answer: *c.*

    a. Means the factors are statistically significant

    b. Means the factors are not different

    c. Only one repetition was run at each treatment combination.

    d. Had no center points

    e. All of the above

11. Why do we replicate our experimental runs? Answer: *b.*

    a. So we can look for special causes

    b. To obtain a better estimate of the error and look at interactions *c.* To determine the factor levels

    d. So we can look at the same thing run again

12. To use a center point in your experimental design, at least one factor must be able to be set at it's midpoint coded value = 0. Answer: *b.*

    a. True

    b. False

13. Why use center points in your experimental design? Answer: *c.*

    a. To check for linearity

    b. To check for interactions

    c. To detect curvature

14. If a center point is significant, its p-value in the ANOVA table will be greater than 0.05. Answer: *b.*

    a. True

    b. False

15. Fractional factorial designs require more runs than full factorial designs given the same number of factors. Answer: *b.*

    a. True

    b. False

16. What is the main reason for using a fractional factorial design? Answer: *d.*

    a. Allows you to test and screen a large number of factors in fewer runs

    b. Gives you good estimates of low order interactions

    c. Gives you relative significance of the factors

    d. All of the above

17. Given three factors, A, B, and C, the highest-order interaction would be ABC. Answer: *a.*

    a. True

    b. False

18. In a four-factor 1/2 fractionated design, the AB interaction is confounded with the CD interaction. Answer: *a.*

    a. True

    b. False

19. What does it mean when A is confounded with BC? Answer: *b.*

    a. A is contributing to the result.

    b. BC is contributing to the result.

c. The computed coefficients are related to the sum of the two individual effects.

d. The sums of squares are related to the sum of the two individual effects.

20. In a resolution IV design, two-factor interactions are aliased with three-factor interactions. Answer: *a.*

  a. True

  b. False

21. In a resolution III design, single factors are not aliased with any other factors. Answer: *a.*

  a. True

  b. False

22. The identity expression I + ABCD is used to generate the confounding pattern. Answer: *a.*

  a. True

  b. False

23. Why are resolution V designs preferred over resolution III and resolution IV designs? Answer: *d.*

  a. No main effect is confounded with any other main effect or second-order interactions.

  b. No second-order interactions are confounded with any other second-order interaction, and second-order interactions are confounded with third-order interactions.

  c. Allows for the differentiation of the effects down to the second order, assuming that the effects of third-=order interactions are negligible.

  d. All of the above.

24. Why should you do a hypothesis test before running a DOE? Answer: *e.*

  a. Statistically test for the correct factors

  b. Find the trivial many

  c. To ensure that your measurement system is good

  d. To ensure that you have all the process steps identified

  e. To identify as many the vital few factors prior to DOE

25. What is the mission of the Improve phase? Answer: *e.*

  a. Find the relationships between X and Y

  b. Validate hypothesis tests

  c. Which inputs to control in the next phase

  d. Run a pilot to validate experiment

    e. All of the above

26. Can you calculate epsilon-square percent contribution for the DOE given that the degree of freedom for each factor is different in the ANOVA? Answer: *b.*

    a. Yes

    b. No

CHAPTER 11 REVIEW QUESTIONS

1. The WECO (Western Electric Company) rules are based on probability. We know that for a normal distribution, the probability of encountering a point outside $\pm 2.5\sigma$ is 0.3 percent. This is a rare event. Therefore, if we observe a point outside the control limits, we conclude the process has shifted and is unstable? Answer: *a*, because it should be outside $\pm 3\sigma$.

    a. True

    b. False

2. Outliers usually have a significant affect on an equation derived with regression analysis. Answer: *a.*

    a. True

    b. False

3. Using $Y = f(X)$, do we set tolerance limits for Y? Answer: *b.* We establish with customer using X's to achieve it.

    a. True

    b. False

4. What is the residual? Answer: *e.* When you find the equaton $Y = f(X)$.

    a. It is the equation from the data.

    b. It is the standard error of the equation.

    c. It indicates how well the equation fits.

    d. It is a calculation of the expected value minus the observed value.

    e. *c* and *d*

5. What are control charts? Answer: *d.*

    a. Design of experiment (DOE)

    b. A plot showing Y over time

    c. Charts showing average control

    d. Charts are used to routinely monitor quality

    e. None of the above

6. What does a P-chart track? Answer: *c.*

    a. Process chart showing the main factors

    b. Sample size of the process over time

    c. Simple chart used to track the number of nonconforming units, percentage of defective parts, assuming sample size is *not* necessarily constant

    d. None of the above

7. A DOE is always needed to solve process issues. Answer: *a.* False. A DOE is needed only if information cannot be obtained from passive analysis of the process.

    a. True

    b. False

8. The purpose of performing a designed experiment is to determine what? Answer: *e.*

    a. The mathematical relationship $Y = F(x1, x2, x3, \ldots)$

    b. Which X's most impact Y and therefore need to be controlled

    c. The level of each X to achieve the desired mean Y

    d. The level of each X to minimize the variability of Y

    e. All of the above

9. Within the DOE, the easiest way to test for curvature is to include center points. Answer: *a.*

    a. True

    b. False

10. The most common response surface design is called the central composite design. Answer: *a.*

    a. True

    b. False

11. Control plans provide a written description of the actions that are required at each phase of the process to ensure that all process inputs and outputs will be in a state of control. Answer: *a.*

    a. True

    b. False

12. Control plans are only generated at the start of the life cycle of a product. Answer: *b.* False. Control plans are living documents and should always be maintained and updated throughout the life cycle of a product.

    a. True

    b. False

13. SPC is a statistically based graphing technique that compares current process data to a set of stable control limits established from normal process variation. Answer: *a*.

    a. True

    b. False

14. Control limits and specification limits are the same thing. Answer: *b*.

    a. True

    b. False

15. Control limits are typically set at plus or minus 2 standard deviations from the target of the control chart. Answer: *b*.

    a. True

    b. False

16. Regular residuals are the actual values of the residuals calculated by subtracting the expected value from the observed value? Answer: *b*.

    a. True

    b. False

17. What is the best description of a data transform? Answer: *e*.

    a. A transformation of the data using a power table to treat linearity in the data

    b. A transformation of the data using a power table to treat nonlinearity in the data

    c. Improves the variance within the data

    d. A transformation of the data using a power table to treat the units of the data

    e. It transforms data into a more approximate normal distribution.

18. Outliers usually have a significant affect on an equation derived with regression analysis. Answer: *a*, True.

    a. True

    b. False

19. When an "out of control" situation is signaled on a control chart, the person using the chart will know why the data are giving the signal. Answer: *b*. False. The signal simply says something appears to be wrong, but it does not say why.

    a. True

    b. False

20. Once the special causes of variation in a process have been discovered and eliminated, the long-term goal of anyone managing a process will be to reduce

common cause variation by improving the process or system itself. Answer: *a*. True. Until special causes are under control, it is difficult to attack the common causes because the special causes represent a confounding influence that hinders our ability to understand what is really needed to improve he process. "Business process re-engineering" is the name given to changing processes.

a. True

b. False

21. An "out of control" situation in a production process may be signaled by a sample *f* output, which generates a data point outside the control limits on either the *Xbar–R* range chart. Answer: *a*.

a. True

b. False

22. Mistakeproofing seeks to gain permanency by eliminating or rigidly controlling human intervention in a process. Answer: *a*.

a. True

b. False

23. Six Sigma product and process design or process changes made to the product or process that eliminate the error condition from occurring are called what? Answer: *c*.

a. TQM

b. Mistakeproofing

c. Mistake elimination

d. Foolproofing

e. All of the above

24. Systems that monitor the process and automatically adjust critical X's to correct settings are called what? Answer: *a*.

a. Full automation

b. Process interruption

c. Mechanism

d. SPC

25. In order for mistakeproofing systems to operate effectively, the following rules must not be observed. Answer: *c*.

a. The systems must be installed and properly adjusted before process startup.

b. The systems must be periodically audited and maintained.

c. Systems are periodically disabled.

d. Inoperative or missing systems must be repaired or replaced before operating the process.

e. System overrides must not be used except in an emergency.

26. The EWMA or Exponentially Weighted Moving Average chart is a variable data control chart: Answer: *a*.

a. True

b. False

CHAPTER 12 REVIEW QUESTIONS

1. By the end of the second year of Six Sigma, how many of the people in your organization should be trained as green belts? Answer: *b*.

a. 5 percent

b. 10 percent

c. One for every black belt

d. Anybody who wants to be a green belt

2. How many of your black belts should be certified in the first year of your initiative? Answer: *c*.

a. 10 percent

b. 50 percent

c. At least 70 percent

d. All who are found to be insane

3. How many projects should each black belt work on in a year? Answer: *b*.

a. One or two

b. Four to six

c. As many as he or she wants to do

d. All of them

4. What should be the maximum dropout rate for black belts? Answer: *b*.

a. 1 percent

b. 5 percent

c. 10 percent

d. 15 percent

5. What is a good way to recognize black belts? Answer: *c*.

a. Special privileges, like assigned parking spaces

    b. Honorary titles

    c. Certification events

    d. Name tags

6. What's a good way to retain black belts? Answer: *b.*

    a. Flattery

    b. Compensation plans

    c. Promises of promotions

    d. Noncompete contracts

7. What is the long-term dynamic mean variation? Answer: *a.*

    a. 1.5 sigma shift

    b. Normal fluctuation in Six Sigma responsibilities

    c. An average black belt attrition rate of 5 percent

    d. Attitude changes over time

8. How can leaders promote and sustain Six Sigma? Answer: *f.*

    a. Develop an ongoing project list that registers savings.

    b. Build Six Sigma goals into companywide strategic plans.

    c. Develop a common metric and reporting/review system for projects.

    d. Both *a* and *b*

    e. Both *b* and *c*

    f. All three—*a*, *b*, and *c*

    g. None of the three—*a*, *b*, and *c*

9. Whatever the purpose or the function or the organization, the following is true. Answer: *f.*

    a. Every process has inputs and outputs.

    b. Every process has suppliers and customers.

    c. Every process exhibits variation.

    d. *a* and *b*

    e. *b* and *c*

    f. All three—*a*, *b*, and *c*

    g. None of the three—*a*, *b*, and *c*

10. Why should you work with your suppliers, contractors, outsource partners, and distributors to improve their products and processes? Answer: *d.*

    a. So they can save money through Six Sigma too

    b. So they like your organization and do more business with you *c.* So they can help your organization save more money

    d. Because it's the right thing to do

CHAPTER 13 REVIEW QUESTIONS

1. What are the "4 sigma barrier," the "4.5 sigma barrier," and the "5 sigma barrier"? Answer: *b.*

    a. Limitations of earlier versions of Six Sigma

    b. Points at which efforts to improve products and services are limited by the capability of the designs

    c. The progressive levels of achievement in the Measure, Analyze, and Improve phases, respectively

    d. Indications on control charts that show natural limits

2. What is Design for Six Sigma? Answer: *a.*

    a. A methodology for designing or redesigning products, services, or processes

    b. A new way to plan for a Six Sigma DMAIC initiative

    c. A master plan for marketing Six Sigma within organizations

    d. Both *a* and *b*

    e. Both *b* and *c*

    f. Both *a* and *c*

    g. None of the above

3. Design for Six Sigma is intended for the following. Answer: *d.*

    a. Manufacturers

    b. Service companies

    c. Research and development firms

    d. All companies

    e. Consultants

4. What is a CTQ flowdown? Answer: *c.*

    a. A means of getting customers to identify their critical-to-quality characteristics

    b. The passing along of critical-to-quality characteristics downstream through the value chain

    c. The diagram of a system to identify the dependencies between Y's and X's at various levels of the system

    d. None of the above

5. Which of the following is a Design for Six Sigma model? Answer: *j.*

   a. IDOV—Identify, Design, Optimize, and Verify

   b. DMADOV—Design, Measure, Analyze, Design, Optimize, and Verify

   c. DMCDOV—Define, Measure, Characterize, Design, Optimize, and Verify

   d. DCOV—Define, Characterize, Optimize, and Verify

   e. DCCDI—Define, Customer, Concept, Design, and Implement

   f. DMEDI—Define, Measure, Explore, Develop, and Implement

   g. DMADIC—Define, Measure and Analyze, Design, Implement, and Control

   h. RCI—Define and Develop Requirements, Define and Develop Concepts, and Define and Develop Improvements

   i. None of the above

   j. All of the above

6. In Design for Six Sigma, SIPOC stands for the following. Answer: *c.*

   a. Start, innovate, practice, overcome, complete

   b. Simplicity, ingenuity, patience, organization, creativity the Five Virtues.

   c. Supplier, input, process, output, customer

   d. None of the above

7. The house of quality is? Answer: *c.*

   a. A nickname for GE when Jack Welch was CEO

   b. Any organization that uses Six Sigma

   c. A tool for ranking factors that affect meeting performance specifications

   d. Jargon for a Six Sigma database

   e. None of the above

8. What are *Cp*, *Cpk*, *Cr*, *Pp*, *Ppk*, and *Pr*? Answer: *d.*

   a. Ratings assigned to a black belt for completing a DFSS project

   b. Classifications of costs and profits in DFSS

   c. Groups of characteristics that are critical or preferred

   d. Process capability indices and process performance indices

   e. None of the above

INDEX